Charleston High School Sports Records Book

Kyle Daubs

CHARLESTON HIGH SCHOOL SPORTS RECORD BOOK

Copyright @ 2018 by Hilltop30 Publishers, LLC

All rights are reserved. No part of this book may be reproduced, copied, stored or transmitted in any form and by any means — graphic, electronic or mechanical, including photocopying, recording or information storage or retrieval system — without the expressed written consent of Hilltop30 Publishers, LLC, Kyle Daubs and/or their assigns.

ISBN Number: 978-1-949616-01-9

Library of Congress Number: Pending

To Contact Hilltop30 Publishers, LLC:
Tom Brew, President & Editor
Email: tombrew@hilltop30.com
Phone: (727) 412-4008
Website: www.hilltop30.com

To contact author Kyle Daubs:
Email: daubs@lwcusd21.com
Phone: (217) 294-3627

For media interviews or bulk purchase orders, please feel free to contact either Hilltop30 Publishers or author Kyle Daubs by email with any requests.

Photo credits: Kyle Daubs (baseball, boys basketball, football, boys soccer, boys tennis, softball, girls soccer, girls track); Kevin Kilhoffer (boys cross country); Mike Estell (girls cross country); Justin Rust (boys golf, girls golf). Yearbook photos were use for girls basketball (1979), girls tennis (1983), wrestling (1999), boys track (2003) and volleyball (2012).

DEDICATION

In tribute to teacher Nell Wiseman for
believing in all Charleston High School students
and giving her heart, mind, and soul to teaching
In short, thank you for believing in me, and
the Charleston community!

- To Nell Wiseman for recognizing that I could be a writer, and always believing me. Thank you for teaching me and influencing me to be a writer.

- To principal Trevor Doughty, who gave me a copy of the first CHS Records Book, and told me that he knew I could rewrite the book one day.

- To my parents, Timothy and Anita Tutt, for being a guide and pushing me to be better.

- To coaches Paul Stranz and Jeff Miller for being role models and molding me into the coach and person that I am today.

- To my wife Jordan for being my rock in my life.

- To the members of Class of 2011 who helped make this book possible by assisting me in donations and advertisements. This book is made because of you and thank you for helping make Charleston athletics better. This is our legacy, and I could not have done it without you.

- Finally, to my daughter Penelope. I hope that when you are older, you get to read this book. Daddy loves you!

THANK YOU

     This book of Charleston High School athletics was compiled for several reasons. I wanted to be the person that rewrote the Charleston Sports Records Book. Former Journal Gazette-Times Courier sports editor, Jim Kimball, wrote the first book 1966, which is still used as a historical reference today. During my senior year of high school, I redid all the records books for Charleston athletics. I was later awarded the Merv Baker scholarship for my efforts. That same year, my former English teacher, Nell Wiseman, and assistant principal, Trevor Doughty, told me they would love to see another one made. I wanted to be that person.

     I eventually began writing for the Journal Gazette-Times Courier thanks to the help of Brian Nielsen, who in my opinion, was the best thing that ever happened to the JG-TC. He allowed me to write, grow, and watch sports unfold and for that I am forever grateful.

     This book was made to accolade the battles of past Charleston athletes and create a background of Charleston athletics for future athletes and fans. It should be understood that in compiling a book such as this, that there is a chance that some material might have been overlooked. It is my hope that little of this has happened.

     Material has been retrieved from reading many past Journal Gazette-Times Courier articles. Main writers for these articles include Jim Kimball, Carl Walworth, Bill Lair, Brian Nielsen, Mike Monahan, Rick Dawson, Justin Rust, Erik Hall, and myself. Kimball's book covered football from 1927-1964, basketball from 1919-1964, baseball from 1947-1964, and track from 1897-1964. The rest came from scrapbooks of newspaper clippings saved by the high school, yearbook entries, and articles from the JG-TC. I took these and compiled the new record book that is used today.

     In conclusion, it's my hope that you find this book enjoyable. I hope it helps paint a picture of Charleston's athletic history, as well as some of the great seasons that have happened in its long tenure.

Sincerely,

The Apollo Conference

      The Apollo Conference was formed in 1970 by charter members Charleston, Newton, Paris, and Robinson from the EI Conference. In 1972, Decatur Lakeview and Mount Zion joined the conference. Effingham and Taylorville eventually joined in 1981. However, in 1982, Lakeview brought the conference to seven teams after the school officially closed.

      In 1993, Taylorville left the conference to join the Central State Eight. The conference remained with six teams until 2003 when Olney and Salem left the North Egypt Conference. The Apollo Conference remained with eight teams until 2013.

      Founding members Newton and Robinson left to join the Little Illini Conference. Olney joined the two teams in leaving the conference. Mattoon would leave the Big 12 Conference and join the Apollo that same year. Teutopolis was asked to join but declined the invitation.

      In 2014, Taylorville rejoined the conference, but Paris would depart, leaving Charleston as the lone founding member of the Apollo. In 2017, Mahomet-Seymour and Lincoln left the Corn Belt and Central State Eight respectively, while Salem left to join the Cahokia Conference. Today, the Apollo contains Charleston, Mattoon, Mount Zion, Effingham, Taylorville, Lincoln, and Mahomet-Seymour.

Trojans Baseball
(1947-2018)

Trojans Baseball
(1947-2018)

In 1947, baseball was added to Charleston's athletic program. It seemed the natural thing to do as Charleston was noted for its summer baseball and softball teams during this time in history. The sport was played on a hit-and-miss basis in 1945 and 1946, and it wasn't until 1947 that Charleston had enough players to field a team.

For the first 30 years of the program, Charleston only had four losing seasons. Darrell Black led Charleston as coach to District titles in 1948 and 1950. In 1948, pitcher Jim Martin tossed a no-hit 2-0 victory over Delavan to send Charleston to the Sectional championship, but the team fell to Danville 3-2. That same year, Dale Heaney cracked the first Trojan home run ever. This came against Mattoon at North Park.

In 1950, Charleston landed in the Sectional championship again behind one of the area's best pitching combos in lefthanders Dale Heaney and John "Harpo" Cook. However, Springfield Cathedral defeated the Trojans and their state hopes with a 12-6 victory. After the 1950 season, Charleston left North Park and began playing all their home games at Trojan Field (now Marty Pattin Field). Black coached for two more seasons and eventually coached at Northern Illinois University.

Charleston had some of the area's most dominant pitchers from 1953 to 1961. Don Moses went 16-2 in two seasons in 1953 and 1954, leading the charge for Charleston to capture District titles in both years. Moses came down with measles on the morning of the 1953 Sectional game as Bloomington defeated Charleston 8-1. The following season, coach, Jim Peerman, was instrumental in forming the EI League. Charleston won their first of five titles in this span with Moses leading the way. However, Charleston fell in the Sectional 4-1 to Decatur.

Charleston's luck in the Sectional turned around in 1956. With Dick Campbell taking over, Charleston went 21-5 and qualified for the state tournament. Pitcher Jerry Davis won 15 of Charleston's 21 games which ranked as the states winningest pitcher that season. His 15 wins are still a CHS single season record. The state run began with Davis no-hitting Jamaica in the District final. Charleston followed that with 7-4 wins over Donovan and 4-3 over Champaign in the Sectional. However, Charleston's season ended with a 10-5 loss to Freeburg. Wayne "Hoot" Metzler was chosen as an all-state selection as an outfielder.

Paul Foreman took over in 1957, leading Charleston for 10 seasons. This included Charleston's last recorded trip to state in 1960. Charleston was led by future MLB pitcher Marty Pattin. The Charleston ace was an innings machine. Pattin pitched Charleston past Champaign Centennial 4-2 and Clinton 2-0 on the University of Illinois diamond in the Champaign Sectional to lead CHS to state. Charleston's last state game was a 9-0 loss to Lane Tech.

Pattin is still the best pitcher in CHS history. Some of Pattin's best moments included striking out 18 Oblong Panthers in seven innings and striking out 23 players in a nine-inning Trojan win over Martinsville. Pattin is one of three players to throw two no-hitters in a career, doing so over Marshall and Martinsville. Pattin still holds the record for strikeouts in a season (167 in 1960) and strikeouts in a career (385).

Former Journal Gazette-Times Courier sports editor Jim Kimball took over for three seasons. Kimball went 37-27 in his career. Gig Walden followed with a 41-30 record in four seasons. After seven seasons of no hardware, longtime football coach, Bill Monken, stepped in as the ninth coach in CHS history.

Monken started his eight-year run by winning the first of three straight Apollo Conference championships. Charleston won the Apollo in 1974, 1975, and 1976. In 1975, Jeff Gossett turned into a ball player at Eastern Illinois University. Gossett eventually was drafted by the New York Mets in 1978 in the fifth round where he played two seasons in the minor leagues. Gossett gave up baseball and became a punter in the NFL. Dennis Conley was a multi-Apollo Conference selection and eventually became the coach at Olney Central Community College.

Charleston capped the 1976 season with a Regional title, the first in 16 seasons. Jim Devers set the then-school record for stolen bases in a season with 36. Myron Richardson pitched a perfect game that season as he is just one of two CHS players ever to accomplish that feat (the other being Rob Brown in 1985). Richardson finished the season with 12 wins, which is the second most wins by a pitcher in CHS history. During the three-year Apollo run, Richardson won 30 games, which is tied with Pattin for most wins by a pitcher in a career in CHS history.

After missing out on the Apollo in 1977, Charleston struck three peats again by winning the Apollo Conference in 1978, 1979, and 1980. Charleston missed out on the Apollo in 1981 but captured a Regional title with a 20-6 record. Brian Jones led Charleston offensively many of those years, eventually going on to play college ball at Eastern Illinois University and played several years in the minor leagues. Monken stepped down after the 1981 season and finished his eight-year career with a 129-50 record.

Harold Royer stepped in and had arguably the best four years run in CHS history as a coach. Despite not winning the Apollo, Royer's teams won Regional titles in 1982, 1984, and 1985. Charleston had one of the best hitters in school history in Stan Royer. The future MLB draft pick led CHS from 1983 to 1985, setting records in career batting average, hits, home runs, and runs batted in. Royers' .510 batting average is still tied as a single season record. His 1984 campaign of 10 home runs and 43 runs batted in led the team, while he batted his .510 average in 1985. The 1985 squad set the school record for wins in a season by going 27-5.

Royer was drafted out of high school in 1985 by the Atlanta Braves, but Royer elected to go to college. He attended Eastern Illinois University and earned his economics degree. The Oakland Athletics drafted Royer in 1988. In 1991, the A's traded Royer to the St. Louis Cardinals. Royer finished his four-year career with 41 hits, four home runs, and 21 runs batted in. Royer spent part of the 1994 season with the Boston Red Sox, which was his last MLB season. He now is the president of Clanis Advisors, an investing firm in St. Louis.

After Royer left in 1985, the future all-time winningest coach in CHS history would step in. Bob Lawrence enjoyed a long 19-year career from 1986 to 2004. Lawrence accumulated a 359-222 record with one Regional title and two Apollo titles. In 11 of the 19 seasons, Lawrence-led teams won 20 or more games.

Lawrence coached the likes of future football coach Brian Halsey and current baseball coach Derrick Landrus. Halsey's five triples in a season in 1988 held as a record for 18 years. Lawrence's son, Ryan, is tied with Royer's .510 batting average for a single season. When he finished his career in 1998, Ryan was the career hits leader with 150. Matt Frankie beat out Royer for single season home runs in 1997 with 12. Frankie had a solid career, coming the closest to Royer's all-time .484 batting average by finishing his career with a .453 average.

Frankie is the all-time home run leader with 30. Ryan Strange was the single season hits leader with 57 in 1999 for ten years until Derek Hennig broke his record with 59 in 2009. Frankie signed with Eastern Illinois University, Strange signed with Lake Land, while Hennig pursued academics instead of college baseball.

Brandon Murphy emerged as the second-best pitcher in CHS history from 2000 to 2003. Murphy's career 296 strikeouts are second to Pattin. However, Murphy did surpass the all-time great in innings pitched by pitching 246 innings in his career. The three-sport athlete is also second in career hits (151), but first in career doubles (40).

Lawrence is a house hold name in Charleston. Lawrence taught math for many years at CHS, retiring in 2012. After Landrus picked up his 300th career victory on May 8, 2018, he told Justin Rust of the Journal Gazette-Times Courier after the game, "I was with my buddy the other day and he would still run through a wall for him. That's how much we respected him. It would be really nice to catch him."

Landrus has led the CHS program the last 14 seasons. Landrus has a 304-171-1 career record and is likely to pass Lawrence for most wins. Landrus began his career in 2005 with a stellar 26-9 season. The season featured a unique moment when Kyle Bess hit two home runs in an inning when CHS played Olney on April 26, 2005. George Von Behren broke Royer's record for runs batted in for a single season with 45.

Charleston avenged Apollo defeats to Effingham by knocking out the Hearts 3-2 in the Regional title game. Future Olney Central Community College recruit Wade Hennig struck out 11 in seven innings for the win. In 2006, the script was reversed. Charleston won the Apollo Conference, but fell 5-4 in the Regional title to Effingham. In 2007, Charleston finished with a 21-11 season, and allowed 13 runs in one inning to Alton to fall 18-8 in Regional play.

Charleston's best season in Landrus' career came in 2008. The 26-12 team topped Mattoon 6-4 in the Regional title game. James Addison hit a home run, while Taylor Nead provided two innings of two hit relief. Charleston followed that performance by winning their first Sectional game since 1960.

CHS defeated Mascoutah 7-5 in extra innings in part to Corey Ames. The senior was coming off a five inning start against Mattoon but came back two days later with 5 1/3 innings of relief. This included an eighth inning jam in which Ames walked the bases loaded with one out; however, Ames struck out the next two batters to clinch a spot in the Sectional championship.

"Just a great job by a senior," Landrus told JG-TC sports editor Brian Nielsen. "He was expecting to close, and he came in the third inning. He gave us the best chance to win." Jamel Johnson and Trey Ryan combined for four hits and three runs batted in, while Derek Hennig scored three times.

The state bid ended against Highland. It came down to a future MLB arm closing out the Trojans. With a 2-2 count on Ryan in the seventh inning and two runners on base, Highland elected to bring in Jake Odorizzi. Odorizzi was coming off a complete game performance over Marion in which he allowed his first run in 77 1/3 innings. However, it took just one pitch to strikeout Ryan to win a 4-1 game for Highland.

"We thought we had a chance as good as anyone else did until they brought in Odorizzi," Landrus told Nielsen. Odorizzi has spent the last seven seasons in the MLB with the Kansas City Royals, Tampa Bay Rays, and Minnesota Twins. The sophomore Nead recorded the third most wins in a season by winning 11 games for CHS.

Despite not winning any Regionals since 2008, CHS has shown some successful seasons and players. Brad Wheeler finished a stellar career in 2010. The future Parkland College product finished his career as the all-time hits leader with 154. Wheeler was the all-time RBI leader until 2017, while he is second most all time in career doubles with 38.

Evan Clark followed Wheeler's career with a memorable season of his own. Clark's bat led the Apollo Conference title team in 2011. Charleston had the two best starters in the conference in Joey Miller and Joe Fricke, with Levi Ebbert serving as the team's closer. Clark's 14 home runs in a season is still a single season record. Clark and Aaron Bence combined to score 99 runs that season. Clark eventually went on to play at Kankakee Community College, while Bence played a year at Lake Land College before going to Murray State University. The teams 25 regular season wins is a single season record as well.

CHS has had only one losing season in the last 14 years. Recently, Sam Gubbins broke CHS's single season mark for doubles with 16. In 2017, Dawson Armstrong became the all-time runs batted in record holder with 109 career RBI. Teammate Kevin Beard joined Armstrong in the record books by stealing a single season record 43, finishing his career as the all-time swiper with 83.

Charleston's 1,123 wins as a school ranks 12th all-time according to IHSA. As of 2018, CHS holds a 1,123-618-1 record with a .645 winning percentage. In 2016, Pattin had the baseball field named after him. Pattin is the most successful CHS alum in baseball. Pattin was drafted in the seventh round of the MLB draft in 1965 out of Eastern Illinois University. Pattin spent 13 years in the MLB pitching for the California Angels, Seattle Pilots, Milwaukee Brewers, Boston Red Sox, and Kansas City Royals. He finished his career with a 114-109 record which included an All-Star game appearance in 1971.

Pattin told Rust after the field ceremony, ""This is one of the greatest days of my life," Pattin said during Saturday's ceremony. "I can't tell you how much this means to me. It's a dream come true to me because I grew up here. Having the opportunity to play Little League baseball here all the way up to high school and even college at Eastern (Illinois University), today was a culmination of all that and I am so happy this happened."

Boys Baseball Seasons (Taken from IHSA Website)

Season	Class	Titles	Place	Won	Lost	Tied	Coach
1946-47				3	6		Harold Hall
		Coach Total		3	6		1 yr .333
1947-48	D			8	4		Darrell Black
1948-49				6	4		Darrell Black
1949-50	D			10	4		Darrell Black
1950-51				6	3		Darrell Black
		Coach Total		30	15		4 yr .667
1951-52				3	5		Jack Whitson
		Coach Total		3	5		1 yr .375
1952-53	D			9	4		Jim Peerman
1953-54	D			9	9		Jim Peerman
1954-55				12	5		Jim Peerman
		Coach Total		30	18		3 yr .625
1955-56	DSQ			21	5		Dick Campbell

Season				W	L		Coach
			Coach Total	21	5	1 yr .808	
1956-57				6	5		Paul Foreman
1957-58				9	3		Paul Foreman
1958-59				9	5		Paul Foreman
1959-60		RSQ		15	3		Paul Foreman
1960-61				8	3		Paul Foreman
1961-62				6	4		Paul Foreman
1962-63				7	6		Paul Foreman
1963-64				9	3		Paul Foreman
1964-65				11	2		Paul Foreman
1965-66				7	6		Paul Foreman
			Coach Total	87	40	10 yr .685	
1966-67				12	3		Jim Kimball
1967-68				12	9		Jim Kimball
1968-69				13	10		Jim Kimball
			Coach Total	37	22	3 yr .627	
1969-70				11	6		Gig Walden
1970-71				8	10		Gig Walden
1971-72				12	8		Gig Walden
1972-73				10	6		Gig Walden
			Coach Total	41	30	4 yr .577	
1973-74				13	5		Bill Monken
1974-75				16	7		Bill Monken
1975-76		R		21	5		Bill Monken
1976-77				7	14		Bill Monken
1977-78				19	5		Bill Monken
1978-79				12	5		Bill Monken
1979-80				21	3		Bill Monken
1980-81	AA	R		20	6		Bill Monken
			Coach Total	129	50	8 yr .721	
1981-82	AA	R		20	10		Harold Royer
1982-83				11	13		Harold Royer
1983-84	AA	R		21	6		Harold Royer
1984-85	AA	R		27	5		Harold Royer
			Coach Total	79	34	4 yr .699	
1985-86				24	10		Bob Lawrence
1986-87				21	9		Bob Lawrence
1987-88				23	10		Bob Lawrence
1988-89				22	9		Bob Lawrence
1989-90				20	8		Bob Lawrence
1990-91				15	10		Bob Lawrence
1991-92				18	16		Bob Lawrence
1992-93				8	25		Bob Lawrence
1993-94				16	11		Bob Lawrence
1994-95				16	15		Bob Lawrence
1995-96				14	12		Bob Lawrence
1996-97				20	10		Bob Lawrence

Year				W	L		Coach
1997-98				24	5		Bob Lawrence
1998-99				22	12		Bob Lawrence
1999-00				22	11		Bob Lawrence
2000-01				16	17		Bob Lawrence
2001-02	AA	R		21	7		Bob Lawrence
2002-03				24	7		Bob Lawrence
2003-04				13	18		Bob Lawrence
			Coach Total	**359**	**222**		**19 yr .618**
2004-05	AA	R		26	9		Derrick Landrus
2005-06				24	9		Derrick Landrus
2006-07				21	11		Derrick Landrus
2007-08	3A	R		26	12		Derrick Landrus
2008-09				22	11	1	Derrick Landrus
2009-10				21	14		Derrick Landrus
2010-11				25	10		Derrick Landrus
2011-12				22	14		Derrick Landrus
2012-13				19	12		Derrick Landrus
2013-14				12	21		Derrick Landrus
2014-15				21	13		Derrick Landrus
2015-16				21	11		Derrick Landrus
2016-17				24	9		Derrick Landrus
2017-18				20	15		Derrick Landrus
			Coach Total	**304**	**171**	**1**	**14 yr .639**
			School Total	**1123**	**618**	**1**	**71 yr .645**

Charleston High School Baseball Records (Single Season)

Batting Average

.510, Stan Royer, 1985
.510, Ryan Lawrence, 1998
.509, Tim Parker, 1980

Runs

52, Derek Hennig, 2009
50, Evan Clark, 2011
49, Aaron Bence, 2011
48, Marty Webster, 1989
48, Corey Ames, 2008
47, Ryan Strange, 1999
47, Matt Frankie, 1999

Hits

59, Derek Hennig, 2009
57, Ryan Strange, 1999
56, Evan Clark, 2011
56, Corey Ames, 2011
54, Aaron Bence, 2011
53, Brad Wheeler, 2009
52, Brad Wheeler, 2008
51, Brad Wheeler, 2010

Doubles

16, Sam Gubbins, 2016
16, Dallas Wilson, 2015
16, Cody Mason, 2007
15, Jamel Johnson, 2008

Triples

6, Josh Wilson, 2006
5, Brian Halsey, 1988
5, Mitch Swim, 1984

Home Runs

14, Evan Clark, 2011
12, Matt Frankie, 1997
12, Corey Ames, 2008
10, Stan Royer, 1984
10, Matt Frankie, 1999

RBI

53, Evan Clark, 2011
52, Dawson Armstrong, 2017

45, George Von Behren, 2005
44, Stan Royer, 1985
43, Stan Royer, 1984

Stolen Bases

43, Kevin Beard, 2017
36, Keith Aten, 1978
31, Kevin Beard, 2016
31, Jim Devers, 1976

Walks

36, Luke Buescher, 2017
31, Marty Webster, 1989

Charleston High School Baseball Records (Pitching Single Season)

Wins

15- Jerry Davis (1956)
12- Myron Richardson (1976)
11- Taylor Nead (2008)

Innings Pitched

99 2/3- Jerry Davis (1956)
90- Rob Brown (1985)

Strikeouts

167- Marty Pattin (1960)

No-Hitters

2- Chris Hanner (1992)
2- Bill Applegate (1966)
2- Marty Pattin (1961)

Perfect Games

1- Myron Richardson (1976)
1- Rob Brown (1985

Charleston High School Baseball Records (Career)

Batting Average

.484, Stan Royer, 1983-1985
.453, Matt Frankie, 1997-1999

Hits

156, Brad Wheeler, 2007-2010
151, Brandon Murphy, 2000-2003
150, Ryan Lawrence, 1995-1998
131, Evan Clark, 2009-2011
127, Nathan Lawrence, 2002-2005
121, Derek Hennig, 2007-2009
120, Mason Mcgahey, 2014-2017
119, Stan Royer, 1983-1985

Home Runs
30, Matt Frankie, 1997-1999
22, Stan Royer, 1983-1985

Stolen Bases

83, Kevin Beard, 2015-2017
68, Aaron Bence, 2009-2012
62, Mason McGahey, 2014-2017
53, Luke Beuscher, 2016-2018
51, Derek Hennig, 2007-2009

Walks

82, Marty Webster, 1988-1990

RBI

109, Dawson Armstrong, 2014-2017
108, Brad Wheeler, 2007-2010
103, Stan Royer, 1983-1985
102, Evan Clark, 2009-2011
97, Matt Frankie, 1997-1999

Runs

116, Marty Webster, 1988-1990

Doubles

40- Brandon Murphy (2000-03)
38- Brad Wheeler (2007-10)
33- Evan Clark (2009-11)
32- Dallas Wilson (2013-15)
32- Ryan Lawrence (1995-98)
32- Sam Gubbins (2015-17)

Triples

10, Brian Halsey, 1986-1988

Wins

32, Brandon Murphy, 2000-2003
30, Myron Richardson, 2974-1976
30, Marty Pattin, 1957-1960

Strikeouts

385, Marty Pattin, 1957-1960
296, Brandon Murphy, 2000-2003

Innings Pitches

242, Brandon Murphy, 2000-2003
205 2/3, Marty Pattin, 1957-1960

Charleston Trojan Baseball Records

Most Wins: 27-1985

Most Wins in Regular Season: 25-2011

Apollo Conference Champs: 1974, 1975, 1976, 1978, 1979, 1980, 1998, 2003, 2006, 2011

EI Champs: 1954, 1955, 1956, 1957, 1958, 1960, 1961

District Champs: 1948, 1950, 1953, 1954, 1956, 1960, 1976

Regional Champs: 1956, 1960, 1976, 1981, 1982, 1984, 1985, 2002, 2005, 2008

Sectional Champs: 1956, 1960

Most Coaching Victories: 359, Bob Lawrence (1986-2004),
                                                        304, Derrick Landrus (2005-present)

Trojans Boys Basketball
(1919-2018)

Trojans Boys Basketball
(1919-2018)

Charleston boys' basketball began in 1919. In year two, Leland Colvin led the Trojans as coach to their first ever state appearance in the 1920-1921 season. Charleston defeated Witt 35-12, Windsor 26-8, Shelbyville 23-12, and Kansas 23-12 in the Shelbyville Sectional to advance to the state tournament. Charleston eventually fell to Galesburg 29-7.

Gilbert Carson led the next state team during the 1933-1934 season by going 24-6. The team won the EI Tournament by defeating Marshall 31-15. Charleston won a District Title by defeating Humboldt 51-14, Shelbyville 37-14, and Mattoon 22-20. Charleston defeated Fisher 28-23, Decatur 18-16, and Mt. Pulaski at the Decatur Sectional. Charleston's only win in the state tournament came over Freeport with a 36-14 win. Charleston would eventually lose to Quincy 29-20 in the Elite Eight. This is the last time ever that a boys' basketball team from Charleston qualified for the state tournament.

Sam Gillespie led CHS for four years from 1936 to 1940. In three of those seasons, CHS ended in the Sectional tournament. Despite finishing at the Regional as runner-up, it was custom for the runner-up to move on in the state tournament during these days. Carl Hance led CHS for two seasons, while Leonard King led CHS to s 46-30 record in a three-year span. In 1946, CHS posted their best season in 12 years by going 24-7. Darrell Black replaced Blackwell in 1947. CHS finished 14-12 in his first season but followed with just eight victories in two more years. Paul Swofford stepped in next and compiled a 35-40 record in three years before leaving in 1953. This led to the greatest basketball coach CHS has ever seen.

Charleston had only three 20-win seasons in the next 34 years before Merv Baker stepped up as coach. Charleston went 14-14 in Baker's first year but followed with a 20-7 and 22-7 record in 1954-1955 and 1955-1956. During that 1955-1956 campaign, Charleston moved into their new gym, which is now called Baker Gymnasium, and christened the gym with a 100-61 win over Casey.

Charleston's best season came in 1956-1957. With Dave Dooley, Junior Kearns, Gary Pals, Dave Shick, and Chuck Parker leading the way, the team ended the season with a school record 27 wins and a berth in the Sweet 16 before losing to undefeated Collinsville in the Salem Super Sectional. The 27 wins are still a school record for wins in a season, and 1957 is the last time a boys' basketball team won a Sectional Championship. Baker won five more Regional titles, including a stretch of four years in a row from 1965 to 1968.

In 1965, Charleston made it to the sectional final. This included a thrilling 69-68 victory over Olney in which Tom Strong's rebound and bucket with two seconds left sent Charleston to a sectional final with Lawrenceville. However, the Indians romped past the Trojans to end their season at 22-7. In 1966, CHS reached the sectional final against Lawrenceville again. Rex Morgan and Paul Plath, both who finished in the 1,000-point club, led the team. Charleston trailed Lawrenceville 48-46 with 3:20 left in the game, but Morgan fouled out with 20 points. Plath eventually fouled out when CHS trailed 52-47 with 1:20 left in the game. CHS finished the game being called for 24 fouls in a 57-49 loss to end their season. In 1967, the Trojans lost to Lawrenceville again in the sectional after the Indians, ranked No. 2 in the state, shot 60% from the field.

Rex Morgan finished with the most prolific basketball career. After spending the 1966-1968 years at Lake Land College in Mattoon, Morgan finished his career at Jacksonville University. He was a part of the team's NCAA Runner-Up Finish. After the 1970 season, Morgan was drafted in the second round with the No. 4 overall pick in the NBA draft by the Boston Celtics. Morgan's playing career in the NBA lasted from 1970 to 1972. He eventually coached five high school state basketball teams. Morgan passed away in 2016.

In 1967, the Trojans lost to Lawrenceville for a third consecutive year in the sectional. The team was led by Jim Renshaw and sophomore Gregg Barcus. In 1968, CHS won their fourth straight Regional. With fans chanting, "Plaster Paris," Charleston was led by a future honorable mention all-state selection in Barcus and point guard Ken Baker. The team had the best defense in the area, holding opponents to 44.5 points-per-game. The 26-2 team has the best winning percentage in school history but fell in the sectional.

Barcus was back in 1969. His best game might have been a 39-point, 24 rebound effort that also featured 13 straight free throws made. However, CHS was upset by Chrisman 62-60 in the Regional title game. Barcus finished his career as the all-time scoring leader with 1,380 points and even had invites by University of Kentucky all-time great Adolph Rupp to play. Barcus went and played at Iowa State University. Jim Richie led CHS to a third consecutive 20-win season in 1970, and Coach Baker resigned after that season. His career record of 322-148 in 17 years is the best mark in CHS history.

After Baker left, Dale Alexander took over and had one winning season in four years. Terry Hanner led CHS in 1971 and went on to play at Southern Illinois University-Edwardsville. Mike Pence led CHS in scoring one year and missed time with a groin injury. Alexander stepped down after a 3-19 season in 1974. In 1975, Randy Coonce's one year as coach, CHS snapped a streak of 17 straight losses to Paris with a 61-59 win in the Regional semi-final but lost to Mattoon 71-65 in the title game. The team had three big time scorers in Dave Balsrud (17.0 ppg and 10.5 rpg), Jeff Gossett (16.0 ppg), and Dennis Conley (15.5 ppg).

Steve Hutton took over a program in 1975 after the program suffered six years of mediocrity and rebuilt the team to greatness. After a 1-22 season his first year, Hutton led Charleston to a 12-13 record in 1976-1977. He followed that with back to back 22-4 seasons. Hutton coached the likes of Mitch Shick, Dave Slifer, Don and Mike Mapes, Rick Scott, and twins Jeff and Jim Miller. Charleston won the Charleston Holiday Tournament those two years.

In 1978, Charleston was ranked No. 1 in the Decatur Herald & Review Large School Rankings at one point. However, Charleston was upset by Mattoon in the Regional title game. In 1979, Scott and Jim Miller were dubbed by the JG-TC as the "greatest thing since burger and fries." Despite losing to Decatur Lakeview for the Apollo title, CHS got the best of Lakeview by defeating the team 77-75, a game that featured Scott going off for 39 points, while Jim Miller added 30 of his own. Charleston fell in the Regional final to Danville in a heartbreaking 80-78 game. Scott finished his career as the all-time points scored leader with 1,367 points.

After Hutton left and four losing seasons under coach Rick Bussard, another eventual IBCA Hall of Famer took over. Steve Simons ended a 16-year Regional drought by leading the team to hardware in the 1983-1984 season. The team went 20-8 that year. Jeff Petersen led Charleston to an undefeated Apollo Conference record, which was the first time since the Apollo started that saw a team go undefeated. Petersen was joined by German foreign exchange student Olaf Blab. The 7'0 center combined with the 6'6 Petersen to formulate a daunting defense. Blab, who was the brother of future NBA center Uwe Blab, signed at the University of Illinois and played under Lou Henson for two years.

Simons followed those years with wins of 24 and 20 in 1985 and 1986. In 1985, CHS entered the Regional title game with a 24-2 record and a 46-35 lead over Paris. However, Paris fought back, and fans saw the game tied at 65-all. With under 10 seconds left, Paris scored a layup on the basket to break the hearts of CHS fans to end their season. Petersen finished with 1,197 points for his career and played at Mineral Area College. In 1986, Jeff Gueldner led CHS to a Co-Apollo Conference title, and played at the University of Kansas, where he was a part of the 1988 NCAA National Championship team.

In 1990, CHS featured one of the best sharpshooters in school history in Tim Montgomery. Montgomery finished as an honorable mention all-state selection and signed with Southern Illinois University-Edwardsville. Montgomery holds the record for three-point field goals in a game (Tied-9) and held the record for most in a season (80). Derrick Landrus followed that season with the best individual season in CHS history. Landrus scored 54 points and 56 points in two separate games in the 1990-1991 season. He finished the 1991 campaign with a single season record of 811 points and finished second on the career list with 1,462 points. Landrus led all Class AA scorers in a two-class system that season and signed with Eastern Illinois University.

Simons finished his career with one more Regional title in the 1993-1994 year. Charleston upset Paris 57-50 in the title game. Daniel Taylor led CHS with 13 points. It was a meaningful win for Taylor, who had missed his sophomore and junior seasons with injuries. The Trojans were knocked out by Carbondale, the state runner-up. Troy Hudson blew past the Trojans for 30 points, as Hudson eventually enjoyed a career in the NBA, playing for the Minnesota Timberwolves. Brian Haberer clipped the 1,000-point club in the loss. Haberer finished the season as the record holder for three-point field goals in a season with 85. He went on to play at the University of Iowa.

In 1995, C.J. Applegate led Charleston in one of the best games fans could ever recall. Applegate led CHS with 27 points in a 106-103 win over Shelbyville. He also added 37 points in the Lake Land All-Star Game. After two 7-18 seasons, Simons stepped down. Simons went 171-187 in 14 years and would later be inducted into the IBCA Hall of Fame, while winning the Chuck Rolinski Basketball Coaching Lifetime Achievement Award, serving 25 years on the IBCA as a board member.

Since 1994, Charleston has recorded just eight winning seasons. Six of which came during the Trevor Doughty-era, who is now the current principal of CHS. Doughty coached Charleston from 2002-2003 to 2011-2012. He finished with a career mark of 150-136, and the only two Regional titles since 1994.

The best season during that span was the 2002-2003 campaign that went 23-7. The team won a Regional title and won a sectional game with a 42-39 win over Edwardsville. The game featured a tie breaking 3-point shot from Quinton Combs with 39-seconds left in the game. Brandon Murphy led Charleston with 12 points and had to cancel a trip to Florida to watch spring training baseball, so he could participate in the Sectional semi-final. This setup a rubber match with Troy Triad.

CHS and Triad split the regular season series. Triad defeated Charleston 54-52 in the Salem Invitational in January, while Charleston defeated Triad on the road 61-53. The Trojans lost narrowly to Triad 62-57. The game came down to the wire. Charleston led 27-26 at halftime to make the second half interesting. Charleston led 53-52 with 2:26 left in the game. Triad would hit a pair of free throws to take a 54-53 lead. Nathan Homann had an opportunity to take the lead but missed a shot with 44 seconds left. Free throws sealed the Triad victory, as the team hit 5 of 6 in the final 44 ticks, as the team shot 21-27 from the charity stripe for the game.

Andrew Shick led CHS for two years in 2005 and 2006. Shick comes from a basketball family, so it was not surprising to see his play on the court. His older brother, Ryan, was a starting forward for the 2003 team. His younger brother, Alex, was a starter on the 2011 squad that finished second in the conference, while his dad, Mitch, was a reserve on the 22-win team in 1979, and his grandpa was Dave Shick who was a part of the school record 27-win team.

Shick was a two-time All-Apollo forward that put on one of the best shows on Senior Night against Coles County for Mattoon. Totaling a 30-point, 11 rebound night, which included 24 points and 10 rebounds in the second half, Shick helped lead CHS to a come from behind victory at Baker Gym to beat Mattoon 65-59. Shick eventually went on to play at Lake Land College, while also receiving interest from Eastern Illinois University's football and basketball teams.

Charleston won another Regional title in the 2008-2009 season in Cinderella fashion. Charleston finished the season 10-18, but had a late postseason run to bring home some hardware. In the Regional title game, Jamel Johnson hit the go-ahead free throw with 4.3 seconds left to give Charleston a 50-49 win over Effingham. Charleston would lose to

Carbondale in the Sectional semi-final as Carbondale was coached by CHS alumni Jim Miller, who also coached Carbondale to a state runner-up finish in 2005.

Joey Miller is the last CHS basketball player to make the 1,000-point club, clipping that feat his senior year. Miller had a stellar basketball career at CHS. Miller won the IHSA King of the Hill three-point contest in 2010 as a junior. He was the starting point-guard for the 2009 team that won a Regional title. After graduating, Miller played at year at Eastern Illinois University under his dad, Mike Miller. He then transferred to the University of Illinois-Chicago, where he played two seasons. Miller finished his collegiate career at the Division II Dallas Baptist University in 2016. Miller has enjoyed some stops professionally, including stints with the G-League affiliate Winchester Knicks in 2017, and the Cape Breton Highlanders of Canadian National Basketball League in 2018.

One of the highest scoring games in recent memory came on February 15th, 2013 in an 88-83 overtime loss to Mt. Zion. Ethan Miller's three-point shot with seven seconds sent the game to overtime, but it was three CHS players that will be remembered for scoring for 74 of the 83 points. Truston Winnett scored a career high 32 points, while twin brothers Ethan and Noah scored 22 and 20 points apiece. Ethan and Noah are the sons of current CHS girls coach Jeff Miller. Ethan went on to be named special mention all-state that season and was offered a walk-on roster spot at Eastern Illinois University.

The 2013 season featured many offensive spurts, which also included a 40-point performance by Zach Steidl in a 76-73 victory over Taylorville at the Taylorville Holiday Tournament, in which Steidl hit all eight three-point field goal attempts. It is the highest scoring game by a CHS basketball player since Derrick Landrus scored 56 points against Casey-Westfield on February 8th, 1991. CHS finished with a 14-12 record that year and is just one of two teams to post a winning season in the last 11 seasons. Darrell Phillips was the first member in five years to sign with a college team when he signed with Lake Land College in 2018.

Other recent members of Charleston basketball lore include IBCA Hall of Fame member Randy Harpster. Harpster became the second ever coach for CHS to be inducted as a coach in the IBCA in 2017. Harpster coached Charleston's 7th or 8th grade basketball teams for 29 years, compiling a 405-166 record. This included an 86-27 record with the seventh-grade team and a 319-139 record with the eighth-grade team. This included a state championship in 2000 with the 8th grade team. Harpster led six other teams to the state tournament during that span.

Boys Basketball Seasons (Taken from the IHSA Website)

Season	Class	Titles	Place	Won	Lost	Tied	Coach
1919-20				5	9		Virgil Ashbury
			Coach Total	5	9		1 yr .357
1920-21		DQ		16	5		Leland Colvin
			Coach Total	16	5		1 yr .762
1921-22				15	4		Virgil Asbury
1922-23				11	8		Virgil Asbury
1923-24				12	7		Virgil Asbury
1924-25				22	2		Virgil Asbury
1925-26				8	7		Virgil Asbury
1926-27				13	10		Virgil Asbury
			Coach Total	81	38		6 yr .681
1927-28				3	15		Errett Warner
1928-29				7	13		Errett Warner

			Coach Total	**10**	**28**	**2 yr .263**
1929-30				3	7	Marvin Smith
1930-31				14	11	Marvin Smith
			Coach Total	**17**	**18**	**2 yr .486**
1931-32				7	14	Gilbert Carson
1932-33				12	13	Gilbert Carson
1933-34		DSQ		24	6	Gilbert Carson
1934-35				12	10	Gilbert Carson
1935-36				3	16	Gilbert Carson
			Coach Total	**58**	**59**	**5 yr .496**
1936-37				19	10	Sam Gillespie
1937-38				15	8	Sam Gillespie
1938-39		R		17	10	Sam Gillespie
1939-40				16	10	Sam Gillespie
			Coach Total	**67**	**38**	**4 yr .638**
1940-41				14	15	Carl Hance
1941-42				18	11	Carl Hance
			Coach Total	**32**	**26**	**2 yr .552**
1942-43				16	7	Leonard King
1943-44				17	8	Leonard King
1944-45				13	15	Leonard King
			Coach Total	**46**	**30**	**3 yr .605**
1945-46				24	7	Sam Blackwell
1946-47				14	13	Sam Blackwell
			Coach Total	**38**	**20**	**2 yr .655**
1947-48				14	12	Darrell Black
1948-49				7	19	Darrell Black
1949-50				1	22	Darrell Black
			Coach Total	**22**	**53**	**3 yr .293**
1950-51				6	17	Paul Swofford
1951-52				15	11	Paul Swofford
1952-53				13	13	Paul Swofford
			Coach Total	**34**	**41**	**3 yr .453**
1953-54				14	14	Merv Baker
1954-55				20	7	Merv Baker
1955-56				22	7	Merv Baker
1956-57		RS		27	5	Merv Baker
1957-58				18	10	Merv Baker
1958-59				19	11	Merv Baker
1959-60				10	18	Merv Baker
1960-61		R		19	9	Merv Baker

Year				W	L		Coach
1961-62				14	11		Merv Baker
1962-63				16	10		Merv Baker
1963-64				10	13		Merv Baker
1964-65		R		22	7		Merv Baker
1965-66		R		25	4		Merv Baker
1966-67		R		19	8		Merv Baker
1967-68		R		26	2		Merv Baker
1968-69				21	5		Merv Baker
1969-70				20	7		Merv Baker
			Coach Total	**322**	**148**		**17 yr .685**
1970-71				7	18		Dale Alexander
1971-72				12	11		Dale Alexander
1972-73				7	15		Dale Alexander
1973-74				3	19		Dale Alexander
			Coach Total	**29**	**63**		**4 yr .315**
1974-75				13	11		Randy Coonce
			Coach Total	**13**	**11**		**1 yr .542**
1975-76				1	22		Steve Hutton
1976-77				12	13		Steve Hutton
1977-78				22	4		Steve Hutton
1978-79				22	4		Steve Hutton
			Coach Total	**57**	**43**		**4 yr .570**
1979-80				9	15		Rick Bussard
1980-81				2	21		Rick Bussard
1981-82				1	21		Rick Bussard
1982-83				6	15		Rick Bussard
			Coach Total	**18**	**72**		**4 yr .200**
1983-84	AA	R		20	8		Steve Simons
1984-85				24	3		Steve Simons
1985-86				20	7		Steve Simons
1986-87				15	11		Steve Simons
1987-88				7	18		Steve Simons
1988-89				6	17		Steve Simons
1989-90				12	12		Steve Simons
1990-91				13	13		Steve Simons
1991-92				8	16		Steve Simons
1992-93				3	21		Steve Simons
1993-94	AA	R		14	14		Steve Simons
1994-95				15	11		Steve Simons
1995-96				7	18		Steve Simons
1996-97				7	18		Steve Simons

			Coach Total	171	187	14 yr .478
1997-98				6	18	Jeff Miller
1998-99				4	20	Jeff Miller
1999-00				4	22	Jeff Miller
2000-01				13	16	Jeff Miller
2001-02				13	16	Jeff Miller
			Coach Total	40	92	5 yr .303
2002-03	AA	R		23	8	Trevor Doughty
2003-04				23	7	Trevor Doughty
2004-05				15	13	Trevor Doughty
2005-06				18	11	Trevor Doughty
2006-07				17	12	Trevor Doughty
2007-08				8	20	Trevor Doughty
2008-09	3A	R		10	18	Trevor Doughty
2009-10				10	18	Trevor Doughty
2010-11				16	13	Trevor Doughty
2011-12				10	16	Trevor Doughty
			Coach Total	150	136	10 yr .524
2012-13				14	12	Jim Wood
2013-14				2	20	Jim Wood
2014-15				5	22	Jim Wood
2015-16				9	17	Jim Wood
			Coach Total	30	71	4 yr .297
2016-17				10	14	Blain Mayhall
2017-18				10	14	Blain Mayhall
			Coach Total	20	28	2 yr .417
			School Total	1276	1216	99 yr .512

Landrus, Morgan, Maples, & Miller Lead CHS Scoring

In 1991, Landrus led all Class AA state scorers with his 31.2 point-per-game average. Landrus is just one of three CHS players to ever score over 600 points in a season. Landrus scored 811 points in 1991, Carl Maples scored 650 in 1959, Rex Morgan tallied 642 in 1966, and Joey Miller scored 618 in 2011. Only nine other players have scored at least 500 or more points in a season. This includes Bob Parkinson in 1955 (551 points), Jim Renshaw in 1967 (523 points), Gregg Barcus in 1968 and 1969 (542 and 535 points), Jim Richie in 1970 (594 points), Mike Pence in 1973 (511 points), Rick Scott in 1979 (503 points), Jeff Petersen in 1985 (501 points), Brian Haberer in 1994 (552 points), and Ryan McDermand in 2004 (525 points). There have only been nine players in the 99-year history that have averaged over 20-points a game, and it has only happened one time since 1991.

Year	Player	Points	Scoring Average
1930-1931	Ken Childress	118	6.2
1931-1932	Robert Holmes	99	5.2

1932-1933	Robert Holmes	147	5.8
1933-1934	Robert Holmes	215	7.1
1934-1935	Mervin Baker	130	5.9
1935-1936	Paul Henry	117	6.5
1936-1937	Vic Seaton	224	8.0
1937-1938	Vic Seaton	322	14.6
1938-1939	Junior Phipps	233	8.9
1939-1940	Tony Shoot	195	7.5
1940-1941	Clark Stirewall	211	7.5
1941-1942	Bill Hutton	158	5.6
1942-1943	Charlie Stansberry	235	10.2
1943-1944	Charlie Stansberry	396	15.9
1944-1945	Eugene Moody	175	8.7
1945-1946	Verny May	272	8.7
1946-1947	Verny May	352	13.5
1947-1948	Verny May	454	17.1
1948-1949	Harvey Shoemaker	330	12.7
1949-1950	Noel Swinford	123	7.6
1950-1951	Noel Swinford	225	9.8
1951-1952	Jim Richie	379	14.1
1952-1953	Jim Richie	366	17.4
1953-1954	Bob Parkinson	453	16.2
1954-1955	Bob Parkinson	550	20.4
1955-1956	Al Walters	471	16.2
1956-1957	Dave Shick	490	15.3
1957-1958	Dave Dooley	394	14.1
1958-1959	Carl Maples	650	21.5
1959-1960	Carl Maples	452	16.1
1960-1961	Jerry Loew	459	16.4
1961-1962	Frank Cooper	438	17.3
1962-1963	Mikey Hartley	324	12.9
1963-1964	Don Pankey	469	20.3
1964-1965	Rex Morgan and Paul Plath	Totals Unknown	
1965-1966	Rex Morgan	642	22.1
1966-1967	Jim Renshaw	523	19.3
1967-1968	Gregg Barcus	542	19.4
1968-1969	Gregg Barcus	535	20.8
1969-1970	Jim Richie	594	22.0
1970-1971	Terry Hanner	463	18.5
1971-1972	Kevin Hussey	360	15.7
1972-1973	Mike Pence	511	23.2
1973-1974	Gary Schull	385	17.5
1974-1975	Dave Balsrud	415	17.2
1975-1976	Daryl Hargis	269	11.7
1976-1977	Don Mapes	410	16.4
1977-1978	Rick Scott	446	17.1
1978-1979	Rick Scott	503	19.3
1979-1980	Mark Moore	336	14.0

1980-1981	Kenny Keefer	Total unknown	
1981-1982	Dave Cox	299	13.6
1982-1983	Jeff Petersen	269	11.2
1983-1984	Jeff Petersen	425	15.1
1984-1985	Jeff Petersen	501	20.1
1985-1986	Jeff Gueldner	494	18.3
1986-1987	Gary Hrvol	478	18.4
1987-1988	Paul Snyder	335	13.4
1988-1989	Tim Montgomery	377	16.4
1989-1990	Tim Montgomery	470	16.4
1990-1991	Derrick Landrus	812	31.2
1991-1992	Chad Isley	438	18.2
1992-1993	Brian Haberer	329	13.7
1993-1994	Brian Haberer	552	19.7
1994-1995	C.J. Applegate	425	16.3
1995-1996	Steven Murphy	445	17.8
1996-1997	Matt Ashmore	389	15.6
1997-1998	Brandon Combs	332	13.8
1998-1999	Brandon Combs	386	16.0
1999-2000	Scott Easterday	409	15.7
2000-2001	Kiel Emberton	343	11.8
2001-2002	Chris Brooks	437	15.0
2002-2003	Brandon Murphy	435	14.0
2003-2004	Ryan McDermand	525	17.5
2004-2005	Andrew Shick	363	13.0
2005-2006	Andrew Shick	451	15.6
2006-2007	Ross Hutchinson	369	12.7
2007-2008	Jamel Johnson	383	13.7
2008-2009	Jamel Johnson	317	11.3
2009-2010	Joey Miller	479	17.1
2010-2011	Joey Miller	618	21.3
2011-2012	T.J. Bell	337	13.1
2012-2013	Ethan Miller & Truston Winnett	357	13.7
2013-2014	Mitchell Huddleston	217	9.8
2014-2015	Will Strader	378	14.0
2015-2016	Blaze Taylor-Lutz	369	14.2
2016-2017	Blaze Taylor-Lutz	403	16.8
2017-2018	Darrell Phillips	460	19.2

Top 15 Single Season Scorers

Points	Name	Season
812	Derrick Landrus	1990-1991
650	Carl Maples	1958-1959
642	Rex Morgan	1965-1966
618	Joey Miller	2010-2011

594	Jim Richie	1969-1970
552	Brian Haberer	1993-1994
550	Bob Parkinson	1954-1955
542	Gregg Barcus	1967-1968
535	Gregg Barcus	1968-1969
525	Ryan McDermand	2003-2004
523	Jim Renshaw	1966-1967
511	Mike Pence	1972-1973
503	Rick Scott	1978-1979
501	Jeff Petersen	1984-1985
494	Jeff Gueldner	1985-1986

All-Time Career Scoring List

Points	Name	Career
1,462	Derrick Landrus	1988-1991
1,380	Gregg Barcus	1966-1969
1,367	Rick Scott	1976-1979
1,254	Joey Miller	2008-2011
1,214	Bob Parkinson	1952-1955
1,197	Jeff Petersen	1981-1984
1,132	Al Walters	1953-1956
1,112	Carl Maples	1958-1960
1,078	Verny May	1945-1948
1,032	Brandon Murphy	2000-2003
1,019	Jamel Johnson	2006-2009
1,017	Rex Morgan	1964-1966
1,011	Brad Haberer	1991-1994
1,000	Paul Plath	1963-1966

Charleston Boys' Basketball Records

Most Points in a Game:

56, Derrick Landrus, 1991
54, Derrick Landrus, 1990
44, Rick Scott, 1979
43, Rick Scott, 1978
40, Zach Steidl, 2012

Most Three Point Field Goals in a Game: 9, Tim Montgomery (1990), Derrick Landrus (1991)
Most Points in a Season: 811, Derrick Landrus, 1991
Most Points Per Game Average: 31.2, Derrick Landrus, 1991
Most Three Point Field Goals in a Season: 85, Brian Haberer, 1994

Most Wins: 27, 1957
El League Titles: 1948, 1961, 1966, 1968
Apollo Conference Titles: 1978, 1985, 1986, 2004

District Titles: 1921, 1933
Regional Titles: 1939, 1957, 1961, 1965, 1969, 1984, 1994, 2003, 2009
Sectional Titles: 1933, 1957
State Appearances: 1921, 1933
Most Coaching Victories: 322, Merv Baker, 1954-1970

IBCA Hall of Fame

There are currently 16 members in the Basketball Museum of Illinois that have been associated with the town of Charleston through Charleston athletics or Eastern Illinois University. There are two coaches, three players, and 11 friends of basketball.

Coaches: Merv Baker (1974), Randy Harpster (2017)
Players: Rex Morgan (1975), Jeff Petersen (1996), Derrick Landrus (2009)
Friends of Basketball: Jake Helton (1993), Terry Noble (1993), Bob Beavers (2002), John Morrisey (2003), Larry Ankenbrand (2008), Steve Simons (2010), Don Schaefer (2010), Steve Hutton (2016)
News & Media: Brian Nielsen (2008), Jack Ashmore (2009), Mike Bradd (2011)

Many Reach All-Apollo Status

The Apollo Conference began awarding All-Apollo Conference awards in 1971. Due to lack of insufficient records, finding all-EI League picks from 1948 to 1970 was not possible. The Apollo Conference used to award first and second team selections until 1985. Kevin Hussey, Rick Scott, Jeff Petersen, and Derrick Landrus are the only members to be selected three times.

One interesting fact: Twins Jeff and Jim Miller have been named all-Apollo with Jeff being named in 1978 and Jim in 1979. Flash forward to the modern day where Ethan Miller was named all-Apollo in 2013. Ethan is the son of Jeff and the nephew of Jim.

All-Apollo Conference Selections

Terry Hanner-1971
Kevin Hussey-1971
Kevin Hussey-1972
Jeff Baker-1972
Mike Pence-1973
Kevin Hussey-1973
Dennis Conley-1974
Dave Ballsurd-1975
Dennis Conley-1975
Daryl Hargis-1976
Don Mapes-1977
Rick Scott-1977
Rick Scott-1978
Don Mapes-1978
Jeff Miller-1978
Rick Scott-1979
Jim Miller-1979
Mark Moore-1980
Jeff Petersen-1983
Jeff Petersen-1984
Olaf Blab-1984
Jeff Petersen-1985
Jeff Gueldner-1985
Jeff Gueldner-1986
Darrell Hite-1986
Rezwan Lateef-1986
Jerry Hamner-1986
Gary Hrvol-1987
Rezwan Lateef-1987
Paul Synder-1988
Derrick Landrus-1989
Rick Royer-1989
Tim Montgomery-1989
Tim Montgomery-1990
Derrick Landrus-1990
Derrick Landrus-1991
Louie Andrew-1991
Chad Isley-1991
Chad Isley-1992
Brian Haberer-1993
Brian Haberer-1994
Daniel Taylor-1994
C.J. Applegate-1995
Jay Ankenbrand-1995
Chad Long-1995
Steven Murphy-1995
Steven Murphy-1996
Jon Hanner-1996
Matt Ashmore-1997
Brandon Combs-1998
Matt Ashmore-1998
Ryan Lawrence-1998
Scott Easterday-2000
Kiel Emberton-2001
Chris Brooks-2002
Brandon Murphy-2003
Ryan McDermand-2004
Nathan Homan-2004
Jason Murphy-2004
Andrew Shick-2005
Brad Reid-2005
Jason Murphy-2005
Andrew Shick-2006
Ross Hutchinson-2007

Jamel Johnson-2008
Jamel Johnson-2009
Joey Miller-2010
Joey Miller-2011
T.J. Bell-2011
T.J. Bell-2012

Ethan Miller-2013
Truston Winnett-2013
Will Strader-2015
Blaze Taylor-Lutz-2016
Blaze Taylor-Lutz-2017
Darrell Phillips-2018

Long gone, but Charleston Holiday Tournament never forgotten

Thanks to former Journal Gazette-Times Courier, Brian Nielsen, many memories from the holiday tournament were kept alive. Nielsen, who eventually was inducted into the IBCA Media Hall of Fame, attended nearly every holiday tournament from 1980 to 2010. The first holiday tournament began in 1975. The 16-team bracket stayed around for 32 years until low attendance and teams leaving forced the tournament to use pool play in 2009. In 2010, the last holiday tournament was ran.

The tournament used to split games at Baker Gym and Eastern Illinois University's Lantz Arena. After years of not making money and lack of interest from the public, the Charleston brass decided to pull the plug. Still, the holiday tournament displayed some great basketball talent from 1975 to 2010. Charleston won the tournament twice, under the leadership of Steve Hutton in 1977 and 1978. CHS has only one tournament MVP and that was Jeff Petersen in 1984.

After reading an article by Nielsen in 2002, I agree that the best game ever played game was in 1980. Lawrenceville had two of the best players in the state in Marty Simmons and Doug Novsek. Lawrenceville was battling Effingham in the championship. This game featured a battle between Novsek's 26 points and a future NBA center in Effingham's 7-foot 2-inch center Uwe Blab. Effingham won a close contested 51-49 game.

However, in 1981 and 1982, Lawrenceville won both tournament titles. Simmons shared tournament MVP honors with Novsek in 1981. Then, in 1982, Simmons won tournament MVP on route to a season in which he led Lawrenceville to their second straight IHSA state title. Simmons finished at the holiday tournament record holder in points scored (135) and career points (351). Simmons was named the Illinois 1983 Mr. Basketball that season. Simmons used to hold the record for points scored in a game (45) until Donnell Bivens scored 48 points in a contest. Lawrenceville brought competitive teams during the late 1970s and 1980s. Led by coach Ron Felling, the Indians won four state titles during his 16-year run as head coach that featured a 358-77 career record.

In 1984, Petersen became the only CHS player to ever win tournament MVP. He did so by averaging over 20 points a game. In 1990, cross town rival brought one of the best athletes that Coles County ever saw in freshman Kevin Trimble. Trimble eventually signed a football and baseball scholarship at the University of Illinois. The freshman paired with the likes of Willie High to win the tournament. That same season, Charleston's Derrick Landrus nearly broke Simmons' points in a tournament by scoring 132 points. A questionable call in a 65-60 loss to Belleville Althoff in the semi-finals kept CHS out of the title game that could have featured a Mattoon-Charleston showdown.

In 2000, Jon Tipton helped Mount Zion win their first and only championship with a last second shot to win a 58-57 thriller. In 2002, Charleston nearly ended a tournament dry spell, but fell to Robinson 50-45, losing to the hot hand of Nick Brooks who eventually played at the University of Butler. CHS made the title game again in 2003, but was blown past by Effingham, a game that didn't even start until 10:10 p.m.

    A stretch of tournament dominance followed that year, a main reason why some believe the tournament disbanded. Class 4A Edwardsville won five of the next six tournaments in convincing fashion. Their only blemish was when Teutopolis won in 2006 thanks to 28 points from tournament MVP Jason Runde. Since ending the tournament in 2010, Charleston boys' basketball teams have played at Taylorville and Effingham Holiday Tournaments. Many fans might remember many of these players and teams, but below is a compilation of all tournament winners with the tournament MVP.

Year	Winner	MVP (Same School as Winner unless denoted)
1975	Chicago St. Ignatius	Jeff Carter
1976	Chicago St. Ignatius	Curtis Evans
1977	Charleston	Mark Fitt (Mattoon)
1978	Charleston	Darnall Jones (Olney)
1979	Lawrenceville	Warren Wendling (Olney)
1980	Effingham	Doug Novsek & Uwe Blab (Effingham)
1981	Lawrenceville	Marty Simmons & Doug Novsek
1982	Lawrenceville	Marty Simmons
1983	Taylorville	Jens Kujawa
1984	Murray, Kentucky	Jeff Petersen (Charleston)
1985	Teutopolis	Bob Zerrusen
1986	Belleville Althoff	Kevin Schwarz
1987	Belleville Althoff	Corey Cox
1988	Belleville Althoff	B.C. Penny
1989	Effingham	Brian Foster (Fairfield)
1990	Mattoon	Willie High
1991	Jerseyville	Kiley Gwaltney (Fairfield)
1992	Belleville Althoff	Mike Rodgers (Olney)
1993	Teutopolis	Matt Fitzsimmons (Belleville Althoff)
1994	Fairfield	Kip Walters
1995	Paris	Josh Virostko
1996	Edwardsville	Jim Doughterty
1997	Edwardsville	Jon Harris
1998	Effingham St. Anthony	Kyle Wente
1999	Teutopolis	Johnny King
2000	Mount Zion	Neil Plank
2001	Robinson	Nick Brooks
2002	Robinson	Nick Brooks
2003	Effingham	Aaron Leonard
2004	Edwardsville	Nick Arth
2005	Edwardsville	Spencer Stewart
2006	Teutopolis	Jason Runde
2007	Edwardsville	Anthony Campbell
2008	Edwardsville	Will Triggs

2009	Edwardsville	Will Triggs
2010	Galesburg	Brandon Thompson

Top Players

Many solid basketball players played in the 36-year tournament history. After reading many articles, and many perspectives, the list of the top players to ever go through Charleston and play in the tournament goes as followed:

10. Rick Scott (Charleston) & Darnall Jones (Olney): Scott finished all tournament both years that Charleston won the tournament. He would have won MVP, but finished runner-up in 1978 to Jones, who eventually finished his career with 1,565 points.

9. Will Triggs & Spencer Stewart (Edwardsville): The two players helped lead Edwardsville to a stretch of tournament dominance. Steward continued his career at the University of Illinois-Chicago, while Triggs played at the University of Southern Illinois-Edwardsville.

8. Nick Brooks (Robinson): Helped lead Robinson to back-to-back tournament championships, including a win over CHS in 2002. Brooks went on to play at Butler University.

7. Jeff Petersen (Charleston): He was named tournament MVP and became a future IBCA Hall of Fame member. He would have likely been a Division I player if injuries didn't hamper his career.

6. Neil Plank: After helping Mount Zion win, he enjoyed a collegiate career at the University of Wisconsin and Illinois State University.

5. Kyle Wente (St. Anthony) & Bob Zerrusen (Teutopolis): Wente helped lead St. Anthony to their only tournament title and eventually became a two-time All-Ivy League player at Princeton University. Zerrusen led Teutopolis to an undefeated 1986 season that won a state title.

4. Derrick Landrus (Charleston): He was three points away from breaking a basketball legend's tournament points record. Plus, he was leading the state in points per game. Landrus went on to play at Eastern Illinois University.

3. Doug Novsek (Lawrenceville): He was a two-time MVP in 1981 and 1982 and was a part of two state title teams. Known as a deadly outside shooter, fans today still remember his game.

2. Uwe Blab (Effingham): Played four years at Indiana University unde Hall of Fame coach Bobby Knight. He helped the team win a Big Ten title his senior year and make the Elite Eight of the NCAA Tournament. Blab was drafted with the 17th pick in the first round of the NBA draft, where he played for the Dallas Mavericks, Golden State Warriors, and San Antonio Spurs from 1985 to 1990.

1. Marty Simmons (Lawrenceville): Simmons was nicknamed "Mule" for his ability to carry teams, including the 34-0 state champion team in 1982. Simmons eventually became Blab's teammate at Indiana University. Simmons transferred the University of Evansville, where he became the coach in 2007 and amassed 282 victories to 2018.

Trojans Boys Cross Country
(1945-2018)

Trojans Boys Cross Country
(1945-2018)

Written by Erik Hall and Kyle Daubs

The history of cross country at Charleston High School began in the fall of 1946. The 1946-1947 school year saw CHS almost double the number of varsity sports. CHS had three varsity sports in 1945-1946 and increased to five varsity sports for the 1946-1947 school year, CHS added cross country to the fall activities and baseball in the spring. The year 1946, the Illinois High School Association introduced cross country as an IHSA sponsored activity. Cross country remained available at Charleston only until 1949. After the 1949 season, Charleston did not offer cross country again until 1967. Since 1967, the sport of cross country has continuously been a part of the fall sports scene at Charleston High School.

The coach for the first year of cross country went unmentioned in the *CHS Recorder* and *The Coles County Daily Times*. Jack Hatfield, 1947 freshman runner, believes that when he ran his freshman year that it was not the coach's first year coaching cross country. So apparently, Darrell Black coached Charleston's cross-country team from 1946-1949. Black also coached the CHS varsity basketball team for three seasons starting in the fall of 1947. According to Hatfield, one of Black's rules for his basketball players was, "If you weren't playing football and were playing basketball, you had to run cross country."

Charleston basketball coach Darrell Black began conditioning six cross country runners in the fall of 1946. The first Charleston cross country team included seniors Dick Hampsten and Albert Anderson; juniors Duane Hunt and Maurice Reed; sophomore Harvey Shoemaker; and freshman Bryce Van Bellehem. Cross country requires five runners for the team to score points in a meet. In Black's first year as coach, he had a mere one extra runner.

The October 16, 1946 article also stated that Charleston and Champaign had scheduled to compete between halves of the Charleston homecoming football game against Marshall on October 18, 1946. Running at halftime of varsity football games occurred frequently during Darrell Black's term as cross-country coach. The 1947 season began with a team twice as large as the 1946 squad. In 1948, Darrell Black again doubled the number of runners he had running cross country. With a large team of 24 runners, the Trojans had a small schedule with only two dual meets against Mattoon. Charleston lost both contests.

The 1949-1950 basketball season was Black's last as the head basketball coach at CHS. In the fall of 1950, Darrell Black said that there would be no cross country that year because there were not enough boys interested in the sport. The loss of Black's ability to influence basketball players to run cross country resulted in cross country being lost from the CHS extra-curricular scene until 1967.

The return of cross country in 1967 would bring an actual cross-country coach. John Schneider joined the Charleston High School staff in the fall of 1967. In 1967, Schneider held the Eastern Illinois University cross country record. Possessing this experience, Schneider was the obvious coach for this reborn sport at CHS. Schneider had a very successful first season by guiding the team to a 5-1 dual record and third place finish in the Eastern Illinois Conference Meet. The formation of the Apollo Conference occurred in 1970. The conference contained four schools at the start in Charleston, Newton, Paris and Robinson. Decatur Lakeview and Mount Zion joined the conference in cross country for the 1972 season.

During the years of 1968 to 1970, the IHSA was shifting the cross-country distance from the original two miles to the current three-mile distance. The state meets in 1968 and 1969 were 2.75 miles, in 1970 the distance was 2.67 miles, and 1971 would complete the transition with the distance of three miles established. Three miles remains the distance run in by men's high school cross country in Illinois.

Charleston won eight straight Apollo Conference titles from 1972 to 1979. In 1979, future Eastern Illinois University head cross country coach John McInerney inherited an experienced CHS men's cross-country team. The men's team contained seven returning lettermen and six of them were seniors. Along with coaching the men's team, McInerney coached Charleston first female athletes to run cross country. Women's cross country began at Charleston in 1979 and McInerny served as the first Charleston women's cross-country coach.

"CHS was an ideal position to coach at with the EIU facilities," McInerney said. "I inherited a very experienced group and they were very mature with six seniors on the team." Senior Jim Crail led the men's team most of the 1979 season. The Trojans won the Apollo Conference Title for an eighth consecutive season. In addition to the Apollo team title, Jim Crail won the individual Apollo championship. "I had a very strong team around me," Crail said. "We all ran together as a team and that is the point of cross country, to run as a team and win the ultimate goal."

Contrasting the struggles of CHS in 1981, the Apollo Conference got boosted by the additions of Taylorville and Effingham high schools. The Apollo Conference increased to seven schools in 1981 instead of eight because Robinson decided to attempt playing as an independent school. After the 1981-1982 school year, Decatur Lakeview High School closed. Those two losses reduced the Apollo Conference to six schools for a short time. Robinson returned to the Apollo Conference for the 1983 conference cross country meet. Robinson returned to the conference in football starting with the 1984 season. With Robinson back, the Apollo Conference had seven schools. The conference maintained those seven schools until Taylorville joined the Central State Eight Conference after the 1992-1993 school year.

After four coaches in five years, Gene Nance provided the program with some stability. Nance came from Donovan High School to become the Charleston cross country coach in 1984. Nance coached men's cross country at CHS for 11 years, compiled an 88-27 record, won eight Apollo Conference Titles and took five teams to the sectional meet. It may have been his familiarity with the runners from serving as Charleston's track coach, but the 1995 men's cross-country team did not lose a step when shifting from Gene Nance to new cross-country coach Todd Vilardo.

The 1995 season introduced a change in the format for the Apollo Conference Meet. Robinson hosted the 1995 Apollo Conference Meet. The 1995 meet was the first time that the Apollo Meet was not in Charleston. The Apollo Meet was held at Eastern Illinois University every year since 1970, except for 1982 when it moved to the Charleston Country Club due to the EIU course being too wet. Starting during the 1995 season, the Apollo Meet began to rotate between the six conference schools. Robinson hosted the first year, Newton the second year, Effingham the third year, Mount Zion the fourth year, Paris the fifth year and back to Charleston every sixth year. Vilardo led the Trojans for four years before stepping down in 1999. Vilardo has risen through the ranks of administration at Charleston as he is now the current superintendent of Charleston School District.

The ties between cross country and basketball at CHS helped to start the sport and continued 50 years later. In 1999, Derrick Landrus, Charleston's season and career varsity basketball scoring leader, was hired as head coach for the men's cross-country team.

Frustration surrounded the 2000 Apollo Meet for Charleston. The meet had originally been scheduled to be run at Fox Ridge State Park. It moved to EIU after objections from some conference schools to such a hilly course. The meet then moved back to its old home of EIU. Charleston tied Robinson for first place based on each team's top five runners, but Robinson's sixth runner finished 16th and Charleston's sixth runner placed 17th. Robinson won their sixth Apollo team title in seven years. The Charleston Regional meet brought some relief as the Trojans earned third to advance to the Centralia Sectional meet. At the sectional meet, Charleston finished ninth of the 20 teams, and sophomore Erik Werden missed an individual state berth by one place and one second.

The 2001 team qualified for state for the first time in nearly 30 years. The team was led by Werden's seventh place all state finish. Werden repeated as an all state runner in 2002 by running a school record 14:45, which placed Werden sixth overall. Both 2001 and 2002 teams won the Apollo. Werden's school record lasted for 11 years.

Charleston missed out on winning the Apollo in 2003 but had the individual champion in Clint Coffey. With 100 yards, Coffey outraced Robinson's Brandon Trimble to secure the individual championship. However, Charleston brought the Apollo home in 2004. Charleston beat Olney 68-73, a team that was ranked 13th in the state a week before the conference meet. Dane Church ran a personal best to get sixth place, while Zach Buxton made the all-conference team by placing ninth. Buxton helped lead Charleston to a 2005 Apollo title by placing third at the Apollo meet. Church joined for a second year in a row, while Kyle Lynch-Klarup also made all-Apollo by placing ninth. Charleston defeated Salem by 15 points. Buxton capped his career making the all-Apollo team for a third time, placing third again.

Aaron Smith led Charleston for the next three years, making all-conference three times, including winning the meet his senior season in 2009. Freshman, Riley McInerney also made all-conference in 2009 and became the first state qualifier since Werden in 2002. McInerney, the cousin of Werden, and son of CHS former coach, John, started a brilliant career his freshman campaign. McInerney became the second all-state cross-country runner in CHS history, and the first to make it three times. McInerney finished 18th his sophomore year, and 3rd his junior and senior years, leading the 2012 team to state his senior year. McInerney went on to run at Eastern Illinois University.

In 2013, Taylor Garrett won the Apollo title after placing fifth his junior season. However, Garrett did this while playing soccer in the fall all four years while he was at CHS. Also, in 2013, coach John McInerney was inducted into the Illinois Track and Cross-Country Coaches Association Hall of Fame.

Charleston then made a run of three straight trips to the state tournament as a team from 2014 to 2016, including winning a Regional title in 2015, which was the first since the 1974 District title. Charleston also won the Apollo Conference for the first time in 10 years in 2015, and then again in 2016. Landrus stepped down in 2016, finishing his coaching career with 67-7 record in dual meets in 17 years, which included going 10 years straight without a loss.

A combination of talented runners led Charleston these years, as Nick Oakley capped off the 2017 season by running to a 15th place at the state tournament to make him the third and final CHS athlete to ever reach all-state honors. As of 2017, Charleston holds a 281-103 career record in dual meets in their 55-year history, which makes a .732 winning percentage.

Boys Cross Country (Taken from the IHSA Website)

Season	Class	Titles	Place	Won	Lost	Tied	Coach
1946-47				2	0		Darrell Black
1947-48				0	2		Darrell Black
1948-49				0	2		Darrell Black
1949-50				1	2		Darrell Black
			Coach Total	3	6		4 yr .333
1967-68				5	1		John Schneider
1968-69				5	4		John Schneider
1969-70				4	3		John Schneider
			Coach Total	14	8		3 yr .636
1970-71				2	6		Bernie Miller
			Coach Total	2	6		1 yr .250
1971-72				13	6		Bill Harbeck
1972-73		SQ		13	1		Bill Harbeck
1973-74				10	1		Bill Harbeck
1974-75		DSQ		10	1		Bill Harbeck
			Coach Total	46	9		4 yr .836
1975-76				4	5		Mark Schmink
			Coach Total	4	5		1 yr .444
1976-77				5	2		Rick Everett
			Coach Total	5	2		1 yr .714
1977-78				7	1		Jim Drake
1978-79				6	2		Jim Drake
			Coach Total	13	3		2 yr .813
1979-80				7	2		John McInerny
			Coach Total	7	2		1 yr .778
1980-81				0	8		Scott Parke
			Coach Total	0	8		1 yr .000
1981-82				1	9		Mike Viano
			Coach Total	1	9		1 yr .100
1982-83				3	4		Duncan McHugh
1983-84				9	3		Duncan McHugh
			Coach Total	12	7		2 yr .632
1984-85				10	2		Gene Nance
1985-86				9	2		Gene Nance
1986-87				12	0		Gene Nance
1987-88				7	5		Gene Nance
1988-89				7	4		Gene Nance
1989-90				9	2		Gene Nance

Year				W	L	Coach
1990-91				7	2	Gene Nance
1991-92				10	1	Gene Nance
1992-93				8	3	Gene Nance
1993-94				5	3	Gene Nance
1994-95				4	3	Gene Nance
			Coach Total	88	27	11 yr .765
1995-96				4	3	Todd Vilardo
1996-97				8	0	Todd Vilardo
1997-98				6	1	Todd Vilardo
1998-99				1	0	Todd Vilardo
			Coach Total	19	4	4 yr .826
1999-00				4	0	Derrick Landrus
2000-01				2	0	Derrick Landrus
2001-02	AA	Q		4	0	Derrick Landrus
2002-03				4	0	Derrick Landrus
2003-04				5	0	Derrick Landrus
2004-05				5	0	Derrick Landrus
2005-06				3	0	Derrick Landrus
2006-07				2	0	Derrick Landrus
2007-08				4	0	Derrick Landrus
2008-09				4	0	Derrick Landrus
2009-10				3	1	Derrick Landrus
2010-11				3	1	Derrick Landrus
2011-12				4	1	Derrick Landrus
2012-13	2A	Q		3	1	Derrick Landrus
2013-14				5	1	Derrick Landrus
2014-15	2A	Q		6	1	Derrick Landrus
2015-16	2A	RQ		0	1	Derrick Landrus
2016-17	2A	Q		1	0	Derrick Landrus
			Coach Total	62	7	18 yr .899
2017-18				5	0	Brian Oakley
			Coach Total	5	0	1 yr 1.000
			School Total	281	103	55 yr .732

Top Ten Individual Times (3.00 Mile Course)

**Boys began running three-mile courses in 1971.

1. Riley McInerney-14:33 (2012)
2. Erik Werden 14:45 (2002)
3. Harold Fudge 14:54 (1974)
4. Nick Oakley 15:00 (2017)
5. Colton Bell 15:11 (2015)
6. Kirby Johnson 15:13 (1986)
7. Tom Titus 15:14 (1974)
8. Jay Carey 15:19 (1990)

9. Austin Ames 15:20 (2016)
10. Mark Riddle 15:26 (1985)

Charleston Boys Cross Country Records

Most Dual Meet Wins in a Season: 13, 1971/1972
Apollo Conference Titles: 1972, 1973, 1974, 1975, 1976, 1977, 1978, 1979, 1983, 1984, 1985, 1986, 1988, 1989, 1990, 1991, 1992, 2001, 2002, 2004, 2005, 2015, 2016

District Titles: 1974
Regional Titles: 2015
Sectional Titles: 1972
State Appearances: 1972, 2001, 2012, 2014, 2015, 2016
All State Runners: Eric Werden-7th Place (2001), Eric Werden-6th Place (2002), Riley McInerney-18th Place (2010), Riley McInerney-3rd Place (2011), Riley McInerney-3rd Place (2012), Nick Oakley-15th Place (2017)
Most Coaching Dual Wins: 88, Gene Nance (1984-1994)

Bill Harbeck Leads Charleston to State Runs in Early 70s

Written by Erik Hall

Charleston shifted their coach search from local EIU to Indiana. Charleston found four-year Valparaiso University track and cross-country runner Bill Harbeck. "It wasn't too difficult to take over the struggling cross-country program. There was only one way to go, up," Harbeck said. "When I started, we ran just against small schools and I added bigger schools and upgraded the schedule. The talent was there, and those kids would work and do a lot of running."

One returning letterman, Steve Connor, and a rookie coach should not have brought the type of success that occurred at Charleston starting in 1971. Harbeck's first year saw CHS compile a 13-6 record, a third place in the Apollo Conference Meet (4th in 1970), and advance from the Mount Zion District meet by finishing third. This berth in the Champaign Centennial Sectional meet marked the first time Charleston had advanced beyond the district meet as a team. The Trojans finished 11th in the 15-team sectional meet, far from a top three finish needed to advance to the state meet at Detweiler Park in Peoria.

Advancement could be the theme of the 1972 season. In 1972, the Apollo conference cross country meet advanced the number of teams competing for the title from four to six by adding Decatur Lakeview and Mount Zion. Also, in 1972, CHS advanced the number of Apollo Conference titles from zero to one and advanced as a team to the state cross country meet for the first time in school history.

The first meet of the year, Charleston competed in a triangular with Tolono Unity and Casey. CHS showed that first meet how dominant they were going to be in 1972 as nine CHS runners came over the last hill holding hands to receive a nine-way first place tie. Charleston rushed to an 8-0 start to a dual season that ended with a 13-1 record. The only defeat in dual competition came against Mattoon. The Apollo Conference Meet would be monumental for not only cross country, but all CHS athletics. The Trojan cross-country team won the sport's first Apollo title ever and this was the first outright Apollo title for any CHS sport. Junior Pearcy, the only senior in CHS's top 10, won the individual Apollo title. Pearcy added a first-place finish at the Saint Anthony Invitational and a 10th place at the 39-team Mattoon Invitational to complement his Apollo success.

The Decatur District meet brought an opportunity for CHS to gain revenge on Mattoon for defeats during the season. "Our main goal was to beat Mattoon. Our sights were set on beating the best," Harbeck said. "To beat Mattoon and their coach Larry Burgess was very important."

Mattoon's district meet victory with 38 points to Charleston's 44 points delayed any revenge opportunity at least one week until the Champaign Centennial Sectional meet. Charleston seized that opportunity to win the first sectional title for CHS men's cross country. Charleston's sectional win created school's first team berth into the IHSA State Cross Country meet. Charleston won the sectional with 63 points, Danville took second with 79 points, and Mattoon got the final state berth for finishing third with 82 points. The Trojan's victory came because the team placed four runners in the top 15.

"That was our goal, to qualify for state," Harbeck said. "In one year for us to win the sectional and beat Mattoon. We went from not even being thought of at the sectional to be the best in the sectional. It shows that we had kids with talent and that wanted to win."

The team of senior Junior Pearcy; juniors Toby Franklin, Terry Lemons and Mike Pence; sophomores Chet Bowers, Harold Fudge and Stu Storm were the seven team members Harbeck took to represent CHS in Peoria for the state meet. The Trojans earned a 22nd place finish and had to see county rival Mattoon earn a 13th place. During the state meet competition, Pearcy fell and was taken to the hospital, unable to complete the race. Without the usual number one runner finishing, Fudge led the Charleston finishers in 87th overall with a time of 15:24.

Nine returning lettermen and expectations of a state berth weighed on the 1973 team. A 10-1 dual record, Paris Invitational Title, overall and junior division titles at the Charleston Jamboree, 28-team St. Jacob Triad Meet Title, Flora Invitational Title, second in the 56-team Crete-Monee Pow Wow, second consecutive team title and perfect score of 15 points at the Apollo Conference Meet, and Harold Fudge's still standing 14:15 time at the Mattoon Invitational all occurred during the 1973 season. The team did not accomplish the season's goal of a return trip to the state meet. Charleston finished fifth at the sectional meet and needed a top three finish to advance to the state meet. Junior Harold Fudge earned an individual state berth that he turned into a 65th place finish.

In 1974, hope of a return to state was again occurring in Charleston. With seniors Tom Titus and Will Cooper back after missing the 1973 sectional with illness and new assistant coach Rick Everett, the hopes were high for the cross-country program. The Trojans had another great regular season collecting a second straight 10-1 dual record, the Olney Invitational Title, the Flora Invitational Title, a third straight Apollo Title, and a third at the Mattoon Invitational.

With a varsity containing five seniors, the team knew that the regular season meant nothing compared to when it came time to run the regional and sectional meets. At Decatur Scoville Park, the Trojans won the district meet, after finishing second the two previous years.

This gave Charleston their first and only district title ever for men's cross country. At the sectional meet, trying to finish as one of the top three teams and advance to the state meet, Charleston instead won the team's second sectional title in three years.

Will Cooper, Gary Egan, Harold Fudge, Stu Storm and Tom Titus were the five seniors, junior Jeff Oakley and sophomore Randy Stearns represented CHS at the IHSA State Cross Country meet in Peoria. Harold Fudge ran in his third consecutive state meet after finishing 87th overall in 1972 and 65th in 1973. Stu Storm made 1974 a return trip to run in Peoria after being a part of the 1972 team. The third sophomore runner from 1972, Chet Bowers, moved away from Charleston during the summer of 1974. "The state meet was cold and very crowded," Tom Titus said. Despite these conditions and CHS having a smaller enrollment than 22 of the other schools competing, the Trojans managed a 20th place finish. Harold Fudge led Charleston in 35th, Tom Titus took 84th, Stu Storm--147th, Gary Egan--174th, Will Cooper--182nd, Randy Stearns--184th and Jeff Oakley--211th.

After the 1974-1975 school year, Bill Harbeck left Charleston to coach and teach at Decatur MacArthur High School, and eventually coach at Mt. Zion. Since Harbeck's departure, it took 28 years for another CHS team to qualify for state.

All-Stater Werden leads CHS Back to State in 2001

After missing out on the state meet by one second as a sophomore, junior Erik Werden came back with the best individual season up to the date. He was surrounded with a squad that could contend for a state berth. Derek Fasnacht gave up soccer to focus solely on cross country. Robert Gooden and Sean McNamara were back and experienced, while Brandt Pence, Sean Kelly, and Andy McCormick rounded out the top seven.

The trio of Werden-McNamara-Gooden was unstoppable in some meets. The three went 1-2-3 at the Olney Invitational, Apollo Conference meet, and the Effingham St. Anthony Invite. Thanks to the trio winning the top three spots, Charleston won the Apollo for the first time in nine years.

Werden followed his conference title with a Regional title when postseason began. This set up a run at the Centralia Sectional. Werden placed fifth with a time of 15:20. Gooden placed 17th, while McNamara and Fasnacht went 21st and 27th. All of Charleston's top seven runners ran under 18 minutes and Charleston punched their ticket to the state meet by placing third. The top five teams qualified for the state meet.

Werden ran his best race of the year by breaking the 15-minute plateau, running a time of 14:55, which secured seventh place overall. Werden's seventh place finish made him all-state, and he became the first ever all-state cross-country runner in CHS history. Werden ran a 4:40 first mile, 5:16 second mile, and clinched the place with a 4:58 third mile. He even did it by running out of one of his shoes with 500 yards left and passed two competitors.

"I was surprised," Werden told Journal Gazette-Times Courier sports editor Brian Nielsen. "I usually don't go under five in my last mile." When asked about the shoe situation, Werden told Nielsen, "A guy's front shoe caught the back of my shoe and then it came off. I was a little embarrassed, but I still passed two guys at the end."

At the end of the meet, all the other all-state finishers changed into dress clothes. Werden was unaware as he was the still in his running gear when he accepted his award for seventh place.

Werden's place led Charleston to 19th overall out of 32 teams. The rest of the team included McNamara running a 15:42 (76th place), Gooden a 15:58 (115th place), Fasnacht a 16:21 (179th place), Kelly a 17:04 (238th place), Pence a 17:08 (240th place), and McCormick a 17:43 (258th place).

McInerney Leads CHS Back to State in 2012

After running to all-state honors for two years in a row, McInerney was missing two things: an Apollo Conference title, and a trip to state with his team. Despite all the success McInerney had in his career, Mt. Zion was a powerhouse in cross country. During McInerney's years, Mt. Zion had won four straight Regional titles, made four trips to state, and won a state championship in 2011. They were coached by former CHS coach Bill Harbeck.

In 2012, it would be Charleston's year. McInerney surged through an undefeated regular season that included winning the Peoria Invite, an invite that features 300+ runners, and the Apollo Conference championship. The senior won the Regional leading his team to a runner-up finish heading into the sectional.

Coach Derrick Landrus told Journal Gazette-Times Courier sports editor Brian Nielsen that he believed Charleston could make it as the fifth and final team. He would end up being right as McInerney continued his unbeaten streak by winning the sectional with a time of 14:53. Taylor Garrett ran what his coached called "the biggest race of all" with his 16th place. "He stepped up," Landrus told Nielsen. "I had him projected as the 28th best time and he got 16th. A lot of the guys ran slower because of the cold, but he ran seven seconds faster." Niko Tadic also broke the 17-minute mark with a time of 16:33. McInerney's brother, Colin, ran a 17:01, while Zach Sanders, Colton Bell, and Val Walker each broke 18-minutes.

McInerney went into Peoria with state title aspirations but ended up finishing third for another straight year. However, in his final race, he broke his cousins school record with a time of 14:33. Glenbard South's John Wold won the state title with a time of 14:16. "I tried to go out and win it, but third is still good," McInerney told Nielsen. "Having my teammates here is amazing. I usually come up Friday and then come back, but we were able to eat dinner altogether. I wouldn't trade this experience for anything."

Rounding out the state team was Garrett's time of 15:46 (90th place), Tadic at 16:18 (150th place), Sanders at 16:27 (169th place), Colin McInerney at 16:34 (172nd), Walker at 16:59 (192nd), and Bell at 17:02 (194th). The team placed 19th overall.

State Berth in 2014 Surprises Many

In what might have been a surprise year in 2014, the CHS boys showed great success. It all started after a one-point loss to Salem 50-51 at the Apollo meet. Ross Osterday led the team with a third-place finish, while teammates Colton Bell (fifth), and Kendal Oliver (ninth) joined him on the all-Apollo team.

The boys ran a sluggish Regional, finishing fourth as a team, but did enough to qualify for the sectional meet. The following week became dubbed as "the greatest day in Charleston cross county history." Both the boys and girls qualified for the state meet as a team.

The boys were led by a complete team effort. Osterday led Charleston with a 13th place with a time of 15:51, while Bell was not that far behind with a time of 15:57 and an 18th place. Oliver was also right in the pack, finishing 26th overall with a time of 16:07. However, it was the backend of the team that led Charleston to their second state appearance in three years. After not running the Regional, Joe McKirahan battled back from an injury to run his best race with a time of 16:14, which was good for 32nd place, while number five runner Jonah Moore ran a 16:58, good for 82nd place.

"We were seeded sixth, seventh, or eighth coming in and we needed top five," Landrus told Nielsen. "The boys have had had a rough year battling injury and to have an excruciating one-point loss in the Apollo. Joe McKirahan is one of our best runners, if not the best, and he has battled injuries and illness. He came back and ran his best race of his career. Nobody understands how Jonah Moore has come along. He could not break 20 minutes his freshman or sophomore year. For him to be our number five runner to get us to state is unbelievable."

Charleston finished 17th as a team. The team was led by Osterday's time of 15:38 (62nd place), Bell at 15:47 (176th), Oliver at 16:01 (101st), McKirahan at 16:07 (114th), Moore at 16:58 (181st), Clayton Redden at 17:31 (204th), and Val Walker at 17:35 (207th).

Seniors lead CHS to first Regional Title since 1974

The nucleus was back from the 2014 team for the 2015 squad. Led by seniors Colton Bell, Ross Osterday, and Joe McKirahan, the team was poised for a solid run. Clayton Redden was ready to make the jump from bottom half to contributing runner, while sophomore Nick Oakley, and freshman Austin Ames were ready to make an immediate impact.

After losing by one point in the Apollo last season, Charleston ran away with the conference title, winning by nine points. The conference championship was the first in 10 years. Bell, Osterday, and McKirahan went second-third-fourth in terms of placing to make all conference. This setup the Regional where the top four teams going in were Charleston, Taylorville, Mattoon, and Salem, all teams that Charleston recently beat in the Apollo, mustering the idea that CHS could possibly win the Regional.

The three seniors stepped up once again. McKirahan led Charleston with a time of 16:11, while Osterday and Bell each ran a 16:13. Ames ran a 16:45, while Oakley ran a personal best of 17:09. The low times were enough for Charleston to capture their first Regional title since 1974.

Charleston followed that performance with a state berth, their third in four seasons by finishing third at the sectional. The seniors led the team with Bell running to a fourth-place finish with a time of 15:17. McKirahan added a 10th place with a time of 15:37, while Osterday was 14th with a time of 15:43. Oakley made his contribution by shredding his PR set a week ago by running a 16:27, shedding 43 seconds.

"These seniors, I was not worried about them at all," coach Derrick Landrus told Journal Gazette-Times Courier reporter Mike Monahan. "They just killed it. Oakley's previous personal best was 17:09, so that tells you the whole story right there. Ryan Chambers and he were 60th and 61st about a mile and a half in. I didn't see them for a while, but when I did Nick was 44th. I knew it was over and were going to go. That's why we advanced so easily."

The team placed 19th as a team. Bell just missed the top-25, which deems runners as all-state by finishing 30th with a time of 15:12. "Colton Bell's goal was to be in the top 25 and gave it everything he had, but came up about three seconds short," said Charleston coach Derrick Landrus. "He knew where he was and with 800 yards to go he was in 21st place, but just couldn't hang on. The last two races were by far his best races of his career. I am really happy with the way he ran."

Osterday finished his career with a time of 16:02 (103rd place), while McKirahan ran a time of 16:18 (134th place). Oakley broke his PR once again by running a 16:10 (119th place). The rest of the team included Ames at 16:18 (160th), Redden at 16:54 (186th), and Chambers at 17:02 (189th).

2016 Makes Three-Peat to State

The team may have lost three seniors but did bring back four of the top seven from the 2015 team. Oakley and Ames rose through the ranks last season as underclassman, which included Oakley finishing at the team's No. 3 runner. Clayton Redden was ready to make the jump from No. 7 runner to top five, as well as Ryan Chambers. The rest of the top seven was to be decided as the season progressed.

The boys won the Apollo Conference for a second straight year thanks to the team's top five all finishing top-20 or better. Oakley and Ames went fifth and sixth respectively to make the all-conference team. Chambers just missed all conference by finishing 12th, while Redden and Lance Niemerg battled their way to 15th and 19th places respectively.

After running a sluggish fifth place at the Regional, Charleston knew they were going to have to run better at the sectional. Charleston had their best races all around to clinch the final fifth spot to advance to state for the fourth time in five seasons. Oakley and Ames led the way with 11th and 13th places respectively. Chambers finished 49th, while Niemerg played hero to run the team's fourth best time to net 56th place, while Redden finished 58th, meaning all of Charleston's top five finished in the top-60.

"Lance, I have one of these stories every year," Landrus told Journal Gazette-Times Courier reporter Justin Rust. "He was not a great runner last year and he bought into it. It's what he wanted to do, and he made himself a runner. Clayton, he battled every day since the start of the year. He had the race he needed to have."

The team tied for the best finish by any CHS state qualifying team by placing 17th (also done in 2014). Five of the seven runners had a personal best. Starting with Ames, the sophomore ran a 15:24 (41st place). Oakley ran a 15:35 (52nd), Chambers a 16:38 (148th), Niemerg a 16:39 (149th), Redden a 16:45 (151st), Luke Buescher a 17:06 (180th), and Jonathan Phillips a 18:06 (207th).

Trojans Football
(1927-2018)

Trojans Football
(1927-2018)

(EXCERT FROM JIM KIMBALL'S SPORTS RECORDS BOOK)

Charleston High School fielded football teams from 1896 through 1904, but the numerous injuries, coupled with the addition of Trojan basketball in 1905, shut things down for a period. Two gridiron teams were organized in the fall of 1896 at Charleston. The high school squad was composed of high school students and alumni while the other team called the Charleston Juniors consisted of freshman and sophomores. The first action resulted in a game on October 7, and the high school team shut out the juniors 4-0. Two days later they would lose to Arcola in a game with two 15-minute halves.

Trojan football died in 1905 until it was revived in 1927 through the efforts of School Superintendent W.W. Akenbrand and CHS's first ever football coach Errett Warner. Forty students came out to make the first roster. Due to the shortage of equipment, most of the players received only partial suits. Some players were only issued a helmet while others only got shoulder pads. Charleston's first game in 1927 was a 12-0 victory over Paris Freemen on October 13. The home games were played on Eastern's Schahrer Field until 1935.

Charleston's first four years were a rough patch going 6-12-4. CHS's first ever winning season came in 1929 when they went 3-2-1. It was also the first time CHS scored more than 18 total points in a season. They scored 95 total points. CHS scored over 100 points in a season for the first time in 1932, coincidentally was the first E.I. League title. Charleston football began to grow under new coach Gilbert Carson, who took over in 1931 and had a 14-1-2 record in that two-year span.

Carson was actually the older brother of Howard "The Horse" Carson. "The Horse" did much of the ball carrying in those two seasons. Leonard J. Kincaide, Terre Haute Tribune sports-editor credited much of their undefeated season success to fullback Carson when he wrote in his column, "He (Carson) possesses wonderful speed and is a cutback artist of the best style. There is no doubt but what he was the brains of the championship outfit." An interesting note shows the defense played a major factor as well. From 1931-1933, Charleston's goal line was crossed only seven times. In 1931, the defense only gave up a total of 15 points.

The 30's played out to be a winning sensation with players such a Bud Ewing and Bill Thissell leading the way. Ewing's six touchdowns and thirty-eight total points in a 92-0 win over T.C. are still records in a game. Charleston just missed out on the E.I. crown in 1937 and 1938 with identical 5-1 conference records.

In 1942, CHS finally got back to the top in the conference. Don Johnson's 91 total offensive points led the way to a 7-2 record, 5-0 in conference, and a E.I. League title. This is one of ten total times where CHS went undefeated in the conference. In 1943, CHS would begin their football downhill spiral. The following 11 years resulted in only 21 wins, 57 losses, and 12 ties. The 1948 team of 0-7-1 is one of four teams in Charleston's 84-year football history where the team went winless.

Coach Mervin Baker, a native Charlestonian, returned to the "Friendly City" in 1953 and almost overnight put the Trojans back in the winning circle. The first season produced one win, but there was no looking back after that. Charleston football wouldn't have a losing season again in fourteen years.

The next ten seasons averaged close to seven wins each year under Coach Baker. Also, CHS captured E.I titles in 1955, 1959, and 1961 giving Charleston six crowns. The Trojan teams didn't have top quality one-two scoring punches of Ewing and Thissell or Johnson and Sellett but had team qualities. After a 7-1-1 record in 1964, CHS managed to get back on top of the conference. ** (End of Excerpt)

Two straight years in 1965 and 1966, Charleston captured the E.I. Title. Charleston was led by halfback Steve Bell. Bell had 144 total offensive points in 1966 which was a record until 2012. Bell's 1966 dream season also set records in a season for most touchdowns (24), highest scoring average (18.00), and he was put second at the time on the all-time career scoring list with 186 points, second to the great Steve Temple.

The team also had the boot of Tom Jenkins. A then-season record of 36 extra points kicked in by Jenkins provided that special "kick" to the team. Jenkins finished with a career 113 extra point. The next two seasons would be nothing, but average. On October 10, 1967, Oblong ended a 27-year losing streak to the Trojans by defeating CHS 14-7. The 1969 season ended on the right note in two different ways. Charleston's 4-0 conference record, 7-1 overall, won the last ever E.I. Title and ended the great coaching career of Coach Baker with a 97-33-9 overall record. Today, his legacy lives on through the high school Gymnasium being named in his honor, as well as a baseball field, and a scholarship.

The year 1970 marked a new tradition for Charleston football. Two things were missing: Coach Baker and the E.I. League were both gone. The Apollo Conference was formed by charter members Charleston, Newton, Paris, and Robinson. In 1972, Decatur Lakeview and Mt. Zion joined the conference after departing the Cenois Conference.

In Jerry Van Bellehem's only successful year as the Trojan coach, Charleston won the first ever Apollo Conference title in 1970 with a 2-1 conference record. Once 1973 rolled around, the Chuck Budde era was donned. Budde coached the Trojans from 1973 to 1979, but in his tenure the stretch of dominance is well remembered. The wishbone offense led Charleston to six Apollo Conference titles, a 31-4 record in that stretch, only one losing season, three state qualifying years, and three final fours in the postseason.

During the 70's, the Trojans had a little of everything. Mark Buckellew, Jon Buckellew Mark Jobe, and Tony Baker were all top ground gainers during the years. All though his high points came from the 1971 and 1972 seasons, which were both losing seasons, Kevin Hussey at one point held nearly every passing record in the school's history. Today, these records are now held by his son, Sean.

The defense during the 70's proved to have some unique record holders. Steve Scholes picked off the quarterbacks seven times in 1976, Mark Wilson blocked six kicks in 1973, and Kevin Clark sacked the quarterback five times in 1973. Even the special teams have names from the 70's in four of the seven record titles thanks to great runners of Daylane Cox and Jon Kniskern.

Jeff Gossett became a popular CHS alum. After a minor stint as a professional baseball player, the 1975 CHS alumni turned into a pro-bowl punter in the NFL. Gossett enjoyed a 16-year career which included punting for the Kansas City Chiefs, Cleveland Browns, Chicago Blitz, Portland Breakers, Houston Oilers, and the Oakland Raiders. The Raiders were where Gossett enjoyed much of his success, playing there from 1988 to 1996, which also featured a

Pro Bowl appearance in 1991, and being the oldest punter in the league at age 39 in 1996.

After a couple of Bill Monken years, former Charleston All-American quarterback, Verlon Myers, was the man hired in 1982. In his first season, Myers had the legs of Mark Heise in the quarterback slot. Heise not only could throw but was able to rush for a then-record 254 yards in a game and he finished with a career 102 total offensive points.

After qualifying for the state tournament in 1982, and two Apollo conference titles later as well as a state qualifying berth in 1984, the Trojans could only muster one state berth and two winning seasons until Myer's departure in 1993. Myers was inducted into the Illinois High School Football Coaches' Association Hall of Fame and passed away in 2012.

Bill Monken would have his shot once again. After years of spending time as a defensive coordinator for the Trojans, Monken was hired in '93. The 90's proved to be anything, but glamorous for Charleston fans. Running back, Chuck Earp proved to be the dynamic player of the decade. Earp set the then-record for most points by a sophomore by scoring 48 points in 1995, and he finished with 138 total points, good for eighth on the all-time list at the time.

Charleston only went to state once during the 90's in 1996. CHS also went on to win the Apollo Conference title and had thrilling 52-0 and 37-6 victories over rivals Paris and Effingham. CHS outscored opponents 336-135 that year. Monken was later inducted into the IHSFA Hall of Fame in 2012.

In 2000, it marked a new century, as well as a new football coach. Brian Halsey was named the new leader, but it took the two years for CHS to become anything close to their stretch of dominance from the old days. In 2000, the team would go 0-9, resulting in only the second time in school history the football team was winless. Charleston won a game in 2001, but it was another daunting season, which included a game where Taylorville's Drew Stephenson sacked the CHS quarterback five times in a game.

From 2002-2004, CHS won three straight Apollo Conference titles for the first time since the 70's. The Trojans had the arm of Jon Adkins leading the way, as well as the running power of Brandon Davis. Davis was named a to the All-State team for his stellar work of scoring a then-CHS record of nineteen touchdowns in 2004.

The Trojans went back to state in 2005, but in 2006 would have a poor 2-7 record, breaking the streak of four straight playoff berths. In 2007, Cinderella made her entrance to Charleston, Illinois. The 5-4 Trojans would go on to upset previously 9-0 Effingham and go on to finish that year making the Elite Eight. Eric Gentry set new passing records by tossing 2,060 yards and setting up 17 touchdowns, 11 of them to Jamel Johnson. Gentry also holds the record for most attempts in a season. Mario Johnson's 88-yard kickoff return is the state record for a playoff game in Class 5A.

In 2008, the team would be picked in the pre-season to win the conference but would finish with disappointing record of 4-5. It ended the remarkable careers of the Johnson brothers. Jamel finished his career 13th on the all-time scorers list with 120 points, as well as the career record holder for catching twenty touchdowns. His brother, Mario Johnson could remind you of the likes of "The Horse" of Howard Carson. Johnson was the sixth Trojan to joining the "100 Point Club" in 2008 as well as finish seventh on the all-time scorers list with 156 career points.

In 2009, sophomore, Chris Creek, totaled 163 tackles in a season to break John Best's 1966 record of most tackles in a season, but the team came up short in the playoffs. The team's star wide receiver, Adam Drake, went on to play football at Eastern Illinois University, and even making it to the practice squad of the Kansas City Chiefs.

The team finished 2011 as the best team in school history by going 11-2, reaching the state semi-final game before eventually falling to state champion Rochester. Creek passed John Best as the career holder in tackles by setting a record of tackles that season, including 169 that year. The old record had been held since 1963. The team was led at quarterback by former Charleston great, Kevin Hussey's son, Sean Hussey. During his junior season, Hussey rewrote the passing record books, including breaking his father's record of most consecutive 100 yard passing games.

With most of the offense back in 2012, the team broke all the offensive records, but fell to Rochester in the second round of the playoffs. Hussey finished with 5,975 career passing yards, and now holds every career passing record. Junior, Josh Cazley, broke Steve Bell's points in a season record with 146 points. Senior wideout, Truston Winnett, broke the receiving touchdowns record. Safety, Dillian Cazley went on to play four years at the University of Illinois. Hussey had a walk-on spot at the University of Illinois before deciding to give up football. Winnett was signed on to play at Monmouth College, but eventually transferred back to Eastern Illinois University for school. Josh Cazley became the all-time scoring leader as a junior, but never played his senior football season at Charleston.

Since those magical runs, Charleston has fallen on hard times. The next five seasons have seen the Trojans win just five games and have featured three different coaches.

- During the 2007 season, athletic trainer, Jennifer Staskiewicz, was pregnant, but still traveled to every game. In their first-round playoff game against Effingham, a Flaming Heart fan threw a bottle at Staskiewicz, and hit her. Needless-to-say, Staskiewicz had to be held by multiple football coaches before teaching this fan a lesson. Staskiewicz stayed in Charleston until 2016 before moving to Florida. She is still loved by all her athletes, and the Charleston community. Her husband, Steve, took pictures of all the football games through his business Speaking Digital and made highlight tapes for the team. Despite living miles away, the Staskiewicz's are true Trojan football fanatics.

- · In 2011, two football games didn't start until after 9:00 p.m. due to heavy rainfall. Charleston came up short in a two-point conversion against Chatham-Glenwood in a 42-41 loss but pounded Mattoon 55-29 at Eastern Illinois University's O'Brien Field.

Season by Season Trojan Football Results
*-Conference Game, ^-Playoff Game

1927

Won 1, Lost 3, Tied 0
Coach: Errett Warner

Opponent	Score
Paris Freeman	12-0
Oakland	0-46
Hindsboro	6-12
T.C.	0-49

Total Points By Opponent-107 (26.8 AVG)
Total Points. By CHS-18 (4.5 AVG)

1928

Won 1, Lost 4, Tied 0
Coach: Errett Warner

Opponent	Score
Chrisman	6-0
Paris	0-33
Hindsboro	0-12

Opponent	Score
Effingham	6-62
T.C.	0-26

Total Points By Opponent-133 (26.6 AVG)
Total Points By CHS- 12 (2.4 AVG)

1929

Won 3, Lost 2, Tied 1
Coach: Errett Warner

Opponent	Score
Chrisman	31-6
St. Joseph	7-9
Hindsboro	19-6
Paris	25-6
T.C.	6-6
Effingham	6-12

Total Points By Opponent-45 (7.5 AVG)
Total Points By CHS-95 (15.6 AVG)

1930

Won 1, Lost 3, Tied 3
EI Won 0, Lost 3, Tied 3
Coach: Errett Warner

Opponent	Score
Lawrenceville	19-19
Chrisman	40-0
Martinsville*	6-19
Paris*	0-6
Newton*	6-6
T.C.*	0-0
Robinson*	0-9

Total Points By Opponents-59 (8.4 AVG)
Total Points By CHS-71 (10.1 AVG)

1931

Won 6, Lost 1, Tied 1
EI Won 4, Lost 1, Tied 1
Coach: Gilbert Carson

Opponent	Score
Casey*	6-7
Martinsville*	20-2
Paris*	6-0
Newton*	12-0
Flora	7-0
T.C.*	20-0
Clinton	7-6
Robinson*	0-0

Total Points By Opponents-15 (1.8 AVG)
Total Points By CHS-78 (9.8 AVG)

1932

Won 8, Lost 0, Tied 1
EI Won 5, Lost 0, Tied 1 (EI Champs)
Coach: Gilbert Carson

Opponent	Score
Ridgefarm	32-0
Casey*	12-0
Martinsville*	19-6
Decatur Reserves	26-0
Paris*	12-0
Flora	33-20
Marshall	0-0
T.C*	46-0
Oblong*	12-0

Total Points By Opponent-26 (2.8 AVG)
Total Points By CHS-192 (21.3 AVG)

1933

Won 6, Lost 2, Tied 1
EI Won 5, Lost 0, Tied 1 (EI Champs)
Coach: Gilbert Carson

Opponent	Score
Marshall*	6-0
Martinsville*	13-0
Casey*	12-0
Gertsmeyer	3-0
Paris*	20-0
Mattoon	0-13
Waite	0-26
T.C*	13-0

Oblong*..0-0

Total Points By Opponent-39 (4.3 AVG)
Total Points By CHS-67 (7.4 AVG)

1934

Won 5, Lost 2, Tied 2
El Won 4, Lost 1, Tied 1
Coach: Gilbert Carson

Opponent	Score
Urbana	0-0
Martinsville*	18-6
Casey*	34-6
Mattoon	0-19
Paris*	52-0
Decatur	7-6
Marshall*	0-14
T.C.	53-0
Oblong	6-6

Total Points By Opponent-57 (6.3 AVG)
Total Points By CHS-170 (18.8 AVG)

1935

Won 2, Lost 6, Tied 1
El Won 2, Lost 3, Tied 1
Coach: Gilbert Carson

Opponent	Score
Urbana	0-19
Decatur	0-8
Martinsville	0-0
Casey*	0-6
Mattoon	0-6
Paris*	39-0
Marshall	12-19
T.C*	26-6
Oblong*	3-33

Total Points By Opponents-97 (10.7 AVG)
Total Points By CHS-77 (8.5 AVG)

1936

Won 3, Lost 4, Tied 1
El Won 3, Lost 2, Tied 1
Coach: Sam Gillespie

Opponent	Score
Champaign	14-33
Martinsville*	13-13
Casey*	0-3
Mattoon	0-6
Paris*	13-0
Oblong*	19-33
Marshall*	33-0
T.C*	58-21

Total Points By Opponents-109 (13.6 AVG)
Total Points By CHS-150 (18.7 AVG)

1937

Won 6, Lost 3, Tied 0
El Won 5, Lost 1, Tied 0
Coach: Sam Gillespie

Opponent	Score
Shelbyville	25-6
Martinsville*	13-0
Casey*	27-0
Mattoon	0-24
Paris*	7-13
Oblong*	19-14
Marshall*	31-6
Quincy	7-13
T.C*	27-6

Total Points By Opponents-82 (9.1 AVG)
Total Points By CHS-156 (17.3 AVG)

1938

Won 8, Lost 2, Tied 0
El Won 5, Lost 1, Tied 0
Coach: Sam Gillespie

Opponent	Score
Shelbyville	47-12
Martinsville*	37-0
Mattoon	18-12
Sidell	27-6

Paris*	0-7
Oblong*	32-7
Marshall	20-12
Casey*	27-0
T.C.	92-0
Centralia	0-13

Total Points By Opponents-69 (6.9 AVG)
Total Points By CHS-300 (30.0 AVG)

1939

Won 6, Lost 3, Tied 0
El Won 3, Lost 3, Tied 0
Coach: Sam Gillespie

Opponent	Score
Oakland	18-0
Martinsville*	32-13
Mattoon	6-0
Carmi	18-0
Paris*	6-12
Oblong*	0-7
Marshall*	19-6
Casey	6-0
Newton*	0-7

Total Points By Opponents-45 (5.0 AVG)
Total Points By CHS-105 (11.6 AVG)

1940

Won 1, Lost 6, Tied 1
El Won 0, Lost 4, Tied 1
Coach: Carl Hance

Opponent	Score
Pana	0-6
Gertsmeyer	6-7
Catlin	25-0
Paris*	0-13
Obong*	6-7
Marshall*	0-33
Casey*	0-7
Newton*	13-13

Total Points By Opponents-86 (10.7 AVG)
Total Points By CHS-50 (6.2 AVG)

1941

Won 6, Lost 2, Tied 0
El Won 4, Lost 1, Tied 0
Coach: Carl Hance

Opponent	Score
Pana	6-0
Arcola	6-0
Gertsmeyer	6-19
Paris*	0-12
Oblong*	6-0
Casey*	12-0
Marshall*	7-0
Newton*	18-0

Total Points By Opponents-31 (3.8 AVG)
Total Points By CHS-61 (7.6 AVG)

1942

Won 7, Lost 2, Tied 0
El Won 5, Lost 0, Tied 0 (El Champs)
Coach: Leonard King

Opponent	Score
Mattoon	0-24
Georgetown	12-6
Tuscola	0-13
Shelbyville	41-0
Paris*	40-7
Oblong*	55-0
Marshall*	38-6
Casey*	7-0
Newton*	46-0

Total Points By Opponents-56 (7.0 AVG)
Total Points By CHS-239 (26.5 (AVG)

1943

Won 4, Lost 3, Tied 2
El Won 3, Lost 1, Tied 1

Coach: Leonard King

Opponent	Score
Champaign	0-43
Georgetown	7-7
Shelbyville	27-0
Paris*	6-2
Oblong*	14-0
Marshall*	0-0
Casey*	12-34
Newton*	12-7
Mattoon	0-19

Total Points By Opponents-112 (12.4 AVG)
Total Points By CHS-78 (8.6 AVG)

1944

Won 3, Lost 3, Tied 2
EI Won 2, Lost 1, Tied 2
Coach: Leonard King

Opponent	Score
Georgetown	0-34
Lincoln	6-20
Shelbyville	45-7
Paris*	7-0
Oblong*	39-0
Marshall*	12-12
Casey*	6-19
Newton*	6-6

Total Points By Opponents-98 (12.2 AVG)
Total Points By CHS-115 (14.3 AVG)

1945

Won 3, Lost 2, Tied 3
EI Won 3, Lost 0, Tied 2
Coach: Sam Blackwell

Opponent	Score
Georgetown	0-13
Lincoln	0-41
Paris*	0-0
Oblong*	21-7
Marshall*	20-6
Casey	13-13
Newton*	6-2
Shelbyville	6-6

Total Points By Opponents-88 (11.0 AVG)
Total Points By CHS-66 (8.2 AVG)

1946

Won 1, Lost 7, Tied 0
EI Won 1, Lost 4, Tied 0
Coach: Sam Blackwell

Opponent	Score
Georgetown	25-0
Mattoon	32-0
Westville	19-6
Paris*	25-0
Oblong*	20-0
Marshall*	13-6
Casey*	29-7
Newton*	13-7

Total Points By Opponents-156 (19.5 AVG)
Total Points By Charleston-46 (5.7 AVG)

1947

Won 2, Lost 5, Tied 1
EI Won 1, Lost 4, Tied 0
Coach: Joe Bressler

Opponent	Score
Urbana	19-0
Mattoon	7-13
Georgetown	13-13
Paris*	6-14
Oblong*	25-6
Newton*	0-20
Casey*	7-21
Marshall*	7-12

Total Points By Opponents-159 (19.8 AVG)
Total Points By CHS-84 (10.5 AVG)

1948

Won 0, Lost 7, Tied 1
EI Won 0, Lost 4, Tied 1
Coach: Joe Bressler

Opponent	Score
Urbana	7-18
Mattoon	0-54
Georgetown	0-33
Effingham*	13-13
Marshall*	6-14
Paris*	7-38
Casey*	0-40
Newton*	0-26

Total Points By Opponents-236 (29.5 AVG)
Total Points By CHS-33 (4.1 AVG)

1949

Won 1, Lost 6, Tied 1
EI Won 1, Lost 4, Tied 0
Coach: Joe Bressler

Opponent	Score
Urbana	12-12
Mattoon	0-46
Georgetown	7-21
Effingham*	6-27
Marshall*	0-39
Paris*	7-0
Casey*	13-32
Newton*	6-48

Total Points By Opponents-225 (28.1 AVG)
Total Points By CHS-51 (6.3 AVG)

1950

Won 1, Lost 7, Tied 0
EI Won 1, Lost 4, Tied 0
Coach: Paul Swoffard

Opponent	Score
Urbana	7-12
Villa Grove	6-7
Effingham	13-40
Marshall*	26-18
Paris*	6-13
Casey*	12-14
Newton*	26-28
Unity High (Tolono)	0-27

Total Points By Opponents-159 (19.8 AVG)
Total Points By CHS-96 (12.0 AVG)

1951

Won 3, Lost 5, Tied 0
EI Won 3, Lost 3, Tied 0
Coach: Paul Swoffard

Opponent	Score
Arcola	12-21
Villa Grove	0-24
Oblong*	28-6
Effingham*	7-6
Marshall*	13-12
Paris*	0-20
Casey	6-26
Newton*	6-13

Total Points By Opponents-128 (16.0 AVG)
Total Points By CHS-72 (9.0 AVG)

1952

Won 2, Lost 5, Tied 2
EI Won 2, Lost 4, Tied 1
Coach: Paul Swoffard

Opponent	Score
Arcola	6-14
Eastern State*	19-19
Oblong*	38-0
Effingham*	0-6
Alumni	12-12
Paris*	7-20
Casey*	6-26
Newton*	13-14
Marshall*	27-6

Total Points By Opponents-117 (13.0 AVG)
Total Points By CHS-128 (14.2 AVG)

1953

Won 1, Lost 7, Tied 0
EI Won 1, Lost 6, Tied 0
Coach: Mervin Baker

Opponent	Score
Oakland	19-26
Robinson*	0-30
Oblong*	20-12
Effingham*	0-28
Marshall*	6-21
Paris*	6-20
Casey	0-39
Newton*	0-35

Total Points By Opponents-231 (28.8 AVG)
Total Points By CHS-51 (6.3 AVG)

1954

Won 7, Lost 1, Tied 0
EI Won 6, Lost 1, Tied 0
Coach: Mervin Baker

Opponent	Score
Oakland	28-0
Robinson*	7-6
Oblong*	19-6
Effingham	27-0
Marshall*	34-0
Paris	19-7
Casey*	14-18
Newton*	34-0

Total Points By Opponents-37 (4.6 AVG)
Total Points By CHS-182 (22.7 AVG)

1955

Won 7, Lost 0, Tied 1
EI Won 6, Lost 0, Tied 1 (EI Champs)
Coach: Mervin Baker

Opponent	Score
Oakland	33-7
Robinson*	12-12
Oblong*	20-12
Effingham*	27-6
Marshall*	47-7
Paris*	26-6
Casey*	7-0
Newton*	20-0

Total Points By Opponents-50 (6.2 AVG)
Total Points By CHS-192 (24.0 AVG)

1956

Won 6, Lost 1, Tied 1
EI Won 5, Lost 1, Tied 1
Coach: Mervin Baker

Opponent	Score
Oakland	33-2
Robinson*	19-6
Oblong*	13-13
Effingham*	19-20
Marshall*	53-12
Paris*	47-12
Casey*	20-0
Newton*	16-6

Total Points By Opponents-71 (8.8 AVG)
Total Points By CHS-220 (27.5 AVG)

1957

Won 6, Lost 1, Tied 1
EI Won 4, Lost 1, Tied 1
Coach: Mervin Baker

Opponent	Score
Oakland	34-12
Robinson*	20-0
Oblong*	28-0
Effingham*	0-0
Marshall*	27-12
Eisenhower	14-0
Casey*	27-13
Newton*	19-33

Total Points By Opponents-70 (8.7 AVG)
Total Points By CHS-169 (21.1 AVG)

1958

Won 4, Lost 3, Tied 1
El Won 3, Lost 2, Tied 1
Coach: Mervin Baker

Opponent	Score
Robinson*	6-6
Oblong*	33-7
Effingham*	26-0
Marshall*	0-15
Eisenhower	6-7
Casey*	6-7
Newton*	21-0
Albion	13-6

Total Points By Opponents-53 (6.6 AVG)
Total Points By CHS-111 (13.8 AVG)

1959

Won 6, Lost 1, Tied 1
El Won 6, Lost 0, Tied 1 (El Champs)
Coach: Mervin Baker

Opponent	Score
Robinson*	12-12
Oblong*	28-0
Paris*	31-7
Marshall	46-0
Eisenhower	0-13
Casey*	33-21
Newton*	33-13
Effingham*	28-0

Total Points By Opponents-66 (8.2 AVG)
Total Points By CHS-211 (26.3 AVG)

1960

Won 5, Lost 2, Tied 1
El Won 3, Lost 0, Tied 1
Coach: Mervin Baker

Opponent	Score
Casey*	13-0
Lawrenceville	7-6
Marshall*	34-13
Paris*	12-14
Martinsville*	33-0
Newton*	7-7
Eisenhower	7-18
Robinson*	33-6

Total Points By Opponents-64 (8.0 AVG)
Total Points By CHS-146 (18.2 AVG)

1961

Won 8, Lost 1, Tied 0
El Won 4, Lost 1, Tied 0 (El Champs)
Coach: Mervin Baker

Opponent	Score
Oblong*	32-12
Casey*	38-13
Lawrenceville	25-0
Marshall*	28-13
Paris*	13-6
Martinsville*	25-0
Newton*	12-21
St. Teresa	14-0
Robinson*	26-7

Total Points By Opponents-72 (8.0 AVG)
Total Points By CHS-213 (23.6 AVG)

1962

Won 6, Lost 2, Tied 0
El Won 5, Lost 2, Tied 0
Coach: Mervin Baker

Opponent	Score
St. Teresa	13-7
Casey*	26-20
Paris*	7-13
Marshall*	20-13
Robinson*	14-0

Palestine..31-0
Newton*..0-24
Oblong*..27-13

Total Points By Opponents-90 (11.2 AVG)
Total Points By CHS-138 (17.2 AVG)

1963

Won 7, Lost 2, Tied 0
El Won 5, Lost 2, Tied 0
Coach: Mervin Baker
Opponent   Score
St. Teresa...20-6
Lanphier of Springfield...................13-12
Casey*..38-0
Paris*..0-7
Marshall*..34-13
Robinson*..13-19
Palestine...54-6
Newton*...53-13
Oblong*..14-0

Total Points By Opponents-76 (8.4 AVG)
Total Points By CHS-239 (29.8 AVG)

1964

Won 7, Lost 1, Tied 1
El Won 4, Lost 1, Tied 1
Coach: Mervin Baker
Opponent   Score
St. Teresa...7-0
Lanphier of Springfield...................6-6
Robinson*..21-0
Casey*..41-7
Cumberland......................................47-0
Paris*..0-13
Newton*...41-7
Marshall*..26-13
Oblong*..27-20

Total Points By Opponents 66 (7.1 AVG)
Total Points By CHS-216 (24 AVG)

1965

Won 7, Lost 1, Tied 0
El Won 5, Lost 1, Tied 0 (El Champs)
Coach: Mervin Baker
Opponent   Score
St. Teresa...21-0
Casey*..26-0
Oblong*..35-0
Paris*..36-6
Marshall*..40-0
Robinson*..28-6
Newton*...28-32
Cumberland......................................35-0

Total Points By Opponents-40 (4.8 AVG)
Total Points By CHS-249 (31.1 AVG)

1966

Won 8, Lost 0, Tied 0
El Won 7, Lost 0, Tied 0 (El Champs)
Coach: Mervin Baker
Opponent   Score
Casey*..45-14
Martinsville*....................................48-0
Marshall*..47-0
Robinson*..42-6
Newton*...27-13
Oblong*..42-0
Paris*..19-0
Cumberland......................................60-19
Total Points By Opponents-52 (6.5)
Total Points By CHS-330 (41.3)

1967

Won 4, Lost 4, Tied 0
El Won 3, Lost 4, Tied 0
Coach: Mervin Baker
Opponent   Score
Casey*..38-0

Opponent	Score
Martinsville*	61-6
Marshall*	12-19
Robinson*	34-7
Newton*	6-21
Oblong*	7-41
Paris*	6-12
Cumberland	33-13

Total Points By Opponents-102 (14.0 AVG)
Total Points By CHS-198 (24.7 AVG

1968

Won 1, Lost 5, Tied 2
EI Won 0, Lost 3, Tied 2
Coach: Mervin Baker

Opponent	Score
Arcola	12-40
Mt. Zion	19-13
Paris*	13-25
Robinson*	7-7
Casey*	9-14
Marshall*	6-6
Newton*	6-13
Unity	14-19

Total Points By Opponents-137 (17.1 AVG)
Total Points By CHS-87 (10.8 AVG)

1969

Won 7, Lost 1, Tied 0
EI Won 4, Lost 0, Tied 0 (EI Champs)
Coach: Mervin Baker

Opponent	Score
Arcola	24-6
Mt. Zion	0-23
Paris*	8-6
Robinson*	44-8
Casey	46-0
Marshall*	40-22
Newton*	6-0
Unity	40-7

Total Points By Opponents-72 (9.0 AVG)
Total Points By CHS-208 (26.0 AVG)

1970-Apollo Conference Originates

Won 6, Lost 2, Tied 0
Apollo Won 2, Lost 1, Tied 0 (Apollo Champs)
Coach: Jerry Van Bellehem

Opponent	Score
Peoria Woodruff	6-10
Mt. Zion	Win
Paris*	8-0
Robinson*	16-18
Casey	36-21
Marshall	Win
Newton*	54-6
Unity	44-16

1971

Won 3, Lost 7, Tied 0
Apollo Won 1, Lost 2, Tied 0
Coach: Jerry Van Bellehem

Opponent	Score
Hoopeston	20-6
Mt. Zion	6-26
Lakeview	12-0
Paris*	6-23
Robinson*	24-22
Bloomington Central Catholic	14-52
Marshall	8-19
Newton*	0-13
Unity	14-34
Olney	14-28

Total Points By Opponents-223 (22.3 AVG)
Total Points By CHS-118 (11.8 AVG)

1972

Won 2, Lost 6, Tied 2
Apollo Won 1, Lost 2, Tied 1

Coach: Jerry Van Bellehem

Opponent	Score
Taylorville	6-28
Marshall	30-7
Lakeview*	7-0
Paris*	7-8
Robinson*	6-6
Bloomington Central Catholic	15-26
Mt. Zion*	12-14
Newton*	20-20
Unity	6-26
Olney	18-19

Total Points By Opponents-154 (15.4 AVG)
Total Points By CHS-121 (12.1 AVG)

1973

Won 8, Lost 1, Tied 0
Apollo Won 5, Lost 0, Tied 0 (Apollo Champs)
Coach: Chuck Budde

Opponent	Score
Taylorville	15-16
Marshall	25-20
Lakeview*	21-6
Paris*	20-15
Robinson*	36-20
Sullivan, IN	31-13
Mt. Zion*	53-6
Newton*	10-0
Unity	40-6

Total Points By Opponents-102 (11.3 AVG)
Total Points By CHS-251 (27.8 AVG)

1974

Won 8 Lost 1, Tied 0
Apollo Won 4, Lost 1, Tied 0 (Apollo Champs)
Coach: Chuck Budde

Opponent	Score
Taylorville	12-7
Olney	14-0
Rantoul	26-13
Benton	40-23
Robinson*	28-7
Paris*	30-0
Mt. Zion	12-13
Newton*	34-0
Lakeview*	57-12

Total Points By Opponents-75 (8.3 AVG)
Total Points By CHS-253 (28.1 AVG)

1975

Won 3, Lost 5, Tied 1
Apollo Won 2, Lost 3, Tied 0
Coach: Chuck Budde

Opponent	Score
Taylorville	20-20
Olney	32-16
Rantoul	7-23
Benton	6-12
Robinson*	35-0
Paris*	19-21
Mt. Zion*	3-18
Newton*	14-27
Lakeview*	18-6

Total Points By Opponents-143 (15.8 AVG)
Total Points By CHS-154 (17.1 AVG)

1976

Won 6, Lost 3, Tied 0 (State Qualifier)
Apollo Won 5, Lost 0, Tied 0 (Apollo Champs)
Coach: Chuck Budde

Opponent	Score
Taylorville	10-16
Olney	15-20
Rantoul	20-14
Robinson*	14-6
Paris*	14-0
Mt. Zion*	7-2

Newton*..22-0
Lakeview*...50-0
Roxana^..7-17

Total Points By Opponents-75 (8.3 AVG)
Total Points By CHS-159 (17.7 AVG)

1977-Final Four

Won 10, Lost 1, Tied 0 (State Qualifier)
Apollo Won 5, Lost 0, Tied 0 (Apollo Champs)
Coach: Chuck Budde

Opponent	Score
Taylorville	42-8
Olney	28-0
Rantoul	36-20
Robinson*	10-0
Pairs*	26-12
Mt. Zion*	6-0
Newton*	17-15
Lakeview*	34-0
McLeansboro^	49-7
Murphysboro^	28-21
Metamora^	6-18

Total Points By Opponents-101 (9.2 AVG)
Total Points By CHS-282 (25.6 AVG)

1978-Final Four

Won 10, Lost 1, Tied 0 (State Qualifier)
Apollo Won 5, Lost 0, Tied 0 (Apollo Champs)
Coach: Chuck Budde

Opponent	Score
Taylorville	25-0
Olney	20-2
Rantoul	21-8
Robinson*	26-7
Paris*	17-6
Mt. Zion*	10-0
Newton*	38-14
Lakeview*	37-20

Olney^..26-12
Murphysboro^...39-0
Kankakee McNamara^..............................0-7

Total Points By Opponents-76 (6.9 AVG)
Total Points By CHS-259 (23.6 AVG)

1979-Final Four

Won 10, Lost 2, Tied 2 (State Qualifier)
Apollo Won 5, Lost 0, Tied 0 (Apollo Champs)
Coach: Chuck Budde

Opponent	Score
Metamora	27-26
Olney	48-7
Rantoul	17-20
Benton	39-6
Robinson*	40-0
Paris*	61-12
Mt. Zion*	14-7
Newton*	14-7
Lakeview*	53-14
Mt. Carmel^	46-14
Harrisburg^	35-14
Mascoutah^	15-21

Total Points By Opponents-142 (11.8 AVG)
Total Points By CHS-409 (34.1 AVG)

1980

Won 3, Lost 6, Tied 0
Apollo Won 2, Lost 3, Tied 0
Coach: Bill Monken

Opponent	Score
Metamora	14-36
Olney	2-0 (Forfeit)
Rantoul	14-15
Quincy	0-6
Robinson*	36-7
Paris*	33-0
Mt. Zion*	10-18
Newton*	0-21

Lakeview*..12-46

Total Points By Opponents-139 (17.4 AVG)
Total Points By CHS-121 (15.13 AVG)

1981

Won 4, Lost 5, Tied 0
Apollo Won 3, Lost 4, Tied 0
Coach: Bill Monken

Opponent	Score
Kankakee Eastridge	6-42
Olney	28-0
Paris*	35-0
Effingham*	25-20
Newton*	16-5
Taylorville*	14-20
Lakeview*	12-46
Robinson*	22-16
Mt. Zion*	14-16

Total Points By Opponents-145 (16.1 AVG)
Total Points By CHS-162 (18.0 AVG)

1982

Won 8, Lost 2, Tied 0 (State Qualifier)
Apollo Won 5, Lost 1, Tied 0
Coach: Verlon Myers

Opponent	Score
Kankakee Eastridge	28-12
Olney	16-7
Paris*	2-0 (Forfeit)
Effingham*	42-7
Newton*	6-0 OT
Taylorville*	28-0
Rantoul	15-14
Robinson*	26-0
Mt. Zion*	7-21
Olney^	15-34

Total Points By Opponents-95 (10.6)
Total Points By CHS-183 (20.3 AVG)

1983

Won 6, Lost 3, Tied 0
Apollo Won 4, Lost 2, Tied 0 (Apollo Champs)
Coach: Verlon Myers

Opponent	Score
Chatham-Glenwood	16-7
Olney	26-7
Paris*	37-14
Effingham*	14-20
Newton*	21-20
Taylorville*	17-6
Rantoul	0-3 OT
Robinson*	27-10
Mt. Zion*	0-21

Total Points By Opponents-108 (12.0 AVG)
Total Points By CHS-158 (17.6 AVG)

1984

Won 8, Lost 1, Tied 0 (State Qualifier)
Apollo Won 6, Lost 0, Tied 0 (Apollo Champs)
Coach: Verlon Myers

Opponent	Score
Mattoon	20-18
Olney	31-14
Paris*	46-0
Effingham*	25-8
Newton*	21-6
Taylorville*	19-13
Robinson*	15-0
Mt. Zion*	22-15
Mt. Carmel^	16-38

Total Points By Opponents-112 (12.4 AVG)
Total Points By CHS-215 (23.9 AVG)

1985

Won 4, Lost 4, Tied 0
Apollo Won 4, Lost 2, Tied 0

Coach: Verlon Myers

Opponent	Score
Mattoon	0-6 OT
Olney	7-10
Paris*	0-2 (Forfeit)
Effingham*	20-6
Newton*	21-20
Taylorville*	28-21
Robinson*	27-6
Mt. Zion*	7-36

Total Points By Opponents-95 (13.6 AVG)
Total Points By CHS-110 (15.7 AVG)

1986

Coach 4, Lost 5, Tied 0
Apollo Won 4, Lost 2, Tied 0
Coach: Verlon Myers

Opponent	Score
Mattoon	8-48
Olney	12-20
Paris*	7-0
Effingham*	24-10
Newton*	0-24
Taylorville*	35-12
Murphysboro	8-34
Robinson*	8-7
Mt. Zion*	7-30

Total Points By Opponents-185 (20.6 AVG)
Total Points By CHS-109 (12.1 AVG)

1987

Won 2, Lost 7, Tied 0
Apollo Won 2, Lost 4, Tied 0
Coach: Verlon Myers

Opponent	Score
Mattoon	0-24
Olney	13-21
Paris*	21-14
Effingham*	14-39
Newton*	2-18
Taylorville*	6-19
Murphysboro	7-17
Robinson*	10-6
Mt. Zion*	6-28

Total Points By Opponents-186 (20.7 AVG)
Total Points By CHS-78 (8.7 AVG)

1988

Won 7, Lost 2, Tied 0 (State Qualifier)
Apollo Won 5, Lost 1, Tied 0
Coach: Verlon Myers

Opponent	Score
Olney	25-0
Paris*	49-0
Effingham*	21-7
Newton*	28-0
Taylorville*	46-0
Murphysboro	23-15
Robinson*	20-12
Mt. Zion*	14-20
Rantoul^	22-33

Total Points By Opponents-87 (9.7 AVG)
Total Points By CHS-248 (27.6 AVG)

1989

Won 6, Lost 2, Tied 0
Apollo Won 4, Lost 2, Tied 0
Coach: Verlon Myers

Opponent	Score
Olney	28-0
Paris*	10-6
Effingham*	41-12
Newton*	42-16
Taylorville*	40-0
Murphysboro	27-7
Robinson*	13-22
Mt. Zion*	14-28

Total Points By Opponents-91 (11.4 AVG)
Total Points By CHS-26.9 AVG)

1990

Won 3, Lost 6, Tied 0
Apollo Won 2, Lost 4, Tied 0
Coach Verlon Myers

Opponent	Score
Mascoutah	14-35
Olney	24-0
Paris*	6-13
Effingham*	21-9
Newton*	7-21
Taylorville*	18-20
Murphysboro	13-34
Robinson*	28-13
Mt. Zion*	14-42

Total Points By Opponents-187 (20.8 AVG)
Total Points By CHS-155 (17.2 AVG)

1991

Won 2, Lost 7, Tied 0
Apollo Won 0, Lost 6, Tied 0
Coach: Verlon Myers

Opponent	Score
Mascoutah	2-0 (Forfeit)
Olney	22-8
Paris*	14-32
Effingham*	32-44
Newton*	12-33
Taylorville*	8-15
Robinson*	22-35
Mt. Zion*	8-26

Total Points By Opponents-227 (28.4 AVG)
Total Points By CHS-130 (16.3 AVG)

1992

Won 4, Lost 5, Tied 0
Apollo Won 2, Lost 4, Tied 0
Coach: Verlon Myers

Opponent	Score
Mascoutah	7-0
Olney	20-7
Paris*	21-20
Effingham*	12-34
Newton*	9-20
Taylorville*	33-7
Murphysboro	7-34
Robinson*	23-59
Mt. Zion*	18-35

Total Points By Opponents-216 (24.0 AVG)
Total Points By CHS-150 (16.7 AVG)

1993

Won 3, Lost 6, Tied 0
Apollo Won 2, Lost 3, Tied 0
Coach: Bill Monken

Opponent	Score
Mascoutah	6-20
Olney	23-13
Paris*	42-20
Effingham*	12-28
Newton*	7-20
Urbana	30-42
Centralia	13-28
Robinson*	0-49
Mt. Zion*	19-6

Total Points By Opponents-226 (25.1 AVG)
Total Points By CHS-152 (16.9 AVG)

1994

Won 1, Lost 8, Tied 0
Apollo Won 0, Lost 5, Tied 0
Coach: Bill Monken

Opponent	Score
Taylorville	6-42
Olney	34-7
Paris*	12-20
Effingham*	8-33
Newton*	0-6
Urbana	6-34
Centralia	6-32

Robinson*......................................18-42
Mt. Zion...27-48
Total Points By Opponents-264 (29.3 AVG)
Total Points By CHS-117 (13.0 AVG)

1995

Won 4, Lost 5, Tied 0
Apollo Won 4, Lost 2, Tied 0
Coach: Bill Monken

Opponent	Score
Taylorville	18-39
Olney	0-7
Paris*	40-8
Effingham*	6-28
Newton*	22-21
Bethalto Civic Memorial	20-42
Centralia	22-7
Robinson*	6-27
Mt. Zion*	26-7

Total Points By Opponents-186 (20.7 AVG)
Total Points By CHS-160 (17.8 AVG)

1996

Won 9, Lost 2, Tied 0 (State Qualifier)
Apollo Won 4, Lost 1, Tied 0 (Apollo Champs)
Coach: Bill Monken

Opponent	Score
Taylorville	27-20
Olney	33-6
Paris*	52-0
Effingham*	32-7
Newton*	33-13
Bethalto Civic Memorial	7-0
Robinson*	36-24
Mt. Zion*	21-28
Champaign Central^	40-7
Springfield^	15-24

Total Points By Opponents-135 (12.3 AVG)
Total Points By CHS-336 (30.6 AVG)

1997

Won 5, Lost 4, Tied 0
Apollo Won 3, Lost 2, Tied 0
Coach: Bill Monken

Opponent	Score
Taylorville	0-28
Olney	35-36
Marshall	43-22
Robinson*	20-44
Newton*	37-16
Effingham*	14-13
Paris*	48-8
Mt. Zion*	23-24
Centralia	73-37

Total Points By Opponents-228 (25.3 AVG)
Total Points By CHS-293 (32.6 AVG)

1998

Won 1, Lost 8, Tied 0
Apollo Won 0, Lost 5, Tied 0
Coach: Jerry Rolson

Opponent	Score
Taylorville	26-40
Olney	18-27
Marshall	15-23
Robinson*	14-20
Newton*	6-35
Effingham*	7-19
Paris*	22-27
Mt. Zion	9-14
Centralia	20-14

Total Points By Opponents-219 (24.3 AVG)
Total Points By CHS-137 (15.2 AVG)

1999

Won 1, Lost 8, Tied 0
Apollo Won 1, Lost 4, Tied 0
Coach: Bill Monken

Opponent	Score
Taylorville	7-40
Olney	21-45
Pontiac	7-53
Mt. Zion*	12-38
Robinson*	15-34
Newton*	0-41
Effingham*	6-43
Paris*	50-20
Centralia	0-48

Total Points By Opponents-362 (40.2 AVG)
Total Points By CHS-118 (13.1 AVG)

2000

Won 0, Lost 9, Tied 0
Apollo Won 0, Lost 5, Tied 0
Coach: Brian Halsey

Opponent	Score
Taylorville	7-40
Olney	0-52
Mahomet-Seymour	0-55
Mt. Zion*	7-54
Robinson	6-46
Newton*	7-40
Effingham*	0-35
Paris*	20-21
Centralia	6-35

Total Points By Opponents-378 (42.0 AVG)
Total Points By CHS-53 (5.9 AVG)

2001

Won 1, Lost 8, Tied 0
Apollo 1, Lost 4, Tied 0
Coach: Brian Halsey

Opponent	Score
Taylorville	20-28
Olney	12-24
Mahomet-Seymour	12-34
Paris*	14-6
Mt. Zion*	6-31
Robinson*	0-34
Newton*	28-30
Effingham*	21-45
Salem	15-48

Total Points By Opponents-280 (31.1 AVG)
Total Points By CHS-128 (14.2 AVG)

2002

Won 7, Lost 4, Tied 0 (State Qualifier)
Apollo Won 3, Lost 2, Tied 0 (Apollo Champs)
Coach: Brian Halsey

Opponent	Score
Taylorville	12-34
Olney	40-14
Mascoutah	49-7
Paris*	7-6
Mt. Zion*	13-20
Robinson*	38-39 2OT
Newton*	21-14
Effingham*	25-13
Salem	35-6
Waterloo^	35-28
Springfield Sacred Heart Griffin	20-53

Total Points By Opponents: 234 (21.3 AVG)
Total Points By CHS: 260 (23.6 AVG)

2003

Won 9, Lost 2, Tied 0 (State Qualifier)
Apollo Won 7, Lost 0, Tied 0 (Apollo Champs)
Coach: Brian Halsey

Opponent	Score
Taylorville	7-21
Olney*	28-6
Mt. Zion*	28-27
Paris*	33-14
Newton*	26-14
Robinson*	27-26
Salem*	41-12

Effingham*......................................21-14
Bethalto Civic Memorial................21-14
Waterloo^..34-14
Highland^..14-17
Total Points By Opponents: 179 (16.3 AVG)
Total Points By CHS: 280 (25.5 AVG)

2004

Won 8, Lost 2, Tied 0 (State Qualifier)
Apollo Won 6, Lost 1, Tied 0 (Apollo Champs)
Coach Brian Halsey

Opponent	Score
Taylorville	16-14
Newton*	28-6
Robinson*	42-26
Salem*	21-14
Effingham*	35-47
Olney*	33-30
Mt. Zion*	28-25
Paris*	39-13
Bethalto Civic Memorial	28-21
Jacksonville^	0-40

Total Points By Opponents-236 (23.6 AVG)
Total Points By CHS-260 (26.0 AVG)

2005

Won 6, Lost 4, Tied 0 (State Qualifier)
Apollo Won 6, Lost 1, Tied 0
Coach: Brian Halsey

Opponent	Score
Taylorville	19-27
Paris*	33-7
Newton*	14-20
Robinson*	28-14
Salem*	21-12
Effingham*	38-35
Olney*	39-6
Mt. Zion*	27-12
Highland	0-14
Cahokia^	0-38

Total Points By Opponents-185 (18.5 AVG)
Total Points By CHS-219 (21.9 AVG)

2006

Won 2, Lost 7, Tied 0
Apollo Won 2, Lost 5, Tied 0
Coach: Brian Halsey

Opponent	Score
Taylorville	14-36
Paris*	49-7
Newton*	37-39
Robinson*	21-28
Salem*	21-55
Effingham*	13-29
Olney*	30-20
Mt. Zion*	13-21
Highland	12-29

Total Points By Opponents-264 (26.4 AVG)
Total Points By CHS-210 (21.0 AVG)

2007-Elite Eight

Won 7, Lost 5, Tied 0 (State Qualifier)
Apollo Won 4, Lost 3, Tied 0
Coach: Brian Halsey

Opponent	Score
Taylorville	30-13
Mt. Zion*	24-27
Paris*	40-6
Newton*	6-15
Robinson*	40-0
Salem*	28-21
Effingham*	28-42
Olney*	41-29
Highland	30-41
Effingham^	22-20
Mt. Vernon^	28-12
Marion^	22-43

Total Points By Opponents-275 (22.9 AVG)
Total Points By CHS-311 (25.9 AVG)

2008

Won 4, Lost 5, Tied 0
Apollo Won 4, Lost 3, Tied 0
Coach: Brian Halsey

Opponent	Score
Taylorville	6-38
Mt. Zion*	21-28
Paris*	14-28
Newton*	44-33
Robinson*	13-11
Salem*	27-26
Effingham*	41-48
Olney*	58-36
Highland	7-40

Total Points By Opponents-288 (32.0 AVG)
Total Points By CHS-231 (25.1 AVG)

2009

Won 4, Lost 5, Tied 0
Apollo Won 3, Lost 4, Tied 0
Coach: Brian Halsey

Opponent	Score
Taylorville	21-28
Olney*	21-0
Mt. Zion*	17-34
Paris*	35-20
Newton*	35-6
Robinson*	32-24
Salem*	7-14
Effingham*	21-26
Highland	32-31 OT

Total Points By Opponents-193 (21.4 AVG)
Total Points By CHS-221 (24.5 AVG)

2010

Won 5, Lost 4, Tied 0
Apollo Won 4, Lost 3, Tied 0
Coach: Brian Halsey

Opponent	Score
Rantoul	24-20
Olney*	27-6
Mt. Zion*	14-42
Paris*	33-36
Newton*	12-7
Robinson*	42-28
Salem*	35-21
Effingham*	6-36
Highland	21-42

Total Points By Opponents: 238 (26.4 AVG)
Total Points By CHS-214 (23.7 AVG)

2011-Final Four

Won 11, Lost 2, Tied 0 (State Qualifier)
Apollo Won 6, Lost 1, Tied 0 (Apollo Champs)
Coach: Brian Halsey

Opponent	Score
Rantoul	68-44
Effingham*	40-14
Olney*	28-16
Mt. Zion*	0-35
Paris*	28-7
Newton*	47-27
Robinson*	48-20
Salem*	46-15
Highland	47-28
Waterloo^	55-35
Herrin^	34-21
Mt. Zion^	28-27
Rochester^	13-41

Total Points By Opponents-358 (27.5 AVG)
Total Points By CHS-482 (37.0 AVG)

2012

Won 9, Lost 2, Tied 0 (State Qualifier)
Apollo Won 5, Lost 0, Tied 0 (Apollo Champs)
Coach: Brian Halsey

Opponent	Score
Rantoul	49-6
Peoria Manual	49-0
Chatham Glenwood	41-42
Effingham*	46-7
Mattoon*	55-29
Mount Zion*	56-28
Paris*	44-0
Salem*	42-7
Highland	46-21
Central Catholic^	55-10
Rochester^	14-42

Total Points By Opponents-191 (17.4 AVG)
Total Points By CHS-497 (45.2 AVG)

2013

Won 1, Lost 8, Tied 0
Apollo Won 0, Lost 5, Tied 0
Coach: Brian Halsey

Opponent	Score
Rantoul	36-22
Massac County	26-45
Chatham Glenwood	7-42
Effingham*	13-26
Mattoon*	28-56
Mount Zion*	7-42
Paris*	14-42
Salem*	19-51
Highland	0-56

Total Points By Opponents-382 (42.4 AVG)
Total Points By CHS-150 (16.6 AVG)

2014

Won 1, Lost 8, Tied 0
Apollo Won 0, Lost 5, Tied 0
Coach: Brian Halsey

Opponent	Score
Rantoul	33-26
Mount Vernon	0-28
Centralia	0-42
Effingham*	7-41
Mattoon*	14-41
Mount Zion*	26-52
Taylorville*	0-21
Salem*	9-26
Highland	14-62

Total Points By Opponents-339 (37.6 AVG)
Total Points By CHS-103 (11.4 AVG)

2015

Won 0, Lost 9, Tied 0
Apollo Won 0, Lost 5, Tied 0
Coach: Tim Hogan

Opponent	Score
Rantoul	7-14
Mount Vernon	6-40
Centralia	14-58
Effingham*	0-9
Mattoon*	14-48
Mount Zion*	20-53
Taylorville*	17-43
Salem*	14-52
Highland	0-45

Total Points By Opponents-362 (40.2 AVG)
Total Points By CHS-92 (10.2 AVG)

2016

Won 3, Lost 6, Tied 0
Apollo Won 1, Lost 4, Tied 0
Coach: Tyler Hanner

Opponent	Score
Rantoul	14-6
Mount Vernon	41-14
Centralia	8-41

Effingham*	7-27	Opponent	Score
Mattoon*	0-27		
Mount Zion*	0-40	Canton	13-18
Taylorville*	0-40	Mahomet Seymour*	12-24
Salem*	20-14 OT	Taylorville*	20-55
Highland	14-46	Mattoon*	24-41

Total Points By Opponents-255 (28.3 AVG)
Total Points By CHS-104 (11.4 AVG)

Mount Zion*..............8-28
Lincoln*..................14-40
Effingham*...............0-28
Quincy Notre Dame....0-51

2017

Highland..................6-63

Won 0, Lost 9, Tied 0
Apollo Won 0, Lost 6, Tied 0
Coach: Tyler Hanner

Total Points By Opponents-348 (38.6 AVG)
Total Points By CHS-97 (10.7 AVG)

- Jon Adkins, former quarterback and Class of 2003, became the youngest head coach in the IHSA when he took the head football coach position at Peoria Heights in 2010. Adkins coached for six seasons before leaving in 2016. Adkins led Peoria Heights to a playoff appearance in his last season.

- Superfan, Kevin James, can be seen at all home football and basketball events. The old Save-A-Lot grocery store used to be across the high school, and Kevin would work as a cashier. Many fans could see Kevin as he loves to talk about Trojan athletics. Many fans in the community have even brought Kevin to road games. He can be seen going on his daily walks, including in the winter when he sports his Charleston letterman jacket.

- Bill Moore, a 1975 CHS graduate, started at strong safety on the 1978 Division II National Championship Eastern Illinois University football team. EIU won the title by defeating Delaware 10-9. Moore, who was a safety under Chuck Budde, went on to coach at CHS for multiple years in the 90s when Bill Monken was head coach. Sports runs in the family as his daughter, Ian, signed as Kaskaskia College for soccer, while his other daughter, Rainer, is a three-sport athlete.

Jack Ashmore and Rob Calhoun: The Voice of Charleston Football

Jack Ashmore has been calling Trojan games for quite some time as he started his career in 1993. Ashmore, an Oakland High School graduate, began his broadcasting career in 1971 at WITT in Tuscola. Ashmore is currently the play-by-play voice for Charleston High School boys' basketball and football, while adding color commentary for EIU football and basketball.

Rob Calhoun began working with Ashmore in 1998. Calhoun adds color commentary for Charleston High School boys' basketball and football, while serving as the play-by-pay voice for EIU women's basketball.

The duo has contributed 20 years to broadcasting Charleston football. The duo used to broadcast through WEIU until mandates prohibited university stations to stream high school athletics. Now, the two can be heard on either 103.9 The Victory, or 92.1 The Axe, which are through Cromwell Radio Group.

Trojan Hill Lucky with Great PA Voices

Paul Slifer was the PA man at Trojan Hill for years until 2013. His infamous, "And, that's another…….Trojan……..first down!" could be heard from blocks away. After Slifer left to take a job in Alabama, longtime Charleston announcer Matt Piescinski took over. Piescinski is an Illinois household name in the announcing field. Piescinski was the Eastern Illinois University PA announcer for basketball and football from 1980-2005. He has also been active calling the IHSA state track meet since 1991, and the IHSA state cross country and badminton tournaments since 2006.

Individual Team Breakdown

Albion (1-0-0)
1958............................. 13-6

Alumni (0-0-1)
1952......................12-12

Arcola (2-3-0)
1941..............................6-0
1951............................12-21
1952..............................6-14
1968............................12-40
1969............................24-6

Benton (2-1-0)
1974............................40-23
1975..............................6-12
1979............................39-6

Bethalto Civic Memorial (3-1-0)
1995............................42-20
1996..............................7-0
2003............................21-14
2004............................28-21

Bloomington Central Catholic (1-2-0)
1971............................14-52
1972............................15-26
2012............................55-10

Cahokia (0-1-0)
2005..............................0-38

Canton (0-1-0)
2017............................13-18

Carmi (1-0-0)
1939............................18-0

Casey (21-18-1)
1931..............................6-7
1932............................12-0
1933............................12-0
1934............................34-6
1935..............................0-6
1936..............................0-3
1937............................27-0
1938............................27-0
1939..............................6-0
1940..............................0-7
1941............................12-0

1942.....................................7-0
1943.....................................12-34
1944.....................................0-19
1945.....................................13-13
1946.....................................7-29
1947.....................................7-21
1948.....................................0-40
1949.....................................13-32
1950.....................................12-14
1951.....................................6-26
1952.....................................6-26
1953.....................................0-39
1954.....................................14-18
1955.....................................7-0
1956.....................................20-0
1957.....................................27-13
1958.....................................6-12
1959.....................................33-21
1960.....................................13-0
1961.....................................38-13
1962.....................................26-20
1963.....................................38-0
1964.....................................41-7
1965.....................................26-0
1966.....................................45-14
1967.....................................38-0
1968.....................................9-14
1969.....................................46-0
1970.....................................36-21

Catlin (1-0-0)
1940.....................................25-0

Centralia (4-8-0)
1938.....................................0-13
1993.....................................13-28
1994.....................................6-32
1995.....................................22-7
1996.....................................40-6
1997.....................................73-37
1998.....................................20-14
1999.....................................0-48
2000.....................................6-35
2014.....................................0-42

2015.....................................14-58
2016.....................................8-41

Champaign Central (1-2-0)
1936.....................................14-33
1943.....................................0-43
1996.....................................40-7

Chatham-Glenwood (1-2-0)
1983.....................................16-7
2012.....................................41-42
2013.....................................7-42

Chrisman (3-0-0)
1928.....................................6-0
1929.....................................31-6
1930.....................................40-0

Clinton (1-0-0)
1931.....................................7-6

Cumberland (4-0-0)
1964.....................................47-0
1965.....................................35-0
1966.....................................60-19
1967.....................................33-13

Decatur MacArthur (2-1-0)
1932.....................................26-0
1934.....................................7-6
1935.....................................0-8

Decatur Eisenhower (1-3-0)
1957.....................................14-0
1958.....................................6-7
1959.....................................0-13
1960.....................................7-18

Decatur Lakeview (9-2-0)
1971.....................................12-0
1972.....................................7-0
1973.....................................21-6
1974.....................................57-12
1975.....................................18-6

1976.....................50-0
1977.....................34-0
1978.....................37-20
1979.....................53-12
1980.....................12-46
1981.....................12-46

Eastern State (8-2-3)
1927.....................0-49
1928.....................0-26
1929.....................6-6
1930.....................0-0
1931.....................20-0
1932.....................46-0
1933.....................13-0
1934.....................53-0
1935.....................26-6
1936.....................58-21
1937.....................27-6
1938.....................92-0
1952.....................19-19

Effingham (20-30-2)
1928.....................6-62
1929.....................6-12
1948.....................13-13
1949.....................6-27
1950.....................13-40
1951.....................7-6
1952.....................0-6
1953.....................0-28
1954.....................27-0
1955.....................27-6
1956.....................19-20
1957.....................0-0
1958.....................26-0
1959.....................28-0
1981.....................15-20
1982.....................42-7
1983.....................14-20
1984.....................25-8
1985.....................20-6
1986.....................24-10
1987.....................14-39
1988.....................21-7
1989.....................41-12
1990.....................21-9
1991.....................32-41
1992.....................12-34
1993.....................12-28
1994.....................9-33
1995.....................6-28
1996.....................32-7
1997.....................14-13
1998.....................7-19
1999.....................6-43
2000.....................0-35
2001.....................21-45
2002.....................25-13
2003.....................21-14
2004.....................35-47
2005.....................38-35
2006.....................13-29
2007.....................28-48
2007.....................22-20
2008.....................41-48
2009.....................21-26
2010.....................6-36
2011.....................40-14
2012.....................46-7
2013.....................13-26
2014.....................7-41
2015.....................0-9
2016.....................7-27
2017.....................0-28

Flora (2-0-0)
1931.....................7-0
1932.....................32-20

Georgetown (1-5-2)
1942.....................12-6
1943.....................7-7
1944.....................0-34
1945.....................0-13
1946.....................0-25
1947.....................13-13
1948.....................0-33

1949.........................7-21

Gertsmeyer (1-2-0)
(Terre Haute, IN)
1933.........................3-0
1940.........................6-7
1941.........................6-19

Harrisburg (1-0-0)
1979.........................35-14

Herrin (1-0-0
2011.........................34-21

Highland (3-10-0)
2005.........................0-14
2006.........................12-29
2007.........................30-41
2008.........................7-40
2009.........................32-31
2010.........................21-42
2011.........................47-28
2012.........................46-21
2013.........................0-56
2014.........................14-62
2015.........................0-45
2016.........................14-46
2017.........................6-63

Hindsboro (1-2-0)
1927.........................6-12
1928.........................0-12
1929.........................19-6

Hoopeston (1-0-0)
1971.........................20-6

Jacksonville (0-1-0)
2004.........................0-40

Kankakee Eastridge (1-1-0)
1981.........................6-42
1982.........................28-12

Kankakee McNamara (0-1-0)
1978.........................0-7

Lanphier Springfield (1-0-0)
1963.........................13-12

Lawrenceville (2-0-1)
1930.........................19-19
1960.........................7-6
1961.........................25-0

Lincoln (0-3-0)
1944.........................6-20
1945.........................0-41
2017.........................14-40

Mahomet-Seymour (0-1)
2017.........................12-24

Marshall (28-12-4)
1932.........................0-0
1933.........................6-0
1934.........................0-14
1935.........................12-19
1936.........................33-0
1937.........................31-6
1938.........................20-12
1939.........................19-6
1940.........................0-33
1941.........................7-0
1942.........................38-6
1943.........................0-0
1944.........................12-12
1945.........................20-6
1946.........................6-13
1947.........................7-12
1948.........................6-14
1949.........................0-39
1950.........................26-18
1951.........................13-12
1952.........................27-6
1953.........................6-21
1954.........................34-0
1955.........................47-7

1956.....................53-12
1957.....................27-12
1958......................6-15
1959.......................46-0
1960.....................34-13
1961.....................28-13
1962.....................20-13
1963.....................34-13
1964.....................26-13
1965.......................40-0
1966.......................47-0
1967.....................12-19
1968........................6-6
1969.....................40-22
1970........................Win
1971.......................8-19
1972......................30-7
1973.....................25-20
1997.....................43-22
1998.....................15-23

Marion (0-1-0)
2007.....................22-43

Martinsville (11-1-2)
1930......................6-19
1931......................20-2
1932......................19-6
1933......................13-0
1934......................18-6
1935.......................0-0
1936.....................13-13
1937......................13-0
1938......................37-0
1939.....................32-13
1960......................33-0
1961......................25-0
1966......................48-0
1967......................61-6

Mascoutah (1-3-0)
1979.....................15-21
1990.....................14-35
1991.......................2-0

1993......................6-20

Massac County (0-1-0)
2013.....................26-45

Mattoon (4-19-0)
1933......................0-13
1934......................0-19
1935.......................0-6
1936.......................0-6
1937......................0-24
1938.....................18-12
1939.......................6-0
1942......................0-24
1943......................0-19
1946......................0-32
1947......................7-13
1948......................0-54
1949......................0-46
1984.....................20-18
1985.......................0-6
1986......................8-48
1987......................0-24
2012.....................55-28
2013.....................28-56
2014.....................14-41
2015.....................14-48
2016......................0-27
2017.....................24-41

McLeansboro (1-0-0)
1977......................49-7

Metamora (1-2-0)
1977......................6-18
1979.....................27-26
1980.....................14-36

Mt. Zion (15-36-0)
1968.....................19-13
1969......................0-23
1970........................Win
1971......................6-26
1972.....................12-14

1973	53-6		2016	0-40
1974	12-13		2017	8-28
1975	3-18			
1976	7-2		**Mt. Carmel (1-1-0)**	
1977	6-0		1979	46-14
1978	10-0		1984	16-38
1979	14-7			
1980	10-18		**Mt. Vernon (2-2-0)**	
1981	14-26		2007	28-12
1982	7-21		2014	0-28
1983	0-21		2015	6-40
1984	22-15		2016	41-14
1985	7-36			
1986	7-30		**Murphysboro (4-5-0)**	
1987	6-28		1977	28-21
1988	14-20		1978	39-0
1989	14-28		1986	8-34
1990	14-42		1987	7-17
1991	8-26		1988	23-15
1992	18-35		1989	27-7
1993	19-6		1990	13-34
1994	27-48		1991	12-34
1995	26-7		1992	7-34
1996	21-28			
1997	23-24		**Newton (38-32-5)**	
1998	9-14		1930	6-6
1999	12-38		1931	12-0
2000	7-54		1939	0-7
2001	6-31		1940	13-13
2002	13-20		1941	18-0
2003	28-27		1942	46-0
2004	28-25		1943	12-7
2005	27-12		1944	6-6
2006	13-21		1945	6-2
2007	24-27		1946	7-13
2008	21-28		1947	0-20
2009	17-34		1948	0-26
2010	14-42		1949	6-48
2011	0-35		1950	26-28
2011	28-27		1951	6-13
2012	56-28		1952	13-14
2013	7-42		1953	0-55
2014	26-52		1954	34-0
2015	20-53		1955	20-0

1956	16-6	2000	7-40
1957	19-33	2001	28-30
1958	21-0	2002	21-14
1959	33-13	2003	26-14
1960	7-7	2004	28-6
1961	12-21	2005	14-20
1962	0-24	2006	37-39
1963	53-13	2007	6-15
1964	41-7	2008	44-33
1965	28-32	2009	35-6
1966	27-13	2010	12-7
1967	6-31	2011	47-27
1968	7-13		
1969	6-0	**Oakland (5-2-0)**	
1970	54-6	1927	0-46
1971	0-13	1939	18-0
1972	20-20	1953	19-26
1973	10-0	1954	28-0
1974	34-0	1955	33-7
1975	14-27	1956	33-2
1976	22-0	1957	34-12
1977	17-15		
1978	38-14	**Oblong (21-4-3)**	
1979	14-7	1932	12-0
1980	0-21	1933	0-0
1981	16-5	1934	6-6
1982	6-0	1935	0-33
1983	21-20	1936	19-33
1984	21-6	1937	19-14
1985	21-10	1938	32-7
1986	0-24	1939	0-7
1987	2-18	1940	6-7
1988	28-0	1941	6-0
1989	42-16	1942	55-0
1990	7-21	1943	14-0
1991	12-33	1944	39-0
1992	9-20	1945	21-7
1993	7-20	1946	20-0
1994	0-6	1947	25-6
1995	21-21	1951	28-6
1996	33-13	1952	38-0
1997	37-16	1953	20-12
1998	6-35	1954	19-6
1999	0-41	1955	20-12

1956	13-13	2001	12-24
1957	28-0	2002	40-14
1958	33-7	2003	28-6
1959	28-0	2004	33-30
1961	32-12	2005	39-6
1962	27-13	2006	30-20
1963	14-0	2007	41-29
1964	27-20	2008	58-36
1965	35-0	2009	21-0
1966	42-0	2010	27-6
1967	7-14	2011	28-16

Olney (28-13-0)
1971	14-28
1972	18-19
1974	14-0
1975	32-16
1976	15-20
1977	28-0
1978	20-2
1978	26-12
1979	48-7
1980	2-0
1981	28-0
1982	16-7
1982	15-34
1983	26-7
1984	31-14
1985	7-10
1986	12-20
1987	13-21
1988	25-0
1989	28-0
1990	24-0
1991	22-8
1992	20-7
1993	23-13
1994	34-7
1995	0-7
1996	33-6
1997	35-36
1998	18-27
1999	21-45
2000	0-52

Palestine (2-0-0)
1962	31-0
1963	54-6

Pana (1-1-0)
1940	0-6
1941	6-0

Paris (52-32-1)
1927	12-0
1928	0-33
1929	25-6
1930	0-6
1931	6-0
1932	12-0
1933	20-0
1934	52-0
1935	39-0
1936	13-0
1937	7-13
1938	0-7
1939	6-12
1940	0-13
1941	0-12
1942	40-7
1943	6-2
1944	7-0
1945	0-0
1946	0-25
1947	6-14
1948	7-38
1949	7-0

1950	6-13	1996	52-0
1951	0-20	1997	48-8
1952	7-20	1998	22-27
1953	6-20	1999	50-20
1954	19-7	2000	20-21
1955	26-6	2001	14-6
1956	47-12	2002	7-6
1959	31-7	2003	33-14
1960	12-14	2004	39-13
1961	13-6	2005	33-7
1962	7-13	2006	49-7
1963	0-7	2007	40-6
1964	0-13	2008	14-28
1965	36-6	2009	35-20
1966	19-0	2010	33-36
1967	6-12	2011	28-7
1968	13-25	2012	44-0
1969	8-6	2013	14-42
1970	8-0		
1971	6-23	**Peoria Manual (1-0-0)**	
1972	7-8	2012	49-0
1973	20-15		
1974	30-0	**Peoria Woodruff (0-1-0)**	
1975	19-21	1970	6-10
1976	14-0		
1977	26-12		
1978	17-6	**Pontiac (0-1-0)**	
1979	61-12	1999	7-53
1980	33-0		
1981	35-0	**Quincy Notre Dame (0-3-0)**	
1982	2-0	1937	7-13
1983	37-14	1980	0-6
1984	46-0	2017	0-51
1985	0-2		
1986	7-0	**Rantoul (11-6-0)**	
1987	21-14	1974	26-13
1988	49-0	1975	7-23
1989	10-6	1976	20-14
1990	6-13	1977	36-20
1991	14-32	1978	21-8
1992	21-20	1979	17-20
1993	42-20	1980	14-15
1994	12-20	1982	15-14
1995	40-8	1983	0-3

1988	22-33	1982	26-0
2010	24-20	1983	27-10
2011	68-44	1984	15-0
2012	49-6	1985	27-6
2013	36-22	1986	8-7
2014	33-26	1987	9-6
2015	7-14	1988	20-12
2016	14-6	1989	13-22

Ridgefarm (1-0-0)
1932.....................32-0

Robinson (37-18-6)
1930.....................0-9
1931.....................0-0
1953.....................0-30
1954.....................7-6
1955.....................12-12
1956.....................19-6
1957.....................20-0
1958.....................6-6
1959.....................12-12
1960.....................33-6
1961.....................26-7
1962.....................14-0
1963.....................13-19
1964.....................21-0
1965.....................28-6
1966.....................42-6
1967.....................34-7
1968.....................7-7
1969.....................44-8
1970.....................16-18
1971.....................24-22
1972.....................6-6
1973.....................36-20
1974.....................28-7
1975.....................35-0
1976.....................14-6
1977.....................10-0
1978.....................26-7
1979.....................40-0
1980.....................36-7
1981.....................22-16

1990.....................13-38
1991.....................22-35
1992.....................23-59
1993.....................0-49
1994.....................18-42
1995.....................6-27
1996.....................36-24
1997.....................20-44
1998.....................14-20
1999.....................15-34
2000.....................6-46
2001.....................0-34
2002.....................38-39
2003.....................27-26
2004.....................42-26
2005.....................28-14
2006.....................21-28
2007.....................40-6
2008.....................13-11
2009.....................32-34
2010.....................42-28
2011.....................48-20

Rochester (0-2-0)
2011.....................13-41
2012.....................14-42

Roxana (0-1-0)
1976.....................7-17

Sacred Heart Griffin (0-1-0)
2002.....................20-53

Salem (9-7-0)
2001.....................15-48
2002.....................35-6

2003..................41-12
2004..................21-14
2005..................21-12
2006..................21-55
2007..................28-21
2008..................27-26
2009...................7-14
2010..................35-21
2011..................46-15
2012...................42-7
2013..................19-51
2014...................9-26
2015..................14-52
2016..................20-14 OT

Shelbyville (5-0-1)
1937...................25-6
1938..................47-12
1942....................4-0
1943...................27-0
1944...................45-7
1945....................6-6

Sidell (1-0-0)
1938...................27-6

St. Joseph (0-1-0)
1929....................7-9

St. Teresa (5-0-0)
1961...................14-0
1962...................13-7
1963...................20-6
1964....................7-0
1965...................21-0

Sullivan, IN (1-0-0)
1973..................31-13

Taylorville (15-23-1)
1972...................6-28
1973..................15-16
1974...................12-7
1975..................20-20

1976..................10-16
1977...................42-8
1978...................25-0
1981..................14-20
1982...................28-0
1983...................17-6
1984..................19-13
1985..................28-21
1986..................35-12
1987...................6-19
1988...................46-0
1989...................40-0
1990..................18-20
1991...................8-15
1992...................33-7
1994...................6-42
1995..................18-39
1996..................27-20
1997...................0-28
1998..................26-40
1999...................7-40
2000...................7-40
2001..................20-28
2002..................12-34
2003...................7-21
2004..................16-14
2005..................19-27
2006..................14-36
2007..................30-13
2008...................6-38
2009..................21-28
2014...................0-21
2015..................17-43
2016...................0-40
2017..................20-55

Tuscola (0-1-0)
1942...................0-13

Tolono Unity (3-4-0)
1950...................0-27
1968..................14-19
1969...................40-7
1970..................44-16

1971.....................14-34
1972.......................6-26
1973.......................40-6

Urbana (1-5-2)
1934.........................0-0
1935.......................0-19
1947.......................19-0
1948.......................7-18
1949.....................12-12
1950.......................7-12
1993.....................30-42
1994.......................6-34

Villa Grove (0-2-0)

1950.........................6-7
1951.......................0-24

Waite (0-1-0)
1933.......................0-26

Waterloo
2002.....................35-28
2003.....................34-14
2011.....................55-35

Westville (0-1-0)
1946.......................6-19

CHS ALL TIME RECORD VS. CONFERENCE

All Time Apollo Conference Members (1970-2018)

Opponent	Win	Lost	Tie	Percentage
Effingham	20	30	2	.406
Lincoln	0	3	0	.000
Mahomet-Seymour	0	1	0	.000
Mattoon	4	19	0	.174
Mount Zion	15	36	0	.294
Newton	38	32	5	.519
Olney	28	13	0	.682
Paris	52	32	1	.618
Robinson	37	18	6	.656
Salem	9	7	2	.563
Taylorville	15	23	1	.397
Totals	218	214	17	.504

CHS vs. Teams in Present Day Conference

Apollo Conference

Opponent	Win	Lost	Tie	Percentage
Effingham	20	30	2	.403
Lincoln	0	3	0	.000

Opponent	Win	Lost	Tie	Percentage
Mahomet-Seymour	0	1	0	.000
Mattoon	4	19	0	.174
Mount Zion	15	36	0	.294
Taylorville	15	23	1	.397
Totals	54	112	3	.323

Big 12 Conference

Opponent	Win	Lost	Tie	Percentage
Champaign Central	1	2	0	.333
Peoria Manual	1	0	0	1.000
Urbana	1	5	2	.125
Totals	3	7	2	.307

Central Illinois Conference

Opponent	Win	Lost	Tie	Percentage
Clinton	1	0	0	1.000
Shelbyville	5	0	1	.833
St. Teresa	5	0	0	1.000
Tuscola	0	1	0	.000
Totals	11	1	1	.884

Central State Eight Conference

Opponent	Win	Lost	Tie	Percentage
Chatham Glenwood	1	2	0	.333
Decatur MacArthur	2	1	0	.666
Decatur Eisenhower	1	3	0	.250
Jacksonville	0	1	0	.000
Springfield Lanphier	1	0	0	1.000
Rochester	0	2	0	.000
Springfield Sacred Heart Griffin	0	1	0	.000
Totals	5	10	0	.333

Dead Opponents

Opponent	Win	Lost	Tied	Percentage
Albion	1	0	0	1.000
Alumni	0	0	1	.500
Catlin	1	0	0	1.000
Chrisman	3	0	0	1.000
Decatur Lakeview	9	2	0	.818
Eastern State	8	2	3	.615
Kankakee Eastridge	1	1	0	.500
Peoria Woodruff	0	1	0	.000
Hindsboro	1	2	0	.333
Total	24	8	4	.722

Illini Prairie Conference (Merger of Corn Belt and Okaw Valley Conference)

Opponent	Win	Lost	Tied	Percentage
Bloomington Central Catholic	1	2	0	.333
Pontiac	0	1	0	.000
Rantoul	11	6	0	.647
St. Joseph-Ogdon	0	1	0	.000
Tolono Unity	3	4	0	.423
Totals	15	14	0	.512

Little Illini

Opponent	Win	Lost	Tied	Percentage
Casey	21	18	1	.525
Flora	1	0	0	1.000
Lawrenceville	2	0	1	.666
Marshall	28	12	4	.636
Newton	38	32	5	.519
Olney	28	13	0	.682
Paris	52	32	1	.618
Robinson	37	18	6	.656
Total	207	125	18	.617

Little Okaw Valley Conference

Opponent	Win	Lost	Tie	Conference
Arcola	2	3	0	.400
Cumberland	4	0	0	1.000
Martinsville	11	1	2	.786
Oakland	5	2	0	.714
Oblong	25	2	3	.756
Palestine	2	0	0	1.000
Villa Grove	0	2	0	.000
Totals	49	10	5	.804

Mississippi Valley Conference

Opponent	Win	Lost	Tie	Conference
Bethalto Civic Memorial	0	2	0	.000
Highland	3	10	0	.230
Mascoutah	1	3	0	.250
Waterloo	3	0	0	1.000
Total	7	15	0	.312

Out of State Opponents

Opponent	Win	Lost	Tie	Conference
Gertsmeyer, IN	1	2	0	.333
Sullivan, IN	1	0	0	1.000
Waite, OH	0	1	0	.000
Total	2	3	0	.666

South Seven

Opponent	Win	Lost	Tied	Percentage
Cahokia	0	1	0	.000
Centralia	4	8	0	.333
Marion	0	1	0	.000
Mt. Vernon	2	2	0	.500
Total	6	12	0	.333

Southern Illinois River to River Conference

Opponent	Win	Lost	Tied	Percentage
Benton	2	1	0	.666
Harrisburg	1	0	0	1.000

Herrin	1	0	0	1.000
Murphysboro	4	5	0	.444
Total	8	6	0	.576

Other Opponents

Opponent	Win	Lost	Tied	Percentage
Carmi	1	0	0	1.000
Georgetown	1	5	2	.125
Hoopeston	1	0	0	1.000
Kankakee McNamara	0	1	0	.000
McLeansboro	1	0	0	1.000
Metamora	1	2	0	.333
Mt. Carmel	1	1	0	.500
Pana	1	1	0	.500
Quincy Notre Dame	0	2	0	.000
Ridgefarm	1	0	0	1.000
Roxana	0	1	0	.000
Sidell	1	0	0	1.000
Westville	0	1	0	.000
Total	9	14	2	.400

TROJAN FOOTBALL RECORDS-INDIVIDUAL SINGLE GAME

Rushing:
Most Times Carried: 46, Myles Decker (CHS 28, Mattoon 56) 2013
Net Yards Gained: Myles Decker 268 (CHS 36, Rantoul 22) 2013
Longest Touchdown Run: 96, Jon Buckellew, (Olney), 1978

Passing:
Attempted: 46, Sean Hussey (Rochester, 42, CHS 14) 2012
Completed: 29, Sean Hussey (Rochester 42, CHS 14) 2012
Net Yards Gained: 392, Sean Hussey (CHS 47, Newton 27
Touchdowns: 5, Sean Hussey (CHS 47, Newton 27), 2011
Longest Scoring Play: 90, Sean Hussey to Aaron Bence, 2010/Jon Adkins to Dustin Culp, 2003
Most Interceptions: 6, Taylor Bartlett, 2008

Total Offense Scoring:
Net Yards Gained: 407, Sean Hussey (CHS 47, Newton 27)-2011
Touchdowns: 6, Bud Ewing, (CHS 92, T.C. High 0) 1938
Extra Points:8, Dalton Runyon (CHS 68, Rantoul 44) 2011
Field Goals: 2, Nick Wilson (CHS 55, Mattoon 29) 2012, Darrell Runnels vs Effingham, 1989

Most Two Point Conversions: 3, Del Cloud (vs. Unity, vs Robinson, vs Marshall), 1969
Most Total Points: 38, Bud Ewing, (CHS 92, T.C. High 0) 1938

Pass Receiving:
Caught: 14, Matt Shonk vs Newton, 2001
Net Yards Gained: 188, Matt Shonk vs Newton, 2001
Touchdowns: 4, Tibet Spencer, (CHS 47, Newton 27) 2011/Truston Winnett(CHS 55, Mattoon 29)2012
Longest Touchdown Reception: 90, Dustin Culp, 2003/Aaron Bence, 2010

Miscellaneous
Longest Kickoff Return: 98 Yards, Drew Campbell vs Paris, 1999
Longest Scoring Kickoff Return: 98 Yards, Drew Campbell vs Paris, 1999
Longest Scoring Interception Return: 95 Yards: Bill Thissell, (CHS 31, Marshall 6) 1936
Longest Punt: 75 Yards: Jerry Curtis, (CHS 6, Newton 2) 1945
Longest Punt Return: 80 Yards, George Clark (CHS 28, Oblong 6) 1951
Longest Scoring Punt Return: 80 Yards, George Clark (CHS 28, Oblong 6) 1951

Defense
Most Tackles: 24, Chris Creek, 2009
Most Sacks: 6, Mel Thomason, vs. Mt. Zion, 1979
Most Interceptions .3, Paul Moffett, vs. Oblong, Oct. 28, 1966
3, Steve Scholes, vs. Decatur Lakeview, Nov. 5, 1976
3, Bob Snider, vs. Effingham, Sept. 20, 1985
3, Bob Snider, vs. Taylorville, Oct. 4, 1985
3, Pat Lynch, vs. Taylorville, Oct. 10, 1986
3, Ross Arnold, vs. Taylorville, Oct. 7, 1988
3, Dustin Culp, vs. Salem, Oct. 25, 2002
Longest Interception Return for a Touchdown: 79 Yards, Brandon Murphy vs Effingham, 2002
Most Fumbles Recovered: 3, Dave Brazzell vs Newton, 1973
Most Blocked Kicks: 2, Sean Wickham (1978), Matt McSparin (1979)

Team Single Game

Scoring:
Most Points: 92, vs. T.C. 1938
Most Touchdowns: 14, vs. T.C.1938
Most Extra Points: 8, vs T.C. 1938/vs. Rantoul 2011.
Most Two Point Conversions: 5, vs. Casey 1969
Most Yards Total Offense: 705 Yards vs Centralia, 1997 (611 rush, 94 pass)

Rushing:
Attempts: 66, vs Champaign Central, 1996
Yards Rushing: 611 vs Centralia, 1997

Passing:
Attempts: 46, vs Rochester, 2012
Completed: 29, vs Rochester, 2012
Most Yards Passing: 392 vs. Newton, 2011
Touchdowns: 5, vs. Marshall, 1955/vs. Newton 2011

Defense:
Fewest Yards Allowed: 4, vs T.C., 1938
Fewest Yards Allowed Rushing: -39 yards, vs Mt. Zion, 1970
Fewest Yards Allowed Passing: -4, vs Taylorville, 1990
Most Punts: 8, vs. Springfield Lanphier, 1964
Most Punting Yards, 287, vs. Newton, 1976

INDIVIDUAL SINGLE SEASON

Rushing:
Times Carried: 260, Myles Decker, 2013
Highest Attempts Per Game Average: 28.8, Myles Decker, 2013
Net Yards Gained: 1,473, Brandon Davis, 2004
Highest Yards Per Attempt Average: 28.33, Frank Keown, 1964
Touchdowns: 22, Josh Cazley, 2012
Most 100 Yard Rushing Games: 9, Brandon Davis, 2004
Most Consecutive 100 Yard Rushing Games: 9, Brandon Davis, 2004

Passing:
Attempted: 268, Eric Gentry, 2007
Completed: 160, Sean Hussey, 2011
Net Yards Gained: Sean Hussey, 2,357, 2011
Touchdowns: 24, Sean Hussey, 2012
Pct. Of Completions: .63.89%, Randy Cooley, 1966
Most Games With 300+ Yards Passing: 2, Chuck Rutan, 1970
Most Games With 200+ Yards Passing: 6, Sean Hussey, 2012
Most Games With 100+ Yards Passing: 13, Sean Hussey, 2011
Most Consecutive Games of 100+ Yards Passing: 13, Sean Hussey, 2011
Yards Per Game: 207.50, Sean Hussey, 2012

Total Offense Scoring:
Touchdowns: 24, Steve Bell, 1966/Josh Cazley, 2012
Most Points: 146, Josh Cazley, 2012
Most Points by a Freshman: 23, Tom Jenkins, 1963 (9 Games)
Most Points by a Sophomore: 72, Josh Cazley, 2011 (13 Games)
Most Points by a Junior: 146, Josh Cazley, 2012 (11 Games)
Most Points by a Senior: 144, Steve Bell, 1966 (8 Games)

Highest Scoring Average: 18.00, Steve Bell, 1966
Extra Points: 47, Nick Wilson, 2012
Most Two Point Conversions: 12, Del Cloud, 1969
Most Consecutive Points After Touchdown Made: 18, John Sellett, 1976 (Sept. 10-Nov. 10)
Field Goals: 4, Brad DeLong, 1983
Most Consecutive Field Goals Made: 4, Brad Delong, September 9-October 14, 1983

Pass Receiving:
Caught: 56, Tibet Spencer, 2011
Net Yards Gained: 1,034, Truston Winnett, 2012
Touchdowns: 14, Truston Winnett, 2012

Special Teams
Kickoffs Kicked: 72, Nick Wilson, 2012
Kickoff Yards Kicked: 3,848, Nick Wilson, 2012
Punting Average: 44.0 Jim Rickie, 1967
Most Punts Returned: 22, Jon Kniskern, 1970
Most Yards On Punt Returns: 244, Jon Kniskern, 1970
Most Punting Yards: 1,450, Jon Buckellew, 1978

DEFENSE
Interceptions: 9, Bob Hillis, 1986/ Truston Winnett, 2011
Most Touchdowns On Interception Returns: 2, Chris Creek, 2010/Adam Drake-2009
Most Blocked Kicks, 6, Mark Wilson, 1973
Most Tackles: 161, Chris Creek, 2009
Most Assist Tackles: 94,Chris Creek, 2011
Most Sacks: 6.5, Mel Thomason, 1979

Team Single-Season
Most Games Played: 13 Games, 2011

Scoring:
Most Points: 497, 2012
Most Touchdowns: 71, 2012
Most Extra Points: 47, 2012
Most Field Goals: 5, 2000
Most Yards Total Offense: 5,283, 2011
Most Two Point Conversions, 22, 1969

Rushing:
Attempts: 505, 1979
Yards: 2,906, 1997

Touchdowns: 43, 2011

Passing:
Attempts: 268, 2007
Completed: 161, 2011
Yards Passing: 2,379, 2011
Touchdowns: 22, 2011

Punting:
Most Punts: 46, 1976
Punting Yards: 1,618, 1976
Highest Punting Average: 37.06, 1971

Defense:
Fewest Points Allowed: 15, 1931
Most Shutouts: 8, 1931
Most Passes Intercepted: 20, 2012
Most Fumbles Recovered: 19, 1974
Most Blocked Kicks: 8, 1973

INDIVIDUAL CAREER

Rushing:
Times Carried: 420, Jon Buckellew, 1976-1978
Net Yards Gained: 2,364, Jon Buckellew, 1976-1978
Highest Average Yards per Game: 89.2, Josh Cazley (2,140 in 24 games), 2011-2012
Highest Yards per Attempt (min 125 att), 9.2, Josh Cazley (2,140 in 233 att), 2011-2012
Most Rushing Touchdowns: 33, Josh Cazley, 2011-2012

Passing:
Attempted: 658, Sean Hussey, 2010-2012
Completed: 397, Sean Hussey, 2010-2012
Net Yards Gained: 5,975, Sean Hussey, 2010-2012
Touchdowns: 52, Sean Hussey, 2010-2012
Most Games with 100+ Passing Yards: 32, Sean Hussey, 2010-2012
Most Games with 200+ Passing Yards, 13, Sean Hussey, 2010-2012
Most Games with 300+ Passing Yards, 2, Chuck Rutan, 1970

Total Offense Scoring:
Net Yards Gained: 2,406, Josh Cazley, 2011-2012
Touchdowns: 36, Josh Cazley, 2011-2012
Extra Points: 113, Tom Jenkins, 1963-66
Field Goals: 7, John Sellett 1976-1978

Points: 218, Josh Cazley, 2011-2012

Pass Receiving
Caught: 128, Matt Shonk, 1999-2001
Net Yards Gained: Matt Shonk, 1,645, 1999-2001
Touchdowns: 20, Jamel Johnson, 2007-09

Punting:
Times Kicked: 38, Dick Young, 1956-57
Yards Kicked: 1,463, Dick Young, 1956-57
Punting Average: 38.4, Dick Young, 1956-57

Defense
Most Completed: 425, Chris Creek, 2009-2011
Most Assists: 251, Chris Creek, 2009-2011
Interceptions: 14, Truston Winnett, 2010-2012
Most Touchdowns on Interception Returns: 2, Page Alexander, 1983-1984

Miscellaneous Records
Longest Overall Road Win Streak: 10...1976-1979
Longest Overall Road Losing Streak: 11..2013-2015
Longest Overall Home Win Streak: 16..1976-1979
Longest Overall Home Losing Streak: 10..1999-2001
Longest Conference Winning Streak: 23...1976-1980
Longest EI Conference Win Streak: 17..1931-1934
Longest Conference Losing Streak: 19..2013-2016
Most Consecutive Losses: 13..1999-2001
Most Consecutive Wins: 14...1973-1974
Highest Regular Season Win Streak: 24..1976-1979
Most Consecutive Shutouts...8, 1932-1933
Longest Home Winning Streak...18, 1963-1967
Longest Home Losing Streak..18, 1998-2002
Best Win Percentage: 1.000...(8-0, 1932)/(8-0-0,1966)
Worst Losing Percentage: .000..(0-9-0, 2000, 2015, 2017)
Best Conference Winning Percentage: 1.000, (5-0, 1942), (7-0, 1966), (4-0, 1969), (5-0, 1973), (5-0, 1976), (5-0, 1977), (5-0, 1978), (5-0, 1979), (6-0, 1984), (7-0, 2003), (5-0, 2012)
Most Wins: 11..2011
Most Losses: 9..2000, 2015, 2017
Most Ties: 3...1930
. . . .

CHS held Oblong to five yards rushing on October 9, 1965 as David Kniskern scored three times. Two seasons later on October 27, 1967, Oblong ended a 27-year losing streak to the Trojans by defeating them 14-7.

. . . .

1977 seemed to be the year of oddities. According to an article in the "Times-Courier", the Trojans game vs. the Olney Tigers on September 17 was delayed an hour due to the officials never arriving. Bob Hussey, Terry Noble, and Ken Baker of Charleston, plus Rick Hartrich of Olney worked the contest and kept everything under control.

Almost exactly one month later on October 15, referees tossed the yellow flag 36 times for a combined 402 yards in penalties between both teams in a game against rival Paris.

. . . .

In 2012, Mattoon and Charleston renewed their rivalry as Mattoon joined the Apollo Conference. The Coles County Clash has been played at Eastern Illinois University O'Brien Stadium with the winner receiving a trophy that is displayed at the winner's school.

All-Apollo Conference List (Compiled by Erik Hall and Kyle Daubs)

The first ever all-conference team was awarded in 1969 with the EI League. When Charleston moved to the Apollo Conference, the all-conference team was announced in 1970. First team and second team selections did not start until 1975. Selections for the list now include first team offense, first team defense, second team offense, and second team defense.

First Team All-Apollo Conference Offense

Jay Ogelsby, Tackle, 1975
Ernie Eveland, End, 1975
Paul Wilson, Guard, 1975
Steve Cougill, Tackle, 1976
Keith Aten, Quarterback, 1976
Mark Buckellew, Halfback, 1976
Steve Scholes, Halfback, 1976
Craig Donna, Center, 1977
Steve Cougill, Tackle, 1977
Bill Beavers, Split End, 1977
Keith Aten, Quarterback, 1977
Jon Buckellew, Fullback, 1977
Mel Thomason, Guard, 1978
Don Plummer, Tackle, 1978
Bill Gibson, Center, 1978
Brian Jones, Quarterback, 1978
Jon Buckellew, Fullback, 1978
Dan Downs, Halfback, 1978
Shon McCray, Running Back, 1982
Ken Huckstep, Lineman, 1982
Jeff Drake, Lineman, 1982
George Birch, Center, 1983
Jerry Hamner, Running Back, 1984
Mike Watson, Lineman, 1984
Eric Craft, Lineman, 1984
Stan Royer, Receiver, 1984
Eric Bomball, Lineman, 1985
Eric Craft, Lineman, 1985
Jerry Hamner, Back, 1985
Tom Padgett, Quarterback, 1985
Blaine Little, Lineman, 1986
Brian Halsey, Receiver, 1987
Walt Bomball, Guard, 1988
Rick Royer, Quarterback, 1988
Ted Trueblood, Running Back, 1988
Deron Kimball, Receiver, 1988
Darrell Rennels, Kicker, 1988
Darrell Rennels, Punter, 1988
Jim Lanman, Lineman, 1989
Tim Montgomery, Receiver, 1989
Louie Andrew, Receiver, 1989
Darrell Rennels, Kicker, 1989
Chad Isley, Receiver, 1991

Jacob Bell, Receiver, 1992
Jacob Bell, Kicker, 1992
Kevin Pearcy, Receiver, 1993
C.J. Applegate, Punter, 1994
Ken Ratliff, Guard, 1995
Steve Plummer, Receiver, 1996
Matt Shober, Lineman, 1996
Marshall Moore, Lineman, 1996
Brandon Beever, Lineman, 1996
Brad Homann, Running Back, 1996
Charlie Logsdon, Punter, 1996
Matt Shober, Lineman, 1997
Brandon Beever, Lineman, 1997
Marshall Moore, Lineman, 1997
Ryan Levenchuck, Lineman, 1997
Chuck Earp, Running Back, 1997
Ben Lawson, Running Back, 1997
T.J. Huddlestun, Kicker, 1997
Scott Parrish, Receiver, 1998
Ryan Levenchuck, Lineman, 1998
Neal DeLude, Lineman, 2002
Matt Shonk, Receiver, 2002
Lee Bollinger, Running Back, 2002
Brandon Murphy, Quarterback, 2002
Colin Smith, Lineman, 2003
Nathan Homann, Running Back, 2003
Dustin Culp, Receiver, 2003
Drew Baker, Lineman, 2004
Brandon Davis, Running Back, 2004
Jon Adkins, Quarterback, 2004
Evan Stoltz, Running Back, 2005
Steve Phillips, Lineman, 2005
Brady Wesch, Lineman, 2006
Kyle Hasbargen, Lineman, 2007
Jamel Johnson, Receiver, 2007
Mario Johnson, Running Back, 2008
Jon Stallons, Lineman, 2009
Adam Drake, Receiver, 2009
Tim Hiser, Lineman, 2010
LJ Welsh, Running Back, 2010
Tibet Spencer, Receiver, 2011
Aaron Bence, Receiver, 2011
Sean Hussey, Quarterback, 2011
Dan Hildebrandt, Lineman, 2012

Cody Margenthaler, Lineman, 2012
Josh Cazley, Running Back, 2012
Truston Winnett, Receiver, 2012
Sean Hussey, Quarterback, 2012
Cody Margenthaler, Lineman, 2013
Myles Decker, Running Back, 2013

First Team All-Apollo Conference Defense:

John Dively, Linebacker, 1975
Tom Sellett, Cornerback, 1975
Craig Donna, Linebacker, 1976
Joe Sanders, Linebacker, 1976
Paul Wilson, Guard, 1976
Craig Donna, Linebacker, 1977
Steve Cougill, Tackle, 1977
Bob Taylor, Nose Guard, 1977
John Sellett, Defensive Back, 1977
Mel Thomason, Tackle, 1978
Mark Daugherty, End, 1978
Sean Wickham, Linebacker, 1978
John Sellett, Halfback, 1978
Gary Davis, Halfback, 1978
Scott Enslen, Middle Linebacker, 1980
Shon McCray, Lineman, 1981
Shon McCray, Lineman, 1982
Randy Craft, Tackle, 1982
Brad DeLong, Linebacker, 1982
Sam Buxton, Secondary, 1982
Mitch Swim, Secondary, 1982
Jerry Hamner, Secondary, 1984
Page Alexander, Secondary, 1984
Jeff Oetting, Linebacker, 1984
Eric Bomball, Lineman, 1984
Eric Bomball, Lineman, 1985
Eric Craft, Lineman, 1985
Jerry Hamner, Back, 1985
Jeff Oetting, Linebacker, 1985
Shane Hunt, Linebacker, 1986
Bob Hillis, Back, 1986
Walt Bomball, Lineman, 1987
Walt Bomball, End, 1988
Brian Little, Linebacker, 1988

Ross Arnold, Back, 1988
Howie Groff, Linebacker, 1989
Tony Logue, Back, 1989
Rob Shrader, Tackle, 1989
Jim Lanman, Lineman, 1990
Tony Logue, Back, 1990
Chad Isley, Safety, 1991
Jay Ankenbrand, Back, 1993
Ruben Perez, Lineman, 1995
Nick Vonlanken, Back, 1995
Chris Rennels, Lineman, 1996
Rubin Perez, Linebacker, 1996
Nick Vonlanken, Back, 1996
Nate Ralston, Back, 1996
Brad Homann, Back, 1996
Matt Robinson, Lineman, 1997
Brandon Matheny, Safety, 1997
Brandon Matheny, Safety, 1998
Hank Hargis, Linebacker, 2001
Michael Payne, Lineman, 2002
Neal DeLude, Linebacker, 2002
Nathan Homann, Back, 2002
Kyle Bess, Lineman, 2003
Josh Campbell, Linebacker, 2003
Nathan Homann, Back, 2003
Jason Murphy, Back, 2003
Kyle Bess, Lineman, 2004
Adam Bonwell, Back, 2004
Jason Murphy, Back, 2004
Chris Darimont, Lineman, 2005
B.K. Leonard, Linebacker, 2005
Justin Rardin, Back, 2005
Evan Stoltz, Back, 2005
Jamel Johnson, Back, 2007
Michael Campbell, Linebacker, 2007
Drew Riley, Lineman, 2007
Adam Drake, Back, 2008
Adam Drake, Back, 2009
Chris Creek, Linebacker, 2010
Chris Creek, Linebacker, 2011
Truston Winnett, Back, 2011
Dillan Cazley, Back, 2011
Jesse Campbell, Lineman, 2012
Noah Miller, Linebacker, 2012

Dillan Cazley, Back, 2012
Truston Winnett, Back, 2012
Josh Cazley, Back, 2012

Second Team All-Apollo Conference Offense:

Bob Dulka, Split End, 1975
John Dively, Center, 1975
Tom Sellett, Halfback, 1975
Craig Donna, Center, 1976
Paul Wilson, Guard, 1976
Bill Beavers, End, 1976
Bob DiPietro, Halfback, 1976
Mike Wozniak, Tackle, 1977
Dan Downs, Halfback, 1977
Mark Daugherty, Tight End, 1978
Chuck Birch, Tackle, 1980
John Hurst, Guard, 1980
John Sullivan, Back, 1980
Mike Duncan, Lineman, 1981
Tony Vavroch, Tight End, 1982
George Birch, Lineman, 1982
Sam Buxton, Running Back, 1982
Tony Vavroch, Receiver, 1983
Jim Morrisey, Lineman, 1983
Brad DeLong, Lineman, 1983
Steve Hankenson, Running Back, 1983
Page Alexander, Running Back, 1984
Mike Watson, Lineman, 1985
Jeff Oetting, Receiver, 1985
Tom Weir, Kicker, 1985
Leon Hall, Lineman, 1986
Shane Hunt, Back, 1986
Pat Whitley, Punter, 1986
Walt Bomball, Lineman, 1987
Fred Hudson, Lineman, 1988
Mike Brown, Lineman, 1988
Lance Tucker, Receiver, 1988
Howie Groff, Back, 1989
Marty Webster, Quarterback, 1989
Andy Hoker, Receiver, 1989
Doug Paige, Lineman, 1989
Darrell Rennels, Punter, 1989

Jim Lanman, Lineman, 1990
Louie Andrew, Running Back, 1990
Andy Hoker, Receiver, 1990
Josh Dowland, Running Back, 1991
Josh Gilbert, Lineman, 1992
Greg Pfeiffer, Lineman, 1993
C.J. Applegate, Punter, 1993
C.J. Applegate, Running Back, 1994
Matt Shober, Lineman, 1995
Ruben Perez, Center, 1995
Chuck Earp, Running Back, 1995
Nick Vonlanken, Receiver, 1996
Chris Franz, Quarterback, 1996
Ben Lawson, Running Back, 1996
Chuck Earp, Running Back, 1996
Chris Franz, Quarterback, 1997
Scott Johnson, Running Back, 1997
Matt Perez, Tight End, 1998
Kermit Boyer, Running Back, 1998
Clayton Bayley, Lineman, 1999
Kyle Frazier, Lineman, 1999
Drew Campbell, Running Back, 1999
Matt Shonk, Receiver, 2000
Matt Shonk, Receiver, 2001
Josh Wurtsbaugh, Lineman, 2001
Collin Smith, Lineman, 2002
Pat Buchar, Receiver, 2002
Tom Peterlich, Receiver, 2002
John Calhoun, Lineman, 2003
Jason Murphy, Receiver, 2003
Jon Adkins, Quarterback, 2003
Daniel Maples, Lineman, 2004
Jason Murphy, Receiver, 2004
Brady Wesch, Lineman, 2005
Daniel Maples, Lineman, 2005
Cody Mason, Running Back, 2005
Cody Mason, Running Back, 2006
Adam Drake, Receiver, 2008
Jon Stallons, Lineman, 2008
Jamel Johnson, Receiver, 2008
Tim Hiser, Lineman, 2009
Aaron Bence, Receiver, 2010
Noah Miller, Running Back, 2011
Jesse Campbell, Lineman, 2011

Dustin Smith, Lineman, 2012
Noah Miller, Running Back, 2012
Austin Cohn, Receiver, 2012
Tristan Brown, Lineman, 2013
Keaton Halsey, Lineman, 2014
Bryce Frederick, Running Back, 2016
Dawson Armstrong, Lineman, 2016

Second Team All-Apollo Conference Defense:

Jeff Johns, Linebacker, 1975
Pat Grant, Linebacker, 1976
Mark Buckellew, 1976
Tim Grant, End, 1977
Anthony Cox, Tackle, 1977
Mark O'Dell, Nose Guard, 1978
Jeff Phillips, Linebacker, 1980
Kenny Keefer, Defensive Back, 1980
Ken Huckstep, End, 1981
Kenny Keefer, Linebacker, 1981
Ken Huckstep, Lineman, 1982
George Birch, Linebacker, 1982
Terry Thomason, Secondary, 1982
Tony Vavroch, Linebacker, 1983
George Birch, Linebacker, 1983
Jim Morrisey, Lineman, 1983
Page Alexander, Back, 1983
Bill Ingle, Linebacker, 1984
Bob Snider, Secondary, 1985
Shane Hunt, Linebacker, 1985
Blaine Little, Lineman, 1986
Tony Peters, Linebacker, 1986
Pat Lynch, Back, 1986
Bob Hillis, Back, 1987
Rob Shrader, Lineman, 1988
Howie Groff, Linebacker, 1988
Doug Krukewitt, Back, 1988
Chris Doherty, Back, 1989
Louie Andrew, Back, 1990
Doug Paige, Lineman, 1990
John Hamner, Linebacker, 1990
Matt Davis, Corner Back, 1991
Rob Myerscough, Linebacker, 1991

Josh Gilbert, Lineman, 1992
Chris Baird, Linebacker, 1992
Todd Bradford, Linebacker, 1993
Colby Kruse, Linebacker, 1994
Nick Vonlanken, Safety, 1994
Joe Shober, Lineman, 1995
Eric Wade, Linebacker, 1995
Earnest Williams, Lineman, 1996
Tony Coffey, Linebacker, 1996
Charlie Logsdon, Linebacker, 1996
Heith Price, Back, 1996
James Warman, Lineman, 1997
Mike Kelly, Linebacker, 1997
Qualtrell Favours, Lineman, 2001
Hank Hargis, Linebacker, 2002
Josh Campbell, Linebacker, 2002
Dustin Culp, Back, 2002
Matt Giles, Lineman, 2003
Dustin Culp, Back, 2003
Nick Davis, Linebacker, 2004
Brad Reid, Back, 2004
Mikey Peterlich, Back, 2004
Clint Tucker, Lineman, 2005
Cody Mason, Linebacker, 2006
Jamel Johnson, Back, 2006
Nick Guinto, Linebacker, 2007
Chris Creek, Linebacker, 2009
Ryan Preston, Linebacker, 2012
Aron Decker, Lineman, 2012
Aron Decker, Lineman, 2013
Forest Rortramel, Linebacker, 2014
Trevor Gibson, Lineman, 2014
Cole Hoover, Linebacker, 2015
Dawson Armstrong, Back, 2016
Griffin Green, Back, 2017

All-Apollo Conference:
Jon Kniskern, Offensive End, 1970
Bob Ballsrud, Offensive Tackle, 1970
Chuck Rutan, Quarterback, 1970
Jerry Baldwin, Offensive Halfback, 1970
Nick Matthew, Defensive End, 1970
Pat Hussey, Linebacker, 1970
Tom Coon, Center, 1971
Rod Franklin, End, 1971
Kevin Hussey, Quarterback, 1971
Kim Ingram, Guard, 1971
Jim Schnorf, Defensive Back, 1971
Kevin Hussey, Quarterback, 1972
Ken Ramsey, Linebacker, 1972
Mike Spaniol, Defensive Back, 1972
Jeff Sanders, Halfback, 1973
Dave Ballsrud, Offensive Tackle, 1973
Mike Snow, Defensive End, 1973
Dave Brazzell, Linebacker, 1973
Bill Moore, Safety, 1973
Scott Allen, Halfback, 1973
Dave Ballsrud, Tackle, 1974
Dave Bough, Running Back, 1974
Jeff Gossett, Quarterback, 1974
Kelly Hussey, End, 1974
Mark Jobe, Fullback, 1974
Jeff Johns, Linebacker, 1974
Bill Moore, Halfback, 1974
Mike Snow, Guard-Tackle, 1974

All-E.I. League Football Team (Large Division):
Tom Jenkins, Interior Lineman, 1966
Gary Cole, Center, 1966
Randy Cooley, Quarterback, 1966
Steve Bell, Back, 1966
Ken Baker, Quarterback, 1967
Jon Kniskern, End, 1969
Dan Hussey, Tackle, 1969
Jerry Myerscough, Guard, 1969
John McCarthy, Quarterback, 1969
Del Cloud, Halfback, 1969
Jim Richie, End, 1969
Tony Robinson, Linebacker, 1969
Brian Keown, Halfback, 1969

All-State:
Gerald "Bud" Ewing, Halfback, 1938

Coach and Athlete Magazine Honorable Mention All-American:
Verlon Myers, Quarterback, 1955

Jon Kniskern, End, 1970

IHSA Academic All-State Team (players must be first-team all-conference and meet academic requirements):
Hank Hargis, Linebacker, 2001
Brandon Murphy, Quarterback, 2002
Lee Bollinger, Running Back, 2002
Nathan Homann, Defensive Back, 2002
Kyle Bess, Defensive End, 2003
Nathan Homann, Running Back/Defensive Back, 2003
Jason Murphy, Defensive Back, 2003
Brandon Davis, Running Back, 2004
Brady Wesch, Lineman, 2005
Tim Hiser, Lineman, 2010
Sean Hussey, Quarterback, 2011
Dillan Cazley, Defensive Back, 2011
Sean Hussey, Quarterback, 2012
Dillan Cazley, Defensive Back, 2012

Illinois Football Coaches Association Class 4A All-State:
Rubin Perez, Linebacker, 1996
Matt Shober, Lineman, 1997
Chris Creek, Linebacker, 2011
Sean Hussey, Quarterback, 2011
Sean Hussey, Quarterback, 2012
Dillan Cazley, Defensive Back, 2012
Truston Winnett, Receiver, 2012

Illinois Football Coaches Association Class 5A All-State:
Brandon Davis, Running Back, 2004

Illinois Football Coaches Association Hall of Fame inductee:
Verlon Myers, 1991, career record 131-104-5

Lincoln Trail Officials Association Sportsmanship Award:
Bill Monken, 1997

Chicago Daily News All-State:
Howard Carson, 1932
Kevin Hussey, Quarterback, 1972
Craig Donna, Center-Linebacker, 1977 (Class 1A-2A-3A Team)

Chicago Daily News Special Mention All-State:
Jon Kniskern, End, 1970
Jeff Sanders, Halfback, 1973
Mark Buckellew, Halfback, 1975
Keith Aten, Quarterback, 1977

Chicago Daily News Honorable Mention All-State:
Dave Brazzell, Guard-Linebacker, 1973
Mark Wilson, End, 1973
Steve Cougill, Tackle, 1977
Jon Buckellew, Running back, 1977
John Sellett, Running back, 1977

Chicago Sun Times All-State Team:
Mark O'Dell, Tackle, 1979
Melvin Thomason, Tackle, 1979

Decatur Herald Coach of the Year
Merv Baker-1969
Chuck Budde-1979
Brian Halsey-2011

Decatur Herald Player of the Year
Craig Donna, Linebacker, 1977
Sean Hussey, Quarterback, 2012

Elite Group Makes up "100-Point Club"

In the many years of Trojan football, only eight stars have gained the exclusive membership to the "100-Point Club." Those who make up this club have accumulated over one hundred total offensive points in a single season.

Howard Carson became the charter member with 106 points in 1932. Carson scored eight touchdowns in a two-week period in Friday wins over Flora, 34-20, and T.C., 46-0. One of Carsons touchdown runs against T.C. was 72 yards.

Bud Ewing followed him in 1938 with 101 points to his credit. Ewing's scoring spectacle is still a record today when he rushed over T.C. The talented halfback raced for six touchdowns and two PAT's. When all the math is done, 38 of Ewings total 101 points came in a single game. Also, Bill Thissell teamed up with Ewing for a powerful one-two scoring combo. Thissell finished the '38 campaign with 99 total points, the two combined for 200 of the total 300 points scored that season.

Members were scarce for the following 17 years until Bob Thomas waltzed his way in with a record, at the time, 113 points. Among Thomas' 113 points is a 14-yard field goal that was only the second in Trojan football history at the time. Thomas, only 5-8 and 140 pounds, came against Paris with a game to never forget. He was on the doubtful to play list with leg troubles, but with his team losing 14-6, Thomas entered the game.

Thomas played with heart. He carried the ball six times for 130 yards, complete a pass for 19 yards, score four touchdowns on runs of 47, 24, 20, and 18 yards, and booting four extra points. CHS hammered Paris for a 47-12 win. Thomas scored four times versus Marshall the previous Friday too.

Four years later Steve Temple, the former all time CHS total offensive points career holder, raced to 102 points. Temple had plenty of memories when scored three touchdowns in four different games his senior year. Nine of those touchdowns came in the first regular season games. In the opening game that season, Temple ran for 220 yards, including an 89-yard dash among his three touchdowns. Temples career 35 touchdowns still tops CHS records.

Only six years later, Steve Bell made an effort for Temples all time mark. Bell would crush Thomas's 113 points, with an outstanding 144 total offensive points scored. This was also in only eight games played.

Bell's 24 touchdowns broke Carson's previous record of seventeen in a season. Nine of Bell's touchdowns were from caught passes from Randy Cooley. Not only did Bell have great success, but the team followed. Twenty-nine Trojan football records were either broken or tied during the '66 season. Bell ranks third on the all-time career list.

Decades would follow until 2009 when Mario Johnson was able to stretch over the hump with 108 points. Johnson rushed into the end zone sixteen times, caught one pass, and scored on a kickoff. He finished with 1,274 rushing yards. Johnson scored five touchdowns in a crucial win versus Olney. At the same time Johnson scored his one kickoff return touchdown by nearly setting the record for a 96-yard score. The team finished 4-5 that season.

For the first time in the school history, two players in the same season accumulated 100 points in a season. During the 2012 campaign, junior running back, Josh Cazley, rushed his way into the record books. Cazley broke Bell's record for points in a season with 146 points. Cazley finished with 1,275 yards on the ground on 144 carries and 22 touchdowns. Cazley also scored one received touchdown, a returned kickoff, and one two point conversion.

Senior, Truston Winnett, had a sensational senior year. Winnett barely made the cut with 102 points. His 14 received touchdowns are a new school record. He also had two interception returns for touchdowns and a kickoff return for a touchdown. Fullback, Noah Miller, nearly made the club. The senior finished the season with 92 points in 2012. His 14 touchdowns and four two-point conversions were enough to send the athlete to fourth on the all-time list in scoring though.

ALL-TIME CAREER SCORERS

1. 218-Josh Cazley
2. 210-Steve Temple
3. 186, Steve Bell
4. 172, Noah Miller
5. 170, Bill Thissel
6. 167, Bud Ewing
7. 163, Bob Thomas
8. 160, Steve Cloud
9. 156, Mario Johnson
10. 138, Chuck Earp
11. 132, Howard Carson
12. 132, Paul Moffett
13. 127, Jeff Sanders
14. 121, Don Johnson
15. 120, Jamel Johnson
16. 120, Brandon Davis
17. 118, Dan Downs
18. 117, John Buckellew
19. 114, L.J. Welsh
20. 113, Tom Jenkins
21. 110, Truston Winnett
22. 104, Jerry Allen
23. 102, Mark Heise
24. 102, Larry Drake

"100 Point Club" (In A Season)

Howard Carson 102, 1932
Bud Ewing 101 1938
Bob Thomas 113, 1956
Steve Temple 102 1960
Steve Bell 144 1966
Mario Johnson 108, 2008
Truston Winnett 102, 2012
Josh Cazley 146, 2012

Scoring Leaders

Football

No. Player	Years Played	Position	TD's	PAT	Total Points
1. Josh Cazley	2011-2012	HB	36	1	218
2. Steve Temple	1959-1961	HB	35	-	210
3. Steve Bell	1964-1966	HB	31	-	186
4. Noah Miller	2010-2012	FB	26	13	172
5. Bill Thissell	1936-1938	HB	26	14	170
6. Bud Ewing	1935-1938	HB	27	5	167
7. Bob Thomas	1954-1956	HB	25	10	163
8. Steve Cloud	1965-1967	HB	26	4	160
9. Mario Johnson	2006-2008	HB	26	-	156
10. Chuck Earp	1994-1996	HB	23	-	138

Football
All-Time Football Coaching Records

Years	Coach	Total Years	Won	Lost	Tied	Percentage
1973-1979	Chuck Budde	7	55	14	1	.793
1953-1970	Mervin Baker	17	93	33	9	.730
1931-1935	Gilbert Carson	5	27	11	6	.682
1936-1939	Sam Gillespie	4	23	12	1	.653
1942-1944	Leonard King	3	14	8	4	.615
1982-1992	Verlon Myers	11	54	44	0	.551
2000-2014	Brian Halsey	15	75	75	0	.500
1981-1982 1993-1997 1999	Bill Monken	7	30	44	0	.405
1940-1941	Carl Hance	2	7	8	1	.468
1970-1972	Jerry Van Bellehem	3	11	15	2	.429
1927-1930	Errett Warner	4	6	12	4	.364
1945-1946	Sam Blackwell	2	4	9	3	.344
1950-1952	Paul Swoffard	3	6	17	2	.280
2016-Present	Tyler Hanner	2	3	15	0	.200
1947-1949	Joe Bressler	3	3	18	3	.188
1998	Jeff Rolson	1	1	8	0	.111
2015	Tim Hogan	1	0	9	0	.000
Totals	17 Coaches	89	416	354	36	.538

All-Time Football Coaching Records For E.I. League

Years	Coach	Total Years	Won	Lost	Tied	Percentage
1942-1944	Leonard King	3	10	2	2	.767
1931-1935	Gilbert Carson	5	20	5	5	.750
1953-1969	Mervin Baker	17	63	23	8	.713
1936-1939	Sam Gillespie	4	16	7	1	.688
1945-1946	Sam Blackewell	2	4	4	2	.500
1940-1941	Carl Hance	2	4	5	1	.450
1950-1952	Paul Swoffard	2	6	11	1	.361
1927-1930	Errett Warner	1	0	3	2	.200
1947-1949	Joe Bressler	3	2	12	1	.167
Totals	Nine Coaches	39	125	72	24	.620

All-Time Football Coaching Records for Apollo Conference

Years	Coach	Total Years	Won	Lost	Tied	Percentage
1973-1979	Chuck Budde	7	31	4	0	.886
2000-2014	Brian Halsey	15	51	48	0	.515

Years	Coach		W	L	T	Pct
1982-1992	Verlon Myers	11	38	28	0	.576
1970-1972	Jerry Van Bellehem	3	4	5	2	.500
1980-1981 1993-1997 1999	Bill Monken	8	18	24	0	.429
2016-Present	Tyler Hanner	2	1	9	0	.166
1998	Jeff Rolson	1	0	5	0	.000
2015	Tim Hogan	1	0	5	0	.000
Totals	Eight Coaches	48	143	116	2	.552

Trojans Coaching Records
Football (Single Season)
Most Wins..11, Brian Halsey, 2011
Most Defeats..............................9, Brian Halsey, 2000, Tim Hogan, 2015, Tyler Hanner 2017
Most E.I. League Wins.....................................6, Mervin Baker, 1954-55-59
Most E.I. Defeats..6, Merv Baker, 1953
Most Apollo Conference Wins..7, Brian Halsey, 2003
Most Apollo Conference Defeats.............................6, Verlon Myers, 1991, Tyler Hanner 2017
Most Consecutive Wins..10, Chuck Budde, 1977
Most Consecutive Defeats..............9, Brian Halsey, 2000, Tim Hogan, 2015, Tyler Hanner, 2017
Best Game Scoring Average...45.2, Brian Halsey, 2012
Best Winning Percentage................................100%, Mervin Baker, 1966 (8-0-0)

Football (Career)
Most Years at CHS...17, Mervin Baker, 1953-1970
Most Wins...97, Mervin Baker, 1953-1970
Most Consecutive Wins...14, Chuck Budde, 1973-74
Most Defeats...75, Brian Halsey, 2000-2014
Most E.I. League Wins..71, Mervin Baker, 1953-1970
Most E.I. League Defeats..23, Mervin Baker, 1953-1970
Most Apollo Conference Wins.......................................51, Brian Halsey, 2000-2014
Most Apollo Conference Defeats...................................48, Brian Halsey, 2000-2014
Best Winning Percentage...793, Chuck Budde, 1973-1980
Most EI Championships............................5, Mervin Baker, 1953, 1963, 1965, 1966, 1969
Most Apollo Conference Championships: 6, Chuck Budde, 1973, 1974, 1976, 1977, 1978, 1979
Most State Qualifications............................7, Brian Halsey, 2002, 2003, 2004, 2005, 2007, 2011, 2012

. . . .

In the fall of 1945, Coach Sam Blackwell had yet to be discharged from the Navy to start football workouts at Trojan Hill. So, Andy Sullivan, Eastern Illinois's grid captain and Charleston native, filled in as the coach for a few days. After business forced Sullivan to quit, Bill Thissell, ex-Trojan great in the late 1930's, guided the Trojans through drills until Blackwell's arrival. CHS won 3, lost 2 and tied 3 that year.

. . . .

After Chuck Budde's departure in 1979, CHS was looking strong at Bill Monken and now retired math teacher, Bob Lawrence, to take over. Monken was picked over Lawrence. Lawrence went on to coach baseball beginning in the spring of 1985 and went on to compile a 359-221 record in nineteen years of coaching. Monken finished his overall coaching career with 18 football victories, and 129 baseball victories. Monken was later inducted into the Hall of Fame. Lawrence holds the most wins in coaching baseball.

. . . .

In 2014, the Charleston School Board voted to fire Brian Halsey despite efforts from the community to try and retain the coach. Former students, coaches, and players went to the school board meeting in defense of Halsey, but the school board voted 6-0 with one ostension to dismiss Halsey.

CHARLESTON FOOTBALL HEADLINERS

1932 Trojan Team First to Win Conference
(Excerpt taken from Jim Kimball's Sports Records Book)

Charleston High's 1932 football team was known as the "Triple Champions," which stemmed from its winning of the EI League, Wabash Valley Conference, and city championship. The latter resulted from its 46-0 win over cross town rival, T.C. The winning of the EI and Wabash were both firsts for the school's football program that dated back only five years to that point. The Wabash was made up of all schools within a 60-mile radius of Terre Haute, Indiana.

There were over 100 schools in this conference of which 25 played football and the championship was decided by an executive committee. Charleston tied Marshall and beat Casey, Martinsville, and Paris in Wabash play. Coach Gilbert Carson led the team to a 5-0-1 record in EI play, and only Martinsville cross the Trojan goal-line in those six games. Charleston beat Casey 12-0, Paris 12-0, T.C. 46-0, Oblong 12-0, and Martinsville 19-6. Charleston played a 0-0 tie with Marshall.

According to a sports article in the Charleston courier, two conditions led to the one blemish on the Trojan record. The article stated, "First, they faced by far the sub honest line this season at Marshall. Second, they were decidedly off color due in a large part to the handicap under which star halfback Howard Carson played.

The game was delayed 20 minutes to await the arrival of Carson who had a short time before submitted to a blood transfusion for his sister who was critically ill in the Olney hospital. Carson had not worked out with the team during its practices of the three days previous to the game, while Coach Carson had not been present in those final practices to prepare his team for battle. Carson would be named to the all-state team that season.

1966 Football Team Goes Undefeated

The 1966 football team is the only team to ever go undefeated in the long program's history under the leadership of Charleston great Merv Baker. Playoffs weren't formed yet so the team only played eight games in the season. The Trojan offense finished the season by scoring 330 points, while the defense held opponents to 52 points.

The Trojans largest margin victory came in the second week of the season in a 48-0 beatdown of Martinsville. Courier-News Sports Editor, Jim Kimball, reported that according to the statistics, CHS showed an overwhelming advantage. The Trojans finished the game with 366-93 total yard advantage.

The Trojans had the arm of Randy Cooley, and a powerful ground game with the legs of Paul Moffett and Steve Bell. Tom Jenkins was the special teams leader by setting a then record of PAT's kicked in a season with 36. The Charleston defense finished the season with four shutouts by shutting out Martinsville, Marshall 47-0, Oblong 42-0, and Paris 19-0.

Charleston claimed the sole right to the EI League title, and placed Cooley, Bell, Jenkins, and Gary Cole on the E.I. League Football Team. The team broke or tied twenty-nine school records. Starting with Steve Bell. Bell might have had the best individual season of any halfback in CHS history.

Bell set records for most touchdowns in a season (24), points scored in a season (144). Those records held strong until 2012. Other records Bells set but have been broken over the years include: receiving yards in a season (569), and touchdown caught in a season (10). Bell finished a career that put him second on the all-time CHS career scorers list with 186 points. Bell is now ranked third on the all-time list. Moffett finished as the all-time CHS career rushing attempts leader at the time with 286 attempts. That record stood until 2011.

CHS's First Final Four Football Team In 1977

The first of three straight trips to the final four started in 1977, the fifth year in head coach Chuck Budde's coaching tenure. The Trojans managed to take a stretch of ten straight victories into the game before losing to Metamora 18-6. The team won the outright Apollo Conference Championship and had to play the 3A's top rated powerhouse. According to Ex-Courier sports editor, Bill Lair, the Trojans were out battled in the rain and mud in front of a crowd of an estimated 3,000 fans at Trojan Hill.

Trailing 12-0 in the third quarter, Craig Donna substituted for injured snapper Bill Gibson in the game. Backed to their own five-yard line, Metamora's punter, Doug Neff, tried to get the punt off, but Charleston's defensive end Tim Grant blocked the kick, and Donna fell on the ball in the end zone for the Trojans first score. In the end, it would not be enough. The Metamora defense held the Trojans to only seven first downs, and reliable quarterback Keith Aten was held to a 2-7 passing night for 22 yards, and one interception.

Lair wrote in his "Time Out" section, "It was a great season for the Trojans. Everyone felt CHS would be strong in 1977 and the Trojans lived up to their advance billing. The "TCP-Taking' Care of Business" attitude helped the squad through 10 straight wins and last week sparked more spirit in this community than we have seen in our five years now."

Seven CHS players were selected to the All-Apollo Football team that year. Donna was tabbed to the first team offensive and defensive units at his tackle positions. Steve Cougill was the other two-way recipient on the team as well. Donna lead the team in tackles with 108, and also was credited with a fumble recovery, and a blocked punt. Cougill recorded 59 tackles and two quarterback sacks.

Other Trojan players selected to the first team were Bill Beavers, Keith Aten, and fullback Jon Buckellew, Bob Taylor, and John Sellett. This would be the second straight year being named all-conference. Beavers would snag 11 receptions for 272 yards, and six touchdowns. Aten carried the ball 88 times for 397 yards and eight rushing touchdowns. He also completed 21 of 48 passes for 432 yards and six touchdown passes.

Buckellew was the top rusher for the Trojans with 721 rushing yards on 105 carries and six touchdown runs. Taylor was credited with 53 tackles, and Sellett had 55 tackles, and five interceptions. Four Trojans were selected to the second team on the offensive and defensive units which included Mike Wozniak, Dan Downs, Tim Grant, and Anthony Cox.

CHS's Advances To Final Four Again In 1978

After a year that had the Trojans in the IHSA playoff record books for 25 first downs in a 49-7 playoff victory against McLeansboro, the Trojans were back for action in 1978. The Trojans were once again undefeated during the regular season, and during the whole year excelled on both sides of the football field. The Trojan offense scored a total 259 points, while the defense held opponents to a total 76 points.

At one point, Charleston were ranked in the UPI Prep Rankings at number three in the state at Class 3A, only to be behind 9-0 schools Geneseo and Sycamore high schools. The Trojans almost did not make it to the Final Four game if it wasn't for great playoff games from the team. In the first round, CHS found themselves trailing 12-7 in the fourth quarter to Olney. Lair wrote in the Courier, "For three periods, the Charleston Trojan offense was dormant." Remember that this is a team that Charleston beat 20-2 in the regular season.

The Trojans scored 19 points in the fourth quarter to mount the comeback. Jon Buckellew's 211 rushing yard, two touchdown night led the Trojans on the ground. Buckellew's 34-yard run, and Dan Down's 32-yard runs in the fourth quarter set up the following weeks matchup vs. Murphysboro. This time, the Trojans never trailed and combined for 237 yards on the ground from Buckellew and Downs to lead a 39-0 win.

Heading into their game vs. Kankakee McNamara, Lair wrote, "It is a strong, deep Charleston team in 1978. A little stronger than, but possible not quite as quick as, the 1977 squad." Lair also quoted coach Chuck Budde about last year's defeat. "I thought last year we were ready to play. Other factors (the weather) stopped what we thought was a ready attitude. I don't think anything will stop that attitude this time. We expect to do whatever it takes to win this game."

The Trojans would do whatever it took to win this game, but a 7-0 defeat sent Kankakee McNamara to the state finals and ended the Trojan season. Downs, who had a touchdown taken away for a clipping penalty earlier in the game, fumbled a handoff with 9:16 remaining in the fourth quarter on the Trojan 32-yard line. Kankakee quarterback, Kelly O'Connor, and tailback Brian Crossely combined to move the ball down before fullback Rob Lyons scored the touchdown.

The Trojans had their chances in the game. The team was inside the McNamara 15-yard line on three separate occasions, but penalties took away possible scores. Also, a 22-yard field goal attempt by John Sellett was blocked. Budde was quoted by Lair saying, "The difference in the game was the failure by our offense to put the ball in the end zone when we were in the four-down area. I felt we could move the ball. They had enough defense to stop us from going in the end zone."

Asked if it was hard to accept compared to last year, Budde responded, "Maybe a little bit because these folks are repeaters. We've been close so long, like a family. It couldn't hurt anymore if my son was playing. We have spent a long time together. Like a family. That's what makes it so hard. We can take consolation in the fact that we did a good job and we are dedicated to do it again. We WILL be back."

The Trojans had eleven players on the All-Conference team, six on offense, and five on defense. Mel Thomason was the lone CHS player named to the offensive and defensive units for his work as a lineman and defensive tackle. Other first team offensive picks included tackle Don Plummer, Thomason, center Bill Gibson, quarterback Brian Jones, fullback Jon Buckelew, and halfback Dan Downs. First Team picks on defense included Mark Daugherty, Thomason, John Sellett, linebacker Sean Wickham, and Gary Davis. Mark O'Dell and Daugherty would be both named on the second team.

Near State Bid Ends in Final Four in 1979

The 1979 squad had high hopes. The Trojans were coming off two straight Final Four appearances. This year, the team looked to win it all. "We never have rebuilding years," Budde told Times Courier Sports Editor Rick Gibson. "We expect to win every year."

Charleston brought back an experienced team with eight starters on defense and six starters on offense returning. Brian Jones returned as an all-conference quarterback, but the team lost all-state running back Jon Buckellew to graduation, as well as fullbacks John Sellett and Dan Downs. However, Rod Helton brought back experience, as well as Tony Clark. Jones, Helton, and Mark Daughtery were the team's tri-captains.

The Trojans began the year with one of the best played games in Trojan history at home against annual football powerhouse Metamora. After going to overtime with the score deadlocked at 20-each, Jones gave the Trojans the lead with a six-yard touchdown run. After Scott Inslen kicked the extra point to make the score 27-20, Metamora needed just one play in OT. The Redbirds scored on a 90-yard pass play. After a timeout, Metamora decided to line up for the two-point conversion.

Mel Thomason proved to be hero for this team in this game. The Redbirds looked to run a trap play for Sam Adami; however, he met Thomason at the one-yard line to seal the Trojans victory. Adami claimed to make it into the end zone, but the official disagreed. "Our kid said he came down on the line with the ball," Metamora coach John Helmich said. "He ran an awful lot of steps to not make it into the end zone."

Defensive coordinator Bill Monken believed the Trojans stopped him, and that they were ready for the play. "We called the touchdown and extra point," said Monken. "We were stacked up for it over there. They just executed on the touchdown, but Thomason got him on the extra point."

You would have thought that was a playoff game, but it was just the season opener. Charleston followed that week blowing out Olney 48-7, and losing a close 20-17 game to Rantoul to set up the Apollo Conference schedule. Charleston ran by Robinson 40-0 and Paris 61-12 before being tested.

Charleston was outgained in a narrow 14-7 victory over Mount Zion to set up an overtime showdown with Newton. Jones scored both touchdowns in a 14-7 win over Newton, including the leading scorer in overtime on the second play. The Trojans sealed the victory and the Apollo Conference when Jeff Matheny intercepted Tom Wolf. "We didn't play mediocre on purpose," said Budde. "Newton had a lot to do with it. They had us pegged pretty good." Charleston clinched the outright title with a 53-14 victory over Decatur Lakeview.

At 8-1, Charleston entered playoff contention ranked No. 2 in the UPI. Charleston drew Mt. Carmel in the first round and blew right past them. The offense racked up 423 total yards, while the defense tackled two Aces in the end zone for safeties. Mt. Carmel was without 1,000-yard rusher, Jon Dardeen, who suffered a broken wrist.

"I think we played well," said Monken after the game to Gibson. "They moved the ball once. They had some tricky stuff on the pass that was bothering us for a while. Then, we shut that down, and that was about it." Tony Baker led the team on the ground with 85 yards and two touchdown scores. The win set up a home game for Charleston with Harrisburg, who defeated Murphysboro 27-7.

Charleston had to battle Harrisburg on a wet, soggy field at Trojan Hill. The 30-degree temperature, combined with the fact that it snowed nearly all day kept the offense on the ground. It was fine with Charleston as the team rushed in all five touchdown scores in a 35-14 win to send the Trojans to the Final Four for a third straight season.

The two teams were tied at 14-14 until Jones ran in a three-yard score to give the Trojans the lead. On the following possession, Matt McSparin batted away a pitch to force a fumble, and the Trojans recovered the ball. CHS marched down the field for another score to force a two-possession lead before padding the lead with a fifth score in the fourth quarter.

"It was the turning point," said Budde to Gibson. "That took the wind out of the sails, and we took it in. I was wondering when we were going to get a big play, and McSparin gave it to us." The win setup a showdown with Mascoutah, who defeated Metamora 21-8.

The Trojans ride would end with the infamous fumble that will forever go down in Charleston lore. After battling back twice to take a 15-14 lead in the fourth quarter, it appeared Charleston was going to make their first trip to the state championship game when Chris Whitley intercepted a Mascoutah pass at the CHS 22-yard line with 6:03 remaining in the game. Five plays later, a handoff from Jones to Clark ended up on the ground, and Mascoutah recovered the ball on the CHS 42-yard line. Mascoutah marched down the field, capping the drive with a quarterback sneak as Mascoutah defeated Charleston 21-15.

Charleston's fumble was the third of the game, and it came at the worst possible time. "There's no question we would have won without the fumble," said Budde. "We were going to eat the clock alive." Mascoutah went on to win the state championship with a perfect 13-0 season. It was the third 10-win season for Charleston. "I'm not going to hang my head," said Budde. "I am proud of our people. The game just didn't go our way."

Charleston dominated the All-Apollo picks at the end of the season. On the first team offensive squad was Mark Daughtery at tight end, Mark O'Dell, Scott Enslen, Mel Thomason, and Mike Helton on the offensive line, Rod Helton at running back, and Brian Jones at quarterback. Cliff Campbell made the second team as an offensive lineman, while Tony Clark made the team as a fullback. The first team defensive team featured Thomason as a defensive end, as well as Matt McSparin. At linebacker, Marc Paap, and Enslen made it, while Helton made it as a defensive back.

Budde left Charleston after the season, accumulating a 55-14-1 record in seven seasons. After a year off, Budde was hired at Salem Community High School. Budde coached at Salem for nine seasons with a 64-26 record and seven playoff appearances. His 10-1 squad in 1985 is still Salem's single season record for wins. Budde was eventually inducted into the IHSCFA Hall of Fame.

1984 Squad Goes Undefeated in Regular Season

The 1984 Trojans capped an undefeated regular season by marching 8-0 in the regular season with an Apollo Conference championship and a trip to the playoffs. A first round playoff loss would finish the year 8-1, but there was still plenty to talk about in the town. Coach Verlon Myers, former All-American CHS quarterback, was back to his Alma mater and led a squad that raised some eyebrows in a season that was not meant to be. The 1984 squad was deeply inexperienced in the offensive and defensive department.

Two returning halfbacks were left from the year before in Ladd Rudell and Page Alexander. Junior, Tom Padget ended up beating out senior Kent Grissom for the starting quarterback job. Defensive Coordinator, Bill Monken, only had four starters left on defense. Former sports editor for the Times-Courier, Carl Walworth, reported Monken saying, "We feel the defense is just coming into its own. We're pleased with what they have been able to do and their overall execution."

The Trojans opened up the season in a non-conference test with their county rivals of Mattoon. CHS used a 20-point second quarter to win 20-18, but it didn't come easy. With winds blowing a reported 40 MPH, the passing game was flat with both quarterbacks combining to go 8-23, and 77 passing yards. Alexander, Ruddell, and emerging junior running back, Jerry Hamner all rushed for a touchdown in the victory.

In their second non-conference test, the status was uncertain. With Olney's teachers on a strike, the game status was up in the air. The teachers ended up delaying the strike, and the Trojans took advantage with a 31-14 win by out rushing the Tigers 249-143. After a 46-0 romp over rival Paris, the Trojans secured a 25-8 victory over Effingham with the help of a blocked punt. Senior Trojan lineman, Dave Stewart, fell on a blocked punt in the end zone for the third touchdown of the game. Effingham punter, John Sites, took a bad snap on the 10-yard line, and Charleston's Shane Thomas broke through to get the block. Then, Stewart, a 215-pound tackle, ran the ball down the end zone. Walworth wrote Monken saying, "There was nothing they could do to move the ball. Everything they tried to do we had them shut down."

After a win over Newton, the Trojans posted a 19-13 overtime thriller over Taylorville thanks to Hamner's one-yard plunge in OT. Alexander's 70-yard touchdown run helped dispose of Robinson, as the game of the year was just a week away.

Charleston, 7-0, and Mount Zion, 7-1, 5-0 in conference, had a date with destiny. The Braves led the offensive stats with running back Darrin Davis leading the way with 959 yards on the ground on 106 carries, and 21 touchdowns. There was a deep underdog feeling considering Alexander was the leading the Trojans with seven touchdowns. In Walworth's preview story, he quoted Myers saying, "I think the key is the ball club and who can maintain consistency and play their brand of ball." Walworth also went on to write, "Both teams are tough. It's just who is going to be tougher tonight."

In the clash of Apollo giants, it was Hamner and Padgett who led the 22-15 victory over the Braves to claim the conference championship. The defense limited Mount Zion to 102 yards on the ground, and quarterback Craig Guest, to a 6-15 passing night, throwing 94 passing yards, and two interceptions. Hamner powered his way for a night to remember. A 124-yard night on 15 carries, and a touchdown led the ground game. Padgett overcame past troubles by hooking up with Stan Royer for 74 of his total 130 yards passed on an 8-12 night.

Both Myers and Monken praised the work of volunteer coach Craig Bezruki who prepared both the offensive line and defensive lines according to Walworth. Myers was quoted saying after the victory, "Our offensive line just ate them alive, and the defense was just super. I think it was our best game on offense and defense."

The Mount Carmel Aces ended the memorable year by defeating the Trojans on their home field 38-16. Aces running backs, Doug Wirth and Brent Tedford, both rushed for two touchdowns, and both played factors with the Aces out rushing the Trojans 428-92.

Eight Trojans landed on the first-team Apollo conference list. Those included offensive lineman Mike Watson and Eric Craft, Royer as a receiver, Hamner as a running back, defensive lineman Eric Bomball, linebacker Jeff Oetting, and Alexander a defensive back. Alexander landed on the second team all-conference list as a running back, and Bill Ingles joined him as a defensive lineman.

Padget finished the season by completing 45 of 92 passes for 712 yards, eight touchdowns, and six interceptions. Hamner finished the year with 683 yards on 112 carries, and eight touchdowns. Royer led all receivers by catching 22 passes for 371 yards, and three touchdowns. Hamner went on to play at the University of Illinois. The seniors came a long way since their 2-4 freshman year that included a 57-0 loss to Mount Zion. Years later, their 22-15 victory over the Braves clinched the conference title, and an undefeated regular season.

1996 Squad Is Dream Team of 90's

The 1996 football team ended up being the only winning team in the 90's. It took Bill Monken some time, but this year gave Charleston something to be happy about. It was the second time since 1984 that the football team would make the playoffs. The year started off with the team thinking big. Literally. The offensive line's starters had the smallest man weighing at 220 pounds, while the biggest was at 315. Sports-editor, Brian Nielsen, quoted Monken talking about assistant coach Todd Miller's new nickname the big guys liked.

"We were in the weight room and the big men stay around each other. Miller walked over to them and said, 'man you guys look like a bunch of rhinos.' He put his thumb up by his nose and said 'hook em rhinos.' The kids laughed. Now we have shirts made up for them that says "Rhinos."

The team also had 1995 offensive player of the year Chuck Earp, and defensive player of the year Rubin Perez. Mike Kelly looked to help take the load off Earp as another returning starter. The year started off with a thrilling come-from-behind victory over Taylorville. Tony Coffey's rush up the gut with 2:27 left in the fourth quarter had the Trojan lead at five. Steve Plummer's jumping catch for the two-point conversion on the throw by quarterback Chris Frantz sealed the victory.

The game was dedicated to assistant coach, Eric Dircks's mom, Mary, who along with her husband never missed a football game. She died earlier in the year, and her thoughts helped fuel a hungry Trojan team. Nielsen quoted Monken saying, "Knowing she would be here in the game with us helped. We said before the game, 'Mrs. Dircks, at a critical time will you help us?" With the Trojans trying to seal the victory by converting a third-and-4, Monken said to his squad, "Mrs., Dircks, the time is now." Charlie Logsden would catch a 20-yard pass, capping

Frantz's 10-19, 197-yard performance.

    The Trojans bulldozed Olney the following week thanks to three touchdowns by emerging star running back Brad Homann. His 92 rushing yards led a Trojan ground game that out rushed Olney 295-2. It was the defense that would shine the following weeks. Starting with Paris, Tony Coffey was able to tackle Tiger halfback, Steve Macke in the end zone for a safety. Defensive back, Chris Rennells picked up Paris quarterback Levi Ray, and returned it 29 yards, and Logsden returned a fumble 15 yards for a touchdown.

    Effingham was held quiet when the defense held them to 23 total yards offense. CHS's Scott Johnson picked up Frantz's off passing night by racking up 108 yards on seven carries. Homann also chipped in 70 yards, Ben Lawson 80 yards, and Earp 62 yards. Safety Heath Price was quoted saying by Nielsen, "We thought this would show the rest of the Apollo conference. People probably said we were just beating easy teams. We thought this would help prove ourselves."

    After a win over Newton, the defense shut down Bethalto Civic Memorial 7-0 with a fourth quarter stand. Two plays after the Trojans lost a fumble on their own 27, Civic Memorial fullback Joe Odom broke away and was heading down the field in front of the Charleston sideline. Cornerback, Nick Ralston, caught up to Odom and with the help of Homann, made the touchdown saving tackle. After three stops, Civic Memorial had to convert the fourth-and-11. The Trojans Matt Robinson, and Justin Brown charged through to make the sack, preserving the win.

    With Robinson next on the schedule, it would be no easy task. The Maroons, once ranked 5th in the Class 2A, was knocking the Apollo Conference door. The Trojans held strong by defeating them 36-24 thanks to Homann's 154 rushing night and clinching the conference title. The Braves ended the perfect regular season for Charleston, but it was playoff time. CHS nabbed Big 12 Conference foe Champaign Central, a team that made the playoffs for the first time since 1988 and was coming in with a streak of three straight shutouts.

    The streak was broken with the Trojans out rushing Central 357-140 to take the 40-7 romp. Offensive play caller, Brian Halsey was quoted by Nielsen saying, "All week long we got dogged by the T.V., radio, and the newspapers. We got no respect. Central thought they were coming down to Mayberry to play Barney and Goober, and they found the Big Red Machine."

    Springfield brought their 9-1 record next up but was more worried about their quarterback that broke his non-throwing arm in their playoff victory. Chad Ruesky was so far having a nice season by throwing 1,267 yards and 18 touchdown passes. With CHS leading 7-6 at half, Ruesky would play through the pain, and lead the 24-15 win over Charleston. The Trojans lost three fumbles, and the Senators turned two of the five turnovers into touchdowns.

    Nielsen wrote in his column a couple days later, "I'm going to use newspaper space for what some might consider a trite thank you to those coaches and players who had grown up and kids making rhino calls for offensive lineman, and cheers in winning football. The Trojans gave fans a satisfying playoff rout over a team from the Big 12 conference and tends to turn up its noses towards schools like Charleston. This team gave the town something to claim for itself all fall. It had to end somewhere sometime."

    The Trojans dominated the all-conference picks. First team members included Matt Trober, Marshall Moore, and Brandon Beever as offensive lineman, Homann as a running back and defensive back, Rennells as a defensive lineman, Perez at linebacker, Van Lanken and

Ralston as defensive backs, and Logsden at punting. The second team had Von Lanken as a wide receiver, Frantz as quarterback, Lawson and Earp at runningback, Ernest Williams as a defensive lineman, Coffey and Logsden as a linebacker, and Price as a defensive back. Perez was also mentioned to the all-state team at linebacker in Class 4A.

Cinderella 2007 Team Makes Elite Eight

It was about redemption in 2007. After qualifying for the state football playoffs four years in a row, a 2-7 record in 2007 brought Charleston back down to Earth. "I think you need to get knocked down the mountain to appreciate things," coach Brian Halsey said to Journal Gazette-Times Courier sports editor Brian Nielsen before the season. "We didn't just get knocked off the mountain, but down the countryside."

There was some reason for optimism though. Senior quarterback Eric Gentry led the JG-TC area in passing yards as a junior but was coming off a 10-14 touchdown-interception ratio. Jamel Johnson and Clayton Murphy went two-three in receiving yards in the area. Twin brother, Mario Johnson, was looking to make a leap at runningback, while Taylor Bradley was looking to play significant minutes.

Charleston started the year defeating Taylorville 30-13 before the Apollo Conference opener. CHS dropped their next game to Mt. Zion 27-24 where the final 80 seconds were gold for a football fan. Charleston was marching down the field looking to upset Mt. Zion, but Jeremy Sy topped a pass intended for Murphy high in the air, where Jordan Grinestaff reeled it in to seal the victory over Charleston. The game was a highlight reel as the first 33 seconds of the contest featured 15 points.

Charleston regained momentum with a 40-6 romp over Paris, but then fell to Newton the following week 15-6. Charleston posted their first shutout in 10 years with a 40-0 victory over Robinson. Then, the team followed that up with a 28-21 win over Salem. Charleston fell to undefeated Effingham 42-28 the following week but won their fifth game to qualify them for the playoffs with a 41-29 win over Olney. However, CHS missed clinching a playoff berth by falling to Highland 41-30 at the end of the season, forcing them to wait until the weekend to see if they qualified for the playoffs.

Charleston was able to breathe a sigh of relief, but it was close. Due to 4-5 teams Pinckneyville and Norridge Ridgeview being upset in week nine, Charleston was the second to last team to qualify for the playoffs but drew what Coach Halsey called "the best-case scenario" when CHS found they were playing 9-0 Effingham in the first round.

A slew of nicknames including "Comeback Kids" and "Cinderella" were thrown at Charleston after the Trojans accomplished the impossible. With a 22-20 win over Effingham, Charleston fans were sent into a frenzy, and for good reason too. Charleston fought back from a 13-point deficit in the fourth quarter. Bradley came back from an injury to have his best game of his career, including a 27-yard touchdown run with 8:20 left in the fourth. Mario Johnson tied the game with 3:51 remaining.

After Gentry lost the snap on the PAT, Gentry scrambled to his feet, and whirled a two-point conversion to Jamel Johnson to give Charleston the two-point lead. Nielsen wrote that Halsey didn't even see the conversion because the coach put his head down after the snap was botched. Halsey saw an incredible finish though from the defense. Effingham marched down from their 43-yard line to the Charleston nine with 11 seconds left. However, on the final play, Effingham quarterback Connor McNeely dropped back and overthrew Steve Keller.

"They were running that play across the middle," defensive end Matt Gooden told Nielsen. "Jamel goes 'Hey, I am going to man up this guy running the crossing route.' It was a player adjustment with me and him, that's all it was. He was on that all day."

Charleston qualified for the Elite Eight by knocking off Mt. Vernon 28-12 at Trojan Hill, which setup another game at home for Charleston after Marion advanced. Charleston's dream of making their first final four since 1979 was crushed when the pass-happy Marion out-rushed Charleston to lead a 43-22 win. Marion running back Micah Markley rushed 152 yards to lead a ground game that nearly rushed 300 yards as a team, while quarterback Matt Brown added 242 yards in the air. "If they are going to give us the run, we have got to take it and win the game on the ground," Marion coach Kerry Martin told Nielsen after the game. "They were going to try and take away a lot of our passing stuff, and they did a good job of that." Mario Johnson's 88-yard kickoff return is still an IHSA Class 5A record for a kickoff return.

Jamel Johnson made the all-Apollo first team on the offensive and defensive side. Kyle Hasbargan joined Johnson on the first team offense, while Drew Riley made it on the first team defense. Nick Guinto made the second team defensive team as a linebacker. Gentry finished the year as the career record holder in all passing categories.

2011 Team Best of All Time

It was three straight underachieving seasons that passed Charleston High School. In 2008, the team was poised to win the Apollo Conference, but finished 4-5. Stumbling losses to Robinson and Salem in 2009 made the team finish under .500, and in 2010, a 5-4 record still wasn't enough for post-season. In 2011 it was different. Many changes came. Coach, Brian Halsey, knew this was crunch time for him. "The pressure is on me," said Halsey in JG-TC sports-editor Brian Nielsen's football preview.

Halsey decided to not call both ends of the field and was able to lure back old defensive coordinator Tim Hogan. Hogan was on Halsey's staff in the early parts of a rebuilding CHS football program that went from two wins in two seasons to three-time Apollo Conference champions. In Nielsen's article, Hogan said, "I had other offers, but it wasn't a fit. I really missed it, and I'm glad to be back."

Hogan had plenty to work with in senior Chris Creek anchoring the defense. Creek was poised to break John Best's 322 career tackles mark this season, having already broken the single season mark as a sophomore. He was joined by returning starters Matt Wolfe and Stephen Majors. The defense took a new look with two new cornerbacks, Truston Winnett and James Hudson, safety Dillian Cazley, and Ryan Preston and Jesse Campbell looking to start somewhere in the middle at linebacker. The Trojans were without leading runningback L.J. Welsh for most of the beginning of the season due to injury but had a seasoned quarterback in Sean Hussey along with veteran receivers in Tibet Spencer and Aaron Bence, along with a new addition in the 6-foot-7 T.J. Bell.

After much hype, the season began with a road game at Rantoul. The Trojans and the Eagles combined for 112 points in CHS's 68-44 victory. It was sophomore Josh Cazley emergence after Welsh's injury rushing for 164 yards in his varsity debut. Rantoul's Terry

Deaville wound up throwing six touchdown passes, but junior Noah Miller worked his way in for four scores on the ground. Dillian Cazley added in a 93-yard kickoff return, and kicker Dalton Runyon broke Tom Jenkins's record for most PAT's kicked in a game by knocking in eight.

The Flaming Hearts were next on the list with plenty of bad blood to go around. It should be noted that both teams were in a near brawl after a late hit on Welsh cost him his final regular season game in 2010, but it was the Trojans who got the last laugh. Dillian Cazley returned another kickoff to the house for 85 yards, and his brother rushed for 167 yards in the 40-14 victory. Halsey said after the game, "I think the thing I'm pleased with the most is how our defense rebounded from last week. The defense staff took it personal and had a great week in practice. It's not very often you hold Effingham to only 14 points."

With a rout over Olney, it was time to go to Mount Zion who held a 25-game Apollo Conference win streak. Welsh was still limited due to his injury, but the Braves had their number one runningback at full capacity. Grant Naylor ran all over the Trojans racking up 235 rushing yards on 29 carries, and three touchdown runs. Quarterback Nick Stroud added over a hundred yards rushing, and the Trojans were held scoreless 35-0. The Trojans offense was held in check at the goal line three times.

Charleston was able to rebound next week as they hosted Paris. Hussey was able to find three different receivers in the end zone to lead the 28-7 victory Creek also recorded career tackle 353 to become the best tackler in school history. In a monster victory over Newton, Hussey and Spencer officially put their names in the record books forever. Hussey's 393 yards beat out his father, Kevin Hussey's, previous record of 353 yards thrown in a game. Spencer played a huge part in helping by collecting four touchdown passes, beating the previous record of three held by six different receivers.

All that aside, the Trojans were too busy focusing in on the upcoming week versus Robinson. A win guaranteed a playoff berth, but the Maroons weren't going to just laydown coming into the Trojan Hill with an identical 5-1 record. Welsh returned at an appropriate time by leading Charleston's ground game, picking up 177 yards on 13 carries. Orion Roberts' three-yard touchdown on an eight minute-32 second drive was one of many key factors in the 48-20 victory. The win clinched the playoff berth. There was plenty more to cheer about as announcer Paul Slifer announced that Effingham pulled the 15-14 victory over Mount Zion. A win next week over Salem would give the Trojans a share of the conference title.

"We have two things we want to accomplish in the next two weeks, and that's to get an Apollo Championship, and a first round playoff game at home," said Halsey. "That's why this game is so important. This is the time of the year you want to be playing your best football." The Trojans played outstanding football. It started off with perhaps the best defensive performance in years. Charleston held Salem to only 54 passing yards, seven first downs, and 0-10 on third down conversions in the 46-15 victory. CHS then beat Highland for only the second time in school history with a 47-28 romp. Bence caught three passes, traveling for 153 yards, turning each catch into a touchdown. Bence caught passes that went for 22, 83, and 49 yards.

Charleston hosted Waterloo in the first round of the playoffs, but before the week started there was much appraisal to the Trojans coaching staff. Twelve assistant coaches joined Halsey's staff including: Bob Black, Cliff Campbell, Shad Ferguson, Tyler Hanner, Tim Hogan, Jim Kuykendall, Cliff McBenge, Jeff Miller, John Pogue, Chris Sczecsniak, Carl Wolfe, and Jim Wood. The Trojans had plenty of big plays against Waterloo. With the game tied 28-28, Matt

Wolfe's strip and recovery on their own 39-yard line gave the team plenty of momentum. Roberts gave the Trojans the upper hand once again by causing another Waterloo fumble, and Hussey's fourth-and-15 conversion touchdown pass to Spencer sealed the victory The Trojans finished the game with 197 yards on the ground too. "In addition to doing well up front, Noah Miller did a great job of blocking," said Halsey.

    CHS hosted another playoff game thanks to Herrin's win over Columbia. The game was pushed back towards the evening so fans could watch Eastern Illinois head coach, Bob Spoo, coach his last game of a 50-year coaching career. Herrin was not happy with the push back. "It's high school football time," said Herrin coach Jason Karnes to Nielsen. "I'm not too happy with it to be honest. We have kids who will be getting home late and have church the next morning. I think the big picture is travel with 75 players and cheerleaders. It's no disrespect to Eastern, it's just safety for the kids."

    The Trojans were in the driver's seat to tie the schools record for wins in a season dating back Charleston's historic 70's teams. Late game or not, they tied the record with a powerful 34-21 victory. Charleston finished with 243 rushing yards, and held Herrin's All-State quarterback, Antuan Davis, to 6-13 passing for 78 yards, and 92 rushing yards.

    Gutsy calls led the win. Facing a fourth-and-6, Welsh took a fake punt and rushed it for 23 yards for the first down. Two plays later, Josh Cazley broke through two tackles for a 25-yard touchdown run. It was Cazley shining once again in the second half by opening the half returning the kickoff 94 yards. Herrin didn't score until 5:00 left in the third quarter, and after Welsh's 13-yard run, and Noah Miller's one yard plunge the score read 34-7 with 11:02 remaining in the game.

    The game of the year was now set. Mount Zion upset number one seed Breese Mater Dei, which meant Charleston would travel back to Mount Zion for a rematch to determine who would play in the Final Four. Mount Zion was without Naylor, but had a super sophomore stud in Austin Rey, who was well over 1,000 rushing yards. When it was all said and done, this possibly could have been the best game ever.

    After Creek's six-yard touchdown run, Winnett gave Charleston the double-digit lead in the first half by picking up a loose fumble and returning it 44 yards for a touchdown. The Braves scored 14 points in under two minutes to send the game tied at halftime but opened the half with a touchdown by Stroud. Welsh kept the Trojans in the game with a 57-yard touchdown run, but Stroud responded by breaking five tackles for a 67-yard touchdown. The failed kick kept the score at 27-20. Facing a third-and-14, Hussey found Winnett for a 37-yard touchdown to bring Charleston within one, but the Trojans weren't done yet.

    Dillian Cazley made up for his fumble late in the fourth quarter by catching the game winner. Facing heavy pressure, Hussey flipped a shuffle pass to Cazley standing in the end zone. The big play put CHS up 28-27, and the crowd could possibly be heard all over town. "It was possibly the best feeling in my life," said Cazley to Nielsen. The Braves couldn't come up on their last drive thanks to two tackles for a loss by Ryan Preston, and Spencer's interception. The win sealed the 11th win, most in school history.

    The Trojans now found themselves hosting the Final Four game. A pep rally was set the day before the game with former coaches and players Ken Baker, Verlon Myers, and Bill Monken all giving motivational speeches. The offensive line was one of the biggest stories so far this season, helping protect Hussey to set a school record for touchdown passes in a season. The offensive line was led by Tevin Brookins, Cody Reeley, Daniel Hildebrandt, Cody Margentaller, Jacob Schrock, and Jesse Campbell.

The Trojans season came to an end against eventual state champion Rochester. Oklahoma State-bound quarterback Wes Lunt (who eventually transferred to the University of Illinois), and All-State wide receiver Zach Grant (who also eventually transferred to the University of Illinois) helped Rochester overcome a second quarter deficit, to a 41-13 win.

The 13-6 second quarter lead by Charleston was helped with the wind gusting, but with Lunt's back to the wind, he was unstoppable. Rochester played villain to spoil a great season. "It's like we were one step away from turf," said Spencer to Nielsen. "We could smell it." Halsey said, "I told them it hurts now, but the tears will eventually turn to smiles. The records that shattered individually, and as a team, it should be nothing, but smiles. It's special. The love and chemistry they have for one another."

The records the team accomplished are amazing. Starting on offense, Hussey broke every passing record. Josh Cazley broke the most points by a sophomore record, and Noah Miller broke the most points by a junior. Spencer broke Matt Shonk's receptions in a season record. Creek set the career tackle records becoming the first ever CHS player to record at least 400 career tackles. Winnett also broke Steve Scholes most interceptions in a season record by picking off nine passes.

Punter, Ethan Miller didn't break any punting records, but was the number one punter in the state when it came to punting yardage.

Hussey held all the career passing records. Creek was named to the class 4A All-State team while Hussey was named honorable-mention. Halsey was eventually named the 2011 Decatur Herald & Review Coach of the Year.

2012 Team the Best to Not Be Hung Up

Coming off a Final Four appearance and a school record 11-2 record setting season, the Trojans were poised to be in the driver's seat to head back to the final four. Charleston had their all-state passing record-holding quarterback in senior Sean Hussey. The team also returned hard-hitting fullback Noah Miller and speedy running back, Josh Cazley. Truston Winnett, Austin Cohn, and Ethan Miller led the receiving corp.

The defense lost all-state linebacker, Chris Creek, but had University of Illinois commit Dillan Cazley at safety. Orion Roberts, Noah Miller, and Ryan Preston were also back for some hard hits at the linebacker spot. Junior Aron Decker, was back after a strong sophomore season at defensive end. Nick Wilson came over to split duty with the golf team to kick PAT's, and both Cazley's and Winnett were to return kicks. Everyone who followed Trojan football knew that this was the year Charleston football was going to shine.

Charleston didn't disappoint in their opener against Rantoul with a 49-6 win. It was the Trojans home opener and forced the cheerleaders to do 196 jumping jacks since they did seven jumping jacks after each touchdown. "They probably were mad," said Josh Cazley who finished with a game high 136 yards rushing on six carries for two touchdowns. "I'd be mad too. It probably felt like practice to them." Noah Miller had 73 of his 95 yards rushing in the first quarter. Hussey needed to complete just seven passes for 176 yards, completing touchdown passes to Winnett twice, Cohn, and Ethan Miller. The defense held Rantoul to 15 yards passing.

The following week, the Trojans had to make the two-hour trip to Peoria Manual. With Olney, Newton, and Robinson leaving the Apollo Conference, Charleston made a contract for two years with Manuel and Chatham Glenwood. Manual was a breeze for Charleston. The Trojans won 49-0 and avoided a tornado warning. Four touchdowns on the ground came from Josh Cazley, and two came from Noah Miller. Winnett also corralled 107 yards of Hussey's 256 yards passing. Outscoring their opponents 98-6 in their first two games the Trojans cracked the top ten, ranking 9th in Class 5A, but faced a test in the fourth best team in Class 6A in Chatham Glenwood in week three. Boy, was it a classic.

Chatham had a duel threat quarterback in Miles McAdams, and a hard runningback in Donovyn Hammonds. Charleston held a 15-14 lead after the first quarter, but a 21-point second quarter paved the way to a 35-29 halftime lead over Charleston. Josh Cazley's 4-yard run with two seconds left in the second quarter gave Charleston the momentum, but neither team scored in the third quarter. Jesse Campbell caught a 15-yard pass for a touchdown to give Charleston the 36-35 lead with under seven minutes to play. Hammonds responded with a seven-yard run with 3:17 left to play, and with the kick, Chatham was up 42-35. After a drive down the field, Josh Cazley was able to punch in the one-yard run. Then, coach Halsey gave the signal to go for two.

"I had to do it," Halsey said. "We'd had a couple of PAT's blocked. We were the underdog and we were at home. We make that and we shock the state. We didn't but hopefully gained some respect." Nathan Hack came up with the game saving tackle to deny Noah Miller, and the Trojans lost the 42-41 heart breaker. Fans had their fill as the game didn't start till 9:15 p.m. due to rain. "I can't give enough respect to Charleston," McAdams said after the game. "I will say they will go deep into the playoffs. We came in giving them respect because we knew they gave Rochester a heckuva game last year. That's easily the best team we've played so far." Charleston couldn't sweat the loss too hard because week four was the tip-off of the Apollo Conference schedule. The hard-fought game against Chatham raised Charleston to a No. 8 state ranking.

Winless Effingham was the Trojans first conference opponent. Charleston beat Effingham with ease in a 46-7 rout at home. Josh Cazley finished the game 178 yards rushing on the ground with two touchdowns, including a 78-yard touchdown run nullified on a holding penalty. Hype surrounded the Coles County area next week for the First Mid Coles County Clash between now Apollo Conference member, and county rival, Mattoon. It would be the first meeting between the two teams since 1987.

Dillan Cazley returned to the starting lineup after missing the first three games and made a splash by making nine tackles. Charleston defeated Mattoon with Winnett leading the way in record setting fashion. Winnett tied Tibet Spencer's record for receiving touchdowns in a game by grabbing four. Hussey only needed to complete nine passes for 254 yards. Once again, the Trojans had to weather a rain delay with the game starting two hours late. The Green Wave held a 10-0 lead, but Josh Cazley's 74-yard kickoff return grabbed the momentum back and the Trojans used a 29-point second quarter to lead a 55-29 victory.

The win moved Charleston up to No. 6 in the Class 4A rankings. Next up on the list was the Homecoming game against Mount Zion. The Braves looked to hoist an upset after leading 13-0 and 22-21 at halftime over Charleston. "Coming into halftime, we were a little down," said Sean Hussey, who finished the game 19-27 for 252 yards with two touchdowns thrown. "We knew that we were a better team than what we were in the first half. It must have been one heck of a halftime speech. Josh Cazley rushed for three second half touchdowns, and the defense intercepted three passes. One being a 64-yard interception return by Winnett. The win made Charleston playoff eligible with their fifth win. Cazley passed Bill Thissell and Bob Thomas for third on the all-time career points list.

Charleston clinched the Apollo Conference in week seven with a 44-0 victory at Paris. It was the third time this season Charleston had to play in the rain, but still managed for four rushing touchdowns. Charleston handled Salem 42-7 the next week on Senior Night. A trip to Highland would determine if Charleston would host a first round playoff game. The Trojans would need a win to put them an 8-1 to cap off the regular season. Charleston could return home happily with a 46-21 win. During the game, Winnett's 68-yard touchdown broke Jamel Johnson's 2007 records of receiving yards in a season.

As playoff brackets were announced the following night, Charleston did clinch a first round home playoff game. While that was nice, others were too busy looking at the possibility of playing Rochester in the second round if Charleston defeated Bloomington Central Catholic.

"My job is to stay focused and right now it's Bloomington Central Catholic," Halsey said. "We've focused one week at a time. Since June everybody talked about week five and we were able to stay focused. "Ending the season as the No. 3 ranked team in Class 4A, Rochester was dropped down to Class 4A, and was ranked No. 1. First, the Trojans had to deal with Bloomington Central Catholic.

Charleston used a 35-point third quarter to blow out Bloomington Central Catholic 55-10. Josh Cazley rushed for two touchdowns, Noah Miller grabbed a touchdown pass after the linebacker blocked a punt, and Winnett added a touchdown reception. Dillan Cazley capped off the third quarter with a 60-yard interception return.

With the win, it was finally time for that showdown between the first and third best teams in Class 4A. "Our kids have been preparing for this game since last year," Halsey said. Rochester entered the game with University of Wisconsin bound linebacker, Garrett Dooley, and future Eastern Illinois University quarterback commit, Austin Green.

Rochester held a 14-0 lead before the CHS offense even touched foot on the playing field. The first play of the game Blake Pasley returned a kickoff for 89 yards. Gabe Ferguson's 78-yard interception return added more frustration. "We made too many mistakes early," Charleston coach Brian Halsey said. "You can't go against a good football team like that and make mistakes. A lot of the mistakes we made, they created."

Austin Cohn's seven-yard touchdown reception cut the deficit to a touchdown, but two of Dooley's three touchdowns came in the second quarter, and Rochester held a 28-7 halftime lead. Two more Rochester touchdowns in the second half broke open the game.

So, ended the season of what could have been. What could have happened if that two-point conversion went through against Chatham-Glenwood? Would it have been a Charleston versus Rochester state final? We will never know. Instead, Charleston had to endure the pain of their season ending in the second round of the playoffs. Halsey said farewell to each of his seniors one by one. The seniors left their marks being a part of teams the last two years that gave Charleston a combined 20-4 record and two conference crowns.

"We told our kids the 2003 group went 17-4 (in 2002-03) and put Charleston football on the map," Halsey said. "Then there was a lull and these kids have brought it back. I'm proud of these kids but I'm also so proud of our staff. We have a staff of volunteer coaches who work their tails off. Charleston football is where it is because of the staff and these kids.

The season was one to remember in the record books. Hussey and Winnett were both all state selections. Hussey left Charleston holding all of the regular season and career passing records. Hussey finished his career with records of 397 pass completions, 658 attempts, 5,975 yards passing, and 52 touchdown passes. Hussey received a walk on position for the University of Illinois, but never played. Dillian Cazley played at the University of Illinois, making the all-academic Big Ten team three times.

Winnett became Charleston's first ever receiver to record over 1,000 yards receiving in a season, finishing with 1,034. Winnett also holds the record for most receiving yards in a game with 193 against Mattoon. Josh Cazley became Charleston's all-time scorer with 218 career points, breaking Steve Temple's all-time mark set from 1964-1966. His career 2,406 net yards, and 36 career touchdowns are also new records. His regular season marks of 144 times carried, 146 total offensive points, and 22 rushing touchdowns were also new records. Nick Wilson broke the record for PAT's kicked in a season with 47. Wilson eventually made the Eastern Illinois University football team and was the kicker.

As a team, the Charleston offense broke the records for points and touchdowns in a season. The 2012 squad scored 497 points and scored 71 touchdowns. The defense recorded the most interceptions in a season by interception 20. Winnett and Josh Cazley were named as two-way Apollo Conference picks. Other selections included lineman Daniel Hildebrandt, and Cody Margenthaler as lineman, Josh Cazley at running back, Hussey at quarterback, Winnett at receiver, defensive lineman Campbell, linebacker Noah Miller, and defensive back Dillan Cazley.

Boys Golf
(1944-2018)

Boys Golf
(1944-2018)

There may be records before the 1944 season, but nothing was found on IHSA. The first ever team to qualify for the state tournament was in 1944. Individual performances for that season cannot be found, but the team finished 10th overall. Regional and Sectional scores were not recorded until 2000.

Greg Petersen could be considered the greatest boy's golfer in CHS history. Petersen made his mark in the record books in 1978, shooting a two-day score of 149 to capture the AA state championship. During the regular season, Petersen lost the Apollo Conference title to current good friend and former Paris alumni, Brad Hamilton. Hamilton went onto to tie for eighth place at the state tournament. The only two events that Petersen did not win his senior year was at conference and at the sectional qualifier.

Today, Petersen still remembers that state tournament that happened nearly 40 years ago. After the sectional qualifier, Petersen jammed his finger in P.E. and couldn't grip the clubs very well. Two days before the state tournament, Petersen was practicing on the course, and remembered a conversation with an Eastern Illinois University men's golf player who worked as a proshop assistant at Lincoln Greens Golf Course near Springfield, which was where high school golf played the final round of the state tournament that year. "We were talking, and he noticed I couldn't grip the clubs very well, and he asked me who he thought was going to win the tournament," said Petersen. "I looked at him and said that I thought I was. He laughed and said 'Seriously, who do you think is going to win?' I said I think I am. He came up to me at the end of the tournament and said 'Congratulations, I guess you weren't kidding!"

Petersen powered through the injury by defeating Springfield (Griffin) J.C. Anderson's score of 152 by three strokes. At this time, there was only a two-class system, Class A for small school, and Class AA for the large school. Petersen won the large school Class AA. Today, high school golf plays in a three-class system.

Petersen eventually golfed at the University of Illinois at the end of his golf career. He also won a state championship in bowling in the spring of 1979. The Bowling Championship was sponsored by the Bowling Proprietors of America. Petersen qualified for the Nationals by winning the State tournament and finished ninth in the National Bowling Championship that next summer, which led to him being voted the Illinois Male Athlete of the Year, beating out the likes of future NBA Hall of Famer, Isiah Thomas, who went to St. Joseph High School in Winchester, Illinois.

After that, Petersen played golf professionally for nearly 20 years, and was ranked in the top 300 in the world during a stretch in the mid-1990s. He played professionally on the PGA Tour, the European Tour, the Ben Hogan Tour/Nike Tour (which is now the Web.com Tour), the Canadian Tour, the South African Tour, the Asian Tour, the South American Tour, and the Central American Tour. During this span, he had several top finishes, including second place finishes on both the Canadian Tour and South African Tour, as well as a fifth-place finish in a European Tour event (1996 South African PGA Championship.

Petersen was coached by coaching legend Stan Adkins. The Decatur Eisenhower native, who actually excelled in football back in the day, coached Charleston for 41 years before retiring in 2014. Adkins taught for 37 years before returning in 2003 but remained as the boy's golf coach. Adkins was a pioneer in starting the Trojan Booster Club Golf Classic in 2004, which generated money for the Booster Club. Today, the money is used towards transportation for Charleston athletics. In 2014, Adkins was awarded Chamber of Commerce Volunteer of the Year. In 2017, Adkins had the Trojan Fall Golf Classic named after him, which is now the Stan Adkins Trojan Fall Golf Classic.

Charleston Makes Three Peat in Early 2000s

In 1993, team won a Regional title, but there are no records of individual performances. Six years later, Adkins led another team to state in 1999. the team was the first of three-straight state appearances. The team placed 15th overall at the state tournament. The team only had one senior on the team. Sophomore Dustin Sloat led the team with a two-day score of 171. Nick Sloat, Ben Wochner, Matt Myerscough, Chris Brooks and Dustin Sloat set the school record for an 18-hole score. Justin LaPlante and Nick Wood were also on the team.

The team qualified in 2000 despite missing out on a Regional. Ben Wochner won Regional medalist honors. At the Alton Sectional, Charleston finished third to move onto the state tournament. Dustin Sloat and Chris Brooks had scores of 75, while Wochner added an 80. Sloat finished his career as an all-state golfer by finishing 10th overall with a two-day score of 155, which included a 5-under on day two. Wochner, Brooks, LaPlante, and Sloat were holdovers, while Scott Frankie, and Nick Meissen contributed.

The 2001 team capped a three-year run with a Regional title with a team score of 303, which was eight strokes better than second place Highland. Dustin Sloat won Regional medalist honors. Charleston hosted the Sectional at the Charleston Country Club and finished third, qualifying for state in part to a spectacular day from sophomore Tony Wochner. Sloat finished with a 75, while Brooks finished with a 79, but Wochner stepped up with a score of 80. LaPlante, Meissen, and Frankie rounded out the team.

The final round of the IHSA golf state finals was called off that year due to heavy rain in the Bloomington-Normal area. Trophies and medals were awarded based on the final results of Friday's play. Brooks just missed all-state, finishing 12th with a score of 74. The team finished 11th overall. Adkins finished his head coaching career with a dual record of 440-109-6. Former Charleston Middle School basketball coach (now CHS JV basketball coach) and 1982 CHS grad, Randy Harpster, took over.

State Champion Golf Team Wins Big in 2017

After going 10-6 and 17-3 in dual meets his first two seasons, Harpster led a young CHS core to the school's first Regional title in 15 years. Charleston won the Charleston Regional with a score of 311, which was nine strokes better than second place Mattoon.

However, Charleston had a rough going at the Sectional. Mattoon would surprise Charleston by finishing ahead of the Trojans and placing third. Charleston finished fifth. Disappointed, Harpster told Tyler Rusk, "The kids never gave up. They competed all the way to the end. Individually, we did not play our best, but we hung in there. We finished fifth and were three shots from making state and that's an accomplishment." Preston Smith would qualify for the state tournament as an individual, but the team had an upside as all top six individuals were sophomores or freshman.

Next season, the 2017 team was hungry. The team finished 19-0 in dual meets and won the Apollo Conference for a second year in a row, this time by 20 strokes over Mattoon. However, Mattoon upset the Trojans again, this time in the Regional. Mattoon beat Charleston by six strokes at the Effingham Regional. The team shot a 321, and they were not happy.

Harpster told Justin Rust after the match, "We came here to move on and that's what we did. We did a good job. The one day where we did not get the four scores that we have had every match, all year long. Going into the Sectional, we know we will get the scores. I know we will come back from this."

He was right. One week later, Charleston won their first ever Sectional championship with a score of 307 at the Salem Country Club. Junior, Keagan Gowin was the headliner as he led the team with a score of 72. His score was 19-strokes better than his Regional effort. Gowin was typically the fourth best golfer on the team. "My team carried me here, so I decided I needed to pick up and contribute," Gowin told Rust.

Ben Lanman shot a 76, Robert Rardin a 79, Preston Smith an 80, Blake Wolfe an 83, and Zach Will an 85 to round out the team. Harpster told Rust, "We are real excited about this. We have been averaging between 300 to 309, but to do it in a sectional, that is pretty impressive. To have all scorers 85 or under, that is really getting it done."

Just when you thought the team couldn't top that, Charleston went even further next week. The Trojans came into Saturday's competition six strokes off pace for first place. The team pulled together and broke the school record for an 18-hole round by six strokes. Their 292-team score on Saturday, combined with their 307 on Friday, won the state championship with a two-day total of 599, nine strokes better than second place. "I don't have the words," said Harpster to Rust. "Unbelievable. More than I expected. I told them to just go out and have fun. Every year, this group has stepped up for the next challenge."

The state title was dedicated to Jordan Holly, a CHS student that passed away in a car crash in May that year. The team bought gold polos before the season in her memory and wore the polos on Friday. "Any time things go tough this season, we would say that Jordan would not want them to make excuses," Harpster told Rust. "She was an inspiration to our whole season."

Robert Rardin placed sixth by shooting a 4-under-par 67 on Saturday to shot a two-day total of 146. His 146 two days score broke former state champion Greg Petersen's two-day score set in 1978. Ben Lanman joined Rardin as an all-state golfer by shooting a two-day score of 147, good for 10th place overall.

"I noticed that Robert was low, but I did not think we could shoot that low," Lanman told Rust. "We have never done that before and it was the perfect time to do it." Rardin was just amazed with the performance. "Honestly, I started hitting shots and they started going where I wanted them to go," Rardin said to Rust. "I thought we were in contention, and that is all I really knew."

Preston Smith just missed all-state honors by finishing 12th overall. "I am excited. I have no words," Smith told Rust. "I knew we had talent, but I thought it would be closer like one or two strokes, but nine. That's a lot."

On a separate phone call with Coach Harpster, he described Smith's gameplay at state the most selfless player he has ever coached. "Preston Smith went into hole 18 and we had a six or seven stroke lead. He was having trouble with the bunker, so I told him to just lay it out there. He ends up getting in on the green, still a little far out. I ask him if he is going to try and sink that putt, and he says 'No, coach. I am just going to try and get it close, so I can putt it in. It's about the team right now.' He ends up sinking the put for a par. Some kids in that situation would say they want to be all-state and fire away. Preston cared about the team. I told him next year if he is in that situation to fire away because no matter what, he can say he is a state champion."

Gowin began the day with a six-over-par 43 on the first nine holes but fought his way back with a 37 on the back nine to finish the day with 80 on Saturday. "I knew I had to turn it around and stick it out for my team," Gowin told Rust. "I am speechless." Blake Wolfe played five strokes better than his Friday score on Saturday. Wolfe and Zach Will each shot two-day scores of 173.

The Trojans will have the spotlight on them for the 2018 season as all six golfers will be back, but Harpster was not thinking about that at the time. "I will just say that is a good thing, but right now we will just enjoy this," Harpster said to Rust. "Assistant coach Ron Rardin has done an amazing job. Assistant coach Stan Adkins and the whole Charleston community has been so supportive. Some kids came out today to watch us, and they drove an hour and a half to support the guys."

As of 2017, Harpster has a career 65-9 record in dual matches. Harpster noted that the last three years, Charleston has had five of their top six place at the Apollo Conference meet, where only eight spots are open for all-conference. Smith is also the only recorded player in the last four years to sink a hole-in-one.

Boys Soccer
(1986-2018)

Boys Soccer
(1986-2018)

Nearly thirty-two years ago, Charleston soccer wasn't what you would have thought it was now. Trojan soccer has grown into one of the best programs in the eastern/central part of Illinois thanks to not having a losing season since 1993. However, back when soccer started at Charleston in 1986, it took the very first ever Trojan soccer team eighteen games to win their first game.

The 1986 team didn't take time to get their names in the stat books. Tim Montgomery led the team with eleven total offensive points. Charleston lost their first regular season game to Blue Mound 6-2. Although, the stats would only get worse for the '86 Trojans. In the schools only no-win season, Charleston allowed a total 105 goals to opponents and scored 16. That's about 7.5 goals allowed each game and 1.1 goals scored. Success wouldn't follow the Trojans immediately. After the 0-14 season, it took Charleston four more losses until the Trojans, led by Darrick Brooks, edged Mt. Zion 3-2 to win their first game in school history. Unfortunately, the team would only win one more game to finish the year 2-11-0.

Chuck Castle lead the Trojans for six years compiling a 17-61-5 coaching record. Although Castle didn't ever have a winning season, he had some quality moments to watch from some of his players. In the 1988 season, Tim Montgomery set a school record by setting up four different goals in a 5-2 victory over Blue Mound. Montgomery was one of the bright spots from the first development of Charleston soccer. He finished his career with 15 goals, 12 assists, and 42 total offensive points. His teammate Brooks was a scoring machine during the 80s. Brooks finished his career after a 4-9-1 1989 season. Brooks led the team all three years he played in goals. He finished with 40 goals, good for eighth best on the all-time list.

Trojan soccer didn't see their first winning season until 1992. In Bob Sanders' only year coaching, the team saw vast improvement by going 7-4-2. It was also the first time the team had a higher goal scored two goals allowed ratio with a 43:20. This was only the start of what would become of Trojan soccer. Some could say Hank Nino was the Merv Baker of Charleston soccer. Nino stepped in 1993, and after one year made Charleston one of the best in the state.

After the 1993's 9-11-0 year, 1994 saw amazing improvement by going 13-5-4. It was Charleston's first ever season with double-digit wins. The following year would once again set the school record with wins thanks to a 16-7-1 record. Charleston had eight different players with at least double digit total offensive point tallies. Wade Starwalt lead the way by netting eighteen goals.

Before Nino took over, it was very uncommon to see more than eight or nine players in the stat books for a goal or an assist. Nino's teams had nearly the whole roster chipping in to a team victory. It didn't matter for which stat either. There was at least one player with a goal or an assist. It wasn't until 1996 when the team made post-season history. Fans had the chance to see Charleston raise their first ever Regional Championship with a 3-0 victory over Lovington.

Team was a key word for this championship team. Tim Hutti, Jay Kilgore, and Lonnie Fitzgerald all had at least 22 total offensive points as Hutti lead the way with 16 goals. Five different players tied for most assists with five. Hutti's career finished on a very high note. He was named to the IHSA All-State team twice, once in 1996 and 1997.

The 1998 team came into question with Hutti's disappearance, but many would forget that he was not the team's leading scorer in 1997's 18-4-2 team. Kevin Zawodniak once again led the team in goals scored with 15 but was not named to the All-Central Team. The team finished with a successful 15-9-1 season and a sectional final 3-1 loss to the Decatur MacArthur Generals. It was also the first of four straight years Charleston was Central Illinois Soccer Conference Champs.

Dustin Adair and Myles Stoner were the next faces of scoring for what would be Hank Nino's last season at the helm of Charleston coaching. Cody Baird had his usual success in the forward position. Adair and Stoner each had 14 and 12 goals apiece and lead the team to a conference title. Hank Nino retired after seven very successful seasons. Nino's remembrance and humbleness are perfect examples of one of the great coaches to go through Charleston, Illinois. In his retirement article written by TC Sports Editor Brian Nielsen, Nino expressed his goals over the year and his first intentions. Nino said, "My intention was when we spoke about is that I wanted soccer to not be treated as a diversion or sidelight to my career. I think my goals were to try to promote soccer to the community and let young men, and now also women of course, to mature as soccer players and have some fun."

Most can say that this was a success. Also mentioned in the article was Nino's wife, Liz, who also retired at the girl's coach. Liz's quote can be arguably the best quote of a perfect vision of Trojan soccer. "I remember when we came in that it was just some extra program for players to go out and play. They were not held in very high esteem. I remember coach Hank saying he was going to make Charleston a soccer town." Nino finished with a coaching record of 109-47-23, two conference titles, two sectional finals berth, a Regional Championship, and the respect of the area for turning Charleston into a premier power. The soccer fields at Sister City Park are named "Nino Fields."

The job change was at first an easy, smooth transition by handing the torch to Nino's assistant Adam Howarth. However, two months down the road Howarth took the vacant Eastern Illinois University men's soccer team head coaching position. Charleston found a coach just mere weeks before practice was scheduled to begin. Paul Stranz was approved by the board. Stranz was a recent referee for seven years and was not shy to the program. His first son Tyler Stranz was the Central Illinois Soccer Conference player of the year in 1994, and his second son Zack Stranz was still playing for the Trojans.

Stanz's first year as coach was as perfect as it could be for a first-time coach. The team went on to win the conference title for a third straight year, and more importantly qualify for the state finals. Curt Hinds handled most of the scoring duties with the help of players like Dallas Bartz, Pat Hutti, and Adair. Charleston didn't lose their first game until the middle of October, and their road to state wasn't as difficult as you would think with blowout wins of five, six, or even seven goals until the super-sectional game vs. Normal University, a game that goalkeeper Charles Johnson will never forget in his life.

Johnson recorded 26 saves in the 2-1 penalty kick shootout win. This is a record that still is held by Johnson today. In Nielsen's article, Nielsen wrote, "Others were running the length of the field, but Charles Johnson was just as exhausted, manning his goal area." "I've never been so busy," the Charleston goalkeeper said to Nielsen. "I've never been so winded playing in goal." Finally, after denying shot after shot from Normal University High, Johnson had to exert a bit more energy in hugs of celebration. Despite having only eight shots to the Pioneers twenty-nine, Charleston qualified for the Elite Eight. Nielsen's article quoted Stranz saying after the game, "I'm numb." The season would come to an end to eventual undefeated state champion Lisle Benet Academy. The teams 22-4-1 record was the best in school history.

The soccer success would continue. Charleston saw a monster development in the career of Curt Hinds. Hinds stat sheet of 40 goals, 21 assists, and 101 total offensive points were mesmerizing. Hinds was the first member of the exclusive "100 Point Club." The 2001 team failed to qualify for state but finished with an undefeated regular season. In 2002, records were broken. It was another year that CHS went to state, but it was more of a spectacle to watch two of the most premier players in the state to play side by side. Hinds finished the year with another quality stat line of 34 goals, 32 assists, and 100 total offensive points. His 32 assists are most in school history for a regular season, and his career 96 assists rank first in CHS history. His teammate Ryan McDermand's 36 goals, 19 assists, and 91 total offensive points, proved that the team had the best one-two punch in the state.

Hinds and McDermand tied the school record for assists in a game a combined three times. McDermand put his name the record books with four assists versus Big 12 foe Champaign Central. Hinds followed up McDermand's performance one day later with four of his own against Rantoul, and then three weeks later against Herscher. The season also marked the emasculation of Nino Fields, of course named after Hank and Liz Nino for their contribution to CHS soccer as coaches. Nino Fields had a winning debut with a 6-0 win over Mt. Carmel and a 4-0 victory over Centralia in the Red & Gold Tournament.

The team's offense was overpowering. Out of Charleston's total twenty-three wins, which is also a school record, only five wins were a two-goal difference. Out of the total twenty-seven contests, only seven games were decided by two goals. Fans would come to watch a blowout usually. One of those blowouts was a 13-0 victory over Rantoul. The team tied the 1995 school record for goals in a game, who beat St. Anthony that year 13-0.

The 2003 season was a year to remember, but in sort of a bittersweet way. The departure longtime reliant scorers in Hinds and Dallas Bartz left the team in McDermands hands. The Decatur Herald & Review Player of the Year led the team in being the only player in CHS history to score over fifty goals in a season. McDermand finished the year setting records by booting 52 goals, accumulating 118 total offensive points, and having a 2.00 goal per game average. His teammate Uzo Obia had a breakout year. He may have been overshadowed over his long four-year career at CHS. Obia had been on the field since 2000, but with two all-state players Obia was just another player on the team of glory.

Obia finished second on the team in each three-offensive category with 29 goals, 16 assists, and 74 total offensive points. McDermand and Obia set the new record for goals scored in a single game with five. McDermand accomplished his feat against Meridian on September 17, while Obia netted his against Teutopolis on October 14.

All was going well for the Trojans as they won their third straight Regional Championship and made it to the Sectional Finals. The talk for the Sectional final was blown up even more when the game was scheduled for a Charleston vs. Mattoon matchup with the winner going to state. Steven Bower's cross to Colin Wallace put Charleston up 1-0 before halftime, until the Green Wave roared back to defeat the Trojans 2-1. It was Mattoon's first state berth, and all the Trojans could do is watch as their season came to an end.

2004 marked the last time Charleston made it to the state tournament. The Trojans had quality scoring in Roo Cudone and sophomore Kevin Hinds. Cudone, the lone representative from the 2002 state squad led the team with 71 total offensive points and 29 goals. The Trojans finished with a 17-8-1 record with a thrilling 2-1 loss to St. Joseph in the state tournament. Charleston was unable to take the rematch game from earlier in the season. Cudone put CHS up 1-0 with his goal in the first half, but the second half doomed the Trojan ball players.

After a down 2005 season, the Trojans were able to get back to their post-season winning ways with another Regional Championship in 2006. Senior, Kevin Hinds capped a career with 51 total goals in which he scored 25 his senior season. Other contributions from Ross Hutchinson and Ian McCausland also helped keep the Trojans on the board. The 2007 season was another remarkable career in McCausland. The future Eastern Illinois University recruit tied the high school record by knocking in five goals in a 6-0 win over Monticello. The Trojans would flail at Regionals. McCausland finished his career with 50 goals.

The next season was a team bonding experience for the team that only had two seniors. The team's star midfielder Coon was injured, and the team finished the year 12-9-3. In 2009, Tommy Ball led the team in goals scored and total offensive points, but Coon's midfield presence, and the pure team effort led the team to seventeen wins for the first time since 2004. All year, the Trojans were solid as they won their first Regional Championship since 2006. The team had solid midfielders on the corners from Chidi Obia and Joey Martinez. The left footed Martinez led the team with eleven assists.

During the Regional Championship game versus Effingham, CHS nearly faltered as the game went to overtime. Faeeq Yousaf's overtime goal lifted fans off their feet in celebration. The celebration ended soon when Charleston found out that Coon would not be playing in the Sectional game due to yellow cards. The hard-fought contest against Marion sent the game to four overtimes and penalty kicks, but to no avail, Charleston was sent home packing.

In 2010, it seemed like the first year in nearly a decade that fans doubted a winning season. Critics were silenced when the 2010 soccer boys mustered a second consecutive Apollo Conference and Regional title. In the Regional Championship game, Alex Finley's game tying goal and two shots to the net from Adam Barker led CHS to a 3-1 victory. They were led by McCausland's little brother, Eric McCausland with ten goals, and leadership from Ryan Dau and goalkeeper Michael Van Popering. The team relied heavily on defense that featured Dau, Van Popering, me, Thorin Blitz, and Ben Hoover. The Trojans did; however, only finish with a 9-9-3 record.

In McCausland's senior campaign in 2011 the team improved to 10-8-2. McCausland followed his brother, Ian, to play at Eastern Illinois University. Ian graduated in 2007 when Eric came in as a freshman. Ian red-shirted one year at EIU, so for one year the two McCausland brothers were able to play together. Blitz led the team in goals that season with 10 and went to Benoit College to play. Hoover went to Blackburn College to play collegiate soccer.

In 2012, the Trojans bounced back with a surprise Apollo Conference championship season. The 2012 squad had lost eight of their scorers, as well as their starting goalie, John Coulton. The team inherited Michael Spencer from Meridian to play goalie for one season as his parents moved to teach at EIU. Elliot Griffin and Taylor Garrett were back and were to fill larger roles as juniors. Speedy, Rhett Hallett, came over to play after a two-year stint in football. The team fell to Mattoon in the Regional semi-final but finished with an 11-9-0 record and share of the Apollo Conference title.

Griffin and Garrett were back for a fourth straight year to lead the 2013 squad, who is the last CHS team to win a Regional title. The team began the season by winning the Red & Gold Tournament, which was the first time since 2009. The team was 8-2-0 at one point but hit a rough patch in the season by losing five in a row, including six of their last eight going into the postseason. However, Charleston conquered past Salem 1-0, and Mattoon 1-0 in the championship game to bring home another Regional title.

Coach Stranz retired after the 2013 season. Since then, Charleston has gone 36-29-17. Longtime JV coach Dave Dunlap stepped up as the coach in 2014, but only stayed for two seasons before taking an open position at Urbana High School. Former player, Josh Garrett, has coached the last two seasons. Charleston has now gone 25 straight years without a losing season in boys' soccer.

Season by Season Boys Soccer Results

1986
Won, 0, Lost 14, Tied 0
Coach: Chuck Castle

Opponent	Score
Blue Mound	2-6
Urbana	0-12
Mattoon	3-4
Blue Mound	2-10
Mt. Zion	1-13
Mattoon	1-3
Taylorville	1-5
Champaign Central	1-7
Champaign Centennial	0-5
Danville	1-8
Urbana University	1-4
Decatur MacArthur	0-15
St. Teresa	1-5
Urbana	2-8

Total Goals By Opponent: 105 (7.5 AVG)
Total Goals By CHS: 16 (1.1 AVG)

1987
Won, 2, Lost 13, Tied 0
Coach: Chuck Castle

Opponent	Score
Mattoon	0-2
Urbana University	0-5
Urbana	0-4
Blue Mound	2-7
Mt. Zion	3-2
Mattoon	2-3
Taylorville	0-2
Blue Mound	5-4
Champaign Central	0-7
Champaign Centennial	1-4
Danville	1-5
Urbana University	2-5
Decatur MacArthur	1-2
Urbana	1-5
Taylorville	2-5

Total Goals By Opponent: 61 (4.1 AVG)
Total Goals By CHS: 19 (1.3 AVG)

1988
Won, 4, Lost 7, Tied 3
Coach: Chuck Castle

Opponent	Score
Mattoon	0-0
Urbana University	0-2
Urbana	3-7
Blue Mound	5-2
Mt. Zion	2-2
Taylorville	3-2
Blue Mound	5-4
Champaign Central	3-2
Champaign Centennial	2-4
Danville	2-4
Urbana University	2-2
Decatur MacArthur	2-5
Urbana	1-2
Taylorville	2-3

Total Goals By Opponent: 41 (2.9 AVG)

Total Goals By CHS: 31 (2.2 AVG)

1989
Won, 4, Lost 9, Tied 1
Coach: Chuck Castle

Opponent	Score
Mattoon	0-0
Mt. Carmel	4-3
Urbana University	3-1
Urbana	0-3
Blue Mound	0-3
Mt. Zion	1-3
Taylorville	0-2
Mattoon	2-4
Blue Mound	6-1
Champaign Central	1-2
Champaign Centennial	1-7
Danville	1-9
Decatur MacArthur	3-4
Taylorville	0-1

Total Goals By Opponent: 40 (2.9 AVG)
Total Goals By CHS: 25 (1.8 AVG)

***There are no other records of the 1990 and 1991 seasons. 1990 finished 3-11-0 and 1991 finished 4-10-1. If there is any other findings contact 217-294-3627.

1992
Won, 7, Lost 4, Tied 5
Coach: Bob Sanders

Opponent	Score
Mattoon	1-1
Mt. Carmel	2-1
Urbana University	4-1
Urbana	3-3
Westville	5-0
Blue Mound	0-1
Mt. Zion	3-3
Mattoon	2-0
Blue Mound	5-1
Champaign Central	0-2
Danville	1-2
Champaign Centennial	2-1
Westville	10-0
Urbana University	4-1
Decatur MacArthur	2-2
Mattoon	0-1

Total Goals By Opponent: 19 (1.2 AVG)
Total Goals By CHS: 43 (2.7 AVG)

1993
Won, 7, Lost 4, Tied 5
Coach: Hank Nino

Opponent	Score
Mt. Carmel	5-0
Mt. Carmel	3-0
Urbana University	1-0
Urbana	0-1
Westville	0-2
Blue Mound	1-3
Mt. Zion	1-2
Mattoon	0-1
Champaign Centennial	2-0
Urbana	1-2
Champaign Central	0-5
Blue Mound	1-0
Champaign Central	3-1
Danville	1-0
Champaign Centennial	/....2-3
Westville	2-3
Urbana University	0-2
Decatur MacArthur	1-0
Decatur Eisenhower	0-3

Total Goals By Opponents: 22 (1.1 AVG)
Total Goals By CHS: 26 (1.3 AVG)

1994
Won, 13, Lost 5, Tied 4
Coach: Hank Nino

Opponent	Score
Mattoon	3-0
Mt. Carmel	3-0
Urbana	0-1
Westville	0-1
Urbana University	3-0
Meridian	3-1

Mt. Zion..1-0
Mattoon...1-1
Champaign Centennial........................1-1
Danville...1-0
Champaign Centennial........................1-0
Champaign Central..............................1-2
Meridian..1-3
Champaign Central..............................0-0
Danville...0-0
Champaign Centennial........................1-0
Westville...8-0
Urbana University................................1-0
Stephen Decatur..................................5-0
Decatur MacArthur...............................5-0
Mt. Zion...2-1
Urbana..0-1
Total Goals By Opponent: 13 (.59 AVG)
Total Goals By CHS: 36 (1.6 AVG)

1995
Won 16, Lost 7, Tied 1
Coach: Hank Nino
Opponent   Score
St. Anthony...13-0
Lovington..6-0
St. Teresa...1-2
Meridian..1-0
Urbana..2-2
Urbana University................................5-1
Mt. Carmel..6-0
Meridian..1-0
Mt. Zion...2-1
Champaign Centennial........................1-3
Danville...1-2
Champaign Central..............................0-5
Meridian..1-0
Champaign Central..............................1-2
Mahomet-Seymour...............................4-1
Lovington..6-1
Danville...0-1
Champaign Centennial........................3-0
Mattoon...1-0
Urbana University................................2-1
Stephen Decatur..................................4-1

Decatur MacArthur...............................5-0
Mt. Zion...1-0
Champaign Central..............................1-2
Total Goals By Opponents: 24 (1.0 AVG)
Total Goals By CHS: 68 (2.8 AVG)

1996
Won, 16, Lost 3, Tied 4 (Regional Champs)
Coach: Hank Nino
Opponent   Score
Mattoon...0-0
Williamsville...1-3
Springfield Southeast..........................1-1
Lincoln..8-0
Mt. Carmel..7-0
Urbana..1-0
Urbana University................................2-2
Meridian..2-0
Mt. Zion...2-0
Lovington..1-2
St. Teresa...4-1
Urbana University................................6-1
Champaign Central..............................1-0
Lovington..3-1
Danville...2-1
Champaign Centennial........................1-1
Altamont...4-0
Argenta...7-0
Stephen Decatur..................................2-1
Decatur MacArthur...............................5-0
Decatur Eisenhower.............................6-2
Lovington..3-0
Bloomington...0-1
Total Goals By Opponents: 22 (.95 AVG)
Total Goals By CHS: 69 (3.0 AVG)

1997
Won, 18, Lost 4, Tied 2
Coach: Hank Nino
Opponent   Score
St. Anthony...7-1
Jacksonville..2-2
Chatham-Glenwood..............................3-2
Champaign Central..............................2-4

Mattoon	6-1
Mt. Carmel	3-1
Urbana	3-0
Urbana University	4-0
St. Anthony	7-0
Meridian	4-0
Mt. Zion	0-5
Argenta	2-1(OT)
Mahomet-Seymour	3-2(OT)
Mt. Zion	1-2
Champaign Central	2-1
Lovington	6-2
Danville	3-3
Champaign Centennial	1-0
Argenta	1-0
Stephen Decatur	6-0
Decatur MacArthur	5-0
Altamont	3-0
Mattoon	6-0
Decatur Eisenhower	2-6

Total Goals By Opponent: 32 (1.3 AVG)
Total Goals By CHS: 79 (3.3 AVG)

1998
Won, 15, Lost 9, Tied 1
Coach: Hank Nino

Opponent	Score
Chatham-Glenwood	0-3
Altamont	2-1
Jacksonville	0-2
Litchfield	6-0
Monticello	6-0
Mattoon	4-1
Mt. Zion	1-2
Urbana	0-6
Teutopolis	5-1
St. Anthony	0-1
Meridian	1-2
Urbana University	2-1
St. Teresa	3-1
Mt. Zion	1-0
Champaign Central	0-2
Lovington	4-2
Danville	0-0
Champaign Centennial	1-5
Altamont	1-0
Argenta	6-0
Stephen Decatur	7-1
Decatur MacArthur	1-1
Teutopolis	6-0
St. Teresa	3-0
Decatur Eisenhower	2-0
Decatur MacArthur	1-3

Total Goals By Opponent: 35 (1.4 AVG)
Total Goals By CHS: 64 (2.6 AVG)

1999
Won, 15, Lost 4, Tied 6
Coach: Hank Nino

Opponent	Score
Chatham-Glenwood	1-1
Olney	4-2
Jacksonville	0-1
Litchfield	1-1
Monticello	7-0
Mattoon	6-0
Mt. Zion	0-0
Urbana	0-1
Altamont	1-0
St. Anthony	2-0
Meridian	3-2
Mahomet-Seymour	2-1 (PK)
Champaign Central	4-2
Danville	2-0
Champaign Centennial	1-1
Lovington	6-0
Argenta	5-1
Teutopolis	0-3
Stephen Decatur	4-1
Decatur	1-1
Mt. Zion	2-1
Mattoon	8-0
Decatur MacArthur	0-3

Total Goals By Opponent: 26 (1.1 AVG)
Total Goals By CHS: 66 (2.6 AVG)

2000
Won, 22, Lost 4, Tied 1 (State Qualifier)

Coach: Paul Stranz

Opponent	Score
Altamont	3-0
Olney	5-0
Jacksonville	3-0
Champaign Centennial	2-0
Monticello	2-1
Mattoon	3-0
Mt. Zion	2-1
Urbana	1-1
Altamont	3-2
St. Anthony	5-1
Meridian	2-1
Mahomet-Seymour	5-0
Altamont	3-1
Teutopolis	3-0
Lovington	6-0
Champaign Central	3-0
St. Teresa	1-3
Danville	0-1
Champaign Centennial	2-0
Teutopolis	6-0
Rantoul	8-0
Decatur MacArthur	0-1
Lovington	7-0
Teutopolis	5-0
Monticello	6-1
Normal University	2-1(PK)
Lisle Benet Academy	0-5

Total Goals By Opponents: 21 (.77 AVG)
Total Goals By CHS: 81 (3.0 AVG)

2001

Won, 21, Lost 1, Tied 5 (Sectional Champs)
Coach: Paul Stranz

Opponent	Score
Jacksonville	4-4
Mt. Carmel	5-1
Centralia	2-1
Olney	4-1
Altamont	6-2
Monticello	7-5
Mattoon	1-1
Mt. Zion	2-1
Urbana	2-2
Altamont	6-1
St. Anthony	9-0
Meridian	4-2
Teutopolis	5-1
St. Anthony	8-0
Altamont	7-0
Sullivan-Lovington	3-0
Champaign Central	1-1
Rantoul	11-0
St. Teresa	3-0
Danville	2-0
Champaign Centennial	1-1
Decatur MacArthur	3-1
Teutopolis	4-1
Tolono Unity	10-0
Danville Schlarman	4-0
Mattoon	3-0
Normal University	0-1

Total Goals By Opponents: 28 (1.0 AVG)
Total Goals By CHS: 117 (4.3 AVG)

2002

Won, 23, Lost 3, Tied 1 (State Qualifier)
Coach: Paul Stranz

Opponent	Score
Mt. Carmel	6-0
Centralia	4-0
Jacksonville	0-1
Effingham	7-0
Monticello	7-1
Mattoon	5-2
Mt. Zion	2-0
Urbana	4-3
St. Anthony	5-0
Altamont	6-0
Meridian	5-0
Decatur MacArthur	0-0
Belleville East	6-1
Chatham-Glenwood	2-0
Decatur MacArthur	5-3
Sullivan-Lovington	7-0
Champaign Central	5-3
Rantoul	3-0

St. Teresa..2-1
Danville..5-1
Champaign Centennial..........................2-0
Teutopolis...2-0
Olney..6-1
Monticello...4-0
Herscher..8-0
Peotone...3-2
Waterloo...0-1
Total Goals By Opponents: 25 (.93 AVG)
Total Goals By CHS: 116 (4.3 AVG)

2003
Won, 21, Lost 5, Tied 0 (Regional Champs)
Coach: Paul Stranz
Opponent   Score
Mt. Carmel..7-0
Centralia...5-0
Jacksonville...4-1
Effingham...9-0
Monticello...7-0
Mattoon..4-2
Mt. Zion...4-1
St. Teresa..6-1
Urbana...5-0
Altamont...10-0
St. Anthony..10-0
Meridian..7-1
Olney..9-1
Rantoul..5-0
Sullivan-Lovington................................3-0
Champaign Central...............................0-4
Peoria Notre Dame.......................4-5 (OT)
St. Joseph...3-1
Waterloo...1-3
Champaign Centennial..........................1-3
Decatur MacArthur...............................1-2
Teutopolis...8-0
Tolono Unity..4-1
Mt. Carmel..4-1
Mahomet-Seymour...............................3-2
Mattoon..1-2
Total Goals By Opponents: 29 (1.1 AVG)

Total Goals By CHS: 131 (5.0 AVG)

2004
Won, 17, Lost 8, Tied 1 (State Qualifier)
Coach: Paul Stranz
Opponent   Score
Mattoon..5-1
Centralia...2-3
Champaign Central...............................2-1
Monticello...5-1
Mattoon..7-0
St. Teresa..1-1
Urbana...0-1
Altamont...10-1
St. Anthony...8-1
Meridian..5-0
Olney..4-1
Mt. Zion...5-0
Sullivan-Lovington................................7-0
Champaign Central...............................0-1
Waterloo...0-3
Springfield Sacred Heart Griffin...........1-2
St. Joseph...0-3
Rantoul..8-0
Champaign Centennial..........................2-3
Decatur MacArthur...............................4-2
Teutopolis...6-0
Monticello...5-1
Mattoon..3-0
Judah Christian......................................3-1
Danville Schlarman...............................5-0
St. Joseph...1-2
Total Goals By Opponent: 29 (1.1 AVG)
Total Goals By CHS: 99 (3.8 AVG)

2005
Won, 15, Lost 6, Tied 3
Coach: Paul Stranz
Opponent   Score
Decatur MacArthur...............................1-0
Dunlap...1-3
Centralia...1-0
Jacksonville...0-0
Monticello...2-2

Opponent	Score
Mattoon	4-1
St. Teresa	9-2
Urbana	1-3
St. Anthony	2-0
Effingham	6-0
Olney	3-1
Mt. Zion	2-0
Danville	5-0
Sullivan-Lovington	12-1
Champaign Central	2-1
St. Joseph	1-2
Springfield Sacred Heart Griffin	0-1
Urbana University	1-4
Rantoul	12-0
Champaign Centennial	0-0
Decatur MacArthur	3-1
Teutopolis	2-0
Mattoon	6-1
Urbana	0-2

Total Goals By Opponent: 26 (1.1 AVG)
Total Goals By CHS: 76 (3.2 AVG)

2006
Won, 16, Lost 7, Tied 2 (Regional Champs)
Coach: Paul Stranz

Opponent	Score
Decatur MacArthur	2-1
Dunlap	1-0
Champaign Central	2-4
Jacksonville	1-1
Monticello	6-0
Mattoon	4-0
St. Teresa	5-1
Urbana	1-1
Mahomet-Seymour	4-0
St. Anthony	2-0
Effingham	7-0
Olney	8-0
Mt. Zion	5-0
Danville	7-0
Sullivan-Lovington	8-2
Champaign Central	2-3
Peoria Notre Dame	2-3 (OT)
Waterloo	0-4
Champaign Centennial	0-1
Decatur MacArthur	4-1
Mattoon	5-0
Urbana	2-1 (PK)
Normal University	0-1

Total Goals By Opponents: 26 (1.1 AVG)
Total Goals By CHS: 85 (3.4 AVG)

2007
Won, 13, Lost 7, Tied 3
Coach: Paul Stranz

Opponent	Score
St. Teresa	2-2
Decatur MacArthur	1-0
Dunlap	0-2
Olney	4-1
Jacksonville	0-1
Monticello	6-0
Mattoon	3-0
Urbana	1-3
Mahomet-Seymour	4-1
St. Anthony	4-0
Effingham	6-0
Olney	5-0
Mt. Zion	2-0
Danville	5-1
Sullivan-Lovington	6-0
Champaign Central	4-2
Springfield Sacred Heart Griffin	0-3
Waterloo	1-2
St. Joseph	1-2
Champaign Centennial	2-2
Decatur MacArthur	2-2
Teutopolis	2-1
Springfield Southeast	0-1

Total Goals By Opponent: 26 (1.1 AVG)
Total Goals By CHS: 61 (2.7 AVG)

2008
Won, 12, Lost 9, Tied 3
Coach: Paul Stranz

Opponent	Score
St. Teresa	3-1
Olney	6-0

Opponent	Score
Centralia	0-0
Decatur MacArthur	1-3
Jacksonville	0-0
Monticello	2-1
Decatur MacArthur	1-6
Mattoon	1-0
Urbana	0-5
Mahomet-Seymour	3-2
St. Anthony	7-0
Effingham	7-1
Olney	3-3
Teutopolis	1-0
Mt. Zion	3-0
Danville	2-1
Sullivan	8-1
Champaign Central	2-3
Quincy Notre Dame	0-2
Peoria Notre Dame	0-4
Waterloo	1-3
Champaign Centennial	1-6
Effingham	4-1
Highland	2-3 (OT)

Total Goals By Opponent: 36 (1.5 AVG)
Total Goals By CHS: 58 (2.4 AVG)

2009
Won, 17, Lost 5, Tied 2 (Regional Champions)
Apollo Won 4, Lost 0, Tied 0 (Apollo Conference Champs)
Coach: Paul Stranz

Opponent	Score
St. Teresa	2-1
Centralia	4-1
Jacksonville	3-0
Teutopolis	4-1
Monticello	3-3
Mattoon	3-0
Decatur MacArthur	5-2
Urbana	3-1
Mahomet-Seymour	1-0
St. Anthony	7-0
Olney*	5-0
Teutopolis	3-0
Mt. Zion*	5-0
Danville	1-1
Champaign Central	3-0
St. Viator	1-6
Quincy Notre Dame	1-2
Waterloo	2-4
Salem*	4-0
Effingham*	1-0
Champaign Centennial	0-3
Salem	4-0
Effingham	2-1 (OT)
Marion	1-2 (PK)

Total Goals by Opponents: 28 (1.3 AVG)
Total Goals by CHS 66 (2.75 AVG)

2010
Won 9, Lost 9, Tied 3 (Regional Champions)
Apollo Won 3, Lost 0, Tied 1 (Apollo Champs)
Coach: Paul Stranz

Opponent	Score
St. Teresa	1-2
Centralia	2-0
Jacksonville	0-2
Teutopolis	0-1
Monticello	0-0
Mattoon	2-0
Decatur MacArthur	1-0
Urbana	0-3
Mahomet-Seymour	2-1
St. Anthony	0-0
Olney*	1-0
Teutopolis	2-3
Mt. Zion*	0-0
Danville	0-1
Champaign Central	0-4
Salem*	6-0
Champaign Centennial	0-1
Effingham*	1-0
Salem	8-0
Mattoon	3-1
Carbondale	0-3

Total Goals By Opponent: 22 (1.1 AVG)
Total Goals By CHS: 29 (1.4 AVG)

2011
Won 10, Lost 8, Tied 2
Apollo Won 3, Lost 1, Tied 0
Coach: Paul Stranz

Opponent	Score
St. Teresa	4-0
Centralia	1-0
Jacksonville	0-3
Teutopolis	3-0
Monticello	0-4
Mattoon	1-1
Decatur MacArthur	7-3
Urbana	0-3
Mahomet-Seymour	0-1
St. Anthony	1-1
Olney*	6-1
Teutopolis	2-1
Mt. Zion*	0-4
Danville	0-4
Champaign Central	0-4
Salem*	6-0
Champaign Centennial	0-6
Effingham*	3-0
Mattoon	2-1 (2OT)
Mt. Zion	0-4

Total Goals By Opponent: 37 (1.6 AVG)
Total Goals By CHS: 37 (1.6 AVG)

2012
Won, 11, Lost 9, Tied 0
Apollo Won 3, Lost 1, Tied 0 (Apollo Champs)
Coach: Paul Stranz

Opponent	Score
St. Teresa	4-0
Teutopolis	1-4
Olney	3-2
Mattoon	0-3
Monticello	3-0
Mattoon*	1-0
Urbana	0-7
Mahomet-Seymour	0-3
St. Anthony	3-0
Decatur MacArthur	9-0
Olney	0-1
Teutopolis	3-2
Mount Zion*	1-3
Danville	1-0
Champaign Central	1-8
Salem*	2-1 (OT)
Champaign Centennial	0-2
Effingham*	5-1
Salem	2-0
Mattoon	3-5

Total Goals By Opponent: 41 (2.1 AVG)
Total Goals By CHS: 41 (2.1 AVG)

2013
Won 12, Lost 9, Tied 0 (Regional Champs)
Apollo Won 2, Lost 2, Tied 0
Coach: Paul Stranz

Opponent	Score
St. Teresa	5-1
Effingham	2-1
Teutopolis	1-0
Mattoon	1-0
Monticello	2-0
Mattoon*	0-2
Decatur MacArthur	7-0
Urbana	0-3
Mahomet-Seymour	4-1
St. Anthony	2-0
Danville	0-2
Olney	0-1
Teutopolis	0-1
Mt. Zion*	1-2 (PK)
Champaign Central	0-5
Salem*	7-0
Champaign Centennial	0-4
Effingham*	2-0
Salem	1-0
Mattoon	1-0
Troy Triad	0-4

Total Goals By Opponent 27 (1.1 AVG)
Total Goals By CHS: 37 (1.6 AVG)

2014
Won 8, Lost 7, Tied 5
Apollo Won 5, Lost 2, Tied 2
Coach: Dave Dunlap

Opponent	Score
Olney	0-0
Teutopolis	2-4
Mattoon	0-1
Teutopolis	2-2
Champaign Centennial	2-0
Newton	1-0
Mahomet-Seymour	2-2
Taylorville*	5-2
Effingham*	1-0
Mt. Zion*	3-2
Salem*	5-0
Mattoon*	1-4
Danville	0-7
Champaign Central	0-6
Taylorville*	5-0
Effingham*	1-0
Mt. Zion*	0-3
Mattoon*	1-1
Mt. Zion	2-0
Mattoon	0-2

Total Goals by Opponents: 35 (1.8 AVG)
Total Goals by CHS: 34 (1.7 AVG)

2015
Won 8, Lost 8, Tied 5
Apollo Won 3, Lost 4, Tied 3
Coach: Dave Dunlap

Opponent	Score
Effingham	0-0
Monticello	4-1
Olney	1-1
Teutopolis	1-0
Champaign Centennial	3-2
Newton	4-1
Effingham*	2-2
Mahomet-Seymour	1-4
Taylorville*	0-1
Mt. Zion *	4-2
Salem*	2-3
Mattoon*	3-2
Danville*	1-7
Effingham*	1-1
Taylorville**	4-0
Champaign Central	0-2
Mt. Zion*	1-4
Salem*	2-2
Mattoon*	1-6
Mt. Zion*	4-0
Danville*	0-7

Total Goals By Opponents: 48 (2.3 AVG)
Total Goals By CHS: 39 (1.7 AVG)

2016
Won 10, Lost 5, Tied 5
Apollo Won 7, Lost 2, Tied 1
Coach: Jason Garrett

Opponent	Score
Mattoon	2-2
Teutopolis	2-1
Monticello	4-1
Champaign Centennial	2-2
Newton	3-1
Effingham*	9-1
Mahomet-Seymour	1-4
Taylorville*	7-0
Mt. Zion*	1-1
Salem**	3-1
Mattoon*	1-2
Taylorville*	5-1
Effingham*	7-1
Champaign Central	1-5
Mt. Zion*	6-0
Salem*	6-2
Danville	3-3
Mattoon*	0-2
Mahomet-Seymour	0-2

Total Goals By Opponent 33 (1.7 AVG)
Total Goals By CHS 65 (3.3 AVG)

2017
Won 10, Lost 9, Tied 2
Apollo Won 6, Lost 6, Tied 0
Coach: Jason Garrett

Opponent	Score
Centralia	2-1
Teutopolis	3-1
Mattoon	1-1
Teutopolis	4-3
Newton	0-1
Lincoln*	0-1
Mahomet-Seymour*	1-6
Taylorville*	9-1
Effingham*	5-1
Mt. Zion*	3-1
Mattoon*	0-4
Olney	3-3
Lincoln*	0-2
Mahomet-Seymour*	0-3
Danville	1-2
Taylorville*	9-0
Effingham*	5-1
Mt. Zion*	0-5
Mattoon*	2-0
Georgetown Ridgefarm	5-0
Urbana	0-6

Total Goals By Opponent: 43 (2.0 AVG)
Total Goals By CHS: 53 (2.5 AVG)

Individual Team Breakdown

Altamont (14-0-0)

1996-1997	4-0
1997-1998	3-0
1998-1999	2-0
1998-1999	1-0
1999-2000	1-0
2000-2001	3-0
2000-2001	3-2
2000-2001	3-1
2001-2002	6-2
2001-2002	6-1
2001-2002	7-0
2002-2003	6-0
2003-2004	10-0
2004-2005	10-1

Argenta (5-0-0)

1996-1997	7-0
1997-1998	2-1 (OT)
1997-1998	1-0
1998-1999	6-0
1999-2000	5-1

Belleville East (0-1-0)
2002-2003......1-6

Bloomington (0-1-0)
1996-1997......0-1

Blue Mound (8-5-0)

1986-1987	2-6
1986-1987	2-10
1987-1988	2-7
1987-1988	5-4
1988-1989	5-2
1988-1989	5-4
1989-1990	3-0
1989-1990	6-0
1992-1993	1-0
1992-1993	5-1
1993-1994	1-3
1993-1994	1-0

Carbondale (0-1-0)
2010-2011......0-3

Centralia (8-1-1)

2001-2002..................2-1
2002-2003..................2-0
2003-2004..................5-0
2004-2005..................2-3
2005-2006..................1-0
2008-2009..................0-0
2009-2010..................4-1
2010-2011..................2-0
2011-2012..................1-0
2017-2018..................2-1

Champaign Centennial (10-16-7)

1986-1987..................0-5
1987-1988..................1-4
1988-1989..................2-4
1989-1990..................1-7
1992-1993..................1-2
1993-1994..................2-0
1993-1994..................2-3
1994-1995..................1-1
1994-1995..................1-0
1994-1995..................1-0
1995-1996..................1-3
1995-1996..................3-0
1996-1997..................1-1
1997-1998..................1-0
1998-1999..................1-5
1999-2000..................1-1
2000-2001..................2-0
2000-2001..................2-0
2001-2002..................1-1
2002-2003..................2-0
2003-2004..................1-3
2004-2005..................2-3
2005-2006..................0-0
2006-2007..................0-1
2007-2008..................2-2
2008-2009..................1-6
2009-2010..................0-3
2010-2011..................0-1
2011-2012..................0-3
2012-2013..................0-2
2013-2014..................0-4
2014-2015..................2-0
2015-2016..................3-2
2016-2017..................2-2

Champaign Central (13-23-3)

1986-1987..................1-7
1987-1988..................0-7
1988-1989..................3-2
1989-1990..................1-2
1992-1993..................1-1
1993-1994..................0-5
1993-1994..................3-1
1994-1995..................1-2
1994-1995..................0-0
1995-1996..................0-5
1995-1996..................1-2
1995-1996..................1-2
1996-1997..................1-0
1997-1998..................2-4
1997-1998..................2-1
1998-1999..................0-2
1999-2000..................4-2
2000-2001..................3-1
2001-2002..................1-1
2002-2003..................5-3
2003-2004..................3-0
2004-2005..................2-1
2004-2005..................0-1
2005-2006..................2-1
2006-2007..................2-4
2006-2007..................2-3
2007-2008..................4-2
2008-2009..................2-3
2009-2010..................3-0
2010-2011..................0-4
2011-2012..................0-4
2012-2013..................1-8
2013-2014..................0-5
2014-2015..................2-0

2015-2016	3-2
2016-2017	2-2

Chatham-Glenwood (2-1-1)

1997-1998	3-2
1998-1999	0-3
1999-2000	1-1
2002-2003	2-0

Danville (12-14-5)

1986-1987	1-8
1987-1988	1-5
1988-1989	2-4
1989-1990	1-9
1992-1993	0-2
1993-1994	1-0
1994-1995	1-0
1994-1995	0-1
995-1996	1-2
1995-1996	0-1
1996-1997	2-1
1997-1998	3-3
1998-1999	0-0
1999-2000	2-0
2000-2001	0-1
2001-2002	2-0
2002-2003	5-1
2005-2006	5-0
2006-2007	7-0
2007-2008	5-1
2008-2009	2-1
2009-2010	1-1
2010-2011	0-1
2011-2012	0-4
2012-2013	1-0
2013-2014	0-5
2014-2015	0-7
2015-2016	1-7
2015-2016	0-7
2016-2017	3-3

Danville Schlarman (2-0-0)

2001-2002	4-0
2004-2005	5-0

Decatur (0-0-1)

1999-2000	1-1

Decatur Eisenhower (2-2-0)

1993-1994	0-3
1996-1997	6-2
1997-1998	2-6
1998-1999	2-0

Decatur MacArthur (18-8-4)

1986-1987	0-15
1987-1988	1-2
1988-1989	2-5
1989-1990	3-4
1992-1993	2-2
1993-1994	1-0
1994-1995	5-0
1995-1996	5-0
1996-1997	5-0
1997-1998	5-0
1998-1999	1-1
1998-1999	1-3
1999-2000	0-3
2000-2001	0-1
2001-2002	3-1
2002-2003	0-0
2002-2003	5-3
2003-2004	1-2
2004-2005	4-2
2005-2006	1-0
2005-2006	3-1
2006-2007	2-1
2006-2007	4-1
2007-2008	1-0
2007-2008	2-2
2008-2009	1-3
2008-2009	1-6
2009-2010	5-2

2010-2011..................1-0
2011-2012..................7-3
2012-2013..................9-0
2013-2014..................7-0

Decatur St. Teresa (12-4-2)

1986-1987..................1-5
1995-1996..................1-2
1996-1997..................4-1
1998-1999..................3-1
1998-1999..................3-0
2000-2001..................1-3
2001-2002..................3-0
2002-2003..................2-1
2003-2004..................6-1
2004-2005..................1-1
2005-2006..................9-2
2006-2007..................5-1
2007-2008..................2-2
2008-2009..................3-1
2009-2010..................2-1
2010-2011..................1-2
2011-2012..................4-0
2012-2013..................4-0
2013-2014..................5-1

Dunlap (1-2-0)

2005-2006..................1-3
2006-2007..................1-0
2007-2008..................0-2

Effingham (19-0-2)

2002-2003..................7-0
2003-2004..................9-0
2005-2006..................6-0
2006-2007..................7-0
2007-2008..................6-0
2008-2009..................7-1
2008-2009..................4-1
2009-2010..............2-1 (OT)
2010-2011..................1-0

2011-2012..................3-0
2012-2013..................5-1
2013-2014..................2-1
2013-2014..................2-0
2014-2015..................1-0
2014-2015..................1-0
2015-2016..................0-0
2015-2016..................1-1
2016-2017..................9-1
2016-2017..................7-1
2017-2018..................5-1
2017-2018..................5-1

Effingham St. Anthony (18-1-2)

1995-1996..................13-0
1997-1998..................7-1
1997-1998..................7-0
1998-1999..................0-1
1999-2000..................2-0
1999-2000..................7-0
2000-2001..................5-1
2001-2002..................9-0
2001-2002..................8-0
2002-2003..................5-0
2003-2004..................10-0
2004-2005..................8-1
2005-2006..................2-0
2006-2007..................2-2
2007-2008..................4-0
2008-2009..................7-0
2009-2010..................7-0
2010-2011..................0-0
2011-2012..................1-1
2012-2013..................3-0
2013-2014..................2-0

Georgetown-Ridgefarm (1-0-0)

2017-2018..................5-0

Herscher (1-0-0)
2002-2003..................8-0

Highland (0-1-0)
2008-2009..................2-3 (OT)

Jacksonville (3-6-4)

1998-1999..........................0-2
1999-2000..........................0-1
2000-2001..........................3-1
2001-2002..........................4-4
2002-2003..........................0-1
2003-2004..........................4-1
2005-2006..........................0-0
2006-2007..........................1-1
2007-2008..........................0-1
2008-2009..........................0-0
2009-2010..........................3-0
2010-2011..........................0-2
2011-2012..........................0-4

Judah Christian (1-0-0)
2004-2005..........................3-1

Lincoln (1-2-0)
1996-1997..........................8-0
2017-2018..........................0-1
2017-2018..........................0-2

Lisle Benet Academy (0-1-0)
2000-2001..........................0-5

Litchfield (1-0-1)

1998-1999..........................6-0
1999-2000..........................1-1

Lovington (9-0-1)

1995-1996..........................6-0
1995-1996..........................6-1
1996-1997..........................1-2
1996-1997..........................3-1
1996-1997..........................3-0
1997-1998..........................6-2

1998-1999..........................4-2
1999-2000..........................6-0
2000-2001..........................6-0
2000-2001..........................7-0

Mahomet-Seymour (11-6-2)

1995-1996..........................4-1
1997-1998..................3-2 (OT)
1999-2000..........................1-1
1999-2000..................2-1 (PK)
2000-2001..........................5-0
2003-2004..........................3-2
2006-2007..........................4-0
2007-2008..........................4-1
2008-2009..........................3-2
2009-2010..........................1-0
2010-2011..........................2-1
2011-2012..........................1-0
2012-2013..........................0-3
2013-2014..........................4-1
2014-2015..........................1-1
2015-2016..........................1-4
2016-2017..........................1-4
2016-2017..........................0-2
2017-2018..........................1-6
2017-2018..........................0-3

Marion (0-1-0)
2009-2010..................1-2 (PK)

Mattoon (30-19-9)

1986-1987..........................3-4
1986-1987..........................1-3
1987-1988..........................0-2
1987-1988..........................0-2
1988-1989..........................0-0
1989-1990..........................0-0
1989-1990..........................2-4
1992-1993..........................1-1
1992-1993..........................2-0
1992-1993..........................0-1
1993-1994..........................0-2

1993-1994	0-1	2016-2017	1-2
1994-1995	3-0	2017-2018	1-1
1994-1995	1-1	2017-2018	0-4
1995-1996	1-0	2017-2018	2-0
1996-1997	0-0		
1997-1998	6-1		

Meridian (11-2-0)

1997-1998	6-0		
1998-1999	4-1	1994-1995	3-1
1999-2000	6-0	1995-1996	0-1
1999-2000	8-0	1995-1996	1-0
2000-2001	3-0	1995-1996	1-0
2001-2002	1-1	1996-1997	2-0
2001-2002	3-0	1997-1998	4-0
2002-2003	5-2	1998-1999	0-2
2003-2004	4-2	1999-2000	3-2
2003-2004	1-2	2000-2001	2-1
2004-2005	5-1	2001-2002	4-2
2004-2005	7-0	2002-2003	5-0
2004-2005	3-0	2003-2004	7-1
2005-2006	4-1	2004-2005	5-0
2005-2006	6-1		

Monticello (15-1-3)

2006-2007	4-0		
2006-2007	5-0	1998-1999	6-0
2007-2008	3-0	1999-2000	7-0
2008-2009	1-0	2000-2001	2-1
2009-2010	3-0	2000-2001	6-1
2010-2011	2-0	2001-2002	7-5
2010-2011	3-1	2002-2003	7-1
2011-2012	1-1	2002-2003	4-0
2011-2012	2-1 (2 OT)	2003-2004	7-0
2012-2013	0-3	2004-2005	5-1
2012-2013	1-0	2004-2005	5-1
2012-2013	3-5	2005-2006	2-2
2013-2014	1-0	2006-2007	6-0
2013-2014	0-2	2007-2008	6-0
20.13-2014	1-0	2008-2009	2-1
2014-2015	0-1	2009-2010	3-3
2014-2015	1-4	2010-2011	0-0
2014-2015	1-1	2011-2012	0-4
2014-2015	0-2	2012-2013	3-0
2015-2016	3-2	2013-2014	2-0
2015-2016	1-6		
2016-2017	2-2		

Mt. Carmel (12-0-0)

2016-2017	1-2

1989-1990..........................4-3
1992-1993..........................2-1
1993-1994..........................5-0
1993-1994..........................3-0
1994-1995..........................3-0
1995-1996..........................6-0
1996-1997..........................7-0
1997-1998..........................3-1
2001-2002..........................5-1
2002-2003..........................6-0
2003-2004..........................7-0
2003-2004..........................4-1

Mt. Zion (24-13-7)

1986-1987..........................1-13
1987-1988..........................3-2
1988-1989..........................2-2
1989-1990..........................1-3
1992-1993..........................3-3
1993-1994..........................1-2
1994-1995..........................1-0
1994-1995..........................2-1
1995-1996..........................2-1
1995-1996..........................1-0
1996-1997..........................2-0
1997-1998..........................0-5
1997-1998..........................1-2
1998-1999..........................1-2
1998-1999..........................1-0
1999-2000..........................0-0
1999-2000..........................2-1
2000-2001..........................2-1
2001-2002..........................2-1
2002-2003..........................2-0
2003-2004..........................4-1
2004-2005..........................5-0
2005-2006..........................2-0
2006-2007..........................5-0
2007-2008..........................2-0
2008-2009..........................3-0
2009-2010..........................5-0
2010-2011..........................0-0

2011-2012..........................0-4
2011-2012..........................0-4
2012-2013..........................1-3
2013-2014..........................1-2 (PK)
2014-2015..........................3-2
2014-2015..........................0-3
2014-2015..........................2-0
2015-2016..........................4-2
2015-2016..........................1-4
2015-2016..........................4-0
2016-2017..........................1-1
2016-2017..........................6-0
2017-2018..........................3-1
2017-2018..........................0-5

Newton (3-1-0)

2014-2015..........................1-0
2015-2016..........................4-1
2016-2017..........................3-1
2017-2018..........................0-1

Normal University (1-2-0)

2000-2001..................2-1 (PK)
2001-2002..........................0-1
2006-2007..........................0-1

Olney (15-2-4)

1999-2000..........................4-2
2000-2001..........................5-0
2001-2002..........................4-1
2002-2003..........................6-1
2003-2004..........................7-0
2004-2005..........................4-1
2005-2006..........................3-1
2006-2007..........................8-0
2007-2008..........................4-1
2007-2008..........................5-0
2008-2009..........................6-0
2008-2009..........................3-3
2009-2010..........................5-0
2010-2011..........................1-0

2011-2012.........................6-1
2012-2013.........................3-2
2012-2013.........................0-1
2013-2014.........................0-1
2014-2015.........................0-0
2015-2016.........................1-1
2017-2018.........................3-3

Peoria Notre Dame (0-3-0)

2003-2004.........................0-4
2006-2007................2-3 (OT)
2008-2009.........................0-4

Peotone (1-0-0)
2002-2003.........................3-2

Quincy Notre Dame (0-2-0)

2008-2009.........................0-2
2009-2010.........................1-2

Rantoul (6-0-0)

2000-2001.........................8-0
2001-2002.......................11-0
2002-2003.......................13-0
2003-2004.........................9-1
2004-2005.........................8-0
2005-2006.......................12-0

Salem (11-1-1)

2009-2010.........................4-0
2010-2011.........................6-0
2010-2011.........................8-0
2011-2012.........................6-0
2012-2013................2-1 (OT)
2012-2013.........................2-0
2013-2014.........................7-0
2013-2014.........................1-0
2014-2015.........................5-0
2015-2016.........................2-3
2015-2016.........................2-2

2016-2017.........................3-1
2016-2017.........................6-2

Springfield Sacred Heart Griffin (0-3-0)

2004-2005.........................1-2
2005-2006.........................0-1
2007-2008.........................0-3

Springfield Southeast (0-1-1)

1996-1997.........................1-1
2007-2008.........................0-1

St. Joseph (0-5-0)

2003-2004................4-5 (OT)
2004-2005.........................3-0
2004-2005.........................1-2
2005-2006.........................1-2
2007-2008.........................1-2

St. Viator (0-1-0)
2009-2010.........................1-6

Stephen Decatur (6-0-0)

1994-1995.........................5-0
1995-1996.........................4-1
1996-1997.........................2-1
1997-1998.........................6-0
1998-1999.........................7-0
1999-2000.........................4-1

Sullivan-Lovington (8-0-0)

2001-2002.........................3-0
2002-2003.........................7-0
2003-2004.........................5-0
2004-2005.........................7-0
2005-2006.......................12-1
2006-2007.........................8-2
2007-2008.........................6-0

2008-2009......................8-1

Taylorville (8-7-0)

1986-1987......................1-5
1987-1988......................1-7
1987-1988......................2-5
1988-1989......................3-2
1988-1989......................2-3
1989-1990......................0-2
1989-1990......................0-1
2014-2015......................5-2
2014-2015......................5-0
2015-2016......................0-1
2015-2016......................4-0
2016-2017......................7-0
2016-2017......................5-1
2017-2018......................9-1
2017-2018......................9-0

Teutopolis (22-6-2)

1998-1999......................5-1
1998-1999......................6-0
1999-2000......................0-3
2000-2001......................3-0
2000-2001......................6-0
2000-2001......................5-0
2001-2002......................5-1
2001-2002......................4-1
2002-2003......................2-0
2003-2004......................8-0
2004-2005......................6-0
2005-2006......................2-0
2007-2008......................2-1
2008-2009......................1-0
2009-2010......................4-1
2009-2010......................3-0
2010-2011......................0-1
2010-2011......................2-3
2011-2012......................3-0
2011-2012......................2-1
2012-2013......................1-4
2012-2013......................3-2
2013-2014......................1-0
2013-2014......................0-1
2014-2015......................2-4
2014-2015......................2-2
2016-2017......................1-0
2016-2017......................2-1
2017-2018......................4-3

Tolono Unity (2-0-0)

2001-2002......................10-0
2003-2004......................4-1

Troy Triad (0-1-0)

2013-2014......................0-4

Urbana (6-22-5)

1986-1987......................0-12
1986-1987......................2-8
1987-1988......................0-4
1987-1988......................1-5
1988-1989......................3-7
1988-1989......................1-2
1989-1990......................0-3
1992-1993......................3-3
1993-1994......................0-1
1993-1994......................1-2
1994-1995......................0-1
1994-1995......................0-1
1995-1996......................2-2
1996-1997......................1-0
1997-1998......................3-0
1998-1999......................0-6
1999-2000......................0-1
2000-2001......................1-1
2002-2003......................2-2
2002-2003......................4-3
2003-2004......................5-0
2004-2005......................0-1
2005-2006......................1-3
2005-2006......................0-2
2006-2007......................1-1

2006-2007.................2-1 (PK)
2007-2008........................1-3
2008-2009........................0-5
2009-2010........................3-1
2010-2011........................0-3
2011-2012........................0-4
2012-2013........................0-7
2013-2014........................0-3
2017-2018........................0-6

Urbana University (11-6-2)

1986-1987........................1-4
1987-1988........................0-5
1987-1988........................2-5
1988-1989........................0-2
1988-1989........................2-2
1989-1990........................3-1
1992-1993........................4-1
1992-1993........................4-1
1993-1994........................1-0
1993-1994........................0-2
1994-1995........................0-3
1994-1995........................1-0
1995-1996........................5-1
1995-1996........................2-1
1996-1997........................2-2

1996-1997........................6-1
1997-1998........................4-0
1998-1999........................2-1
1999-2000........................1-4

Waterloo (1-6-0)

2002-2003........................0-1
2003-2004........................3-1
2004-2005........................0-3
2006-2007........................0-4
2007-2008........................1-2
2008-2009........................1-3
2009-2010........................2-4

Westville (4-2-0)
1992-1993........................5-0
1992-1993......................10-0
1993-1994........................1-0
1993-1994........................2-3
1994-1995........................1-0
1994-1995........................8-0

Williamsville (0-1-0)

1996-1997........................1-3

CHS ALL TIME RECORD VS. CONFERENCE

Apollo Conference

Opponent	Win	Loss	Tie	Percentage
Effingham	19	0	2	.952
Lincoln	1	2	0	.333
Mahomet-Seymour	11	6	2	.631
Mattoon	30	19	9	.712
Mt. Zion	24	13	7	.625
Taylorville	8	7	0	.533
Total	93	47	18	.646

**Charleston 119-50-5 against all-time Apollo opponents, which includes Olney and Salem, which is a .698 winning percentage.

Big 12 Conference

Opponent	Win	Loss	Tie	Percentage
Bloomington	0	1	0	.000
Champaign Central	13	23	3	.371
Champaign Centennial	10	16	7	.312
Danville	12	14	5	.468
Peoria Notre Dame	0	3	0	.000
Urbana	6	22	5	.258
Total	41	79	20	.364

Central Illinois Conference

Opponent	Win	Loss	Tie	Percentage
St. Teresa	12	4	2	.722
Meridian	11	2	0	.846
Sullivan	8	0	0	1.000
Total	31	6	2	.820

Central State Eight Conference

Opponent	Win	Loss	Tie	Percentage
Chatham Glenwood	2	1	1	.625
Decatur Eisenhower	2	2	0	.500
Decatur MacArthur	18	8	4	.666
Jacksonville	3	6	4	.231
Normal University	1	2	0	.333
Springfield Sacred Heart	0	3	0	.000
Springfield Southeast	0	1	1	.250
Total	28	23	10	.540

Dead Opponents

Opponent	Won	Loss	Tie	Percentage
Blue Mound	8	5	0	.615
Decatur	0	0	1	.500
Lovington	9	0	1	.900
Stephen Decatur	6	0	0	1.000
Total	23	5	2	.800

Illini Prairie Conference

Opponent	Won	Loss	Tie	Percentage
Monticello	15	1	3	.868
Rantoul	6	0	0	1.000
St. Joseph	0	5	0	.000
Tolono Unity	2	0	0	1.000
Total	23	6	3	.766

Independent

Opponent	Won	Loss	Tie	Percentage
Teutopolis	22	6	2	.767

Little Illini Conference

Opponent	Won	Loss	Tie	Percentage
Newton	3	1	0	.750
Olney	15	2	4	.810
Total	18	3	4	.800

Mississippi Valley Conference

Opponent	Won	Loss	Tie	Percentage
Highland	0	1	0	.000
Troy Triad	0	1	0	.000
Waterloo	1	6	0	.166
Total	1	8	0	.125

South Seven Conference

Opponent	Won	Loss	Tie	Percentage
Carbondale	0	1	0	.000

Centralia	8	1	0	.889
Marion	0	1	0	.000
Total	8	3	0	.727

Other Opponents

Opponent	Won	Loss	Tie	Percentage
Argenta	5	0	0	1.000
Belleville East	0	1	0	.000
Danville Schlarman	2	0	0	1.000
Dunlap	1	2	0	.333
Georgetown Ridgefarm	1	0	0	1.000
Herscher	1	0	0	1.000
Champaign Judah Christian	1	0	0	1.000
Lisle Benet Academy	0	1	0	.000
Litchfield	1	0	1	.750
Mt. Carmel	2	0	0	1.000
Peotone	1	0	0	1.000
Quincy Notre Dame	0	2	0	.000
Salem	11	1	1	.884
St. Viator	0	1	0	.000
Urbana University	11	6	2	.632
Westville	4	2	0	.666
Williamsville	0	1	0	.000
Total	41	18	4	.683

TROJAN SOCCER RECORDS

Individual Single Game

Goals Scored in a Game: 5, Ryan McDermand (CHS vs. Meridian) 9-17-03
    Uzo Obia (CHS vs. T-Town) 10-14-03
    Ian McCausland (CHS vs. Monticello) 8-28-07
Assists in a Game: 4, Tim Montgomery (CHS vs. Blue Mound) 1988
    Ryan McDermand (CHS vs. Champaign Central) 10-2-02
    Curt Hinds (CHS vs. Rantoul) 10-3-02
    Curt Hinds (CHS vs. Herscher) 10-26-02

Goalie Saves in a Game: 26, Charles Johnson (CHS vs. Normal University) 10-31-00

Team Single Game

Most Goals Scored in a Game: 13, (CHS vs. St. Anthony) 8-28-95/
(CHS vs. Rantoul) 10-3-02
Most Goals Allowed in a Game: 15, (CHS vs. Decatur MacArthur) 1986
Most Shots on Goal in a Game: 61, (CHS vs. Altamont) 9-11-04
Most Shots on Goal Allowed in a Game: 33, (CHS vs. Taylorville) 9-24-86
Most Fouls Committed in a Game: 29, (CHS vs. Danville) 9-24-05
Most Goals Scored in the First Half in a Game: 8, (CHS vs. Altamont) 9-13-03
Most Goals Scored in the Second Half in a Game: 8, (CHS vs. St. Anthony) 9-15-03

Individual Single Season

Most Goals Scored: 52, Ryan McDermand-2003
Highest Goals Per Game Average: 2.00, Ryan McDermand-2003
Most Assists: 32, Curt Hinds-2002
Most Total Offensive Points: 118, Ryan McDermand-2003
Most Goalie Saves: 192, Corey Brinkmeyer-1992
Most Non-Goalie Saves: 7, Trevor Belzer-1993
Goals Against/Game: .65, Jeremy Hill-1994
Most Goals Scored as a Junior: 40, Curt Hinds, 2001
Most Goals Scored as a Sophomore: 19, Curt Hinds, 2000
Most Goals Scored as a Freshman: 8, Kevin Hinds-2003

Team Single Season

Most Goals Scored: (131)-2003
Fewest Goals Allowed: (13)-1994
Shutout Wins: (14)-2002
Most Goalie Saves: (194)-1986
Most Shots on Goal: (767)-2003
Most Shots on Goal Allowed: (353)-1986
Most Fouls Committed: (364)-2004
Most Goals Allowed in the First Half: (76)-2003
Most Goals Allowed in the Second Half: (65)-2001
Fewest Goals Allowed in the First Half:(2)-1994
Fewest Goals Allowed in the Second Half: (9)-1996
Most Wins: (23)-2002
Fewest Wins: (0)-1986
Most Losses: (14)-1986
Fewest Losses: (1)-2001
Most Ties: (6)-2000

Career

Most Goals Scored: 96, Curt Hinds (1999-2002)
Most Goals/Game: 1.34, Ryan McDermand (2001-2003)
Most Assists: 74, Curt Hinds (1999-2002)
Total Offensive Points: 266, Curt Hinds (1999-2002)
Most Goalie Saves: 434, Charles Johnson (1999-2001)
Non-Goalie Saves: 15, Trevor Belzer (1992-1994)
Most Goals Against/Game: .96, Adam Cooper (1995-1996)

. . . .

Dallas Bartz might have been living in a shadow during his high school soccer career. Bartz is third on the all-time career scoring list with 52 goals from 2000-2002. Bartz's seasons goals of, in this order, 15, 14, and 17 goals would make him the team's leading, or co-leading, scorer of at least twelve different teams throughout Charleston history.

. . . .

Despite a four year absent period, from 1992 to 2014, a Stranz was been associated with CHS soccer. Tyler Stranz (1992-1994), Zack Stranz (1998-2000), and head coach Paul Stranz (2000-2014).

Miscellaneous Records

Longest Overall Road Win Streak	14, (2002-2003)
Longest Overall Road Losing Streak	10, (1986-1987)
Longest Overall Home Win Streak	15, (2002-2003)
Longest Overall Home Losing Streak	10, (1986-1987)
Most Consecutive Losses	18, (1986-1987)
Most Consecutive Wins	16, (2003)
Most Consecutive Games Won Without Loss/Tie	21, (2001)
Best Win Percentage	.852, (2002)
Worst Losing Percentage	.000, (1986)
Most Wins	23, (2002)
Most Losses	14, (1986)
Most Ties	6, (2000)
Fewest Wins	0, (1986)
Fewest Losses	1, (2001)

. . . .

When looking at the records, it took eight attempts for Charleston to beat their neighboring county foe, Mattoon. Five losses, and three ties later, everything went the Trojans ways. Mattoon beat Charleston only once in the next 17 years.

. . . .

Kevin Hinds earned all-state honors the Illinois Soccer Coaches Association four years after his older brother, Curt, earned his second all-state selection. Kevin led the Trojans to an upset over Urbana for the Regional Championship and went on to play at Western Illinois University. After Curt graduated in 2002, he went on to Vanderbilt University.

. . . .

In a 2002 contest vs. Mattoon at Nino Fields, Dallas Bartz was issued his second yellow card with 4.9 seconds left on the clock in the first half, making him ineligible to play in the Trojans following game against Mount Zion. Charleston would still knock off the Braves 5-2.

. . . .

In a 2010 contest vs Mattoon at the now named Stranz Field, myself (Kyle Daubs) went to clear a ball and tore apart the top from the bottom of my soccer cleats. The game went on and I had to play with torn shoes. We defeated Mattoon 2-0, and on the front page of the sports section for the JG-TC, you can see me turning to kick a ball with my socks showing through the torn shoes. Many parents would then contact my mom asking if we could afford shoes and offered to buy me new soccer cleats.

. . . .

In 2012, three former Charleston players were pinned against each other in collegiate ball. Ian and Eric McCausland at Eastern Illinois took on Jason Coon who was at Bradley once during the regular season.

All-Apollo Conference List

The first Apollo Conference team did not come out until 2009. First team and second team selections did not start until 2014. Since 2009, the following winners of the Apollo Conference have gone as followed: Charleston-2009, Charleston/Mt. Zion-2010, Mt. Zion-2011, Charleston/Mt. Zion-2012, Mt. Zion-2013, Mattoon-2014, Mattoon-2015, Mattoon-2016, Mattoon-2017.

All-Apollo Conference

Tommy Ball, Midfield, 2009
Jason Coon, Midfield, 2009
Quinn Hussey, Defender, 2009
Joey Martinez, Midfielder, 2009
Chidi Obia, Forward, 2009
Aaron Smith, Goalkeeper, 2009
Ryan Dau, Defender, 2010
Ben Hoover, Defender, 2010
Michael Van Popering, Goalkeeper, 2010
Eric McCausland, Midfielder, 2010
Thorin Blitz, Forward, 2011
Eric McCausland, Midfielder, 2011
Ben Hoover, Defender, 2011
Taylor Garrett, Forward, 2011
Elliott Griffin, Midfielder, 2012
Taylor Garrett, Forward, 2012
Michael Spencer, Goalkeeper, 2012
Elliott Griffin, Midfielder, 2013
Taylor Garrett, Forward, 2013
Isaac Dallas, Defender, 2013

Drew Smith, Goalkeeper, 2013

All-Apollo Conference First Team

Reece Bell, Forward, 2014
Vincent Hoover, Midfielder, 2014
Wade Spence, Defender, 2015
Reece Bell, Forward, 2015
Drew Mejdrich, Forward, 2016
John Larouere, Defender, 2016
Wyatt Garrett, Midfielder, 2016
Jack Thain, Forward, 2016
Grant Cline, Midfielder, 2017
Jack Thain, Forward, 2017

All-Apollo Conference Second Team

Jack Thain, Forward, 2014
Brandon Peterson, Midfielder, 2014
Dillon McClelland, Defender, 2014
Drew Mejdrich, Midfielder, 2015
Jack Thain, Forward, 2015
Gabe Oetting, Midfielder, 2016
Michael Smith, Midfielder, 2016
Jack McGrath, Midfielder, 2017

IHSA All State Selections

Curt Hinds, Midfielder, 2001
Curt Hinds, Midfielder, 2002
Ryan McDermand, Forward, 2003
Kevin Hinds, Midfielder, 2006
Ian McCausland, Forward, 2007
Jason Coon, Midfielder, 2009

Decatur Herald & Review Coach of the Year

Paul Stranz-2009
Paul Stranz-2009

Decatur Herald & Review Player of the Year

Tyler Stranz, Midfielder, 1994
Curt Hinds, Midfielder, 2001
Curt Hinds, Midfielder, 2002
Ryan McDermand, Forward, 2003
Andrew Cudone, Midfielder, 2004
Kevin Hinds, Midfielder, 2006
Jason Coon, Midfielder, 2009

McDermand, Hinds, Cudone, Highlight Soccer Scoring

Modern soccer scoring stars Ryan McDermand, Curt Hinds, and Andrew (Roo) Cudone dominated the current 32-year Trojan scoring totals. The three make up the top five single season scoring totals, while Hinds and McDermand are a one-two punch in career scoring.

These mighty three, joined by Kevin Hinds, Uzo Obia, Jason Jones, Darrick Brooks, and Ian McCausland are the only CHS players to finish a season with at least a 1.00 goal scored per game average. McDermand is the only player in CHS history to have at least a 2.00 goal scored per game average. Hinds' 96 goals in 1999-2002 stands as the all-time season high while McDermand's 52 goals in 2003 are good enough to capture the single-season scoring title. Hinds 40 goals in 2001 and 34 goals in 2002 claimed second and fourth ranks in a season, and McDermands 36 total is set for third place.

Roo Cudone, one of the key factors in the 2004 state qualifying team, stepped forward to round out the top five with his 29 boots to the goal. Cudone would only finish his career with 38 goals, putting him 10th on the all-time leaderboards. Recent graduate Jack Thain capped a four-year varsity career by finishing third on the all-time list with 53 goals. His junior and senior seasons of 18 and 19 goals propelled him to the top part of the leaderboard.

Uzo Obia ranks eighth in career totaling by scoring 27 of his career 41 goals in 2003. Obia added sixteen assists that year as well. The current list of scoring leaders from 1986 through 2018 is supplemented by several two-time winners. Darrick Brooks (1987-1989) was one of the few bright spots during Charleston's beginning soccer program in the late 80's. Thain and him are the only player in CHS history to lead the team in scoring three straight seasons. Brooks finished with 40 goals, good enough for ninth on the all-time scoring list.

The only others who led Trojan scoring in at least two seasons was Kevin Zawodniak (1997-1998), Hinds (2000-2001), and McDermand (2002-2003). Jason Coon was only four goals away from joining the club in 2009.

SEASON SCORING LEADERS

BOYS SOCCER

Year	Player	Games	Goals	Scoring Average
1986	Tim Montgomery	14	5	.36
1987	Darrick Brooks	15	13	.86
1988	Darrick Brooks	14	10	.71
1989	Darrick Brooks	14	17	1.21
1992	Jason Jones	13	16	1.23
1993	Tim Condron	20	9	.45
1994	Tyler Stranz	22	10	.45
1995	Wade Starwalt	24	18	.75
1996	Tim Hutti	23	16	.70
1997	Kevin Zawodniak	24	18	.75
1998	Kevin Zawodniak	25	14	.56
1999	Dustin Adair	25	14	.56
2000	Curt Hinds	27	19	.70
2001	Curt Hinds	27	40	1.48
2002	Ryan McDermand	27	36	1.33
2003	Ryan McDermand	26	52	2.00
2004	Andrew Cudone	26	29	1.16
2005	Ben Hussey	24	13	.54
2006	Kevin Hinds	25	25	1.00
2007	Ian McCausland	23	24	1.04
2008	Jason Coon	24	15	.63
2009	Tommy Ball	24	18	.75
2010	Eric McCausland	21	10	.48
2011	Thorin Blitz	22	10	.45
2012	Taylor Garrett	21	9	.43
2013	Taylor Garrett	21	13	.62
2014	Reece Bell	20	7	.35
2015	Jack Thain	21	11	.52

Year	Coach			
2016	Jack Thain	20	18	.90
2017	Jack Thain	21	19	.90

TOP TEN (Single Season)

2003 Ryan McDermand.....................52
2001 Curt Hinds...............................40
2002 Ryan McDermand.....................36
2002 Curt Hinds...............................34
2004 Andrew (Roo) Cudone..............29
2003 Uzo Obia..................................29
2006 Kevin Hinds..............................26
2007 Ian McCausland........................24
2000 Dallas Bartz.............................20
1999 Kevin Zawodniak......................19
2017 Jack Thain...............................19

TOP TEN (Career)

1999-2002 Curt Hinds................96
2001-2003 Ryan McDermand......90
2014-2017 Jack Thain................53
2003-2006 Kevin Hinds..............51
2004-2007 Ian McCausland.........50
2006-2009 Jason Coon...............48
2000-2002 Dallas Bartz..............46
2000-2003 Uzo Obia..................41
1987-1989 Darrick Brooks..........40
2002-2004 Andrew Cudone.........38

All-Time Points Leaders

No.	Player	Years Played	Goals	Assists	Total Points
1.	Curt Hinds	1999-2000	96	74	266
2.	Ryan McDermand	2001-2003	90	34	214
3.	Kevin Hinds	2003-2006	51	35	137
4.	Jack Thain	2014-2017	53	21	129
5.	Ian McCausland	2004-2007	50	26	126
6.	Dallas Bartz	1999-2002	52	18	122
7.	Jason Coon	2006-2009	34	26	122
8.	Andrew (Roo) Cudone	2002-2004	39	22	100
9.	Dustin Adair	1998-2001	36	27	99
10.	Uzo Obia	2000-2003	39	18	96

Boys Soccer
All-Time Boys Soccer Coaching Records

Years	Coach	Total Years	Won	Lost	Tied	Percentage
2000-2013	Paul Stranz	14	219	90	26	.693
1993-1999	Hank Nino	8	109	47	23	.673
1992	Bob Sanders	1	7	4	5	.594
2016-Present	Jason Garrett	2	20	14	7	.573
2015-2016	Dave Dunlap	2	16	15	10	.512
1986-1991	Chuck Castle	6	17	61	5	.250
Total	6 Coaches	33	388	231	76	.613

All-Time Boys Soccer Coaching Records for Apollo Conference

Years	Coach	Total Years	Won	Lost	Tied	Percentage
2009-2013	Paul Stranz	4	15	4	2	.762
2016-Present	Jason Garrett	2	13	8	1	.614
2014-2015	Dave Dunlap	2	8	6	5	.553
Total	3 Coaches	8	36	18	8	.645

Trojans Coaching Records
Boys Soccer (Single Season)

Most Wins	23, Paul Stranz, 2002
Fewest Wins	0, Chuck Castle, 1986
Most Defeats	14, Chuck Castle, 1986
Fewest Defeats	1, Paul Stranz, 2001
Most Ties	6, Paul Stranz, 2000
Most Apollo Conference Victories	7, Jason Garrett, 2017
Most Consecutive Wins	16, Paul Stranz, 2003
Most Consecutive Games Won Without Loss/Tie	21, Paul Stranz, 2001
Best Win Percentage	.852, Paul Stranz, 2002
Worst Losing Percentage	0, Chuck Castle, 1986

Boys Soccer (Career)

Most Regional Titles..........8, Paul Stranz (2001, 2002, 2003, 2004, 2006, 2009, 2010, 2013)
Most Sectional Titles..4, Paul Stranz (2000, 2001, 2002, 2004)
Most Times Qualified For State...............3, Paul Stranz (2000, 2002, 2004)
Most Apollo Conference Titles..3, Paul Stranz (2009, 2010, 2012)
Most CISC Titles..................2, Hank Nino (1998, 1999)/Paul Stranz (2000, 2001)
Most Soccer Tournament Titles.....5, Paul Stranz (Red & Gold: 2001, 2002, 2003, 2009, 2013)

CHARLESTON BOYS SOCCER HEADLINERS

2000 squad starts new millennium and success

Just weeks before practice was to start, Paul Stranz was named the head coach of both soccer teams at Charleston High School. "I hear the boys talk about wanting to go past the sectional title," Stranz said to JG-TC sports editor Brian Nielsen. "I just want to continue Hank Nino's success." Nino compiled a 109-46-23 record in eight years of coaching the boys team. Stranz inherited 18 lettermen from a team that went 15-4-6 the year before.

The team returned an all-sectional pick, and son of the coach, Zack Stranz. Also, back was forwards Miles Stoner, who was honorable-mention all-sectional; defenders Chris Potsch and David Stumpf and midfielder Pat Hutti, who were named all-Central Illinois Soccer Conference. The team also had a seasoned goalkeeper in Charles Johnson.

Charleston began the season with a 4-0 record to claim the Red & Gold Tournament title. Champaign Central also went 4-0 during the two-day tournament, but Charleston won the tie breaker since they allowed fewer goals. Potsch and Johnson were two of the Trojans all tournament picks and were key contributors that held teams to zero goals. Sophomore, Curt Hinds, had three goals and four assists in Saturday's three games and was Charleston's other representative on the tourney team. The four wins were victories over Altamont, Olney, Jacksonville, and Champaign Centennial.

Charleston allowed their first goal of the season with just 23 seconds left in the game against Monticello, but still won 2-1. The game was delayed one hour due to the hot, humid weather. Charleston endured the heat again with a 3-0 win over Mattoon. Charleston followed that up with a 2-1 win over Mount Zion, and a 1-1 tie against Urbana.

Just a week later after his penalty kick helped seal the win over Mattoon, Dallas Bartz had to play hero after the Trojans were trailing for the first time all season against Altamont. "I think we were too confident and thought we could win without trying," Bartz said to Nielsen. After Altamont's second goal put the Trojans down, Bartz scored with 31 minutes left, and then scored nearly three minutes later, and Charleston held on for the 3-2 win.

Charleston notched two more victories with a 2-1 win over Meridian and a 5-0 victory against St. Anthony. At his point, the Trojans had a 10-0-1 record through their first ten games of the season. Curt Hinds put on a show against Mahomet-Seymour by scoring four goals by himself in a 5-0 win. He nearly set the record, but he missed a point black shot that sailed over the goal. "It wasn't a big deal since we were winning," Hinds said of his near miss to Nielsen "But you always want to put the ball in the net.

The Trojans could keep celebrating as their 3-0 win over Teutopolis clinched the Central Illinois Soccer Conference boy's championship. During the tournament, Bartz and Hinds each had two goals. It was less drama-filling this season. Last season, the Trojans had to go to a shootout with Mahomet-Seymour in which Charleston won.

In the following week, Charleston added wins over Lovington and Champaign Central, but finally saw their unbeaten streak end with a 3-1 loss to Decatur St. Teresa. The Bulldogs', Toney Douglass, scored three first half goals. If that wasn't enough, a 1-0 loss to Danville added some frustrations, but Charleston recovered with a 2-0 win against Champaign Centennial. Stoner led Charleston with a goal and assist, and Johnson had 13 saves. Bartz had his second hat trick of the season in a 6-0 win over Teutopolis and then the team erupted for eight goals in an 8-0 win over Rantoul. A 1-0 loss to Decatur MacArthur was a damper as Charleston prepared for the Sectional.

All the teams that defeated Charleston were in different Sectionals, and Charleston was the host in which they were the number one seed, tying the school record for wins with a 18-3-1 regular season record. Before the Sectional, Zach Stranz and Pat Hutti were named all sectional picks.

Charleston handled Lovington in the first round with a 7-0 win. Dustin Adair, who had to miss eight games this season with a knee injury, led Charleston with two goals. Charleston's 20th win of the season sent Charleston to the school's first sectional title game with a 5-0 win over Teutopolis. Adair finished the game again with two goals. For the sectional championship, Charleston was to play Monticello, a team that they defeated 2-1 earlier in the season. Monticello was playing for their first Sectional title and was just in their fourth year of existence in terms of the boys' soccer program.

Five second half goals lifted Charleston to the school's first sectional title. "She (Monticello coach Lois Cryder) gets them very motivated," Stranz said to Nielsen. "I wanted to do it in a convincing manner." Adair continued to have the hot foot by scoring the half's first goal. Bartz shortly followed with a goal off an assist by Adair and Hinds. Adair and Zach Stranz also scored for the other goals. Next up on the list was state power Normal University.

Not only were they fighting against a good team, but against superstition as well. All three of the Trojans' losses have come on football fields, which is where the super-sectional match was played. "We're going to practice at night on the football field," Stranz said of his team's practice plans. "It's probably better not to tell him the game will be on Halloween."

Charleston practiced on Trojan Hill three times and were getting ready for a possible Sweet 16 spot if they were to win. Stranz said to Nielsen: "It's a private school where they seem to get the best athletes," Charleston coach Paul Stranz said. "We're going to have our challenge. No doubt about it, they have a track record like Teutopolis does in basketball. I guess anyway you look at it we're underdogs. But hopefully, that will be a way to get the boys up and motivated. We've had a great season and we hope to make it last a little longer."

Not only did the Trojans make their season last longer, but they won in the best way possible. With a state berth on the line, and a shootout, Charles Johnson prevailed in the goal. "I've never been so busy," the Charleston goalkeeper said. "I've never been so winded playing in goal." Finally, after denying shot after shot from Normal University High, Johnson also had to exert a bit more energy in hugs of celebration. Curt Hinds and Pat Hutti converted the Trojans' last two penalty kicks in a tiebreaker and Charleston had a 2-1 boys' soccer win over Normal University High Tuesday night in the IHSA Class an Urbana Super-Sectional.

"This is the most fun I've ever had in my life," said Dallas Bartz to Nielsen, who had the Trojans' only goal in regulation that ended tied 1-1. "I'm numb," first-year head coach Paul Stranz said. "I'm elated. Fantastic game." "This is what I've been dreaming of my whole career," the coach's son and a senior co-captain Zack Stranz said.

Charleston maintained its 1-0 lead until 8:13 remained. U-High's Trevor White took a lead pass from all-stater Ryan Singer and zoomed the ball into the right corner of the net to tie the game. Charleston had some scoring opportunities of its own during the second of the 10-minute overtime periods and was on a run just past midfield when the whistle blew signaling that time had run out.

Then Charleston fans started chanting "Charlie, Charlie, Charlie!" as their goalkeeper prepared for the sudden death shootout in which five players from each team take penalty shots. Only for a bit did the CHS backers get quiet when U-High's first shooter Sean LaBounty bounced in a shot past Johnson. "You just don't think about it again," Johnson said to Nielsen. "It's one shot at a time." Fenger stepped out to bat away the first three shots by the Trojans while Johnson made two saves, including a dive to his left, to keep Charleston behind just 1-0 in the shootout.

Then Hinds, the sophomore who led Charleston's scoring during the year, drove the ball in the air to the left of Fenger to make things even. Johnson knocked away another shot, setting the stage for Hutti. "I watched him against everyone else," Charleston's senior midfielder said to Nielsen. "He was going by the plant foot so I started one way and chipped it the other way." Hutti's kick hit the inside of the left post and bounced in putting the Trojans ahead with only U-

High's Chris Spong left to kick.

This time, Johnson did not even have to touch the ball as the attempt sailed wide to the left setting the stage for the Trojans' players and fans to go wild while U-High's season ended 17-3-3. "Pure enjoyment," Johnson said to Nielsen. "It's great."

The Elite Eight berth came in the first year when Charleston soccer was funded by the school rather than a soccer booster organization. Assistant coach, Bill Jeremiahs, was going to be 15 minutes away from his hometown of O'Fallon when Charleston traveled down to play Lisle Benet Academy in the Elite Eight. The dream season ended when Charleston was defeated 5-0. Just under a minute, Lisle's scoring leader, Luke Rojo, drove down and smashed a ball, but Johnson dived to stop in, stimulating thoughts that this could be another repeat of the game against Normal University. Instead, reality kicked in. Lisle went on to win the state championship.

The year was one to remember. The team finished 22-4-1 and scored 86 goals and set a record for 13 shutouts in a season. Hinds led the team in offensive points with 55. He was also the leader in goals (19) and assists (17). Bartz finished with 15 goals. Hutti had 10 goals and 15 assists. Adair had 10 goals. Johnson finished with 180 goalie saves.

No state, but team picture hangs with undefeated 2001 regular season

The team was coming off the school's first trip to state. The Trojans lost an all sectional pick in Hutti, but Hinds was back for his junior season. Adair played the year healthy to provide extra scoring, and Bartz was also back for a scoring/leadership role. Defenders Potsch and Kellen Fasnacht were back with Johnson in goal. It was another twenty-win season for the Trojans. The 2001 squad is the first and only team to go undefeated during the regular season.

Charleston began the year with a tie to Jacksonville. Then followed with wins over Mount Carmel, Centralia, Olney, Altamont, and a high scoring 7-5 win over Monticello. Charleston then tied in two of their next three games. During Charleston's next seven wins, the Trojans outscored their opponents 42-4. Headlining the win steak were a 9-0 and 8-0 win over St. Anthony, and a 7-0 win over Altamont. After a 1-1 tie to Champaign Central, Charleston went back to work with a record 11-0 win over Rantoul. Finishing the season with a 19-0-5 record, Charleston claimed the number one seed and were to play Danville Schlarman in the first round of the IHSA Class A Sectional game.

Curt Hinds celebrated his special day in a big way with two goals and assist for a 4-0 victory. Before the game, Hinds had been told he was named to the all-state team. Stranz waited until after the game to tell his players of the post-season honors. Adair and Potsch were named to the all sectional team. Charleston claimed the Sectional with a 3-0 win over rival, Mattoon. The win set up Charleston with a rematch against Normal University, a team they defeated in penalty kicks a year ago to make it to state.

Normal University entered the game having lost 12 seniors from their team a year ago, but still had Adam Hage who was headed to Bradley on a soccer scholarship. No magic was to happen this year as Normal defeated Charleston 1-0

Hinds finished the year setting a then school record with 40 goals and 21 assists, good for 101 offensive points. Adair finished his senior season with 12 goals and 13 assists. Bartz had another solid year with 14 goals. As a team, Charleston finished with a ratio of 117-28 goals scored/goals against.

2002 squad returns to state

Going into the season, the plan was to improve from a season ago. Going into the tip of the preseason, 25 of the players attended an Experiential Leadership Camp at Homer. "They said any high school or college team that has been there has come back the next year and set school records," Stranz said to Nielsen. "It needs to be proved yet but I think that set the stage for this year. We're all headed in the right direction for the year."

Back to lead the team was all state selection, and senior, Curt Hinds. During the off-season, Hinds played for the Illinois U-17 Olympic developmental team. Back to help was Bartz for his senior season, and a future powerful offensive workhorse in Ryan McDermand. Leading the midfield was Andrew "Roo" Cudone.

To help strengthen the schedule, Stranz added the Trojans to a Chatham Glenwood tournament that included Springfield, Springfield Southeast, Belleville East, Danville, Decatur MacArthur and Williamsville. Before the tip-off of the Red and Gold Tournament, the booster club named the fields at Sister City Park after former coaches Hank and Liz Nino. McDermand shined in the celebration day scoring four goals, and the debut of Nino Fields was a success. A 1-0 loss to Jacksonville cost the Trojans a tournament championship.

Charleston followed the loss with an eight-game winning streak. One of the wins included a 5-2 victory over Mattoon that featured more than seven yellow cards and an ejection in the last five seconds. An official stopped the game with 4.9 seconds showing on the clock to issue Bartz his second yellow card, meaning he had to sit out one game. The win streak also featured a close 4-3 victory over Urbana. Hinds scored three goals.

In the Chatham Glenwood tournament, Charleston received the tough games they wished. They began with a 0-0 tie to Decatur MacArthur and a 6-1 loss to Belleville East but recovered with a 2-0 win over Chatham. The Trojans claimed third place with a 5-3 win over MacArthur. Hinds was gone on a college visit during the first game against MacArthur, but this time led Charleston with three goals.

Hinds had his second four goal game in a 5-3 victory over Champaign Central. Charleston finished the regular season on a ten-game winning streak to give them their third straight number one seed in the Sectional. Their first opponent was Olney. After 55 scoreless minutes, the Trojans erupted for six goals in a 6-1 victory. "We knew we were getting the shots and it was just a matter of time," Hinds said. Hinds had three goals in the game. "You get a little worried but when it rains it pours with us," Charleston defender Jake Dively said.

Charleston advanced to the Sectional semi-final game with a 4-0 victory over Monticello to claim the Regional title. Charleston held Monticello's all-state selection, Toney Cook, to no goals. "We feel pretty good about shutting down one of the area's leading scorers," all-sectional sweeper Adam Brimner said. "We just tried to help on the side he'd be on and not let him beat us." During the week, Hinds was a repeat all-state selection. McDermand led Charleston with two goals in the win over Monticello.

Charleston made a statement in the sectional semi-final with an 8-0 win over Herscher. Charleston held a 5-0 halftime lead. "Right now, the seniors are playing pretty much like it's our last game because it could be," Bartz said. "They were a good team. We just played some of our best soccer."

Peotone was next up and were the No. 2 team in the sectional. Peotone, a state quarterfinalist a year ago, put the Trojans behind for the first time in four postseason games when Jayson Schippits fired in a shot with 9 minutes, 49 seconds into the game. For the game, Hinds sported a blonde hairdo. Fans were in awe of his soccer rather than his hair, as Hinds tied the game with his goal. Then, he put the Trojans ahead after Andy Barnhart stole a pass and connected with Hinds for the assist. McDermand's goal gave Charleston a 3-1 advantage.

Peotone scored one goal, but the Trojans held of the comeback bid to make it back to state. "I think Kyle was a big part of our defense tonight," Charleston senior Jake Dively said to Nielsen after Wilson's nine-save game. "They had us on our heels at the end," Stranz said. "I was just glad the time ran out."

Waterloo Gibault was to be Charleston's opponent in the Elite Eight. The winner would go to the Class A's Final Four. The ride ended as Gibault defeated Charleston 1-0. With a state tournament audience watching Friday afternoon, Hassan Nurie's corner kick sailed toward the net and his brother Mike Nurie headed the ball in the goal 16 minutes, 38 seconds into the game. "We worked very hard on corner kicks," Waterloo Gibault coach Jim Corsi said to Nielsen. "We heard from other coaches of schools (Charleston) played and they said that could be a weakness so we worked hard on that for two days."

Both Hinds and McDermand entered the game with more goals, 34 and 36 respectively, than the 33 totals of Gibault's tournament roster. But for the second time this year the Trojans lost a 1-0 game, this one ending their season at 23-3-1. Charleston couldn't get anything past Waterloo's 6-foot-6 goalkeeper, Lance Stemler. "He had a couple of great saves most keepers haven't made against us, Stranz said. Corsi said of Stemler: "Soccer is his second sport. Basketball is what he loves. He almost didn't play soccer."

Hinds finished the season with 32 goals and 34 assists, good for 100 offensive points. His career had finally come to a close. The two-time all-state selection finished on top of the Charleston goals list with 96 goals, assist list with 74 assists, and offensive points with 266. After many college visits, Hinds chose to play for Vanderbilt University. Vanderbilt's head coach was former EIU's head coach, Tim Clements. Hinds also looked at Dartmouth, New Mexico, and Marquette that year. As of today, Hinds career 74 assists ranks fifth on the all-time list on IHSA., while his 34 assists is ninth best in all IHSA play.

McDermand, a Region 15 selection, also wowed spectators. The junior finished the year with a line of 36 goals and 19 assists. Bartz ended his career with a senior year of 17 goals. Currently, Bartz is fifth on the all-time goals scored list with 52 goals.

2003 team denied state by county rival

The whole year soccer fans were spoiled with the scoring ability of McDermand. The senior led Charleston with 52 goals, and 118 offensive points, which are school records that still stands today. McDermand was named to the all-state team that season. McDermand's 52 goals in a season is tied for 18th most in an IHSA season. Charleston also had another deadly scorer in Uzo Obia who finished with 26 goals after an injury riddled season in 2002.

After losing 10 seniors from their team a year ago, the unthinkable happened. A Mattoon vs Charleston, cross county matchup, would determine who would go to state. Charleston commanded a 1-0 halftime lead when Steven Bower launched a throw over and Collin Wallace headed it in at the 20:50 mark. Everything fell apart when Mattoon's Jacob Kimery tapped in a loose ball with 19:09 left in the second half to tie it.

"We were panicking," Charleston coach Paul Stranz said to Nielsen. "We didn't play our game. We didn't do what we were practicing and that happens. They took advantage of it. They've got a lot of heart and they really went after it." With 8:14 left, Alex Hesse lofted a shot from the far left that put Mattoon ahead.

Charleston finished the year 21-5-0 and was denied a second trip to state. A strong group of seniors, including McDermand and Uzo Obia, played their last high school match. McDermand and Obia had record setting moments that year. McDermand initially broke Hind's record of goals in a game by scoring five by himself in a 7-1 over Meridian on September 17th. Obia tied the record by scoring five himself in an 8-0 win over Teutopolis on October 14th. Bower had 23 assists to lead the Trojans. For McDermand, he was named the Decatur Herald & Review player of the year. At the time, only ten players in the state of Illinois had a better season then McDermand.

2004 team makes last recorded state run

Going into the season, Charleston had lost 60 percent of its scoring along with 13 seniors. Someone was going to have to replace scoring threats in McDermand and Obia. Senior captain, Roo Cudone, led Charleston to a season to remember.

The team featured Curt Hinds' little brother, Kevin Hinds. As a freshman, Hinds had eight goals and eight assists. Others to step up were Andy Murphy, Ross Hutchinson, Ben Bates, Colin Wallace, Jeff Nilsen, Phil Norton, and freshman, Ian McCausland. Replacing two-year goalkeeper, Kyle Wilson, was junior, Jonathan Cartwright.

After a 5-1 opening, revenge victory over Mattoon, the team that bounced Charleston in the sectional final in 2003, Charleston stumbled to a 3-2 loss in penalty kicks to Centralia that sent the Trojans to the third-place game in the Red & Gold Tournament. Charleston claimed third with a 2-1 win over Champaign Central.

After the tournament, Charleston added a 5-1 win over Monticello, and a very happy 7-0 win over Mattoon. Up this point, Cudone had already notched seven goals and an assist. A tie to St. Teresa, and a narrow 2-1 loss to undefeated Urbana sent Charleston to a 4-2-1 record, but the Trojans regained their winning ways with a six-game winning streak where they outscored their opponents 39-3.

Cartwright's 13 saves weren't enough as Charleston's win streak ended with a 1-0 loss to Champaign Central. Next up, was some grueling opponents at the Mid-State Soccer Classic, and the losses piled up from there. Three straight losses to Waterloo, Springfield Sacred Heart Griffin, and St. Joseph pushed the losing streak to four games. The offense was averaging 4.7 goals a contest up the tournament, but only managed to score one. "What we need to do is we need to gather up as a team and regroup," Stumpf said to Nielsen. "We know what we have to do from here. We need to just use this as a learning experience."

The four-game losing streak was the longest losing streak in coach Stranz's tenure coaching at Charleston. "We've had four physical games in a row. Now maybe it's taken its toll," Stranz said Saturday. "We got a game on Monday, so we don't have much time. We just got to suck it up and that's part of playing soccer. If you're going to play with the big boys, you got to run with them."

The offense recovered with an 8-0 victory over Rantoul, but the defense squandered in a 3-2 loss to Champaign Centennial. The loss dropped Charleston to 11-7-1 on the season, but Centennial improved to 15-0-3. Cudone scored both of the goals to improve his impressive total to 23 on the season. Charleston ended their regular season with wins over Decatur MacArthur and Teutopolis before facing Monticello in the Regional semi-final. A 5-1 win over Monticello sent Charleston into the Regional championship against the Mattoon Green Wave.

The Trojans played their game for a 3-0 over Mattoon to move on to the Sectional. Josh Wilson executed a perfect header on assist from Cudone for an insurance goal. In their opening sectional win, Charleston defeated Champaign Judah Christian 3-1. Charleston held a 2-1 lead, and with under four minutes left, Kevin Hinds scored a goal on a pass from Andy Murphy to seal the victory. Murphy soon jumped into Wallace's arms, knowing the Trojans had made the Sweet 16. "It was awesome," Murphy said to Nielsen. "It was just the greatest feeling. We had it right there. It was just awesome."

For the championship, Charleston was to face undefeated Danville Schlarman. The team came in with a 19-0-3 record but was still considered the underdog. Danville Schlarman defeated Olney 3-0 in the sectional semi-final, a team that Charleston defeated 4-1 during the regular season. "What we're really going to work on is guarding against not being ready," Stranz said to Nielsen. "I don't want our team to take them too lightly because they have a good team and they have a good record." Charleston was ready with a 5-0 thumping to return back to state. Charleston scored two goals within the first seven minutes on a mud covered, slippery field. Corey Schultz, Hinds, Cudone, Wilson, and Nathan Sweeney all scored.

Charleston was back off to Naperville to play at North Central College, and they were to play against a familiar opponent. During their four-game losing streak, Charleston was defeated by St. Joseph 3-0. "After the game I said, 'Hopefully we'll see each other at state and play again. (St. Joseph coach Ray Fligel) said I know it will be a different game then," Stranz said. The coach received his wish against the school of 1,020 students.

Charleston took a 1-0 lead late in the first half with a goal from their senior leader, Cudone. The Trojans took that lead into halftime, and the first 3:13 of the second half. Then, St. Joseph tied it, and added their second goal with 8:21 remaining. "We knew they were going to be pumped up because they're not used to trailing," said Stranz to Nielsen. "They're not used to allowing anybody to score against them. We knew they would come out pumped up and they did." The Trojans fought back, but were "close, but no cigar." The 2-1 loss ended Charleston's season at 17-8-1.

Cudone's final game had him finishing with a career of 39 goals, 22 assists, and 100 points. At the time, he was tied with Uzo Obia for fourth in goals, Pat Hutti in eight for assists, and fourth in career points. Cudone was named the Decatur Herald & Review Player of the Year. Cudone went on to play soccer at Millikin University. Charleston may not consider their 2004 Regional win over Mattoon revenge for ending their season it 2003, but the Trojans of the future made sure they didn't stumble to their rival. After 2003, the boys' soccer team defeated Mattoon 16 straight times. Their winning streak over the Green Wave ended in the Regional semi-final in 2012, when the team lost 5-3. Mattoon ended up winning the Regional that year.

Boys Tennis
(1980-2018)

Boys Tennis
(1980-2018)

Charleston featured a tennis team in 1954. The team won a District title, but there was no record of tennis teams that came after. However, Charleston tennis officially became an IHSA-affiliate in 1980 with Vicki Preston as the coach. She was also coaching the girl's tennis team when the girls program started in 1978, so it was a no brainer for Coach Preston to lead the charge. After the first year, Charleston won the Apollo Conference four consecutive seasons, including a Sectional championship in 1984. Jim Sexton, John Whittenbarger, Ian Barford, Rob Weidner, and Rezwan Lateef were mainstays during those runs. Preston stepped down after the 1987 season.

The Apollo crown returned to Charleston in 1989, and it came down to a close match. John Smith and Irfan Lateef broke 4-4 tie with Effingham after winning their doubles match to clinch the Apollo title for CHS. Mark Emberly won the singles competition. Emberly qualified for state in 1988 and was ranked 24th in the Wester Tennis Association boys 16s that year. He qualified for state again in 1989. Scott Holycross qualified for state in 1990 and 1991, while Chris Collins and Brian Haberer made it to state as a doubles team in 1992. From 1993 to 1996 there are no records showing any member for CHS made state. IHSA did not start keeping track of sectionals until 1996.

The Apollo returned to CHS in 1997, but it was the following season that proved to be the best in CHS history. The 1998 squad, coached by Doug Reynolds, won a Sectional title and is considered the best finish by a team in CHS history. CHS featured two individual state qualifiers that year and two doubles team. The 1998 squad finished 41st as a team in the state tournament when the IHSA offered a one-class system. Blaze Taylor Lutz and Keegan Gowin paired as a doubles team to finish 34th at the state tournament, but that was in a two-class system, which started in 2016.

There have been some other notable players that are on record. Ryan Shick, class of 2003, won the team MVP award three years in a row, including leading the 2003 team to their first Apollo Conference championship in six years. Shick eventually came back to coach Charleston's boy's tennis team for three years. Sean Hussey, class of 2013, led CHS to their last Apollo Conference championship in 2013. Hussey, and Alex Gowin, CHS class of 2014, are the only CHS tennis players on record to qualify for the state tournament three times.

Boys Tennis Records

Apollo Conference Titles: 1982, 1983, 1984, 1985, 1989, 1997, 1998, 1999, 2003, 2013
Sectional Titles: 1984, 1998

State Qualifiers
1980s: Mark Emberly (singles)-1988, Mark Emberly (singles)-1989.
1990s: Scott Holycross (singles)-1990, Scott Holycross (singles)-1991, Chris Collins & Brian Haberer (doubles)-1992, Matt Horney & Eric Fister (doubles)-1997, Josh Griswold & Clark Miller

(doubles)-1997, Kasey Wagoner (singles)-1998, Eric Fister (singles)-1998, Shariq Kathawala & Clark Miller (doubles)-1998, Jon Schubert & Josh Griswold (doubles)-1998.

2000s: Ryan Shick (singles)-2003, AJ Schubert (singles)-2006, Andy Bays (singles)-2008, Quinn Hussey & Adam Drake (doubles)-2009.

2010s: Quinn Hussey & Adam Drake (doubles)-2010, Alex Shick & Sean Hussey (doubles)-2011, Sean Hussey & Alex Gowin (doubles)-2012, Sean Hussey & Alex Gowin (doubles)-2013, Alex Gowin (singles)-2014, Blaze Taylor-Lutz & Keegan Gowin (doubles)-2017

Trojans Boys Track & Field
(1897-2018)

Trojans Boys Track & Field
(1897-2018)

The first track meet took place on May 10, 1897 against Mattoon, Tuscola, and Paris at Charleston. Charleston won the meet with 50 points. Charleston used to hold their practice sessions at the Coles County Fairgrounds track in the early 1900s. Trojan Hill took form in 1935. Charleston finally began to compete in conference play in 1928 when the EI League was formed. Charleston won their first EI League in 1937. Competition was held on a 440-yard track instead of the 400-meter track that is used today.

Charleston won another EI League title in 1939 after finishing runner-up in 1938. Edgar Smith and Fery Bushue led the team in sprints and throws respectively. Bushue threw the javelin, which was a regulated high school event back in the day. Charleston won their first district title in 1941, and then won another EI League title in 1943. Charles Sellett led Charleston nearly by himself. He won the 100-yard dash, 220-yard dash, and the broad jump. Sellett clinched the narrow victory at the end of the meet by jumping to a first place to give CHS a 38 1/2 to 37 win over Paris. Sellett only lost five times in three years of competing at CHS. Sellett never competed his senior year because he was drafted by the Army.

CHS won the EI League title again in 1953 but produced perhaps their best season in a decade was in 1956 under the leadership of coach Mervin Baker. The nucleus of Bob Thomas, Ben Butler, Jon Kibler, Jerry Easter, Dave York, and Wayne Prince rattled off six straight dual and tri meet wins, one which was over Danville who won the Big 12 Conference. Charleston won the EI League title that year, and then again in 1964. The 1964 team barely beat Newton in a 50-49 squeaker. Jim Drake set an EI League meet record in the discus.

Charleston went over 10 years before winning another conference title, but this time it was in the Apollo. In 1974, Charleston won their first Apollo title, and it was on their way to a sweet 70s ride. Charleston won the Apollo seven straight years from 1974 to 1980. On top of that, Charleston went 25-0 from 1972 to 1975 in dual or tri meets.

In 1974, Charleston swept all five invites, won the District title, and featured three outstanding performances by Dave Bough in the 220-yard dash, Curt Homason in pole vault, and Jeff Towles in triple jump. Bough followed that year with a bigger 1975. Bough, Steve Malehorn, Paul Wilen, and Mark Moutrey were unstoppable in the 4X100 relay, and still hold the school record to the present day. The time of 43.0 is the oldest boy's record in school history.

The second oldest record is by Marty Mizner in the 100-meter-high hurdles. Mizner ran a 14.9 in 1979. Jim Docter, Robert Snoddy, Neal Highland, and Larry Durham broke the school record in the 4X800 that year, while Anthony Cox placed fourth in the state in discuss in 1978. In 1982, Mark Heise ran a 49.98, which was the school record or nearly 20 years. Heise was just a sophomore that year. Heise paired with Page Alexander to lead the 1984 team. Alexander finished as the school record holder in the pole vault, and even vaulted to a seventh-place finish at the state meet.

In 1986, Bob Snider set the school record in the 200-meter dash with a time of 22.3. The year after, Mark Riddle suffered a tragic end to his career. Riddle qualified for state in the 800 and 1600 meter runs but was disqualified in the preliminaries. In 1988, Bob Black vaulted to a sixth-place finish at state, while Jim Bales set the then-school record in the 800-meter run.

Charleston won the Apollo in 1983, and then five straight seasons in from 1985 to 1989. Tony Logue helped the 1989 squad as he was a part of the winning 4X100, 4X200, and 4X400 relays, while winning the triple jump.

The 90s featured two of the best throwers in school history, and the best sprinter/jumper. In 1990, Dave Myerscough surprised many by qualifying for state as a sophomore. In 1991, Myerscough finished fourth in discuss, and then sixth his senior year in 1992. The 1992 season also featured a strange moment when coach Gene Nance found that Charleston had really won the Olney Invite because of a scoring error.

Mark Fleming eventually became the best shot-put thrower from 1994 to 1996. A finger injury kept Fleming out of the state meet his sophomore year, but he returned his junior and senior year, finishing as the runner-up in discuss. Despite not placing, Fleming is still the school record holder in shot put. He was the school record holder in discuss, but James Williams broke that record in 1999. Williams became a two-time all-state discus thrower.

In 1998, the Iheanyi Obia show began. Obia, who holds four track records, set the school record for triple jump that year. He finished as the state runner-up as a junior. His senior season saw the 100-meter dash, 200-meter dash, and long jump records broken by Obia. He capped his season off by placing fourth in the long jump.

Charleston won the Apollo Conference in 2002. The team was led by the future state champion 4X800 team of Clint Coffey, Nathan Homann, Erik Werden, and Derek Fasnacht. Werden eventually became the school record holder in the 800 and 1600-meter runs. Fasnacht is one of the most decorated track athletes in school history. He is a member of the school record 4X200, 4X400, and 4X800 relays, as well as the school record holder for the 300-meter low hurdles. Teammate Dustin Culp was a contributor during the 2002 and 2003 seasons, including breaking Heise's 400-meter record by just .28 seconds.

It took 10 years before CHS won the Apollo again. The 2012 squad was led by sprinters LJ Welsh, Jake McSparin, Dylan Cazley, Josh Cazley, and Tibet Spencer. Riley McInerney, who won the state championship in the two mile in 2013, commanded the distance events, while Chase Black was a successful pole vaulter. McInerney and Black finished their careers as multi-all-state finishers. Charleston did not see another all-state finish until 2017. Nick Oakley placed ninth in 2017 and third in 2018 in the 800-meter run, while Dayton Black placed eighth and fifth in the pole vault those two years.

The Early Champs

Records that stretch all the way to the early 1900s do not include complete names. However, Charleston has three state champions on record. This includes "Clark" who won a state championship in the standing broad jump in 1902. R. Glasco won a state title in the one mile run in 1900, while C. Morris won a state title in the 220-yard low hurdles in 1906.

4X800 Meter Relay Wins State in 2003

For the first time in nearly 100 years, Charleston had a state champion. The 4X800 meter relay team of Clint Coffey, Nathan Homann, Erik Werden, and Derek Fasnacht ran a time of 7:51.21 to win the Class AA title. Charleston had a fantastic showing at the state meet this season, as the team tied for sixth overall.

Coffey led the race and had the team in 10th place. Coffey told Journal Gazette-Times Courier reporter Erik Hall, "I got spiked and they went out kind of slow. I just tried to stay as close as I could. I knew we had three awesome runners after me. I knew we could pull it off if I stayed close."

After Homann took the baton from Coffey, the junior closed the gap. Homann led the second leg at one point but was outkicked in the final 300 meters. Still, Homann took the relay from 10th to third thanks to his 1:57 split time as he handed off to Werden. "I was just trying to stay towards the front and on the last lap, I tried to get the lead for Derek and Erik. I got pretty close, but it was good enough to win."

Werden's kick proved to be too much for his competition. Werden stayed in third place until the final 300 meters where he kicked it home to have Charleston in first place as he handed off to Fasnacht. Werden finished with an amazing 1:54.69 split time. "Once I got the baton, I knew I should just sit on him and start running and give it all I got with 300 meters left because that is what we have been practicing is 300s," Werden told Hall. "I strived to do my best."

Fasnacht went onto clinch the state title for the relay team. Fasnacht led the entire 800 meters, and outkicked Elmhurst York's Mike Corry to bring home the title. Fasnacht told Hall, "I heard the guy right behind me and I didn't know if he was going to pass me or not. I had to push as hard as I could. It was awesome when I cross the finish line."

Charleston had one of their best showings ever that year. Werden placed state runner-up in the 800-meter run with a time of 1:56.99. Fasnacht finished all-state in two other events. Fasnacht placed eight in the 300-meter hurdles, while also helping the 4X400 meter relay team place eighth. The relay team also featured Homann, Quinton Combs, and Dustin Culp.

Riley McInerney Wins 3200 Meter Run Title in 2013

After a decorated cross-country career that featured making all-state honors three times, McInerney upped the ante by winning an individual state title in the 3200-meter run. He became the first individual from Charleston to win a state championship since C. Morris in 1906. Not only did he win state, he set a new Class 2A record in the 3200 with a time of 9:08.49, which is still a record today.

McInerney ran his first mile in 4:35 and was just a step and a half ahead of Chatham Glenwood's Marc Maton heading into the final lap. "I originally thought it was (Jake) Brown (Mt. Zion runner) and not Maton," McInerney told Journal Gazette-Times Courier reporter Mike Monahan. "Then, the announcer said it was Maton and not Brown. I knew Maton had a strong kick. About the 250 mark, he came right up on my shoulder, so I knew I had to pick it up. I just let my kick finish it off."

McInerney also placed fourth in the 1600 meter run that year, leading Charleston to a seventh-place finish as a team. McInerney placed sixth in the 3200 and fourth in the 1600 when he was a junior. McInerney, Werden, and Fasnacht are the only CHS track athletes to ever place at state four times.

Pole Vaulting Runs in Black Family

Some inter-family competition never hurt anyone, especially when your family could possibly be one of the greatest pole vaulting families in Illinois history. Bob Black, a 1988 CHS grad, was an all-state selection in the pole vault when he vaulted to a sixth-place finish in 1988. Fast forward, Black had two sons who picked up the family tradition.

The older son, Chase, was a three-time all-state selection in pole vault. This included a fourth-place finish in 2012, third place finish in 2013, and state runner-up in 2014. Black was a part of the seventh-place team finish in 2013. Chase eventually went on to participate on the track team for Southern Illinois University-Edwardsville. His younger brother, Dayton, won an IESA state championship as an eighth grader in pole vault. Then in high school, Dayton placed 8th as a sophomore in 2017, and fifth as a junior in 2018.

Team Records

EI League Titles: 1937, 1939, 1943, 1953, 1956, 1964
Apollo Conference Titles: 1974, 1975, 1976, 1977, 1978, 1979, 1980, 1983, 1985, 1986, 1987, 1988, 1989, 1996, 1998, 2002, 2012
District Titles: 1941, 1953, 1956, 1973, 1974, 1975
Sectional Titles: None

Individual Records

Event	Name	Time/Finish	Year
100 Meter	Iheanyi Obia	10.49	1999
200 Meter	Iheanyi Obia	22.2	1999
400 Meter	Dustin Culp	49.7	2003
800 Meter	Erik Werden	1:54.79	2002
1600 Meter	Riley McInerney	4:12.23	2013
3200 Meter	Riley McInerney	9:06.41	2013
100 High Hurdles	Marty Mizner	14.9	1979
300 Low Hurdles	Derek Fasnacht	38.9	2003
4X100 Relay	Steve Malehorn Paul Wilen David Bough Mark Moutrey	43.0	1975
4X200 Relay	Kellen Fasnacht Dustin Culp Derek Fasnacht Quinton Combs	1:30.14	2002
4X400 Relay	Dustin Culp Nathan Homann	3:22.26	2003

Event	Name	Mark	Year
4X800 Relay	Quinton Combs Derek Fasnacht Clint Coffey Nathan Homann Eric Werden Derek Fasnacht	7:44.23	2003
Shot Put	Mark Fleming	56-10	1996
Discus	James Williams	185-03	1999
High Jump	Pat Kelly Brad Reid	6-07	1995 2004
Long Jump	Iheanyi Obia	23-05.5	1999
Triple Jump	Iheanyi Obia	46-09	1999
Pole Vault	Chase Black	15-03	2014

Charleston All-State Finishes

Name	Year	Class	Place	Event
RELAY TEAMS	1977-78	AA	6	2-mile relay
	2001-02	AA	8	4x800-meter relay
	2002-03	AA	8	4x400-meter relay
			1	4x800-meter relay
Page Alexander	1983-84	AA	7	pole vault
Herb Anderson	1913-14	B	4	hammer throw
	1915-16	B	3	pole vault
Paul Bailey	1914-15	B	2	220-yard low hurdles
	1915-16	B	2	100-yard dash
Kyle Baumgartner	2000-01	AA	6	pole vault
Bob Black	1987-88	AA	6	pole vault
Chase Black	2011-12	2A	4	pole vault
	2012-13	2A	3	pole vault
	2013-14	2A	2	pole vault
Dayton Black	2016-17	2A	8	pole vault
	2017-18	2A	5	pole vault
Eric Bomball	1985-86	AA	6	discus throw
Howard Carson	1932-33		5	discus throw
Clark	1899-00		3	standing broad jump
	1901-02		1	standing broad jump
P. Clark	1898-99		3	standing broad jump
Clint Coffey	2002-03	AA	1	4x800-meter relay
Quinton Combs	2002-03	AA	8	4x400-meter relay
Anthony Cox	1977-78	AA	4	discus throw
Crispin	1902-03		2	hammer throw
Dustin Culp	2002-03	AA	8	4x400-meter relay
Derek Fasnacht	2001-02	AA	8	4x800-meter relay
	2002-03	AA	8	4x400-meter relay
			1	4x800-meter relay
			8	300-meter intermediate hurdles

Name	Year	Class	Place	Event
Kellen Fasnacht	2001-02	AA	8	4x800-meter relay
L. Fenish	1898-99		3	hammer throw
Mark Fleming	1994-95	AA	2	discus throw
	1995-96	AA	2	discus throw
Fuller	1900-01		2	hammer throw
	1901-02		3	hammer throw
			3	880-yard run
Taylor Garrett	2013-14	2A	8	800-meter run
R. Glasco	1899-00		1	1-mile run
Hawkins	1924-25	B	5t	high jump
Bob Holmes	1933-34		5t	high jump
Nathan Homann	2002-03	AA	1	4x800-meter relay
			8	4x400-meter relay
Sean Kelly	2001-02	AA	8	4x800-meter relay
Riley McInerney	2011-12	2A	4	1600-meter run
			6	3200-meter run
	2012-13	2A	1	3200-meter run
			4	1600-meter run
Miles	1899-00		3	180-yard low hurdles*
Montgomery	1899-00		3	880-yard run
C. Morris	1905-06		2	long jump
			1	220-yard low hurdles
Dave Myerscough	1990-91	AA	6	discus throw
	1991-92	AA	4	discus throw
Nick Oakley	2016-17	2A	9	800-meter run
	2017-18	2A	3	800-meter run
Iheanyi Obia	1997-98	AA	4	triple jump
	1998-99	AA	2	long jump
Purtill	1900-01		3	440-yard dash
			3	50-yard dash
			3	100-yard dash
C. Purtill	1898-99		2	440-yard dash
Smith	1897-98		3	50-yard dash
Erik Werden	2001-02	AA	8	4x800-meter relay
			5	800-meter run
	2002-03	AA	1	4x800-meter relay
			2	800-meter run
James Williams	1997-98	AA	4	discus throw
	1998-99	AA	5	discus throw

**Taken from IHSA Website

Wrestling
(1974-2018)

Wrestling
(1974-2018)

Wrestling began in 1974 with Renny Garshelis as the first coach. In 1975, Charlie Tripp became the first ever Regional champion in the 185-pound weight class. Organized wrestling stayed with Charleston for three years until it took a break due to lack in numbers. In 1982, wrestling came back with Lew Hankenson as the coach. Steve Hankenson became the first CHS grappler to make the state tournament in 1984. His senior season ended with a 29-2 record, and Steve became the all-time wins holder with a career 75-15-1 record. His 1984 campaign was highly successful as he won the Regional and Sectional championship in the 155-pound division and wrestled his way to a fourth-place all-state finish. He wrestled at the University of Illinois after high school.

Ed McKinney followed Hankenson's season with another Regional championship, but he did so in the 105-pound weight division. In 1986, wrestling was not recognized as a club. CHS wrestling finally was given a full IHSA schedule. It was the first time the team finished with a winning dual meet record with an 11-9 mark. The 1986 season was one of the most successful seasons in school history despite no state qualifiers. McKinney finished his season with a 30-11 record, while Brad Baptist finished 30-8. Kurt Hankenson won a Regional title in the 155-pound weight division to go with his 27-7-1 record, while Leon Hall won the heavyweight Regional title in a successful 22-3 campaign.

Hall repeated as a Regional champ in 1987 and was joined by Bob Hillis. Hillis finished as a two-time Regional champ, but just missed state in 1988. Despite going 30-4 that season, Hillis finished fourth at the Sectional meet to miss state. The 1988 season was also the first time CHS defeated Mount Zion in a dual meet. Mike Brown capped the 1989 season with a Regional title in the 189-pound weight division.

In 1990, Mark Metzger broke the record for career wins by finishing with an 86-43 record. Fast forward to 1999, Clay French became the first CHS wrestler to qualify for the state tournament in 15 years. French did more than just qualify. French became the second CHS wrestler to ever win a sectional championship, and then finished fourth overall in the 145-pound weight division.

It took four years, but Andy McGilliard put CHS back on the map by winning a Regional title in 2003 and qualified for the state tournament in the 103-pound weight division. McGilliard came back in 2004 with a fantastic season, winning the Regional title, and the Sectional championship in the 112-pound weight division. He is the last CHS wrestler to ever win a Sectional and made the state tournament that year.

Despite numerous wrestlers winning a Regional title, CHS took a dry spell for 12 years before someone qualified for the state tournament. In 2005, CHS had three wrestlers win a Regional title. Ian McCausland won the 103-pound weight division, Justin Rardin won the 145-pound weight division, and Clint Tucker won the 160-pound weight division. Then, in 2006, CHS featured four Regional champions. This included Mick Wurtsbaugh in the 112-pound weight division, Garrett Buell in the 130-pound weight division, Chris Darimont in the 145-pound weight division, and Clayton Osborn in the 189-pound weight division. Wurtsbaugh won the 119-pound weight division in 2007; however, none of these wrestlers made it to state. Despite not making state from 2011 to 2014, Zac Lawyer finished his career as one of the all-time bests at CHS. In the 113-pound weight division, Lawyer qualified for the Sectional all four years and accumulated a 90-31 overall record.

Kevin Reddish end the streak in 2016. Reddish won the Regional in the 160-pound weight division, and then qualified for state. Quinten Carver, who was a teammate of Reddish and missed state, finished with a huge senior season. In 2017, Carver won the 152-pound weight division, and qualified for state. Carver ended up finishing fifth in the state, becoming the third and final member of all-state wrestlers in school history.

The coaches at CHS have given a lot to the program. Charleston's first coach, Renny Garshelis, eventually enjoyed a long career as a wrestling official. In 2009, Garshelis was inducted into the Illinois Chapter of the National Wrestling Hall of Fame. He was also named to the Hall of Fame for Illinois Wrestling Coaches and Officials Association, Eastern Illinois University athletics, and the Charleston High School Wrestling Hall of Fame. His career featured officiating numerous large collegiate tournaments, as well as the NCAA West Regionals for 20 years, two NAIA national tournaments, and a stop in 1979 where he officiated all three NCAA levels of Nationals in Division I, Division II, and Division III.

The practice facility that CHS uses is named after coach Lew Hankenson. The Lew Hankenson Wrestling Gym was formerly named in 2015 for all the years that Hankenson served as head coach and as a wrestling volunteer. Another coach that many CHS wrestlers will remember includes Ralph McCausland. The former All-American was a NCAA Division II champion at 142 pounds at Eastern Illinois University. McCausland eventually became the EIU wrestling coach, and then became the head CHS coach in his later days. His sons Ian and Eric both played soccer at EIU.

In 2005, Charleston adopted the Charleston High School Wrestling Hall of Fame. Today, the club features 19 members. These members that are included in the Hall of Fame are Renny Garshelis, Lew Hankenson, Bud May, Steven Hankenson, Clay French, Bob Hillis, Susan Hankenson, Dave Baumgartner, Leon Hall, Paul Stranz, Andy McGilliard, Mark Metzger, Ed McKinney, Brad Baptist, Kurt Hankenson, Chris Darimont, Clayton Osborn, Brandon Rardin, and Garrett Buell. No one has been inducted since 2015.

Regional Champions: Charlie Tripp at 185 pounds (1975), Steve Hankenson at 155 (1984), Ed McKinney at 105 (1985), Kurt Hankenson at 155 (1986), Leon Hall at HWT (1986), Bob Hillis at 138 (1987), Leon Hall at HWT (1987), Bob Hillis at 138 (1988), Mike Brown at 189 (1989), Randy Reed at 145 (1994), Corey Edington at 145 (1995), Clay French at 145 (1999), Andrew Coffey at 275 (1999), Andy McGilliard at 103 (2003), Tony Gross at 135 (2003), Andy McGilliard at 112 (2004), Garrett Buell at 103 (2004), Ian McCausland at 103 (2005), Justin Rardin at 145 (2005), Clint Tucker at 160 (2005), Mick Wurtsbaugh at 112 (2006), Garrett Buell at 130 (2006), Chris Darimont at 145 (2006), Clayton Osborn at 189 (206), Mick Wurtsbaugh at 119 (2007), Kevin Reddish at 160 (2016), Quinten Carver at 152 (2017)

Sectional Champions: Steve Hankenson at 155 (1984), Clay French at 145 (1999), Andy McGilliard at 112 (2004)

State Qualifiers: Steve Hankenson at 145 (1983), Steve Hankenson at 155 (1984), Clay French at 145 (1999), Andy McGilliard at 103 (2004), Andy McGilliard at 112 (2004), Kevin Reddish at 160 (2016), Quinten Carver at 152 (2017)

All-State Wrestlers: Steve Hankenson-4th (1984), Clay French-4th (1999), Quinten Carver-5th (2017)

Trojans Girls Basketball
(1976-2018)

Girls Basketball
(1976-2018)

John Easter became the first ever coach in Charleston High School History during the 1976-1977 season. The team won a Regional title in the school's second season by going 10-6. Kathy Tait led Charleston the first four years, becoming the school's first ever member of the 1,000-career points club. After winning the Regional in 1978, Charleston lost in the Sectional to Mattoon 67-36. Mattoon came into the game 18-1 and forced Charleston to commit 49 turnovers.

In 1979, Charleston fell to Paris in the title game, but had a memorable semi-final. Taitt's baseline jumper with four seconds left in second overtime sent CHS past Shiloh. In 1980, Taitt and Carol Pence had what newspapers were calling the area's best inside-outside game, but CHS fell to Mattoon in the Regional, ending the career of Taitt. Tait finished with 1,125 points, tallied from 1977-1980, which is currently 7th all time. Taitt also holds the record for most points in a game, when she scored 45 points against Casey-Westfield on February 18th, 1977. Tait is the only Lady Trojan to ever score more than 40 points in a game.

Janna Oetting set the mark for rebounds in a game when she pulled down 27 rebounds in a game against Robinson on January 20th, 1981. Oetting's 27 boards is still the school record for rebounds in a game. The following season, Charleston lost to Mattoon for a sixth straight year in the Regional. Amy Rogers led Charleston at center and eventually signed a basketball scholarship at Rice University after receiving offers from Baylor, Arizona State, and Wichita State. After three losing seasons, Charleston got back on the winning track in 1984 by finishing 14-8. Carol Chapman (15.5 ppg) and Jamie Ambrose (15.3 ppg) led Charleston as juniors. If Chapman did not pick up a fourth foul in the first half against Paris in the Regional title game that year, who knows what could have happened?

Chapman scored the second most points in school history (at the time) by scoring 34 points in a game versus Neoga on January 24th, 1985. The team set the then-school record for wins by going 17-8. Chapman (17.5 ppg) and Ambrose (16.8 ppg) once again led CHS in scoring. However, Mattoon got the best of CHS again in the Regional. CHS trailed by two with just 23.8 seconds left, but a missed free throw that was corralled by Mattoon sent the Lady Wave to the free throw line, where two free throws stretched the lead to four and CHS lost 51-45. The following season Charleston finished 6-14.

The 1986 season was just growing pains though as sophomores, Kari Young, Rhonda Ritz, and Heather Landrus played in nearly every game. Charleston rebounded to a 12-9 record their junior year and succeeded their senior years by going 17-8 in 1988. Despite their success, Charleston could not get past Mattoon once again. Charleston led by five at one point, but Mattoon's future points scored record holder in Barb Blume scored 28 points to lead Mattoon. In her final game, Ritz scored 14 points and pulled down 17 rebounds. Ritz is currently third all-time in career rebounds. Landrus finisher her career leading CHS in points three years straight.

Charleston's postseason woes finally changed, as CHS won three Regional titles in four years from 1990 to 1993. Jenny Osborn gave CHS some hope in 1988 after tallying 10 points, 15 rebounds, and seven blocks in the Regional loss. Combined with Kristy Haberer, a sophomore led lineup led Charleston to a 15-9 record in 1989. In 1990, Charleston took a turn.

Charleston claimed the Regional title in an intense 53-47 overtime victory over Effingham. Then, Charleston won their Sectional opener against Mount Vernon 74-53. Haberer scored 24 points, while Shelby Dycus added 11 points. This was with Osborn on the bench due to strep throat. The season came to an end with a 58-52 loss to Olney. Charleston led 28-22 at halftime, and 41-37 at the end of the third quarter, but a 21-11 fourth quarter by Olney downed CHS. Charleston ended the season 20-7, a new school record for wins.

Charleston upped the ante in 1991. Charleston set the school record for wins again by finishing 23-5 and won another Regional title. Haberer ended up passing the 1,000-career point mark. Charleston knew they could make a run after beating undefeated 19-0 Olney 75-67 at the end of the season. With a well-balanced attack of Haberer, Holly Pearcy, and Osborn, Charleston won the Regional easily. CHS won the Sectional opener over Centralia 61-50. Charleston led just 42-40 at the end of the third quarter but outscored the Orphans 19-10 in the fourth. The win made up for the bus breaking down two blocks from the high school.

This set up a cross-country Sectional title game with Mattoon. Charleston had beaten Mattoon in December during the regular season 63-51. However, the script was flipped this go around. The game featured Pearcy taking a hit to the eye which required her to get stiches. Charleston trailed 30-17 at one point, and fought back to trail 45-37, but could never get over the hump. Haberer led CHS with 18 points, finishing with 1,147 in her career.

After a 12-13 year in 1992, Charleston won another Regional title in 1993. CHS came into the postseason ranked as the six seed. However, Tammy Strong sank eight three-point shots to send CHS over Salem 65-62, while Holly Deremiah added 21 points. In the Regional title game, Kara Lowell was on a mission. Normally a role player, Lowell erupted for a 29-point, 14 rebound effort to lead CHS over Marion 62-53. Easter would conclude his coaching tenure after this year with a 219-156 record in 17 seasons.

Haberer had help though. Heather Lewis was a deep threat from outside. Lewis ranks sixth all time in three-point field goals (stat began being recorded during 1987-1988 season). Jenny Osborn and Holly Pearcy were forces inside the post. Osborn and Pearcy rank seventh and eighth all time with 480 and 475 career rebounds respectively.

Trevor Doughty became Easter's replacement for the next eight seasons. In 1994, Deremiah finished as an all-area, all-Apollo member and finished with 1,035 career points. In 1995, and 1996, CHS was led by Steffanie Davis who led the area in scoring in 1996 on her way to over 1,000 career points. After a 1997 season that featured no CHS player averaging double-digit points, and a 1998 season that featured some growing pains, Charleston nearly won a Regional title in 1999.

Charleston held a five-point lead with 5:30 left to play, but Collinsville eventually won the game 53-48. Coach Doughty was very upset at the end as Collinsville was not whistled for a foul in the final seven minutes of gameplay. The game was very physical. CHS was already without second leading scorer Nancy Rogers. Emily Garrett took an elbow to the face that nearly blinded her, and Danice Johnson rolled her ankle, and was already dealing with a knee injury. The following two seasons enjoyed winning records as Sara Fisher broke her way to the record books. Fisher's 580 points scored in 2001 was the school record for 15 years. Garrett graduated in 2000 and is still the single season steals, single season assists, and career assists record holder. Doughty stepped down after the 2001 season and finished with a 114-94 record.

Charleston saw some down years the next six years. Jody Smith and Sam Root coached CHS for three seasons a piece, but Charleston saw a 35-116 record during that stretch. There were some memorable performances during this span. Ashley Duzan had a breakout 2002 season when she pulled down 16 rebounds three times that year. Despite her sensational games, Duzan never made the top-ten in rebounds. However, Duzan had a defensive night to remember when she recorded 12 blocks versus Altamont, which is believed to be a school record. In 2006, the career of Stephanie Harper began as she led the team in scoring as a freshman.

Charleston basketball turned around when Jeff Miller came back to coach Charleston in 2007. Miller had resigned from coaching the boys in 2002 to spend more time with family, but the itch to coach had come back. From 2008-2010, Charleston won games of 20, 24, and 25 (school record-twice). Charleston had some dynamic players to help lead the way, beginning with Stephanie Harper. A four-time varsity letter winner, Harper is the only player in school history to record over 1,000 points and 1,000 rebounds in a career. Harper finished her career with 1,767 career points and 1,000 rebounds. Harper is also the career steals record holder with 268. At one point, Harper held the records for career points, single season points, career rebounds, single season rebounds, and career steals.

In 2010, the Lady Trojans had a four headed monster in Holly Wholtman, Haley Sparks, and sisters Brittany and Megan O'Dell. The team surprised many by breaking the school record for wins after Harper had graduated. Wholtman just missed 1,000 career points and is 10th on the all-time list. Wholtman was a part of some electrifying games. Wholtman scored 17 points in a quarter against Salem, which was state ranked at one point. She also scored 14 straight free throws against Decatur Eisenhower, a game that featured 30 made free throws by Charleston.

Brittany O'Dell finished that season with the 7th best single season rebound mark, which included a 16-rebound performance against Mt. Carmel. Haley Sparks finished her career second in career assists at the time (4th all-time today), and third in career steals. Sparks is currently an assistant coach for Miller's team after playing at Lake Land College and making a run to the NJCAA Division II National Tournament. Megan O'Dell lit up the scene as a sophomore when she scored eight 3-point field goals in a game against Paris. However, the real shooting performance was when the squad defeated Galesburg 89-83 in the Charleston Holiday Tournament. The 172 combined points was once ranked in the top 20 for points combined by two teams.

Unfortunately, all three seasons saw defeats to Effingham in regional play. The next four seasons were lackluster for Charleston but had some bright spots. Mary Jackson defied the odds in 2011. Jackson went 0-10 that season from three-point range but would make a Cinderella run and qualify for the IHSA Three-Point Shootout, even making nine in competition and miss making finals by one trey. Megan O'Dell finished her career in 2012 with 1,119 points, which is eighth all time. She was the single season and career record holder for three-point field goals. O'Dell capped her senior year off by finishing second in the IHSA Three Point Shootout in Class 3A. Her picture still hangs in the hallway.

In 2013, Charleston started three freshmen in Morgan Sherwood, Dakota Crowder, and Kyler Rennels, who eventually turned into key contributors. Coach Miller had a proud moment as a coach-father in 2014 when daughter, McClain Miller, led Charleston with 29 points in an 80-68 victory over Decatur Eisenhower, which included a 6-7 night from three-point range. The

12-12 team that year ended the three losing seasons and helped transform Charleston's success today. Allison Gossett signed with Black Hawk East College after the season.

The 2014-2015 season broke a 22-year Regional drought. The 23-6 team was led by Sherwood, who set a single season record for points in a season with 586. Sherwood has gone down as one of the best girls' basketball players in history. Her senior year, Sherwood broke her own record with 587 points. She is the all-time leading scorer with 1,876 points. She is also second all-time in career rebounds with 908, which included games where she pulled down 19, 18, and 17 in one game. Sherwood is also second all-time in career steals, and third all-time in career assists.

The 2015 Regional team eventually lost to state runner-up Rochester in the Sectional semi-final, a game that Charleston led at one point. Charleston lost to Rochester the following season (2016) in the Regional title game, a game that came down to a last second shot by Aislinn Parrish rimming out. Sherwood was named the Decatur Herald and Review Player of the Year that season. She is the only player in CHS history to be given that honor. Sherwood went on to play at Southern Indiana University, while Crowder played at Lake Land College.

The Lady Trojans had another good season in 2017, going 20-7, but lost to Paris in the Regional final. Parish in the top five in career assists and signed with Lake Land College. However, 2018 would be a record setting year. The Lady Trojans tied the single season mark for wins, going 25-3. The team won a Regional title and made the school's first ever Sweet 16 appearance. The team was led by freshman Shae Littleford, who finished with the 4th best single season points scored mark.

Paige Swango finished her career by making 95 three-point field goals that season, which is a school record. Swango is the career record holder with 292 made three-point field goals, which is 11th best in IHSA history. Swango signed with Rose Hulman Institute of Technology. The 25-win team's three losses all came to Effingham. Charleston would defeat Effingham once in the Charleston Holiday Tournament championship, but lost twice in conference season, and in the Sectional championship.

Miller brought success back to girls' basketball since taking over in 2007. Miller has a 195-101 mark in 11 seasons at CHS, and 311 career wins in coaching basketball altogether. He is likely to break Easter's all-time win's record soon. Miller's offense has ranked high in the state in recent years. According to Maxpreps.com, the 2016 team's 1,881 points (69.7 average per game) was ranked third in the state, and his 2018 team's 1,964 points (70.1 average per game) was ranked first in the state. Despite all his success, Miller would be the first to attribute his success to his assistant coaches, Amy Jackson and Ceci Brinker, who have helped coach since 2007, and Haley Sparks, who started in 2013. There's also his wife, Kelly, who can be seen at nearly every home game.

Girls Basketball (Taken from IHSA Website)

Season	Class	Titles	Place	Won	Lost	Tied	Coach
1976-77				6	6		John Easter
1977-78		R		10	6		John Easter
1978-79				15	6		John Easter
1979-80				13	9		John Easter

Year			W	L	Coach
1980-81			7	12	John Easter
1981-82			10	11	John Easter
1982-83			9	11	John Easter
1983-84			14	8	John Easter
1984-85			17	9	John Easter
1985-86			6	14	John Easter
1986-87			12	9	John Easter
1987-88			17	8	John Easter
1988-89			15	9	John Easter
1989-90	AA	R	20	7	John Easter
1990-91	AA	R	23	5	John Easter
1991-92			12	13	John Easter
1992-93	AA	R	13	13	John Easter
		Coach Total	**219**	**156**	**17 yr .584**
1993-94			10	14	Trevor Doughty
1994-95			17	10	Trevor Doughty
1995-96			13	13	Trevor Doughty
1996-97			13	14	Trevor Doughty
1997-98			15	10	Trevor Doughty
1998-99			17	10	Trevor Doughty
1999-00			15	11	Trevor Doughty
2000-01			14	12	Trevor Doughty
		Coach Total	**114**	**94**	**8 yr .548**
2001-02			3	20	Jody Smith
2002-03			5	20	Jody Smith
2003-04			3	22	Jody Smith
		Coach Total	**11**	**62**	**3 yr .151**
2004-05			5	20	Sam Root
2005-06			8	18	Sam Root
2006-07			11	16	Sam Root
		Coach Total	**24**	**54**	**3 yr .308**
2007-08			20	8	Jeff Miller
2008-09			24	4	Jeff Miller
2009-10			25	4	Jeff Miller
2010-11			7	19	Jeff Miller
2011-12			8	18	Jeff Miller
2012-13			8	16	Jeff Miller
2013-14			12	12	Jeff Miller
2014-15	3A	R	23	6	Jeff MIller
2015-16			23	4	Jeff Miller
2016-17			20	7	Jeff Miller

2017-18	3A	R		25	3		Jeff Miller	
		Coach Total		195	101		11 yr	.659
		School Total		563	467		42 yr	.547

Harper & Sherwood Lead Scoring

Stephanie Harper and Morgan Sherwood are the only girls in CHS history to lead the team in scoring all four years. Heather Landrus, Kristy Haberer, and Holly Deremiah led for three consecutive seasons. Sherwood's 22.6 points-per-game leads all Charleston scorers. A side note for the readers: Charleston girls basketball began in 1977; however, records of scoring leaders were not made available until 1982.

Year	Player	Points	Scoring Average
1982	Janna Oetting	278	14.6
1983	Amy Rogers	343	17.1
1984	Carol Chapman	341	15.3
1985	Carol Chapman	434	16.8
1986	Heather Landrus	287	14.3
1987	Heather Landrus	305	14.7
1988	Heather Landrus	377	15.1
1989	Kristy Haberer	245	10.2
1990	Kristy Haberer	398	14.7
1991	Kristy Haberer	463	16.5
1992	Holly Deremiah	327	13.1
1993	Holly Deremiah	333	13.3
1994	Holly Deremiah	435	15.0
1995	Steffanie Davis	454	16.8
1996	Steffanie Davis	386	17.5
1997	Kari McKechnie	220	8.9
1998	Nancy Rogers	289	11.6
1999	Danice Johnson	338	12.5
2000	Sara Fisher	447	17.1
2001	Sara Fisher	580	22.3
2002	Ashley Duzan	273	11.4
2003	Patty Bennett	263	10.5
2004	Lisa Harper	212	8.4
2005	Coartney McKinney	270	12.3
2006	Stephanie Harper	364	14.0
2007	Stephanie Harper	470	17.4
2008	Stephanie Harper	372	16.3
2009	Stephanie Harper	543	19.1
2010	Holly Wholtman	421	14.5
2011	Megan O'Dell	294	11.3
2012	Megan O'Dell	368	14.2
2013	Morgan Sherwood	328	13.7
2014	Morgan Sherwood	359	15.0
2015	Morgan Sherwood	586	20.2

2016	Morgan Sherwood	587	22.6
2017	Paige Swango	487	18.0
2018	Shae Littleford	547	19.5

All Time Scorers

Morgan Sherwood	1876	12-16
Stephanie Harper	1767	05-09
Paige Swango	1658	14-18
Sara Fisher	1184	97-01
Kriste Haberer	1147	87-91
Steffanie Davis	1132	93-96
Kathy Taitt	1125	76-80
Megan O'Dell	1,119	08-12
Holly Deremiah	1035	91-94

Single Season Points

Morgan Sherwood	587	15-16
Morgan Sherwood	586	14-15
Sara Fisher	580	00-01
Shae Littleford	547	17-18
Stephanie Harper	543	08-09
Paige Swango	487	16-17
Paige Swango	483	17-18
Stephanie Harper	470	06-07
Kriste Haberer	463	90-91
Steffanie Davis	456	94-95

Single Game Points

Kathy Taitt	45	Vs. Casey 2/18/76
Sara Fisher	35	Vs. MacArthur 1/11/01
Stephanie Harper	35	Vs. St. Anthony 1/24/07
Carol Chapman	34	Vs. Neoga 1/24/85
Sara Fisher	34	Vs. Oakland 11/25/00
Morgan Sherwood	34	Vs. Urbana 12/28/15
Megan O'Dell	33	Vs. Paris 1/17/12
Morgan Sherwood	33	Vs. Salem 1/14/16
Paige Swango	33	Vs. Salem 12/8/16
Stephanie Harper	32	Vs. Robinson 11/24/05
Sara Fisher	32	Vs. Eisenhower 2/5/01
Paige Swango	32	Vs. Altamont 11/16/17

Career 3 Point Basket (Began 87-88)
Paige Swango	292	14-18
Megan O'Dell	196	08-12
Haley Sparks	97	07-10
Rachell Augon	93	96-00
Rebekah Clark	80	92-95
Heather Lewis	72	89-92
Erin James	71	97-01
Holly Wholtman	69	06-10
Allyson O'Dell	69	13-17

Single Season 3 Point Baskets
Paige Swango	95	17-18
Megan O'Dell	75	11-12
Paige Swango	74	16-17
Paige Swango	66	15-16
Megan O'Dell	64	09-10
Megan O'Dell	58	10-11
Paige Swango	57	14-15
Erin James	55	00-01
Rachel Augon	54	99-00
Haley Sparks	47	09-10

Career Rebounds
Stephanie Harper	1000	05-09
Morgan Sherwood	907	13-16
Rhonda Ritz	549	85-88
Emily Garrett	538	97-00
Brittany O'Dell	487	06-10
Sarah Crimmins	483	94-97
Jenney Osborn	480	88-91
Holly Pearcy	475	88-91
Sara Fisher	468	98-01
Carol Chapman	454	82-85

Single Season Rebounds
Stephanie Harper	286	08-09
Morgan Sherwood	281	14-15
Stephanie Harper	249	07-08
Stephanie Harper	248	06-07
Sarah Crimmins	246	95-96
Morgan Sherwood	240	15-16
Brittany O'Dell	233	09-10
Kara Lowell	231	92-93

Rhonda Ritz	223	87-88
Stephanie Harper	217	05-06

Single Game Records

Janna Oetting	27	Vs. Robinson 1/20/81
Stephanie Harper	21	Vs. Mattoon 1/13/07
Morgan Sherwood	19	Vs. Effingham 1/11/16
Stephanie Harper	18	Vs. Eisenhower 2/9/09
Stephanie Harper	18	Vs. Mattoon 1/18/08
Morgan Sherwood	18	Vs. Salem 1/15/15
Morgan Sherwood	17	Vs. Taylorville 12/14/15
Rhonda Ritz	17	Vs. Mattoon 2/11/88
Stephanie Harper	16	Vs. Mahomet 1/15/08
Ashley Duzan	16	Vs. Eisenhower 1/4/02
Ashley Duzan	16	Vs. Cumberland 11/18/02
Ashley Duzan	16	Vs. Casey 11/30/02
Brittany O'Dell	16	Vs. Mt. Carmel 11/29/08

Career Assists

Emily Garrett	301	97-00
Dakota Crowder	288	13-16
Morgan Sherwood	282	13-16
Haley Sparks	255	07-10
Aislinn Parish	248	13-17
Paige Swango	230	14-18
Holly Wholtman	224	06-10
Megan O'Dell	204	08-12
Hope Griffin	200	14-18
Claire Dau	191	04-08

Single Season Assists

Emily Garrett	131	98-99
Haley Sparks	117	09-10
Haley Sparks	110	08-09
Aislinn Parish	107	16-17
Emily Garrett	107	99-00
Dakota Crowder	107	14-15
Shae Littleford	106	17-18
Morgan Sherwood	99	14-15
Claire Dau	97	06-07
Jessie Titus	95	00-01

Career Steals (Record Began 93-94)

Stephanie Harper	268	05-09
Morgan Sherwood	248	13-16
Emily Garrett	247	97-00
Dakota Crowder	197	13-16
Hope Griffin	188	14-18
Haley Sparks	180	07-10
Aislinn Parish	144	13-17
Paige Swango	144	14-18
Rachel McCarthur	138	96-99
Jessie Titus	138	97-01

Single Season Steals

Emily Garrett	110	98-99
Stephanie Harper	87	08-09
Haley Sparks	86	08-09
Holly Deremiah	85	93-94
Emily Garrett	81	99-00
Hope Griffin	79	16-17
Stephanie Harper	77	06-07
Hope Griffin	77	17-18
Rebekah Clark	76	93-94
Haley Sparks	74	09-10

Team Records

Lowest Points Scored: 17	Vs. T-Town	1/17/85
Most Points Scored: 99	Vs. Casey	1978
Lowest Points Scored by an Opponent: 11	Vs. Robinson	11/23/87
Most Points Scored by an Opponent: 96	Vs. Paris	1/27/96

Charleston Girls' Basketball Records

Most Wins: 25, 2010 and 2018
Regional Titles: 1978, 1990, 1991, 1993, 2015, 2018
Most Coaching Wins: 219, John Easter (1977-1993), 195, Jeff Miller (2007-2018)

Charleston Holiday Tournament is a Christmas Tradition

Budget cuts could not stop the girls Charleston Holiday Tournament from disbanding. The Charleston Booster Club continues to support the holiday tournament that spans a course of three days with games at Baker Gym. Up until 2010, games used to be played at Baker Gym and Lantz Arena at Eastern Illinois University. Today, teams play up to four to five games and features some of the top competition in Class 3A and Class 4A.

The first Charleston Holiday Tournament took place in 1993 where Teutopolis won.

Teutopolis left the holiday tournament after 2009 tourney. Teutopolis has won the tournament seven times, which tops all other teams. Teutopolis was led by Dennis Koester as their coach. Koester-led teams were always a scare. Koester coached Teutopolis from 1982 to 2006, amassing 635 career wins to go along with five state championships, four state runner-up finishes, and a third-place finish to go along with 13 total trips to state.

The tournament has brought some iconic coaches to Charleston. Before leaving the tournament in 2013, Galesburg used to bring their unique sub-five style and three-point shooting. Coach Evan Massey, who has a career 897-337 record over a span from 1975-2018 saw success, winning the tournament two times. Another Hall of Fame coach in Carey McVickers coached Taylorville's girls' teams for many years before taking over the boys' program.

Charleston and Galesburg played in one of the highest scoring affairs in IHSA history. To keep their undefeated season alive, Charleston outplayed Galesburg 89-93 to make the championship game. Despite turning the ball over 34 times, CHS was paced by nearly four 20-point scorers. Holly Wholtman led CHS with 24 points, Haley Sparks added 20 points, while Brittany O'Dell added 19 points, and April Lunt with 18 points. Charleston eventually lost to Teutopolis in the title game, but the combined 172 points is just outside the top 20 in highest scoring games in IHSA history.

Three Charleston players have earned MVP status. Those include Stephanie Harper in 2008, Morgan Sherwood in 2014 and 2015, and Paige Swango in 2017. Charleston and Effingham have played in the tournament championship game for six straight seasons, while Effingham has made the title game every year since 2012. Charleston first won the holiday tournament in 2015 despite many runner-up finishes, and then again in 2017.

Many fans might remember many of these players and teams, but below is a compilation of all tournament winners with the tournament MVP.

Year	Winner	MVP (Same as Winner unless denoted otherwise)
1993	Teutopolis	Carrie Weber
1994	Teutopolis	Gine Bloemer
1995	Teutopolis	Amy Niebrugge
1996	Teutopolis	Maria Niebrugge
1997	Mount Zion	Dottie Bradley
1998	Altamont	Jodi Heiden
1999	Altamont	Jodi Heiden
2000	Nokomis	VaNicia Waterman
2001	Teutopolis	Alicia Ordner
2002	Effingham	Julianne McMillen (Pana)
2003	Pana	Brittany Johnson (Olney)
2004	Paris	Emily Maggert
2005	Teutopolis	Katrina Swingler
2006	Edwardsville	Emily Maggert (Paris)
2007	Edwardsville	Anya Covington
2008	Edwardsville	Stephania Harper (CHS)
2009	Teutopolis	Jessica Wendt
2010	Galesburg	Jessica Howard

2011	Galesburg	Jessica Lieber
2012	Effingham	Josie Zerrusen
2013	Effingham	Caitlin Kaufman
2014	Effingham	Morgan Sherwood (CHS)
2015	Charleston	Morgan Sherwood
2016	Effingham	Carsyn Fearday
2017	Charleston	Paige Swango

Top Players

In the long history of the tournament, I have read and watched some of the finest girls' basketball players in the state. To this day, I still return to the tournament as my vacation. After researching and watching, I have concluded that these are the top players that have went through the Charleston Holiday Tournament.

10. Megan O'Dell (Charleston) & Carsyn Fearday (Effingham): O'Dell led a bad 8-18 team to the championship game her senior year and finished as the all-time three-point record holder when she graduated. Fearday is one of the most clutch players Effingham has displayed. Fearday helped lead Effingham to their first Elite Eight in 2018.

9. Jessica Lieber (Galesburg): Potentially one of the toughest basketball players to ever play at Baker Gym. Lieber left a game with a bloody nose to come back to make seven three-point field goals. Lieber was diagnosed with diverticulitis and gluten sensitivity after graduating, but still went on to play college basketball at Carl Sandberg College.

8 .Paige Swango (Charleston): The all-time leader in three-point field goals at CHS helped knock off Effingham in a battle of future top ten state ranked teams. Swango signed with Rose Hulman in Terre Haute, Indiana.

7. Jenny McMillian (Pana): Helped Pana accomplish the impossible in 2003. The unranked Pana team knocked off second see Teutopolis, third seed Salem in double overtime, and ran past one seed Paris 65-48 to win the title game.

6. Anya Covington (Edwardsville): Helped lead Edwardsville to back-to-back tournament championships in 2006 and 2007. Covington finished as the school's all-time rebounder, and played four years at the University of Wisconsin, finishing her senior year as an honorable-all Big Ten selection in 2012.

5. Emily Maggert (Paris): Led Paris to a title in 2004 and played so well in a year that Edwardsville won to be named MVP again in 2006. Maggert, a Ball State recruit, led the 29-3 Paris team that qualified for state.

4. Stephanie Harper & Morgan Sherwood (Charleston): It is impossible to say one is better than the other. Harper is one of a handful of players to ever finish her career with at least 1,000 career points and 1,000 career rebounds. Sherwood is one of three players to be named MVP twice and she is the school's all-time point holder.

3. Jodi Heiden (Altamont): Leading Altamont to back-to-back championships in 1998 and 1999, Heiden at one point was averaging 28.0 points and 13.8 rebounds a game. The six-foot center eventually played at Southern Illinois University-Carbondale.

2. Amy Niebrugge (Teutopolis): The 1995 MVP had a stellar career at McKendree University where she became the school's leader in points (2,245), rebounds (1,107), and field goals (995). She was instrumental in leading the team to NAIA Division I National Championship appearances in 1998 and 1999.

1. Brittany Johnson (Olney): She eventually became the winner of Ms. Illinois Basketball 2007 and played at Ohio State University. Johnson was the career record holder for points in Illinois until that record was broken in 2014. She averaged 36.4 points per game her senior year and was the holiday tournament MVP as a freshman.

GIRLS BASKETBALL HEADLINERS

First Sweet 16 Appearance Accomplished in 2017-2018

Three seniors were had sour tastes in their mouth. Paige Swango, Hope Griffin, and Kaitlyn Coffey were coming off two straight seasons with 20-plus wins and a loss in the Regional championship game. The team had a strong freshman class entering that was coming off a Class 3A state championship as eighth graders, led by future all-state selection Shae Littleford. The senior group had finished fourth in the state as eighth graders in 2014.

Charleston was untested to start the year, winning their first seven games by an average of 36.8 points per game. This set up an undefeated showdown between two state-ranked teams in Effingham and Charleston. Charleston trailed 23-20 at halftime, but couldn't get over the hump, losing 63-57. Charleston had 17 turnovers for the game. "We pride ourselves on taking care of the basketball," coach Jeff Miller told JG-TC reporter Justin Rust after the game. "We have to do a better job moving forward. Bernie Jackson had a heck of a game. Without her, it would have been an uphill battle."

After blowing out Mt. Zion, Charleston had another test against state ranked Lincoln, the new addition to the Apollo. Charleston gutted out a 63-61 victory at home over Lincoln, with a lot of credit going to Swango's 29 points. Two more wins over Mattoon and Marshall, and Charleston was gearing up for the Charleston Holiday Tournament.

Charleston positioned themselves in the championship game to gain a rematch with Effingham after defeating Pekin, Urbana, Rantoul, and Paris in two days. Charleston came out hot to start the game, scoring the first nine points, and leading 17-7 after the first quarter. Charleston came back down to Earth in the second quarter, but still led 34-21 at halftime. Effingham brought it back to 46-38, but Charleston held off the Flaming Hearts to win 67-57.

Charleston led by just six points with a minute left to play, and Swango launched a 3-point shot in transition. Miller could be heard screaming, "No, no, no!" As the ball swished in to give Charleston a nine-point advantage, Miller high fived the entire first row (fans included) saying, "Great shot, great shot!" The holiday tournament championship was the second in the school's history. Swango was named the tournament MVP and Littleford was name all-tournament team.

The Lady Trojans won the month of January by an average of 26.5 points. With Effingham returning the first week of February, Charleston trailed one game. A win would give Charleston a share of the Apollo. With six seconds remaining and the score tied at 57-57, Hope Griffin's layup try rolled off. Jackson recovered the rebound, but her shot was short. Coffey grabbed the rebound, but her shot was off, meaning the game went to overtime. Effingham defeated CHS in the extra period to win 71-61.

"That's the Apollo Conference," Miller told Rust. "For whatever reason, that was the story of the night, missing point-blank shots." Swango broke the school record for single season 3-point shots, but Miller quickly pointed out "she would rather have the win than the accolade."

After blowing out Decatur Eisenhower by 50 points to win on Senior Night, Charleston was ready for the postseason. Charleston cruised to a 58-38 win over Mt. Zion in the opening round to make it four straights of making the championship round. The team thought they were going to have a test, playing Mahomet-Seymour a third time this season, but Charleston put the beatdown on M-S with a 72-35 victory.

"I am really proud of the girls," Miller told Rust. "How about that defense? We forced 31 turnovers. That was tremendous team effort." Swango led CHS with 18 points, while Littleford added 17 points, but it was reserve, Elizabeth Buescher, who stepped up off the bench and added 15 points.

The win setup a Sectional semi-final match between Charleston and Springfield Lanphier. Lanphier upset their way to a Regional title, as the team was the seven seed in their regional. However, Lanphier was playing as no seven seed, as Charleston only led 40-38 at halftime. Midway through the third, the score read 49-46, but CHS used a 9-0 run to pull away going into the fourth. Littleford led Charleston by hitting nine of 11 free throws in route to her career high 30 points in the 71-59 win. The win gave Charleston their first appearance in the Sweet 16.

"We battled. We are fast, but Lanphier sped us up to the point that we were out of control," Miller told Rust. "I am so proud of the girls. We thought we could be pretty good, but I never dreamed we would win 25 games and a Sectional game."

Of course, that meant Charleston had to play nemesis Effingham in the Sectional Championship, and the fourth time this season. Effingham would give CHS their third loss of the season, amounting for all of Charleston's losses by defeating the Lady Trojans 63-54. Swango and Littleford were held to a combined nine points with under four minutes to play in the third quarter. "Give Effingham all the credit in the world," said Miller to Rust. "They are a solid basketball team. It stinks we had to lose to them three times, but we had great effort, but we just didn't have it."

Miller was named the co-Apollo Coach of the Year and went on to coach the IBCA All-Star game. The 25 wins tied the school record for wins. Littleford was named as an all-state selection, while Swango was named as a special mention.

Trojans Girls Cross Country
1979-2018

Trojans Girls Cross Country
1979-2018

Written by Erik Hall and Kyle Daubs

The fall of 1979 saw the addition of the sport of women's cross country at Charleston High School. Men's cross country had been a sport continuously at CHS since 1967 and offered by the IHSA since 1946. Women's cross country has brought success and notoriety to Charleston and its athletes. The first year of the sport at CHS coincided with the first year the Illinois High School Association offered women's cross country.

Until 1995, the CHS men's and women's cross country teams shared the same head coach. During the first year of women's cross country at CHS, future Eastern Illinois University head cross country coach John McInerney served as Charleston's head cross country coach.

The 1979 CHS women's cross country team was a four-member team. The four inaugural athletes were seniors Patty Carmichael and Robin White; junior Katie McFarland; and freshman Karla Weidner. With only the four team members, and a minimum of five runners needed for a team competition, the Lady Trojans did not compete in their own meets.

Instead, the ladies ran with the men's team on three-mile courses – until the final meet of the season. The Tolono Women's District Meet provided the Lady Trojans with their own meet for the first time. Patty Carmichael led CHS with 15th place finish. Carmichael missed a state berth that went to the top 10 runners.

After 1979, McInerney left CHS's young women's cross country program to new coach Scott Parke. Though most area teams did not have enough runners to have team competitions, the Apollo conference schools possessed necessary numbers. CHS won the first women's Apollo cross country title in 1980. CHS scored 32 points, and Paris finished a distant second with 54 points. (Cross country team competitions are won by the team with the lowest score.)

Mike Viano became men's and women's cross country coach at CHS for the 1981 season. On September 22, 1981, the Lady Trojans won their first cross country dual meet by beating Newton at Newton. Carol Chapman qualified for state that season as a freshman. In 1982, Duncan McHugh stepped in as coach and Charleston qualified for their first trip to state, while winning a Regional title in 1983.

In 1984, Gene Nance led a stretch of dominance for the Lady Trojans. With Nance at the helm, Charleston won two Regional titles and qualified for state five times during his tenure from 1984 to 1994. His 58-2 record in dual meets is the most ever by a CHS coach, and his 58 career dual meet wins is tied for 16th most in IHSA history.

Going into the 1988 season, the CHS women's cross country team possessed a 16-0 all-time dual meet record. Yet in the first meet of 1988, a triangular with Decatur Eisenhower and Rantoul, Eisenhower won the triangular meet and CHS suffered the first dual meet loss for women's cross country. Later in 1988, CHS lost to Paris at EIU's course. After the loss to Paris on September 6, 1988, the Lady Trojans did not lose a dual meet again until 1996.

In 1989, Nance increased the number of scheduled meets and added Steve Craig as an assistant coach for both the men's and women's teams. These changes helped the Lady Trojans compile an 8-0 dual record (tied for 12th most dual victories in a single season in IHSA women's cross country history). In 1991, the team went 10-0 which is tied for 10th most dual meets in a season for IHSA women's cross country history.

The talented 1991 freshman class never reached their full potential. All four of the runners did not remain healthy and injury free for an entire season. Kendra Pickens suffered a hip injury for the first part of 1991. In 1992, Colleen Vandever missed the season's second half due to injury. Then, Shalimar Lewis's injuries caused her to miss the entire 1993 season and virtually all of the 1994 season. After collapsing at the Bloomington Invitational, Kendra Pickens missed five meets during the middle of the 1993 season and did not return to previous form until the 1994 Apollo Conference meet. With all four runners healthy all four years, the women's cross country team could have achieved unprecedented success for any CHS team.

With the 1993 season came the transition of Steve Craig from assistant cross country coach to becoming head women's tennis coach. Barb Sharp joined Nance's staff as the women's assistant coach and Mark Dombrowski became the men's assistant coach. Sharp would later replace Craig again in 2003 when she became CHS women's cross country head coach under her married name, Barb Heitka.

Despite having the largest team in CHS history to that point with 13 runners, the team struggled in 1993 at major meets without Shalimar Lewis and frequently without Kendra Pickens. The women's cross country team went 7-0 in dual meets and the only major meet won by the Lady Trojans came at the St. Anthony Invitational. By just one point, CHS missed winning the Apollo team title. Paris claimed the team victory with 39 points, but Colleen Vandever did win the Apollo individual title. However, the team qualified for state in 1994, which would be Nance's last season.

In 1995, following Nance's coaching retirement, former cross country assistant Steve Craig became the first coach to only coach women's cross country at CHS. Todd Vilardo assumed Nance's position as the men's cross country coach. Craig enjoyed a successful first year as his team posted a 6-0 record in dual meets and won a second consecutive Apollo team title. Entering the 1996 season, expectations were high. CHS had won 51 consecutive dual meets, two consecutive Apollo Team Titles and the women's team had gone to five consecutive sectional meets. The Effingham Flaming Hearts put out two of the three streaks. CHS possessed a 7-0 record entering the season's final dual meet where Effingham defeated CHS 26-31 on October 7, 1996. The 58 consecutive dual meet wins stands as the third longest streak ever in IHSA women's cross country.

Effingham also won the 1996 Apollo team title with 28 points and CHS finished second with 33 points. The highlight of the 1997 Apollo Meet for CHS came when seniors Carmen Owens and Emily Vandever earned all-Apollo honors for the fourth consecutive year. For the 1998 season, the IHSA lengthened the distance for women's cross country races from 2 miles to 2.5 miles.

The women's cross country team did not compete in any dual meets in 1998. The team tried to develop experience entirely from running at invitationals. This strategy proved unsuccessful for the Lady Trojans, who finished third in the Apollo Conference meet. CHS had not finished lower than second place in the Apollo Conference meet since they finished third in 1986.

In 2002, the IHSA chanced the girl's race from 2.5 miles to 3.0 miles, a move towards equality. Charleston had some lackluster years from 2002 to 2010, which included five different coaches in eight years. Derrick Landrus, who coached the boys since 1999, took over at the girls coach also in 2010.

The program featured some growing pains in the first four years, going 5-12 in dual meets. However there were some good moments. Sarah Gisondi reached all-Apollo as a freshman and sophomore. Gisondi decided to forgo her junior and senior campaigns, while Hayley Plummer reached all-conference as a junior in 2012.

In 2013, the team began to turn a corner, making the sectional meet for the first time in many years. Grace Oetting was convinced to give up volleyball her junior season to run cross country. It was a good decision on her part as her senior year she led the team to qualify for state in 2014, the first girls' team to qualify for state in 20 years. Oetting became the third ever Lady Trojan to reach all-state status, finishing ninth.

Since then, Landrus stepped down in 2016, finishing his seven year coaching career with a 13-12 dual meet record. The first ever girl's coach in McInerney came back in 2017 to lead the team after serving as a volunteer assistant for many years.

Girls Cross Country (Taken from IHSA Website)

Season	Class	Titles	Place	Won	Lost	Tied	Coach
1979-80				0	0		John McInerny
			Coach Total	0	0		1 yr
1980-81				0	0		Scott Parke
			Coach Total	0	0		1 yr
1981-82				2	0		Mike Viano
			Coach Total	2	0		1 yr 1.000
1982-83		Q		3	0		Duncan McHugh
1983-84		RQ		1	0		Duncan McHugh
			Coach Total	4	0		2 yr 1.000
1984-85		RQ		3	0		Gene Nance
1985-86		RQ		3	0		Gene Nance
1986-87				1	0		Gene Nance
1987-88				3	0		Gene Nance
1988-89				3	2		Gene Nance
1989-90				8	0		Gene Nance
1990-91				5	0		Gene Nance
1991-92	AA	Q		10	0		Gene Nance
1992-93	AA	Q		8	0		Gene Nance
1993-94				7	0		Gene Nance
1994-95	AA	Q		7	0		Gene Nance
			Coach Total	58	2		11 yr .967
1995-96				6	0		Steve Craig
1996-97				7	1		Steve Craig
1997-98				7	1		Steve Craig
1998-99				0	0		Steve Craig
1999-00				1	2		Steve Craig
2000-01				2	2		Steve Craig
2001-02				2	1	1	Steve Craig
			Coach Total	25	7	1	7 yr .773
2002-03				1	3		Barb Heitka
			Coach Total	1	3		1 yr .250
2003-04				4	0		Bob Edwards
			Coach Total	4	0		1 yr 1.000
2004-05							Rob Ulm
2005-06							Rob Ulm

Year							Coach
2006-07							Rob Ulm
2007-08					2	2	Brad Oakley
2008-09					0	4	Brad Oakley
Coach Total					2	6	2 yr .250
2009-10					0	4	Chad Miller
Coach Total					0	4	1 yr .000
2010-11					1	3	Derrick Landrus
2011-12					1	3	Derrick Landrus
2012-13					0	3	Derrick Landrus
2013-14					3	3	Derrick Landrus
2014-15	2A	Q			6	0	Derrick Landrus
2015-16					1	0	Derrick Landrus
2016-17					1	0	Derrick Landrus
Coach Total					13	12	7 yr .520
2017-18					5	0	John McInerney
Coach Total					5	0	1 yr 1.000
School Total					114	34	1	36 yr .765

Top Five Individual Times (3.00 Mile Course)

***Keep in mind that girls ran a two-mile course from 1979 to 1997. Then, from 1998 to 2001, the girls ran a 2.5-mile course. Girls did not start running three miles in cross country until the 2002 season. Molly Jackson ran a 10:54 two mile in 1985, while Carol Chapman ran an 11:20 in 1982.

   a. Grace Oetting-17:46 (2014)
   b. Megan Garrett 18:40 (2017)
   c. Hope Griffin 18:58 (2014)
   d. Sheridan Noll 19:14 (2014)
   e. Elizabeth Buescher 19:19 (2016)

Charleston Cross Country Records

Most Dual Meet Wins in a Season: 10-0, 1991
Apollo Conference Titles: 1980, 1981, 1983, 1984, 1989, 1990, 1991, 1992, 1994, 1995, 1999, 2014
Regional Titles: 1983, 1984, 1985
Sectional Titles: None
State Appearances: 1982, 1983, 1991, 1992, 1994, 2014
All-State Runners: Carol Chapman-10th Place (1983), Molly Jackson-5th Place (1985), Grace Oetting-10th Place (2014)
Most Coaching Dual Meet Wins: 58, Gene Nance (1984-1994)

Carol Chapman Leads CHS in early 80s

Written by Erik Hall

The fourth year of women's cross country at CHS brought the sport's fourth coach, Duncan McHugh. McHugh guided CHS to a 3-0 dual record his first season. During the 1982 season, the Apollo Conference did not hold a women's cross-country conference meet because there were too few Apollo schools with five-member teams. The Springfield Sectional meet would produce history for the Lady Trojan cross country program. The CHS women's cross-country team finished fourth and earned the last spot that advanced to Peoria for the state cross country meet from the Springfield Sectional. The week after the sectional meet, sophomore Carol Chapman earned all-state honors at Peoria's Detweiler Park. Chapman finished in 10th place while running a time of 11 minutes and 54 seconds on the 2.1-mile course. This would be Chapman's fastest cross-country time at Charleston.

Chapman and CHS's other runners helped Charleston earn a 17th-place team finish at the state meet. This marked the best any CHS women's team sport finished in a state competition. The six runners who represented the scarlet and gold of Charleston were Chapman, Kate Jackson, Becky Woodall, Molly Jackson, Robin Harris and Karla Weidner.

The 1983 season returned the top five runners from the 1982 state-qualifying team. Their experience showed when CHS won its only dual meet of the season, a meet against Champaign Central. Moreover, the Lady Trojans won their third Apollo Conference team title in the third season the meet was held. The Lady Trojans also won the Decatur MacArthur Invitational and Centralia Regional meet. By winning the Centralia Regional, the Lady Trojans advanced to the sectional meet. The results from the Springfield Sectional meet showed Charleston in second with 95 points behind East Saint Louis with 81 points.

CHS's second consecutive state meet appearance included a second consecutive 17th-place team finish. The CHS runners were Libby Black, Carol Chapman, Robin Harris, Kate Jackson, Molly Jackson, Becky Woodall and Mara Checkley. Through windy and wet weather, Chapman led the Lady Trojans on a muddy course by finishing 42nd in 12:23.

Gene Nance Leads Ten Years of Lady Trojan Success

Written by Erik Hall

Gene Nance's tenure got a shaky start as senior Carol Chapman opened the season unable to compete because of an injury. Junior Molly Jackson stepped up to replace the injured veteran. In 1984, Jackson won the individual titles at the Paris Invitational, Robinson Invitational, Apollo Conference meet and Mount Vernon Regional meet. Also, during the 1984 season, Jackson led CHS to team titles at the Paris Invitational, Bloomington Invitational, Apollo Conference meet and Mount Vernon Regional meet.

By the Springfield Sectional meet, the Lady Trojans had been reduced to five runners after starting the season with eight runners. These five runners managed a fourth-place finish and the cross-country program's third consecutive state meet appearance at Peoria's Detweiler Park.

The five runners representing Charleston were seniors Carol Chapman (who had returned late in the season) and Becky Woodall, and juniors Robin Harris, Molly Jackson, and Valerie Marble. Marble was the only CHS runner without experience running at the state meet. The other four runners had run with the CHS team at both the 1982 and 1983 state cross country meets. This experienced group finished 20th in the state and Chapman led the team by finishing 32nd in 12:15. (Women's cross country still used a single class system in 1984.)

For Molly Jackson as well as the Lady Trojans, 1985 brought additional success. The Charleston team ranked 21st in the state at mid-season according to the running publication *Timely Times*. The team won the Bloomington Invitational, a fifth consecutive Apollo team title, their third consecutive regional title and a fourth consecutive team trip to the state meet. After finishing third at the Springfield Sectional meet, the Lady Trojans placed 24th of the 25 teams competing in Peoria. CHS took only six runners to Peoria led by seniors Robin Harris, Molly Jackson, Sheila Lenihan and Valerie Marble along with junior Libby Montgomery and freshman Amy Jackson, younger sister of Molly Jackson.

Senior Molly Jackson won every meet in 1985 until the state meet where she finished fifth. Jackson's fifth place finish at the cross-country state meet is the best finish by a CHS cross country runner--male or female. Other successes for Molly in 1985 included repeating as Apollo individual champion, repeating as the individual regional champion and winning an individual sectional title.

Possibly the most talented and definitely the most successful class of freshmen began running for Nance in 1991. This talented freshman class included Tara Horseman, Shalimar Lewis, Kendra Pickens and Colleen Vandever. In 1991, the Lady Trojans won every meet they entered during the regular season. Ten dual victories (tied for 10th most in IHSA women's cross-country history) and a third consecutive Apollo team title highlighted the undefeated regular season. The Lady Trojans returned home with team titles from the Danville, Olney, Bloomington, Robinson and St. Anthony Invitationals.

At the 1991 Rantoul Regional, Decatur MacArthur won, Champaign Centennial placed second and CHS took third. All three teams earned one of five sectional berths. The next weekend at the Springfield Sectional meet, Decatur MacArthur won, Champaign Centennial placed second and CHS took fourth. East Saint Louis Lincoln finished third.

By finishing among the top five teams at the 1991 Springfield Sectional, the Lady Trojans earned their first trip to the state cross country meet since 1985. CHS's seven runners at Peoria were juniors Jessica Niles and Tori Pschirrer; sophomore Beth Frazier; and freshmen Tara Horseman, Shalimar Lewis, Kendra Pickens and Colleen Vandever. Without the experience or support of seniors, freshman Kendra Pickens ran the team's fastest time of 13:26 on the muddy and snow-covered Detweiller Park course. The team finished 22nd in Class AA.

For the 1992 season, the goal was to reproduce a trip to the state meet. While winning all eight dual meets, CHS won a fourth consecutive Apollo team title and the Lady Trojans finished third in the Rantoul Regional behind winner Decatur MacArthur and runner-up Champaign Centennial. CHS could not repeat the fourth-place finish at the Springfield Sectional that they earned in 1991, but the Lady Trojans still qualified for a second consecutive state berth by finishing fifth.

The seven runners for CHS at the 1992 state meet were seniors Tori Pschirrer and Anne Swartzbaugh; sophomores Tara Horseman, Shalimar Lewis and Kendra Pickens; and freshmen Missy Eich and Molly Ware. CHS finished 19th at Detweiller Park and Kendra Pickens led the Lady Trojans as she finished 84th in 13:09.

The size of the 1994 women's cross-country team reached 15 runners in what would be Gene Nance's 11th and final year as men's and women's cross-country coach at CHS. The 1994 team went 7-0 in dual meets. The Apollo individual title had an exciting storyline as the 1991 individual champion Bessie Fulk of Paris, 1992 individual champion Kendra Pickens of CHS and 1993 individual champion Colleen Vandever of CHS all ran in 1994's Apollo Meet. CHS reclaimed the Apollo Team Title with 21 points and Paris stood a distant second with 61 points. Kendra Pickens showed she had returned to form as she crossed the finish line first to claim the individual Apollo title for a second time.

At the Mattoon Invitational, which had added a women's race in 1993, CHS won the women's team title of the 29th annual event. Then at the regional meet, CHS finished second just three points behind winner Decatur MacArthur, but more importantly, the CHS ladies advanced to the Decatur Eisenhower Sectional.

The Lady Trojans finished second with 119 at the Eisenhower Sectional. East St. Louis Lincoln won with 89 points and Decatur MacArthur finished third with 127 points. All three earned state meet berths that went to the top five teams and the top seven individuals not on advancing teams. The seven CHS runners who ran at Peoria's Detweiler Park were seniors Tara Horseman, Kendra Pickens, Colleen Vandever and Lesley Wells; sophomore Nicole Luft; and freshmen Carmen Owens and Emily Vandever. The CHS women placed 18th at state led by Kendra Pickens in 97th place with a time of 13:16 for the two-mile course.

Grace Oetting's Runs All-State; Team Qualifies in 2014

In 2013, Oetting made the switch from volleyball to cross country. After a year of running, which included running all-Apollo and qualifying for the state track meet in the 3200 as a junior, Oetting was back to make her senior splash. Another senior in Sheridan Noll was returning for a fourth year, but the rest of the team had question marks as the rest of the top six were either freshman or new to the sport. Sophomores Megan Woodruff and Sabrina Ryan were new faces, while freshman twins Hope and Julia Griffin had no experience.

As the season began, Oetting broke the school record in the early weeks. Oetting ran a 17:58 at the Peoria First to the Finish Invitational. However, Oetting sustained an injury the following week, but the team showed progression without her. Charleston won the 17-team Mattoon Invitational without Oetting. Hope Griffin placed fifth overall with a time of 19:53. Recognizing there might be some talent, the team placed their sights on the Apollo. Charleston hadn't won the Apollo Conference in 15 years.

With Oetting back, Charleston ruled the conference meeting, beating out second place Mt. Zion 38-62. Three CHS runners placed all-conference, which included Oetting winning the individual title. Griffin and Noll each made the team by placing third and fifth respectively, while sister Julia Griffin just missed all-conference by placing 11th.

Oetting and Hope Griffin led Charleston to a second-place finish at the Regional. The team did not have their best race. Oetting ran in the mid 19s, while Griffin was in the mid-20s. The back half of the team featured two girls in the 22-minute range, while one girl was in the high 24-minute range.

This setup a great story when Charleston slashed their times at the sectional meet. The day that has been dubbed "the greatest day in Charleston cross country history" occurred when both boys and girl's teams qualified for the state meet.

Oetting rebounded with a time of 18:05 to finish as the sectional runner-up. Hope Griffin ran a 19:37 (24th place) and Noll broke the 20-minute mark with a time of 19:56 (37th place). The three runners had led Charleston all year, but it was the back part of the team that stepped up when they needed them. Julia Griffin and Megan Woodruff ran two minutes faster than their Regional team, and each ran a personal best. Julia ran a 20:07 (43rd place), while Woodruff ran a 20:21 (57th place). Despite not scoring, No. 6 runner Sabrina Ryan shed nearly three minutes off her regional time.

"Grace, Hope, and Sheridan all ran well, but it was Julia and Megan who ran a personal best, Julia by 39 seconds, and Megan by 46 seconds," coach Derrick Landrus told Journal Gazette-Times Courier sports editor Brian Nielsen. "We told them we needed one or two people to do that. The whole team just ran so hard at the end. They were really gutting it out."

Oetting finished her high school career in style by becoming the third ever CHS runner to capture all-state honors. Oetting went out fast, running a 5:30 first mile. The senior gutted out the final two miles to break her own school record with a time of 17:46, and a 10th place finish.

"The first mile happened to be five seconds faster than my mile time in track last year, so it was kind of embarrassing," Oetting told Nielsen. "I thought I would go out and lead the pack, and if I died, I died."

CHS placed 19th as a team. Hope Griffin finished a fantastic freshman season by running an 18:58 (91st place), a feat that Oetting never accomplished her junior season. The rest of the team ran well, starting with Noll at 19:14 (109th), Julia Griffin at 20:05 (167th), Woodruff at 20:44 (197th), and Ryan at 21:32 (208th). Oetting went on to run at the Division I school, University of Lipscomb, after graduating.

Trojans Girls Golf
(1985-2018)

Trojans Girls Golf
(1985-2018)

Karen Petersen became the first ever Lady Trojan to qualify for the state golf tournament in 1985. It was only fitting given that her older brother won the state championship on the boy's side in 1978. Petersen played a year at the University of Southern Illinois University-Carbondale.

Charleston won their first ever Regional title in 1994. After that, Charleston girl's golf was put on the map thanks to Laura Myerscough, who finished her career with three all-state finishes. In 1995, Myerscough finished 15th overall as a sophomore. She followed that season with a 2nd place state runner-up finish in 1996, shooting six strokes off the state champion. Myerscough capped her senior season in 1997 by finishing 4th overall. Myerscough went on to play at the University of Arizona as she was a part of the 2000 National Championship team. Myerscough (now Ianello) enjoyed some time on the LPGA tour, but then came back to her alma mater in 2011 to coach, leading the team to a National Championship in 2018.

Three years later, Charleston won their second Regional title. It was a great year for Adkins as the boy's team qualified for state that season. CHS was led by Kelsey Hinds, who shot an 89 to finish third overall at the Charleston Country Club. Chelsie Hill added a 98, Laura Becker a 107, Sara Wagoner a 114, Tosha Wrye a 115, and Andrea James a 116. Charleston missed out on state in the Sectional, but Wrye and Baker returned two years later as seniors to lead Charleston to another Regional title.

Adkins stepped down as the girl's coach but remained on as the boys coach after 2001. Coach Todd Keating had been assistant for Adkins for five years and stepped up. Wrye led CHS with an 86, while Baker shot a 91 to lead CHS to their third Regional title. The rest of the team was Katie Alexander (104), Caitlin Robinson (110), Jill Clark (113), and Nikki Schenck (119). Keating stepped down after the season.

Coach Deb Landsaw took over and has led the Lady Trojans the last 15 years. After going 14 years with no representation in the state golf tournament, Maddy Burgett broke the drought in 2011 by qualifying as a junior. Her two-day score of 181 at the state tournament had her finish tied for 47th overall. Burgett returned in 2012 as senior. She shot a 173 which had her in a tie for 37th overall. Burgett went on to play at Rend Lake College. After Burgett's senior season, CHS has put on one of the best five year runs out of any CHS sports program.

Lady Trojans Make First Trip to State in 2013

Coach Landsaw thought that CHS could be competitive despite having short numbers. The team featured just six golfers, and three of them were freshman. "We only have six girls, but for a short supply, we are going to be mighty," Landsaw said before the season.

Lauren Chappell, now a legend in the golf community, had moved from Arizona thanks to her father Rand Chappell being hired by Eastern Illinois University men's basketball coach Jay Spoonhour to join his staff as an assistant. Joining Chappell as freshman were Allyson O'Dell and Aislinn Parish. Two sport athlete Morgan Sherwood was going to play volleyball and golf once again, while junior Abby Youngblood and senior Lynnsey Veach were the team's co-captains. "The only thing that is going to hurt us is injury," Landsaw said.

Chappell got to work quickly by winning the Olney Invitational by setting a record with a 2-under-par 33 in near record heat. "I am pretty used to hot weather coming from Arkansas," 2bChappell said. Chappell was hot on the golf course, placing third in the Eisenhower Invite, and winning the Apollo Conference with a score of 74. The team had a rough go at the Apollo, finishing fifth out of five teams, but had good news going into Regional play as their enrollment placed Charleston in Class 1A.

Charleston dominated their own Regional with a team score of 367, which beat out second place Mt. Zion's team score of 436. Chappell was the Regional champion with a 1-under-par 71. "It means that all the time I practiced has paid off," Chappell said. O'Dell added, "She skips out on hanging out with us to go golf."

O'Dell had her best match of the season, while Parish played unsung hero. The normal No. 6 golfer on the season shot a 103, which was fourth best on the team. "She shot a 103 even with a penalty shot for hitting the wrong ball," Landsaw said with a laugh. "For her to shoot that is great. Ally O'Dell had her best score of the season. For us to shoot a 367, it just tops it off."

Charleston followed that performance with one better at the Gibson City-Melvin-Sibley Sectional. Chappell took home fourth overall, while Parish played clutch again, shooting the team's third highest score as Charleston finished third to advance to their first ever state tournament as a team.

Qualifying for state was great news for a team that didn't have a full team until Parish saved the say. "My dad wanted me to do golf," said Parish. "I came out for the summer program with Stan Adkins. It is not the first time I have golfed, but the first time I have done it every day."

The season was capped with one of the best runs by a CHS girl's golfer. Chappell finished day one at Red Tail Run Golf Course in Decatur (the host for the state meet), in second place with a score of 68. She was just one stroke behind the leader. Chappell hit all 18 greens, birdied four holes, and was on even-par the rest of the way. Chappell told Scott Richie of the Decatur Herald & Review, "I was not nervous at all. It helped that my team was here. They kept me pretty relaxed."

Chappell fought harsh winds on Saturday to shoot a 73, which was two strokes better than anyone else to win the state championship, becoming the first ever Lady Trojan to win a state title. Chappell's stretch featured the freshman bogeying hole No. 17. However, Chappell drilled the game winning putt on hole No. 18.

"I have chewed off all my fingernails," Landsaw told Aren Down of the Decatur Herald & Review. "It started at the Regional. Then, the Sectional. My feeling after she bogeyed that hole was to just don't lose it. She came back and played well."

Chappell won by five strokes to end the historic day. "I am really surprised I have done this well," Chappell told Dow. "I was really afraid I was going to blow up. It is just really surprising." The rest of the team capped an 8th place finish as a team for Charleston. Sherwood shot a 201 which was good for 83rd overall, O'Dell a 203 (86th), Parish a 208 (89th), Youngblood a 221 (99th), and Veach a 221 (101st).

Chappell Repeats to Lead 2014 Team's State Berth

Five of the top six were back for CHS. Chappell was back to defend her state title. The sophomore had a busy summer, placing third at the Illinois Junior Girls Golf Championship, and tied for fourth in the Girls North & South Finish, a tournament that featured some of the nation's best, as well as international entries. Sherwood was back to play volleyball and golf for a third straight season, while O'Dell and Parish returned as sophomores. Abby Youngblood was the lone senior and captain. Freshman, Haley Walker, rounded out the top six.

"The nucleus is back," Landsaw said before the season. "Lauren played a lot this summer. Morgan is looking strong and has been hitting some long balls. Abby and Aislinn look better. Plus, we have some freshman who are eager to play."

Charleston played to an undefeated 14-0 season, which included a school record for team score (170) in a dual meet versus Mattoon on Senior Night. Coach Adkins returned from retirement to help coach as Coach Landsaw was hospitalized for 11 days due to surgery. The school record score came at a good time as CHS was entering the Apollo Conference tournament next. Charleston was looking to rebound from a last place finish a year ago, despite finishing 8th in the state as a team.

Those wounds healed from last year as Charleston won the Apollo. Chappell repeated as champion, winning by seven strokes. Sherwood joined Chappell as All-Apollo by placing third. "Everything fell apart last year at Apollo," Sherwood told Journal Gazette-Times Courier sports editor Brian Nielsen. "This year we knew we had to do better and show this was where we belonged as a team."

The Regional provided a little bit more excitement, at least on the individual side. Chappell and Mt. Zion's Ashley Miller were deadlocked at the end of 18-holes with a score of 73. This forced a playoff as Chappell won a consecutive Regional by finishing with a par, while Miller bogeyed. "Ashley Miller was ahead most of the day," Landsaw told Journal Gazette-Times Courier reporter Mike Monahan. "Lauren was down by four strokes at one time and came back to tie it on hole No. 18. It was fantastic to watch."

The team won a second consecutive Regional with a team score of 344, which was 57 strokes better than second place finisher Pana. Going into the Tuscola Sectional, Charleston knew they could make another run to state. For a consecutive year, an unlikely freshman hero stepped up. This time, it was Walker. Walker, playing typically as the No. 6 golfer, finished with the third best individual score for CHS with a 100. Led by Chappell's runner-up finish 75, and Sherwood's 91, Charleston placed second to make another trip to state.

I was asked to write a state preview that season, but a miscommunication had me at the Country Club with no team in sight. Apparently, practice had been cancelled, but guess who was rolling in as I was beginning to leave. Chappell had golf clubs in hand as she was practicing putting. "I have to practice," Chappell told me. "We have state in two days."

Maybe the practice paid off as Chappell led the field after day one with a 3-over-par 75. The following day, Chappell repeated in dramatic fashion. Chappell had a rough Saturday. Chappell bogued holes No. 8 and No. 9, having the defending winner think she had lost the chance of winning state. However, Chappell sunk a 25-foot birdie putt on hole No. 12, and a 15-footer on hole No. 15.

As Chappell was resting for about an hour, her teammates, friends, and family went to watch Rochester's Morgan Savage putt on hole No. 18. As Savage putt the ball in, Chappell thought she had tied her, forcing an overtime.

Instead, her teammate O'Dell came over to tell Chappell she had won and that the putt was actually a par, not a birdie, meaning Chappell had defeated Savage by one stroke 149 to 150 to repeat as state champion. To make the day better, Charleston finished seventh as a team. O'Dell shot a 182 (54th place), Sherwood a 188 (71st), Parish a 198 (88th), Walker a 215 (105th), and Youngblood a 223 (109th).

"I hugged my teammates and celebrated," Chappell told Nielsen after the win. "We beat our team score by 65 strokes from last season. I can't wait for next year."

First team trophy brought home in 2015

Coming off back to back years finishing in the top eight, Charleston had their eyes on something bigger this season: a state trophy. State trophies are only awarded to the top three teams. Once again, Charleston had five of their top six golfers back. The team had two-time state champion in Chappell, while Sherwood played volleyball and golf for a fourth straight season. O'Dell and Parish were back as juniors, while Walker was a seasoned sophomore. Lauren's sister, Paige, a freshman, rounded out the top six.

"The team is stronger than last year because they have matured a lot," Landsaw told Journal Gazette-Times Courier reporter Justin Rust before the season. "The freshman and sophomores are better and we have 12 girls on the team. They expect to be successful."

CHS entered the Apollo Conference tournament with a 12-0 record on the season and ran away with the conference. Chappell won for a third year in a row, while teammates Sherwood, Parish, and sister, Paige, made the All-Apollo team. The team's 329 team scored romped past second place Effingham's score of 383. "Four out of the top eight for this team shows some good consistency," Landsaw told Journal Gazette-Times Courier reporter Keith Stewart. "Of course, this is our home course, at least the front nine is. The back nine we have only played twice this season."

Charleston followed that performance with another successful Regional. The team's 335 score beat second place Lincolnwood by 56 strokes. Chappell won a third straight Regional with her score of 68. Sherwood was the runner-up, while Paige finished in a tie for third. Lauren hit a 34 on the front nine and 34 on the back nine to clip the 60s.

"There was a lot of pretty easy holes where I could birdie," Chappell told Rust. "I birdied a lot of those holds and made a lot of long putts. I was really zoned in because I wanted to get into the sixties."

Charleston had to battle winds of 15 MPH and 20 MPH at the Rochester Sectional. The team did not have their best outing, but still finished second in the sectional to advance to state for a third year in a row. O'Dell came back from her 108 at the Regional to shoot a 91, while the freshman Paige tied O'Dell for second best. Lauren missed out winning the Sectional by one stroke to Rochester's Morgan Savage, who Chappell beat out by one stroke a year before for the state title. Landsaw told Rust that the wind messed with the approaches, but nerves were really the issue. O'Dell told Rust that the team was just saving their best for state.

All jokes aside, Charleston was looking their best after day one. Chappell led the field after day one with a one stroke lead over Mackenzie Hahn of Richwood and a four-stroke lead over Savage. The team sat in second place overall going into Saturday.

Saturday was a bittersweet day for Charleston. Chappell missed out on winning a historic third state title, but CHS shot well enough to bring home the school's first ever state trophy as the team finished third overall. "Earlier, I was crying because we weren't happy with our scores," Sherwood told Rust. "Then, Lauren's dad came over and said we got second or third. Then, we started crying again."

Chappell had a rough go on Saturday, shooting a 9-over-par 81 which dropped her to a tie for fourth overall. "It just wasn't my day," Chappell told Rust. "I couldn't get anything going. I couldn't really play how I like to play. It does make it positive that we have something to celebrate. I am really proud of our team."

Rounding out the team's scores after Chappell's two-day score of 155 was O'Dell at 177 (28th overall), Sherwood at 180 (42nd), Paige Chappell at 188 (60th), Walker at 193 (68th), and Parish at 197 (73rd).

Chappell leads Charleston to State Championship in 2016

Going in their senior seasons, you had three of the top six golfers who had been a part of three state qualifying teams, a third-place finish in 2015, and a leader who had two state titles on her resume. How do you top that if you are Chappell, O'Dell, and Parish? Maybe, winning a state title as a team? "I think we have a good chance with the people we have coming back and the progress the underclassman has made," Landsaw told Journal Gazette-Times Courier reporter Justin Rust. "I know other teams that have girls who have worked hard all summer, but with the run we have had the last couple years, that experience when it comes down to it is good to have." The team lost Sherwood, but brought back the senior seniors, the junior in Walker, and the sophomore sister of Lauren in Paige. Junior Bailey Taylor rounded out the varsity squad.

Chappell had a busy summer gearing up for her senior season. Chappell won the Illinois Women's Amateur Championship in June, placed third in the AJGA Lockton Kansas City Junior Tournament, and verbally committed to golf at Southern Methodist University. The hard work paid off again for the senior as she won the Apollo Conference for a fourth straight year. The team standings were closer, but Charleston edged Effingham 371 to 391.

However, this day belonged to Chappell. "I am excited to get another Apollo win," Chappell told Rust. "It's been an exciting ride. It's been fun and really exciting. I am sad that it is over, but it has been an awesome experience." Joining Chappell on the All-Apollo team was her sister Paige and O'Dell.

If winning four Apollo titles was not enough, how about winning four Regional titles? That is exactly what Chappell did the following week by shooting a score of 73 to win the Pana Regional. The day was a difficult day for all golfers. Water was pooled in many areas due to heavy rainfall, and team scores did not come out until 5:00 pm.

That didn't stop Charleston from running away with their fourth straight Regional title as a team, shooting 73 strokes better that second place Sullivan. "The 333 is good," Landsaw told Rust. "With slow play, you can lose concentration, which makes for a long day. The girls did well on the front nine, had trouble on the back nine, but we had four girls in the 80s which was even better."

The following week, Chappell finally got the sectional monkey off her back. After failing to win a sectional title in her first three years, Chappell shot a 33 on the back nine on route to her medalist score of 71 to win the Lincoln Sectional. What made things better was that

Charleston's seniors in Parish and O'Dell stepped up to shoot an 83 and 84 respectively to lead Charleston to their first ever Sectional Championship as a team.

Charleston rode the momentum going into the final week, and they were in the best position as team as ever had. Charleston held an 11-stroke lead after day one over second place Nashville. Chappell's score of 74 led all competitors, but her teammates were stealing the show. Parish hit a career best score of 80, including a front nine score of 39, which was only one stroke behind Chappell's front nine score. Paige Chappell hit an 85, while O'Dell added an 87. "I told the girls you don't win after day one," Landsaw told Rust. "You have to come back the second day and shoot a good round, and I have a feeling we can do it."

Landsaw was right. Charleston's three seniors stepped up once again. The team's score of 350 was four strokes worse than Nashville, but their huge lead gave some room for error as Charleston's two-day score of 676 was seven strokes better than Nashville. Charleston didn't just win their first ever state championship in golf, but first ever state championship in any sport that CHS provided.

"I am getting goosebumps just thinking about what they accomplished and I just wanted it so much for these girls. They've worked hard," Landsaw said told Rust. "I know that every coach thinks their girls are great and deserve and I say I am so proud of them so many times, but there's something special about these girls. I am going to miss the seniors, but the underclassmen, we are going to work hard to play to the potential that they have.

Chappell's won her third state championship with a two-day score of 149, which was three strokes higher than second place. By winning, Chappell became the first high school boys or girl's golfer in Illinois to win three individual state championships. It's amazing. At the start of the day I struggled a little bit and tripled the fourth hole," Chappell said to Rust. "I went one-under for the rest of the day, so it's awesome. I am really proud of how I fought back. This is just amazing."

According to Rust, "Chappell started the day with a bogey and had a triple-bogey on number four to open the door for Hahn a bit, but Chappell shut the door with two birdies, a number of pars and only one bogey the rest of the way. The ninth hole started the slide for Chappell last season and it was the game-changing hole for her again this season, but this time in a more positive way. Chappell's first shot rolled down the cart path into the edge of the rough, but she handled it well and her second shot gave her a long but makeable putt. Chappell then went on to conquer the back nine. She had a bogey on the 12th hole, but she parred the rest of the holes except for the birdie on No. 17."

"I'm almost speechless. It's been a dream all weekend and it came true. We all worked so hard and I am so proud of this group of girls. We all fought back together and it was awesome," Chappell said to Rust. "It's amazing. I've been looking forward to it all year and I knew we could do it, even with some people weren't sure. It's just really exciting. When I first moved here, I didn't know how well the girls would be, so it's crazy to see how far we've come in the last four years.

O'Dell was happier about seeing her good friend's success. "I am so excited and happy for her," O'Dell told Rust. "She's done so well over the past four years, so it's nice to top it off for her. We all like Lauren a lot, so it was really nice." Though a few moments later, the state title began to sink in. "I didn't think we would come close to this, so this is perfect. It's just weird thinking you can. I knew we were good, but I never thought we were this good, so it's nice,"

O'Dell said to Rust. "I'm jacked. I'm excited. It's pretty awesome just to be able to have this forever. Whenever we have little kids, we can say we won a state title and that's just going to be cool to say."

Parish told Rust she did not know how to feel by saying, "I mean, it's just icing on the cake. Winning it was enough, but to be the first, that's amazing," Parish said. "It's fun because I think of past state champions and they felt what we felt right now. It's just insane to think we won."

To go along with Chappell's two-day state champion score of 149, Paris hit a 172 (36th overall), O'Dell a 173 (40th overall), Paige Chappell a 188 (69th overall), Taylor a 192 (76th overall), and Walker a 197 (83rd overall).

The era finally came to an end when Chappell officially signed with Southern Methodist in November. "It's amazing, just the whole community and all of my friends always support me," Chappell said to Rust. "My basketball coaches and my golf coaches, everybody supports me and works with me. It's so amazing. I just want to thank coach Mike Moncel for always being there for me and to coach (Deb) Landsaw and coach (Stan) Adkins for their amazing support system." Parish went on to play basketball at Lake Land College in Mattoon, while O'Dell went on to play softball at Olney Central Community College. The three finished their golf careers with four Regional titles, four trips to state, and two state trophies, marking the best run by three CHS athletes in school history.

Charleston records fifth trip to state in a row in 2017

Some might have felt that expectations would be down in 2017. It was a justified statement. CHS lost three-time state champion in Lauren Chappell, while mainstays Allyson O'Dell and Aislinn Parish were also graduated and playing sports in college. However, Charleston brought back three pieces from last year's state title team. Hannah Walker and Bailey Taylor were back as seniors, while Paige Chappell returned as a junior. Senior Abby Logsdon put in a lot of work, while freshman Hannah Harpster and Shekinah Moore rounded out the varsity squad.

"I have some girls who have worked really hard over the summer," said Landsaw to Journal Gazette-Times Courier reporter Justin Rust. "Haley, Bailey, and Paige have really put in the work. Haley wants to end her career on a high. The freshman saw what we have done, and they want to get back to state."

CHS missed out on the Apollo Conference title by two strokes to winner Effingham. Walker finished as the runner-up and was joined on the All-Apollo team by Taylor and Harpster. Chappell, who had played at the No. 1 or No. 2 golfer all season, finished with the fourth best score and missed all-conference honors.

However, Chappell responded well the following week, leading Charleston with a score of 92 to lead CHS to a fifth straight Regional title. The team's score of 393 was 43 strokes better than second place Tuscola. Walker shot a 96, while Harpster added a 100.

The Springfield Sectional was hit was rain, but there was a rainbow on the other side as Charleston clinched the second-best team score to advance to state for a fifth year in a row. After about 10 holes, play was suspended due to heavy rain and heavy winds. After an hour and a half delay, golfers could resume play, and Taylor stepped up as a senior for CHS.

"After the suspension, that is when Bailey started to kick it in," Landsaw told Rust. "She fired off four or five straight pars. To play in that stuff and get pars on some of those holes was rough. Bailey came through in a big way." Her teammate Walker shed off nine strokes from her Regional score to lead CHS with a score of 87, while Taylor shed 13 strokes. "Haley kept it together," Landsaw told Rust. "Haley and Bailey were a big part of today. I can't say enough about them. They did their job as seniors."

Despite missing out on a trophy, CHS finished another great season by finishing sixth overall. Their score of 704 was two strokes behind Effingham St. Anthony for fifth place, but Charleston could not have asked for much more. "In August, I would have never dreamed they would get this far, so this is really good," Landsaw told Rust. "They had determination and didn't give up. When we got here, I looked at all the sectional scores. We were ninth. I ask for much more for what we did."

Chappell led Charleston with a two-day score of 169 which was 32nd overall. Walker added a 171 (40th), Harpster a 145 (48th), Taylor a 189 (70th), Logsdon a 224 (102nd), and Moore a 230 (106th).

Trojans Girls Soccer
(1997-2018)

Trojans Girls Soccer
(1997-2018)

In 1997, girls' soccer was added to the Charleston High School athletic program. It seemed like the right thing to do considering the rise of the boy's team winning their first Regional championship in 1996. Now all the sisters and cousins had their shot. The sport was played on a small schedule with only eight games scheduled at the beginning of the season until more were added down the stretch.

Lady Trojan soccer saw their first game Monday, April 6, 1997 vs. the Morton JV in which the team tied 1-1. Anna Wheeler scored the first goal in Charleston High School history. CHS finished the season 7-2-2 with a Central Illinois Soccer Conference Championship. Charleston teams have suffered only two losing seasons in their history and were also back to back. They were the second and third years of Paul Stranz's coaching career. In 2002, the team went 7-11-1. Then in 2003, CHS finished 6-12-1.

Liz Nino led the way for the first four years of girls' soccer. Nino never had a losing record in her varsity coaching career. She began her coaching as the JV boys coach for five years while her husband, Hank Nino, lead the varsity. Charleston followed their first year with mush success. The 1998 season was led by three players who finished the season with at least forty total offensive points.

Emily Garrett, Bobby Jo Buchar, and Anna Wheeler finished the 1998 campaign scoring 49 of the team's total 65 goals. Garrett also set the teams assists record with 22, which has not been broken up to the present day. Also, during the 1998 season, Garrett set a school record setting up four goals in a win over Urbana University on May 19.   .

The Lady Trojans scored a whopping fourteen goals vs. Stephen Decatur in a 14-0 victory. The team scored a record eight goals in the first half. Other accomplishments came from setting season records by scoring 39 total goals in the second half and allowing five goals to other teams in the same half. This was a 39:5 ratio. The 1998 also set a record for the highest goals per game average, 3.8 and fewest losses in a season. CHS won the St. Teresa Invitational, Central Illinois Soccer Conference Championship, and the school's first Regional Championship all in just a year after the school started the program.

The following two seasons proved to continue the well noted winning ways by going a combined 29-8-3 with two second place finishes in the St. Teresa Invitational and two championships at the Mahomet-Seymour Invitational. The year 2000 marked the end of two very successful CHS soccer careers in Emily Garret and coach Liz Nino. Emily Garrett finished the year leading the team with forty total offensive points of ten goals and twenty assists. Garrett went on to win the Decatur Herald & Review Player of the Year. Along with her teammates Bobby Jo Buchar and Sara Fisher, Garrett joined the club of being named All-Conference First Team three times.

Garrett wasn't alone on receiving awards. Her coach won the Decatur Herald & Review Coach of the Year as she led her team to a 17-3-1 record. The seventeen wins was the lone school record until 2007 when the team tied the record. Nino decided to retire after the year was over with her husband. Nino finished her coaching career with a 49-13-8 record. Other numbers that stood out was that in her four-year tenure, CHS only allowed 51 total goals in a total of sixty-eight games total. That would be an average 1.3 goals allowed over the course of those four years. Nino's defense never let more than fourteen goals go past the keeper, and the offense would reward their efforts by scoring at least 53 goals in three of those four seasons.

Paul Stranz became the second coach in school history. The 2001 season campaign had the scoring weapons of Sara Fisher and Kelly Best, who both ended their soccer careers in the top ten career scoring list. The teams also finished the season by setting a record of most shutout wins in a season, twelve, despite finishing with a 15-7-0 record.

Despite the next two seasons being the only two years in the school's history with losing records, there were still some bright spots. Coartney McKinney set a school record by recording twenty-four saves in one game in a 3-0 loss to Champaign Central in 2003. In 2002, it marked the beginning of an outstanding career by Alex Singer. All four years, Singer lead the team in goals scored and total offensive points. In 2004, she was practically the total offense. Singer booted in sixteen of the teams thirty goals and contributed 35 of the teams 76 total offensive points. The closest girl next on the list was Lindsey Gardner with four goals and nine total offensive points.

Gardner stepped up during Singer's senior season as they both combined for 29 goals, 14 assists, and 72 total offensive points. Singer was named the team's Offensive Player of the Year in 2005. The two players combined with other offensive threats Emma Dively and Colleen Hussey won the school's first Regional Championship in seven years by defeating Mattoon 1-0. The game after set the record for worst defeat by losing to Normal West in the Sectional Game 9-0. Paul Stranz was named the Area Coach of the Year, and this seemed to be the beginning an offensive oriented team after a three year "drought" of not scoring at least fifty goals in a season.

The next three years left CHS opponents at the hands of mercy to Molly Ball. She was freshman on the Regional Championship team, but her reign came from 2006-2008. Ball holds the record for most goals scored in a game, most goals in a season, goals per game, goals in her career, total offensive points in a season and career, goals scored by a sophomore, junior, and senior. She also ranks in the top three for all the regular season records she holds, as well as being number three on the all-time list for assists per game in her career.

She was named the team's Offensive Player of the Year, Decatur Herald & Review All-Area Team, and IHSSCA All-Sectional Team three times. She was the All-Area Player of the year in 2008 by scoring the school record 42 goals and racking up 92 total offensive points. Ball's school record of six goals in a match is tied for ninth best in IHSA history.

The 2007 team tied the school's record for wins in a season by going 17-3-4. The team won the school's second Regional Championship in three seasons by defeating powerhouse Champaign Centennial 2-1. Other accomplishments came from winning the St. Teresa Invitational by defeating longtime foe Decatur Eisenhower 2-0 and winning the school's first Dunlap Invitational. Although Ball was a force for most defenders, the team's MVP award went to goalie Selina Satterfield for allowing only 23 goals, six of which only came in the second half. Stranz was then named the Area Coach of the Year for what would be the second time of his three-time awarding. Holly Wholtman set the schools record for most goals by a freshman, destroying the previous record of five.

In 2010, CHS got back to winning their winning ways after an average 2009 season. Wholtman lead the team in goals once again and had a lot of help on the right side of the field from speedy Joy Hall. The defense was much credited to goalkeeper Brittany O'Dell, who eventually was recruited by Eastern Illinois University to play soccer. O'Dell in the back helped preserve nine shutout wins and only fifteen total goals allowed all year. Sweeper, Sarah Bower accredited three non-goalie saves. Bower's most prestigious save came from the thrilling 1-0 victory over Mattoon in the Regional Championship game. O'Dell came out of the goal, but as the ball got past her, Bower swept right in to boot the ball away.

Along, with O'Dell and Bower, and Trojans had other solid defenders in the starting roles with Ashlyn Sweeney, Anika Guinto, and Kristen Elsila. Elsila is the record holder for most games played in her career. It was also the bench players that filled voids such as Jessica Simpson and Macy Coffey on defense and Mary Jackson scoring three goals. Stranz was again awarded the Area Coach of the Year. In the Journal Gazette/Times-Courier, Stranz was quoted by Nielsen giving much of the team's success to his goalkeeper, "Her enthusiasm carried over to the entire team. She could have said, "I'm already committed to Eastern' and got back on her heals. But she didn't. She worked hard and perfected what she did."

The success poured in during the 2011 campaign. Megan Hjort made a sophomore splash season, leading the team in scoring with 21 goals. Junior, Janel Hutton, patrolled the midfield, and finished with eight goals and seven assists. Seniors, Madison Spence, and Brittany Irwin, chipped in a combined 13 goals. The team tied the then-school record for wins, going 17-4-3, but a 1-0 double overtime loss to Mattoon in the Regional Championship soured the season. It was the fourth time the Lady Trojans played Mattoon that season. Ashlyn Sweeney went on to play at Oakland City College and Sarah Bower went to play at Milwaukee School of Engineering.

In 2012, Charleston went back and reclaimed their post-season hardware. Charleston defeated Litchfield 2-0 to claim the second Regional title in three years. Before the season, no one knew who sophomores Madi Fisher, Ali Carlson, and Makenzie Burgess were. The trio led a young team in offensive categories in an injury-riddled season for the junior, Hjort. Fisher led the team in all three offensive categories with 17 goals, eight assists, and 42 offensive points. Hjort still managed 16 goals but was off her sophomore total. Carlson added 10 goals, while Burgess finished with eight. Hutton came back after an injury and played her way to winning the Team's MVP trophy. Goalkeeper, Kristen Gisondi, was named all sectional.
The team was playing in Class A due to their enrollment class. With hopes of a far post-season run, the team was humbled by eventual state champion, Quincy Notre Dame, in an 8-0 defeat in the sectional-semifinal.

Most of the offensive fire power was back to lead the 2013 squad to the best performance in Charleston girls' soccer history. Hjort was a senior and had committed to Kaskaskia, and eventually played two more years at Eastern Illinois University. Fisher and Carlson had verbally committed to Eastern Illinois University. An undefeated regular season made the 2013 team the first team to ever have their picture hung up on the wall for their success. A 19-1-2 season gained everyone's attention. The dream season came to a halt in a 7-1 loss in the Sectional Championship game at Normal West.

Despite the rocky ending, the team had monumental success. The team smashed the team single season goal mark, scoring 104 goals. The trio of three juniors once again were an offensive force. Fisher had 22 goals and 10 assists, Burgess had 18 goals, and Carlson had 15 goals and nine assists. Kristen Gisondi was once again all-sectional, and her sister had a great year in the field, netting nine goals.

In 2014, Fisher, Carlson, Gisondi, and Burgess were a strong offensive core that led the team to breaking the team record for goals scored in a season with 105. The team tied the school record for wins by going 19-3-0 but fell to Champaign St. Thomas More in the Regional title game. Stranz retired with a 194-83-28 record and the two first ever Apollo Conference championships. Charleston would later win the Apollo again in 2017. Ali Hosey scored her way into the top ten scoring.

Season by Season Girls Soccer Results

1997
Won 7, Lost 2, Tied 2
Coach: Liz Nino

Opponent	Score
Morton JV	1-1
St. Teresa	6-2
Urbana University	4-0
Champaign Central	1-0
Danville	6-0
Monticello	2-1
Urbana	0-3
Monticello	0-0
Urbana University	5-3
Mahomet-Seymour	1-0
Urbana	1-2

Total Goals By Opponent: 12 (1.1 AVG)
Total Goals By CHS: 26 (2.4 AVG)

1998

Won 13, Lost 2, Tied 2 (Regional Champs)
Coach: Liz Nino

Opponent	Score
Decatur Eisenhower	1-0
Monticello	4-0
Decatur MacArthur	3-0
Stephen Decatur	14-0
St. Teresa	4-0
Monticello	3-2
Urbana University	3-2
Champaign Central	4-0
Danville	4-0
Jacksonville	0-1
Monticello	2-2
Urbana	2-2
Decatur Eisenhower	1-1
Urbana University	9-0
Springfield Ursuline	5-0
Normal Community	2-1 (PK)
Springfield Sacred Heart Griffin	0-6

Total Goals By Opponent: 14 (.82 AVG)
Total Goals By CHS: 65 (3.8 AVG)

1999

Won 12, Lost 5, Tied 2
Coach: Liz Nino

Opponent	Score
Monticello	3-0
Decatur Eisenhower	0-1
Decatur MacArthur	1-0
Decatur Eisenhower	0-2
Stephen Decatur	11-0
Monticello	1-1
St. Teresa	3-0
Urbana University	9-0
Judah Christian	1-3
Danville	3-0
???	0-1
Herscher	5-0
Mahomet-Seymour	2-0
Urbana	3-2
Decatur Eisenhower	1-0
Decatur MacArthur	0-0
Urbana	1-2

Total Goals By Opponents: 13 (.68 AVG)
Total Goals By CHS: 53 (2.8 AVG)

2000

Won 17, Lost 3, Tied 1
Coach: Liz Nino

Opponent	Score
Decatur MacArthur	2-1 (OT)
Monticello	2-0
Decatur Eisenhower	0-1
Stephen Decatur	12-0
St. Teresa	3-2
Monticello	5-0
Urbana University	5-0
Champaign Central	1-1
Springfield	0-1
Danville	2-0
Jacksonville	5-1
Mt. Zion	6-1
Mahomet-Seymour	4-0
Monticello	3-0
Mahomet-Seymour	5-0
Urbana	3-0
Decatur Eisenhower	4-1
Decatur MacArthur	3-2
Monticello	6-0
Normal West	0-1 (PK)

Total Goals By Opponent: 12 (.57 AVG)
Total Goals By CHS: 71 (3.4 AVG)

2001

Won 15, Lost 7, Tied 1
Coach: Paul Stranz

Opponent	Score
Decatur MacArthur	1-2 (PK)
Meridian	2-1
Warrensburg-Latham	3-0
Decatur MacArthur	1-0
Decatur Eisenhower	1-0
Rantoul	6-0
St. Teresa	1-3
Urbana University	5-0
Champaign Central	0-1
Springfield	0-4
Danville	1-2
Mt. Zion	0-3
Jacksonville	3-2
Meridian	5-0
Mt. Zion	0-3
Urbana University	6-0
Monticello	7-0
Mahomet-Seymour	2-0
Urbana	1-1
Decatur MacArthur	2-0
Mattoon	6-0
St. Teresa	2-1
Champaign Central	1-6

Goals By Opponent: 26 (1.1 AVG)
Goals By CHS: 58 (2.5 AVG)

2002

Won 7, Lost 11, Tied 1
Coach: Paul Stranz

Opponent	Score
Mt. Zion	0-2
Forfeit	1-0
Rantoul	6-0
St. Teresa	0-4
Mattoon	0-0
Urbana University	1-0
Decatur Eisenhower	3-0
Champaign Central	0-6
Olney	3-0
Danville	0-4
Mt. Zion	1-0
Jacksonville	0-1
Meridian	2-1
Warrensburg-Latham	0-3
Monticello	2-1
Mahomet-Seymour	0-2
Urbana	0-6
Decatur MacArthur	0-1

Springfield Sacred Heart Griffin.........0-4

Goals By Opponent: 35 (1.8 AVG)
Goals By CHS: 18 (.95 AVG)

2003

Won 6, Lost 12, Tied 1
Coach: Paul Stranz

Opponent	Score
Meridian	3-2
Mattoon	0-2
Decatur Eisenhower	1-3
Rantoul	6-0
St. Teresa	2-5
Mattoon	2-1
Urbana University	0-0
Champaign Central	0-3
Danville	1-3
Mt. Zion	1-4
Meridian	2-1
Mahomet-Seymour	0-3
Urbana University	0-1
Monticello	2-0
Mahomet-Seymour	0-1
Decatur MacArthur	0-2
Olney	4-0
Mattoon	1-2

Goals By Opponent: 34 (1.8 AVG)
Goals By CHS: 25 (1.3 AVG)

2004

Won 11, Lost 9, Tied 1
Coach: Paul Stranz

Opponent	Score
Mt. Zion	1-2
Warrensburg-Latham	2-0
Decatur MacArthur	1-0 (PK)
Decatur Eisenhower	1-0
Rantoul	1-0
St. Teresa	2-1
Mattoon	1-0
Urbana University	1-1
Champaign Central	0-4
Olney	3-1
Danville	0-2
Mt. Zion	1-5
Dunlap	0-2
Dundee-Crown	0-4
Galena	1-0 (forfeit)
Macon-Meridian	4-0
Monticello	1-0
Mahomet-Seymour	1-5
Urbana	1-2
Decatur MacArthur	2-1
Mt. Zion	1-3

Goals By Opponent: 34 (1.6 AVG)
Goals By CHS: 32 (1.5 AVG)

2005

Won 13, Lost 6, Tied 3 (Regional Champs)
Coach: Paul Stranz

Opponent	Score
St. Teresa	1-0
Decatur MacArthur	1-2
Decatur Eisenhower	5-2
Decatur Eisenhower	2-1
St. Teresa	1-1
Mattoon	5-1
Champaign Central	1-1
Olney	3-0
Danville	1-0
Mt. Zion	5-1
Dunlap	1-2
Dundee-Crown	1-2
Galena	3-1
Macon-Meridian	5-0
Mahomet-Seymour	2-3
Urbana	1-5
Decatur MacArthur	3-2
Urbana University	1-1
Mt. Zion	6-1
Mattoon	1-0
Normal University	0-9

Goals By Opponent: 36 (1.6 AVG)
Goals By CHS: 55 (2.5 AVG)

2006

Won 15, Lost 7, Tied 0
Coach: Paul Stranz

Opponent	Score
Mt. Zion	4-3 (PK)
St. Teresa	3-2 (PK)
Decatur MacArthur	0-3
Decatur Eisenhower	5-3
St. Teresa	3-2
Mattoon	2-1
Urbana University	5-0
Champaign Central	2-0
Olney	1-2
Danville	3-2
Mt. Zion	5-2
Dunlap	0-2
Dundee-Crown	1-6
Galena	7-1
Macon-Meridian	8-0
Urbana	1-0
Monticello	6-0
Mahomet-Seymour	0-1
Decatur MacArthur	0-1
Taylorville	8-0
Mattoon	3-2
Bradley Bourbonnais	3-4

Goals By Opponents: 37 (1.7 AVG)
Goals By CHS: 70 (3.2 AVG)

2007

Won 17, Lost 3, Tied 4 (Regional Champs)
Coach: Paul Stranz

Opponent	Score
Decatur Lutheran	4-1
Warrensburg-Latham	2-1 (2OT)
Decatur MacArthur	2-1
Decatur Eisenhower	2-0
St. Teresa	4-1
St. Thomas More	5-0
Mattoon	0-0
Urbana University	7-1
Champaign Central	0-0
Danville	5-0
Mt. Zion	5-1
Dunlap	0-0
Galena	8-0
Elgin Academy	2-0
Olney	1-1
Centralia	4-0
Urbana	1-5
Decatur MacArthur	0-1
Taylorville	8-0
Mahomet-Seymour	1-0
Champaign Centennial	2-1
Normal West	0-8

Goals By Opponent: 23 (.96 AVG)
Goals By CHS: 71 (3.0 AVG)

2008

Won 13, Lost 6, Tied 2
Coach: Paul Stranz

Opponent	Score
Decatur Eisenhower	8-0
Mattoon	3-4
Urbana University	1-3
Olney	1-6
Danville	5-3
Mt. Zion	6-0
Glenbrook South	1-7
Princeton	3-0
Dunlap	1-2
Centralia	5-0
Warrensburg-Latham	1-1
St. Thomas More	5-1
St. Teresa	8-1
Monticello	6-1
Mahomet-Seymour	2-1
Urbana	2-2

Opponent	Score
Champaign Central	6-1
Decatur MacArthur	4-3
Taylorville	8-0
Mattoon	3-0
Chatham-Glenwood	0-4

Goals By Opponent: 40 (1.9 AVG)
Goals By CHS: 79 (3.8 AVG)

2009

Won 12, Lost 6, Tied 4
Coach: Paul Stranz

Opponent	Score
Warrensburg-Latham	0-2
Mt. Zion	1-0 (PK)
Decatur Lutheran	2-1 (PK)
Bloomington Central Catholic	2-3
Decatur Eisenhower	8-0
St. Thomas More	9-0
Mattoon	1-2
Urbana University	4-1
Olney	1-1
Mt. Zion	3-1
Danville	5-1
Centralia	4-0
Champaign Central	1-1
Dunlap	2-2
Mattoon	1-1
Monticello	2-4
Mahomet-Seymour	2-1
Urbana	2-0
Decatur MacArthur	3-0
Taylorville	7-0
Mattoon	3-0
Urbana	0-1

Goals By Opponent: 24 (1.1 AVG)
Goals By CHS: 61 (2.8 AVG)

2010

Won 15, Lost 3, Tied 5 (Regional Champs)
Coach: Paul Stranz

Opponent	Score
Mattoon	3-0
Warrensburg-Latham	2-1
Decatur MacArthur	2-0
Bloomington Central Catholic	4-1
Olney	3-0
Decatur Eisenhower	6-0
St. Teresa	3-0
Mattoon	1-1
Champaign Centennial	0-3
Urbana University	0-0
Danville	3-1
Mt. Zion	2-0
Champaign Central	0-0
Dunlap	0-0
Mattoon	2-0
Monticello	1-1
Mahomet-Seymour	0-1
Urbana	2-1
Decatur MacArthur	6-2
Taylorville	8-0
Mattoon	1-0
Normal University	0-3

Goals By Opponent: 15 (.65 AVG)
Goals By CHS: 56 (2.4 AVG)

2011

Won 17, Lost 4, Tied 1
Coach: Paul Stranz

Opponent	Score
Mattoon	4-0
Mt. Zion	1-0 (PK)
St. Teresa	3-0
Bloomington Central Catholic	6-0
Decatur Eisenhower	3-0
Centralia	4-1
St. Teresa	3-0
Mattoon	2-0
Champaign Centennial	0-2
Mt. Zion	3-0
Urbana University	4-1

Champaign Central	2-0
Dunlap	1-2
Mattoon	2-0
Monticello	7-0
Mahomet-Seymour	1-1
Urbana	0-2
Danville	2-0
Decatur MacArthur	3-1
Taylorville	9-0
Mattoon	0-1 (2OT)

Goals By Opponent: 11 (0.52 AVG)
Goals By CHS: 70 (3.3 AVG)

2012

Won 15, Lost 5, Tied 3 (Regional Champs)
Coach: Paul Stranz

Opponent	Score
Decatur Eisenhower	5-0
Mount Zion	2-3 (PK)
Decatur Lutheran	0-1
Bloomington Cent. Catholic	7-0
Urbana	1-1
Centralia	7-1
Olney	1-0
St. Teresa	4-0
Mattoon	3-0
Champaign Centennial	2-2
Urbana University	1-0
Danville	7-0
Mount Zion	6-0
Decatur MacArthur	8-0
Champaign Central	2-0
Dunlap	0-1
Mattoon	2-0
Monticello	10-1
Mahomet-Seymour	0-2
Meridian	10-0
Litchfield	2-0
Quincy Notre Dame	0-8

Goals By Opponent: 19 (0.83 AVG)
Goals By CHS: 80 (3.5 AVG)

2013

Won 19, Lost 1, Tied 3 (Regional Champs)
Apollo Won 3 Lost 0 Tied 0 (Apollo Champs)
Coach: Paul Stranz

Opponent	Score
Decatur Lutheran	8-0
Mount Zion	3-2 (OT)
St. Teresa	2-0
Urbana	8-0
Centralia	6-0
Olney	8-0
St. Teresa	4-1
Mattoon*	4-0
Champaign Centennial	2-1
Urbana University	9-0
Decatur MacArthur	9-0
Salem*	8-0
Champaign Central	0-0
Dunlap	2-2
Mattoon	5-0
Mount Zion*	3-2 (OT)
Monticello	7-1
Mahomet-Seymour	2-2
Danville	8-0
Decatur MacArthur	7-0
Mattoon	1-0
Morris	3-0
Normal West	1-7

Goals By Opponent: 17 (0.73 AVG)
Goals By CHS: 104 (4.5 AVG)

2014

Coach: Paul Stranz
Won 19, Lost 3, Tied 0
Apollo Won 3, Lost 0, Tied 0 (Apollo Champs)

Opponent	Score
Danville	6-0
Mt. Zion	1-2

Opponent	Score
Danville	7-0
Warrensburg-Latham	7-0
Salem*	7-0
Urbana	4-0
Centralia	7-0
Olney	7-1
St. Teresa	5-1
Mattoon*	3-0
Champaign Centennial	8-0
Urbana University	2-0
Danville	8-1
Mt. Zion*	3-1
Decatur MacArthur	8-0
Champaign Central	3-1
Dunlap	1-3
Mattoon	8-0
Mahomet-Seymour	3-2
Monticello	8-0
Champaign St. Thomas More	1-4

Goals By Opponent: 15 (0.68 AVG)
Goals By CHS: 105 (4.7 AVG)

2015
Coach: Dave Dunlap
Won 14, Lost 6, Tied 1
Apollo Won 3, Lost 3, Tied 0

Opponent	Score
Pana	1-0 (PK)
Warrensburg-Latham	1-0
Mt. Zion	0-2
Urbana	2-0
Centralia	10-1
Olney	4-1
Salem*	2-1
Mt. Zion*	1-3
Champaign Centennial	1-2
Urbana University	4-0
Salem*	6-0
Mattoon*	1-2
Decatur MacArthur	0-0
Mt. Zion*	2-3
Champaign Centennial	2-1
Urbana	2-0
Mattoon	1-0
Monticello	1-3
Mahomet-Seymour	0-4
Mattoon*	5-0
Judah Christian	5-0
Champaign St. Thomas More	1-3 (OT)

Goals By Opponent: 23 (1.1 AVG)
Goals By CHS: 53 (2.5 AVG)

2016
Coach: Dave Dunlap
Won 13, Lost 8, Tied 1
Apollo Won 4, Lost 2, Tied 0

Opponent	Score
Danville	0-2
Decatur LSA	2-1
Mattoon	1-0 (PK)
Warrensburg-Latham	1-2 (PK)
Urbana	4-2
Centralia	2-2
Olney	5-0
Salem*	3-1
Mt. Zion*	0-2
Mattoon*	2-1
Champaign Centennial	2-3
Urbana University	2-1
Salem*	2-1
Mattoon*	4-1
Mt. Zion*	0-2
Champaign Centennial	0-4
Urbana	2-1
Mattoon	3-1
Monticello	4-3
Mahomet-Seymour	0-4
Mattoon	5-0
Mahomet-Seymour	0-6

Total Goals By Opponent: 39 (1.8 AVG)
Total Goals By CHS: 43 (1.9 AVG)

2017

Coach: Tony Meza
Won 10, Lost 4, Tied 1
Apollo Won 5, Lost 0, Tied 1 (Apollo Champs)

Opponent	Score
Danville	2-3 (PK)
Centralia	4-1
Olney	10-1
Mt. Zion*	4-2
Mattoon*	1-1
Champaign Centennial	0-4
Urbana University	2-1
Salem*	5-1
Mattoon*	4-0
Mt. Zion*	4-1
Salem*	7-0
Monticello	6-2
Mahomet-Seymour	0-2
Danville	3-0
Champaign Centennial	1-2

Goals By Opponent: 20 (0.8 AVG)
Goals By CHS: 48 (3.2 AVG)

2018
Coach: Jason Garrett
Won 15, Lost 4, Tied 1

Apollo Won 7, Lost 3, Tied 0

Opponent	Score
Monticello	4-0
Danville	3-1
St. Teresa	3-2
Monticello	7-1
Mahomet-Seymour*	2-3
Centralia	6-0
Mt. Zion*	2-1
Taylorville*	5-0
Lincoln*	4-0
Mattoon*	3-0
Urbana University	2-2
Mattoon*	4-1
Mahomet-Seymour*	1-4
Mt. Zion*	2-3
Taylorville*	5-0
Olney	7-2
Lincoln*	3-0
Urbana	4-2
Centralia	9-0
Carbondale	1-3

Goals By Opponent: 25 (1.3 AVG)
Goals By CHS: 77 (3.9 AVG)

Individual Team Breakdown

Bloomington Central Catholic (3-1-0)

2008-2009	2-3
2009-2010	4-1
2010-2011	6-0
2011-2012	7-0

Bradley Bourbonnais (0-1-0)

2005-2006	3-4

Carbondale (0-1-0)

2017-2018	1-3

Champaign Centennial (4-6-3)

2006-2007	2-1
2009-2010	0-3
2010-2011	0-2
2011-2012	2-2
2012-2013	2-1
2014-2015	8-0
2015-2016	1-1
2015-2016	2-1
2016-2017	0-4

2017-2018......................0-4
2017-2018......................1-2

Champaign Central (7-5-6)

1996-1997......................1-0
1997-1998......................4-0
1999-2000......................1-1
2000-2001......................0-1
2000-2001......................1-6
2001-2002......................0-6
2002-2003......................0-3
2003-2004......................0-4
2004-2005......................1-1
2005-2006......................2-0
2006-2007......................0-0
2007-2008......................6-1
2008-2009......................1-1
2009-2010......................0-0
2010-2011......................2-0
2011-2012......................2-0
2012-2013......................0-0
2014-2015......................3-1

Chatham Glenwood (0-1-0)

2007-2008......................0-4

Centralia (10-0-1)

2006-2007......................4-0
2007-2008......................5-0
2008-2009......................4-0
2010-2011......................4-1
2011-2012......................7-1
2012-2013......................6-0
2014-2015......................2-0
2015-2016......................10-1
2016-2017......................2-2
2017-2018......................6-0
2017-2018......................9-0

Danville (17-6-0)

1996-1997......................6-0
1997-1998......................4-0
1998-1999......................3-0
1999-2000......................2-0
2000-2001......................1-2
2001-2002......................1-4
2002-2003......................1-3
2003-2004......................0-2
2004-2005......................1-0
2005-2006......................3-2
2006-2007......................5-0
2007-2008......................5-3
2008-2009......................5-1
2009-2010......................3-1
2010-2011......................2-0
2011-2012......................7-0
2013-2014......................6-0
2013-2014......................7-0
2013-2014......................8-1
2015-2016......................0-2
2016-2017....................2-3 (PK)
2016-2017......................3-0
2017-2018......................3-1

Decatur Eisenhower (16-4-0)

1997-1998......................1-0
1997-1998......................1-0
1998-1999......................0-1
1998-1999......................0-2
1998-1999......................1-0
1999-2000......................0-1
1999-2000......................4-1
2000-2001......................1-0
2001-2002......................3-0
2002-2003......................1-3
2003-2004......................1-0
2004-2005......................5-2
2004-2005......................2-1
2005-2006......................5-3
2006-2007......................2-0
2007-2008......................8-0
2008-2009......................8-0
2009-2010......................6-0

2010-2011..................3-0
2011-2012..................5-0

Decatur Lutheran (4-1-0)

2006-2007..................4-1
2008-2009..................2-1 (PK)
2011-2012..................0-1
2012-2013..................8-0
2015-2016..................2-1

Decatur MacArthur (17-8-2)

1997-1998..................3-0
1998-1999..................1-0
1998-1999..................0-0
1999-2000..................2-1(OT)
1999-2000..................3-2
2000-2001..................1-2(PK)
2000-2001..................1-0
2000-2001..................2-0
2001-2002..................0-1
2002-2003..................0-2
2003-2004..................1-0(PK)
2003-2004..................2-1
2004-2005..................1-2
2004-2005..................3-2
2005-2006..................0-3
2005-2006..................0-1
2006-2007..................2-1
2006-2007..................0-1
2007-2008..................4-3
2008-2009..................3-0
2009-2010..................2-0
2009-2010..................6-2
2010-2011..................2-1
2011-2012..................8-0
2012-2013..................9-0
2012-2013..................7-0
2014-2015..................0-0

Dundee-Crown (0-3-0)

2003-2004..................0-4

2004-2005..................1-2
2005-2006..................1-6

Dunlap (0-7-4)

2003-2004..................0-3
2004-2005..................1-2
2005-2006..................0-2
2006-2007..................0-0
2007-2008..................1-2
2008-2009..................2-2
2009-2010..................0-0
2010-2011..................1-2
2011-2012..................0-1
2012-2013..................2-2
2013-2014..................1-3

Elgin Academy (1-0-0)

2006-2007..................2-0

Galena (4-0-0)

2003-2004..................1-0
2004-2005..................3-1
2005-2006..................7-1
2006-2007..................8-0

Glenbrook South (0-1-0)

2007-2008..................1-7

Herscher (1-0-0)

1998-1999..................5-0

Jacksonville (2-3-0)

1997-1998..................0-1
1998-1999..................0-1
1999-2000..................5-1
2000-2001..................3-2
2001-2002..................0-1

Lincoln (2-0-0)

2017-2018.......................4-0
2017-2018.......................3-0

Litchfield (1-0-0)
2011-2012.......................2-0

Mahomet-Seymour (10-14-2)

1996-1997.......................1-0
1998-1999.......................3-0
1998-1999.......................2-0
1999-2000.......................4-0
1999-2000.......................5-0
2000-2001.......................2-0
2001-2002.......................0-2
2002-2003.......................0-3
2002-2003.......................0-1
2003-2004.......................1-5
2004-2005.......................2-3
2005-2006.......................0-1
2006-2007.......................1-0
2007-2008.......................2-1
2008-2009.......................2-1
2009-2010.......................0-1
2010-2011.......................1-1
2011-2012.......................0-2
2012-2013.......................2-2
2013-2014.......................3-2
2014-2015.......................0-4
2015-2016.......................0-4
2015-2016.......................0-6
2016-2017.......................0-2
2017-2018.......................2-3
2017-2018.......................1-4

Mattoon (30-6-4)

2000-2001.......................6-0
2001-2002.......................0-0
2002-2003.......................0-2
2002-2003.......................2-1
2002-2003.......................1-2
2003-2004.......................1-0
2004-2005.......................5-1
2004-2005.......................1-0
2005-2006.......................2-1
2005-2006.......................3-2
2006-2007.......................0-0
2007-2008.......................3-4
2007-2008.......................3-0
2008-2009.......................1-2
2008-2009.......................1-1
2008-2009.......................3-0
2009-2010.......................3-0
2009-2010.......................1-1
2009-2010.......................2-0
2009-2010.......................1-0
2010-2011.......................4-0
2010-2011.......................2-0
2010-2011.......................2-0
2010-2011.............0-1 (2OT)
2011-2012.......................3-0
2011-2012.......................2-0
2012-2013.......................4-0
2012-2013.......................5-0
2012-2013.......................1-0
2013-2014.......................3-0
2013-2014.......................8-0
2014-2015.......................1-0
2014-2015.......................1-2
2014-2015.......................5-0
2015-2016.......................2-1
2015-2016.......................4-1
2015-2016.......................5-0
2015-2016..................1-0 (PK)
2016-2017.......................1-1
2016-2017.......................4-0
2017-2018.......................3-0
2017-2018.......................4-1

Meridian (9-0-0)

2000-2001.......................2-1
2000-2001.......................5-0
2001-2002.......................2-1
2002-2003.......................3-2

2002-2003......................2-1
2003-2004......................4-0
2004-2005......................5-0
2005-2006......................8-0
2011-2012......................10-0

Monticello (24-2-3)

1996-1997......................2-1
1996-1997......................0-0
1997-1998......................4-0
1997-1998......................3-2
1997-1998......................2-2
1998-1999......................3-0
1998-1999......................1-1
1998-1999......................6-1
1999-2000......................2-0
1999-2000......................5-0
1999-2000......................3-0
1999-2000......................6-0
2000-2001......................7-0
2001-2002......................2-1
2002-2003......................2-0
2003-2004......................1-0
2005-2006......................6-0
2006-2007......................6-1
2007-2008......................6-1
2008-2009......................2-4
2009-2010......................1-1
2010-2011......................7-0
2011-2012......................10-0
2012-2013......................7-0
2013-2014......................8-0
2014-2015......................1-3
2015-2016......................4-3
2016-2017......................6-2
2017-2018......................4-0
2017-2018......................7-1

Morris (1-0-0)

2012-2013......................3-0

Morton JV (0-0-1)

1996-1997......................1-1

Mt. Zion (22-15-0)

1999-2000......................6-1
2000-2001......................2-0
2000-2001......................0-3
2001-2002......................0-2
2001-2002......................1-0
2002-2003......................0-1
2002-2003......................1-4
2003-2004......................1-2
2003-2004......................1-5
2003-2004......................1-3
2004-2005......................5-1
2004-2005......................6-1
2005-2006................4-3(PK)
2005-2006......................5-2
2006-2007......................5-1
2007-2008......................6-0
2008-2009................1-0(PK)
2008-2009......................3-1
2009-2010......................2-0
2010-2011................1-0 (PK)
2010-2011......................3-0
2011-2012..............2-3 (PK)
2011-2012......................6-0
2012-2013..............3-2 (OT)
2012-2013..............3-2 (OT)
2013-2014......................1-2
2013-2014......................3-1
2014-2015......................0-2
2014-2015......................1-3
2014-2015......................2-3
2015-2016......................0-2
2016-2017......................4-2
2016-2017......................4-1
2017-2018......................2-1
2017-2018......................2-3

Normal Community (1-0-0)

1997-1998................2-1(PK)

Normal University (0-2-0)

2004-2005..................0-9
2009-2010..................0-3

Normal West (0-2-0)

1999-2000................0-1 (PK)
2006-2007..................0-8
2012-2013..................1-7

Olney (12-2-2)

2001-2002..................3-0
2002-2003..................4-0
2003-2004..................3-1
2004-2005..................3-0
2005-2006..................1-2
2006-2007..................1-1
2007-2008..................1-6
2008-2009..................1-1
2009-2010..................3-0
2011-2012..................1-0
2012-2013..................8-0
2013-2014..................7-1
2014-2015..................4-1
2015-2016..................5-0
2016-2017..................10-1
2017-2018..................7-2

Pana (1-0-0)

2014-2015..................1-0 (PK)

Princeton (1-0-0)

2007-2008..................3-0

Quincy Notre Dame (0-1-0)

2011-2012..................0-8

Rantoul (4-0-0)

2000-2001..................6-0
2001-2002..................6-0
2002-2003..................6-0
2003-2004..................8-0

Salem (8-0-0)

2012-2013..................8-0
2013-2014..................7-0
2014-2015..................2-1
2014-2015..................6-0
2015-2016..................3-1
2015-2016..................2-1
2016-2017..................5-1
2016-2017..................7-0

Springfield High (0-2-0)

1999-2000..................0-3
2000-2001..................0-4

Springfield Sacred Heart Griffin (0-1-0)

2001-2002..................0-4

Springfield Ursuline (1-0-0)

1997-1998..................5-0

St. Teresa (19-3-1)

1996-1997..................6-2
1997-1998..................4-0
1998-1999..................3-0
1999-2000..................3-2
2000-2001..................1-3
2000-2001..................2-1
2001-2002..................0-4
2002-2003..................2-5
2003-2004..................2-1
2004-2005..................1-0
2004-2005..................1-1

2005-2006.................3-2(PK)
2005-2006....................3-2
2006-2007....................4-1
2007-2008....................8-1
2009-2010....................3-0
2010-2011....................3-0
2010-2011....................3-0
2011-2012....................4-0
2012-2013....................2-0
2012-2013....................4-1
2013-2014....................5-0
2017-2018....................3-2

St. Thomas More-Champaign (3-2-0)

2006-2007....................5-0
2007-2008....................5-1
2008-2009....................9-0
2013-2014....................1-4
2014-2015..................1-3 (OT)

Stephen Decatur (3-0-0)
1997-1998....................14-0
1998-1999....................11-0
1999-2000....................12-0

Taylorville (8-0-0)

2005-2006....................8-0
2006-2007....................8-0
2007-2008....................8-0
2008-2009....................7-0
2009-2010....................8-0
2010-2011....................9-0
2017-2018....................5-0
2017-2018....................5-0

Urbana (11-10-4)

1996-1997....................0-3
1996-1997....................1-2
1997-1998....................2-2
1998-1999....................3-2
1998-1999....................1-2

1999-2000....................3-0
2000-2001....................1-1
2001-2002....................0-6
2003-2004....................1-2
2004-2005....................1-5
2005-2006....................1-0
2006-2007....................1-5
2007-2008....................2-2
2008-2009....................0-2
2008-2009....................0-1
2009-2010....................2-1
2010-2011....................0-2
2011-2012....................1-1
2012-2013....................8-0
2013-2014....................4-0
2014-2015....................2-0
2014-2015....................2-0
2015-2016....................4-2
2015-2016....................2-1
2017-2018....................4-2

Urbana University (19-2-5)

1996-1997....................4-0
1996-1997....................5-3
1997-1998....................6-0
1997-1998....................9-0
1998-1999....................9-0
1999-2000....................5-0
2000-2001....................5-0
2000-2001....................6-0
2001-2002....................1-0
2002-2003....................0-0
2002-2003....................0-1
2003-2004....................1-1
2004-2005....................1-1
2005-2006....................5-0
2007-2008....................1-3
2008-2009....................4-1
2009-2010....................0-0
2010-2011....................4-1
2011-2012....................1-0
2012-2013....................9-0
20133-2014....................2-0

2014-2015.......................4-0
2015-2016.......................2-1
2016-2017.......................2-1
2-017-2018......................2-2

Warrensburg-Latham (6-3-1)

2000-2001.......................3-0
2001-2002.......................0-3

2003-2004.......................2-0
2006-2007.................2-1(OT)
2007-2008.......................1-1
2008-2009.......................0-2
2009-2010.................2-1(PK)
2013-2014.......................7-0
2014-2015.......................1-0
2015-2016.......................1-2 (PK)

-In 37 meetings that have dated back to the 1999-2000 season, Charleston and Mt. Zion have never tied. Another longtime foe that Charleston has faced, but never tied is Danville. The two teams have been playing each other since the 1996-1997 season.

CHS ALL TIME RECORD VS. CONFERENCE

Apollo Conference

Opponent	Won	Lost	Tie	Percentage
Lincoln	2	0	0	1.000
Mahomet-Seymour	10	14	2	.423
Mattoon	30	6	4	.800
Mt. Zion	22	15	0	.595
Taylorville	8	0	0	1.000
Total	72	35	6	.664

*Charleston never played Olney in the Apollo Conference. Olney left after the 2012-2013 season, and the first Apollo Conference was in 2014. Charleston holds an 8-0 mark over Salem, who left after the 2016-2017 season. Effingham has never fielded a girls' team, as girls typically play on the boy's team in the fall.

Big 12 Conference

Opponent	Won	Lost	Tie	Percentage
Champaign Centennial	4	6	3	.423
Champaign Central	7	5	6	.555
Danville	17	6	0	.739
Normal Community	0	2	0	.000
Normal West	0	3	0	.000

Urbana	11	10	4	.520
Total	39	32	9	.558

Central Illinois Conference

Opponent	Won	Lost	Tie	Percentage
Meridian	9	0	0	1.000
St. Teresa	19	3	1	.848
Warrensburg-Latham	6	3	1	.650
Total	34	6	2	.833

Central State Eight Conference

Opponent	Won	Lost	Tie	Percentage
Chatham Glenwood	0	1	0	.000
Decatur Eisenhower	16	4	0	.800
Decatur MacArthur	17	8	2	.666
Normal University	0	2	0	.000
Jacksonville	2	3	0	.400
Springfield High	0	2	0	.000
Springfield Sacred Heart Griffin	0	4	0	.000
Total	35	23	2	.600

East Central Conference

Opponent	Won	Lost	Tie	Percentage
Judah Christian	1	0	0	1.000
Urbana University	19	5	5	0860
Total	20	2	5	.8333

Illini Prairie Conference

Opponent	Won	Lost	Tie	Percentage
Bloomington Central Catholic	3	1	0	.750
Monticello	24	2	3	.879
Rantoul	4	0	0	1.000

Champaign St. Thomas More	3	2	0	.600
Total	34	5	3	.845

South Seven Conference

Opponent	Won	Lost	Tie	Percentage
Centralia	10	0	1	.954
Carbondale	0	1	0	.000
Total	10	1	1	.875

Other Opponents

Opponent	Won	Lost	Tie	Percentage
Bradley-Bourbonnais	0	1	0	.000
Decatur LSA	4	1	0	.800
Dundee-Crown	0	3	0	.000
Dunlap	0	7	4	.182
Elgin	1	0	0	1.000
Galena	4	0	0	1.000
Glenbrook South	0	1	0	.000
Herscher	1	0	0	1.000
Litchfield	1	0	0	1.000
Morris	1	0	0	1.000
Morton JV	0	0	1	.500
Olney	12	2	2	.813
Pana	1	0	0	1.000
Princeton	1	0	0	1.000
Quincy Notre Dame	0	1	0	.000
Salem	8	0	0	1.000
Springfield Ursuline	1	0	0	1.000
Stephen Decatur	3	0	0	1.000
Total	41	17	7	.685

LADY TROJAN SOCCER RECORDS

Individual Single Game

Goals Scored in a Game: 6, Molly Ball (CHS vs. Decatur Eisenhower) 3-29-08
Assists in a Game: 4, Emily Garrett (CHS vs. Urbana University) 5-19-98
Goalie Saves in a Game: 24, Coartney McKinney (CHS vs. Champaign Central) 4-17-03

Team Single Game

Most Goals Scored in a Game: 14, (CHS vs. Stephen Decatur) 4-4-98
Most Assists in a Game: 7, (CHS vs. Stephen Decatur) 4-4-98
Most Goals Allowed in a Game: 9, (CHS vs. Normal Community) 5-21-05
Most Shots on Goal in a Game: 57, (CHS vs. Centralia) 4-28-07
Most Shots on Goal Allowed in a Game: 35, (CHS vs. Champaign Central) 4-17-03
Most Fouls Committed in a Game: 16, (CHS vs. Mattoon) 5-19-09
Most Goals Scored in the First Half in a Game: 9, (CHS vs. Centralia) 5-14-18
Most Goals Scored in the Second Half in a Game: 7, (CHS vs. Stephen Decatur) 4-3-99
                                         (CHS vs. Urbana University) 4-17-07
                                             (CHS vs. MacArthur) 4-20-13

Individual Single Season

Most Goals Scored: 42, Molly Ball-2008
Highest Goals Per Game Average: 2.00, Molly Ball-2008
Most Assists: 22, Emily Garrett-1998
Most Total Offensive Points: 92, Molly Ball-2008
Most Goalie Saves: 129, Shanna Davis-2003
Goals Scored as a Junior: 39, Molly Ball-2007
Most Goals Scored as a Sophomore: 25, Molly Ball-2006
Most Goals Scored as a Freshman: 11, Holly Wholtman-2007

Team Single Season

Most Goals Scored: (105)-2014
Fewest Goals Scored: (18)-2002
Fewest Goals Allowed: (12)-1997/2000
Shutout Wins: (17)-2013
Most Goalie Saves: (182)-2003
Most Shots on Goal: (427)-2007
Most Shots on Goal Allowed: (269)-2003
Most Fouls Committed: (153)-1999
Most Goals Scored in the First Half: (56)-2014
Most Goals Scored in the Second Half: (50)-2013
Fewest Goals Allowed in the First Half: (3)-2000
Fewest Goals Allowed in the Second Half: (5)-1998
Highest Goals Per Game Average: (4.95)-2014
Most Wins: (19)-2013, 2014
Fewest Wins: (6)-2003
Most Losses: (12)-2003
Fewest Losses: (1)-2013
Most Ties: (5)-2010

Career

Most Goals Scored: 107, Molly Ball (2005-2008
Most Goals/Game: 1.41, Molly Ball (2005-2008)
Most Assists: 50, Emily Garrett (1997-2000)
Most Assists/Game: 0.98, Emily Garrett (1997-2000)
Total Offensive Points: 239, Molly Ball (2005-2008)
Most Goalie Saves: 358, Shanna Davis (2000-2003)
Most Games Played: 89, Kristen Elsila (2007-2010)

Miscellaneous Records

Longest Overall Road Win Streak	15 (2013-2015)
Longest Overall Road Losing Streak	4, (2002-2003)
Longest Overall Home Win Streak	10 (2013-2015)
Longest Overall Home Losing Streak	3, (2003)
Most Consecutive Losses	4, (2002/2004)
Most Consecutive Wins	12, (2013)
Most Consecutive Games Won Without Loss/Tie	13, (2007)
Best Win Percentage	.891, (2013)
Worst Losing Percentage	.318, (2003)
Most Wins	19,(2013) (2014)
Most Losses	12, (2003)
Most Ties	5, (2010)
Fewest Wins	6, (2003)
Fewest Losses	1, (2013)

. . . .

According to a 1998 sports story by Brian Nielsen in the Journal Gazette-Times Courier, Bobby Jo Buchar became the first player in the Lady Trojan's history to head the ball in for a goal. She converted Emily Garrett's corner kick for one of her two goals in a 4-0 victory over Monticello.

By the end Liz Nino's tenure as head coach, CHS had a combined girls soccer record of 73 wins, 18 losses and 14 ties for the varsity and junior varsity efforts.

There are only 14 members of the "Over Eighty Games Played Club" in Charleston High School history. Four of them came from the class of 2010 and the class of 2014. From the class of 2010, Holly Wholtman had 82, Theresa Bates 83, Anika Guinto 84, and Kristen Elsila are the all-time leader in games played with 89, just beating previous record holder Raven Mott's 86 (Class of 2009). From the class of 2014, Mackenzie Burgess, Sarah Gisondi, Madi Fisher, and Ali Carlson finished with over 80 games played.

All-Apollo Conference

The first All-Apollo Conference team was awarded in 2014. First team and second team selections began being awarded in 2017. The first Apollo Conference title was not awarded until 2013. The winners of the Apollo Conference have gone as followed: Charleston-2013, Charleston-2014, Mt. Zion-2015, Mt. Zion-2016, Charleston-2017, Mahomet-Seymour-2018.

All-Apollo Conference

Makenzie Burgess, Midfielder, 2013
Ali Carlson, Midfielder, 2013
Madi Fisher, Forward, 2013
Kristen Gisondi, Goalkeeper, 2013
Sarah Gisondi, Midfielder, 2013
Laura Pritschet, Defender-2013
Makenzie Burgess, Midfielder, 2014
Ali Carlson, Midfielder, 2014
Madi Fisher, Forward, 2014
Sarah Gisondi, Midfielder, 2014
Codi Martin, Defender, 2014
Catherine Smith, Defender, 2015
Brooke Tozer, Defender, 2015
Emily Bumpus, Midfielder, 2015
Ali Hosey, Forward, 2015
Lyndsey Hunt, Midfielder, 2015
Brooke Tozer, Defender, 2016
Ali Hosey, Forward, 2016
Maya Caltry, Midfielder, 2016
Aislinn Parish, Midfielder, 2016

First Team All-Apollo Conference

Julia Griffin, Forward, 2017
Ali Hosey, Forward, 2017
Aislinn Parish, Goalkeeper, 2017
Maya Caltry, Midfielder, 2018
Julia Griffin, Forward, 2018
Rainer FullerMoore, Defender, 2018

Second Team All-Apollo Conference

Maya Caltry, Midfielder, 2017
Taylor Gadus, Defender, 2017
Maya Ruffolo, Midfielder, 2017
Hope Griffin, Midfielder, 2018
Bernie Jackson, Defender, 2018
Emily Sweeney, Midfielder, 2018

IHSA All State Selections

Madi Fisher, Forward, 2013
Madi Fisher, Forward, 2014

Decatur Herald & Review Coach of the Year

Liz Nino-1999
Liz Nino-2000
Paul Stranz-2005
Paul Stranz-2007
Paul Stranz-2010
Paul Stranz-2013

National Soccer Coaches Association of America Regional Coach of the Year

Paul Stranz-2014

Decatur Area Player of the Year

Emily Garrett, Midfielder, 2000
Molly Ball, Forward, 2008

**Madi Fisher missed out being named in 2014. She lost to Mt. Zion's McKayla Harder, who won the award four years in a row.

Ball, Singer, Fisher, & Hosey Lead Scorers

Molly Ball's 2.0 goals per game scoring average is the best in school history. Her 42 goals are a single season record. Alex Singer is the only member in history to lead the team all four years of high school. Ball, Madi Fisher, and Ali Hosey led CHS teams in scoring for three straight years. In 2018, Julia Griffin surged her way to the third best scoring single season to cement her place in the top ten in all-time career scorers.

SEASON SCORING LEADERS

Girls Soccer

Year	Player	Games	Goals	Scoring Average
1997	Anna Wheeler	11	13	1.18
1998	Bobby Jo Buchar	17	20	1.18
1999	Bobby Jo Buchar	15	19	.79
2000	Sara Fisher	21	12	.57
2001	Sara Fisher	23	18	.78
2002	Alex Singer	19	5	.26
2003	Alex Singer	19	6	.32
2004	Alex Singer	21	16	.76
2005	Alex Singer	22	17	.77
2006	Molly Ball	23	25	1.14
2007	Molly Ball	24	39	1.63
2008	Molly Ball	21	42	2.00
2009	Holly Wholtman	22	12	.80
2010	Holly Wholtman	23	19	.87
2011	Megan Hjort	22	21	.95
2012	Madi Fisher	22	17	.77
2013	Madi Fisher	23	22	.96
2014	Madi Fisher	22	27	1.22
2015	Ali Hosey	21	17	.81
2016	Ali Hosey	22	12	.55
2017	Ali Hosey	15	16	1.0
2018	Julia Griffin	20	29	1.5

TOP TEN (Single Season)

2008 Molly Ball…………………42
2007 Molly Ball…………………39
2018 Julia Griffin………………29
2014 Madi Fisher………………27
2006 Molly Ball…………………25
2013 Madi Fisher………………22
2011 Megan Hjort………………21
1998 Bobby Jo Buchar…………20
2010 Holly Wholtman…………19
1999 Bobby Jo Buchar…………19
2014 Makenzie Burgess………19

TOP TEN (Career)

2005-2008 Molly Ball…………107
2011-2014 Madi Fisher…………68
2014-2017 Ali Hosey……………56

2007-2010 Holly Wholtman......53
2010-2013 Megan Hjort.........52
2011-2014 Makenzie Burgess...51
1998-2001 Sara Fisher...........48

2002-2005 Alex Singer............48
2015-2018 Julia Griffin............47
2011-2014 Ali Carlson...............41

Top Five All-Time Scorers

No. Player	Years Played	Goals	Assists	Total Points
1. Molly Ball	2005-2008	107	25	239
2. Madi Fisher	2011-2014	68	41	138
2. Holly Wholtman	2007-2010	53	29	135
4. Ali Hosey	2015-2017	56	21	133
5. Megan Hjort	2010-2013	52	21	125

Stranz Headlines Trojan Coaching Records

Stranz nearly didn't have a head coaching job when he started. Hank Nino's assistant for a number of years, Adam Howarth, was picked first to fill the shoes of soccer coaching at the helm of Charleston. It was just months after when Howarth was picked to be Charleston's Eastern Illinois University men's soccer coach, leaving a vacant coaching spot just weeks before the season was scheduled to begin.

Stranz was still a good choice. Stranz's demand for discipline and respect for the game led him to 219 victories for the guys and 194 victories for the girls. Stranz also has had both teams win a combined 13 Regional Championships. The girls have never been to state, yet of course, but the guys have four Sectional Championships and three state qualifying years. Stranz led the undefeated regular season team in 2013, while guiding the team to a school record for wins with 19 in 2013 and 2014.

Girls Soccer All-Time Girls Soccer Coaching Records

Years	Coach	Total Years	Won	Lost	Tied	Percentage
2018-Present	Jason Garrett	1	15	4	1	.775
2017	Tony Meza	1	10	4	1	.750
1997-2000	Liz Nino	4	49	13	8	.757
2001-2014	Paul Stranz	14	194	83	28	.681
2015-2016	Dave Dunlap	2	27	14	2	.651
Totals	5 Coaches	22	280	144	40	.647

All-Time Girls Soccer Coaching Records for Apollo Conference

Years	Coach	Total Years	Won	Lost	Tied	Percentage
2013-2014	Paul Stranz	2	6	0	0	1.000
2017	Tony Meza	1	5	0	1	.917
2018-Present	Jason Garrett	1	7	3	0	.700

2014-2015	Dave Dunlap	2	7	5	0	.583
Totals	4 Coaches	6	25	8	1	.750

Girls Soccer (Single Season)

Most Wins..19, Paul Stranz, 2013, 2014
Fewest Wins..6, Paul Stranz, 2003
Most Losses..12, Paul Stranz, 2003
Fewest Losses..1, Paul Stranz, 2013
Most Ties...5, Paul Stranz, 2010
Most Consecutive Wins..19, Paul Stranz, 2013
Most Consecutive Games Won Without Loss/Tie..13, Paul Stranz, 2007
Best Win Percentage..0.891, Paul Stranz, 2013
Worst Losing Percentage..318, Paul Stranz, 2003

Girls Soccer (Career)

Most Regional Titles..5, Paul Stranz (2005, 2007, 2010, 2012, 2013)
Most Central Illinois Soccer Conference Titles (Disbanded)..................2, Liz Nino (1997, 1998)
Most Soccer Tournament Titles: 6, Paul Stranz (St. Teresa Champs-2007, 2010, 2011, 2013; Lady Trojans Spring Classic Champs-2010, Dunlap Invite Champs-2007)
Most Apollo Conference Titles…………………………………..2, Paul Stranz (2013, 2014)
Decatur Herald and Review Coach Of the Year...............4, Paul Stranz-2005, 2007, 2010, 2014)

Stranz's Legacy Cemented with Field Naming

The all-time winningest coach for the boy's and girls' soccer teams at Charleston High School had the field named after him March 24th, 2018. "Paul Stranz Field" was born in front of 250 people to honor Stranz and his accomplishments. Stranz dedicated this moment to his wife, who he has celebrated 42 years of marriage.

Justin Rust of the JG-TC wrote as Stranz choked up as he directed his wife "I really do appreciate it because there were a lot of times I would get up at 4 or 4:30 in the morning and then after a game, it would be 9:30 or 10 at night I would get home. Soccer consumed my life, and she was able to keep me on the straight and narrow."

Stranz was instrumental in fundraising. Donations were taken for lights and shelters. Stranz created the annual "Kick for the Cure" girls soccer match between Charleston and Mattoon, which raised money for cancer awareness. To this date, Rust reported that more than $15,000 was raised for the Sarah Bush Regional Cancer Center due to the match.

"I really didn't think about it because none of the teams were about me or my wins," said Stranz. "It was about how we could improve and what we could do as a team. This was the furthest thing from my mine, but a fantastic honor."

CHARLESTON GIRLS SOCCER HEADLINERS

Girls Soccer Team's First Regional in 1998

In just their second year of existence, the Lady Trojans won the school's first Regional. Charleston opened the season by winning their first nine games. The winning streak was snapped with a 1-0 loss to Jacksonville. After the loss, Charleston tied Monticello and Urbana. Then wins over Decatur Eisenhower and Urbana University put them back on track before the IHSA tournament. Leading the way all season was junior Bobby Jo Buchar, and sophomores, Anna Wheeler, and Emily Garrett. Before the Regional game, Garrett was coming off a three goal, four assist performances against Urbana University.

Charleston's first opponent was Springfield Ursuline (now Sacred Heart Griffin), a private school made up 268 students at the time. This was the first time the two teams ever met. "I think it's kind of exciting to play a team we haven't played during the season," said head coach Liz Nino to Nielsen. "If you play a team you've already beaten you can get overconfident."

Wheeler led the way with a hat trick, and Charleston won a 5-0 decision. The win set Charleston into the championship game against Normal Community. The game was to be played at Eastern Illinois University's Lakeside Field. "It should be an excellent game," said Nino after the game to Nielsen. "Last year we were eliminated in the second round of regionals. We hope to win regionals this year. It should be a very competitive game, and we look forward to having the hometown advantage."

To win the championship, the Lady Trojans were going to have to gut it out. Charleston outlasted Normal Community in a 2-1 win in penalty kicks after playing in regulation and overtime. Goalkeeper, Sarah Toberman, had to leave the game with a bloody nose. Normal held a 1-0 lead in the first half, but Wheeler was able to take a pass from Garrett to score in the second half to knot it up at one. Two ten-minute overtimes were played, and by the end, seven Lady Trojans had played 100 straight minutes.

To decide the victory, penalty kicks were shot. Jill Buchar replaced Toberman in goal. "Sarah didn't want to come out," said Nino to Nielsen. "Somebody kicked her in the face during a shot. She stuck a tissue in her nose and said she could keep playing, but there was blood running all over her uniform. There's also a rule where if the coach runs in, the player has to be taken out."

Garret sank the first goal. After that, every CHS shooter, which included Wheeler, freshman Sarah Fisher, and sophomore Ashley Hutti, made their goals for the satisfying win. "We didn't do much more conditioning for this bigger field," said Coach Nino to Nielsen. "We actually had them lay off a bit because we have them run as much as cross-country teams do during the season. Today was just great. Any team can beat anybody else on a given day."

The marathon game might have hurt Charleston's chances in an upset of Springfield Sacred Heart-Griffin. The Lady Trojans bowed out with a 6-0 loss. "It was a very physical game on Tuesday," said Nino to Nielsen. "It took a lot out of the players, and some were still tired. I told the girls, there's very few teams left in the sectional and I'm very proud of them."

If fatigue wasn't enough, then Springfield's 6-foot 4-inch goalie, Jamie Smith in goal added insult to injury. Charleston only managed one shot on goal and were shut out for the second time that season. "I was impressed with Charleston." said Springfield High coach Bob Wharton. "For a second-year team, they are amazing. This is my 10th year coaching the (Springfield) girls.

Charleston was still happy to make it that far. "We are a very young team," said Nino to Nielsen. "This was a good learning experience. I want to give credit to Missy Doudna (on defense) today. We set a lofty goal of winning the regional and we did that. For these girls to get to sectionals, it's wonderful."

Buchar led the team in goals with 20, and offensive points with 45. Garrett set two records. Her four assists in a game, and 22 assists in the '98 season are still records today. She finished with 44 offensive points. Wheeler had marks of 18 goals, and five assists for 41 offensive points.

2013 Team Gets Hung Up on Wall

This was the deepest Charleston had coming back in years. Charleston lost only four seniors from a team that went 15-5-2. Before the season even started, the team had three future collegiate soccer players. Senior, Megan Hjort, elected to sign with Kaskaskia College. Juniors, Ali Carlson and Madi Fisher, both verbally committed to Eastern Illinois University.

The team also had returning third year starter, and all-sectional goalie, Kristen Gisondi, who was receiving interest from Monmouth College, as well as her junior sister, Sarah Gisondi. Makenzie Burgess was back in the midfield, and the defense looked solid with senior captains Ashtan Marucco and Laura Pritschet leading the way, along with juniors Cody Martin, and Ian FullerMoore. Catherine Smith and Emily Bumpus each came back with experience.

While the chatter of the games the team would win circulated, the team just wanted to practice on the field. A snow storm and multiple rainy days hit Charleston hard to keep the Lady Trojans confined to the gym.

"It is horrible. I have never had to deal with weather this bad before during the season," said Stranz to Nielsen. "We are just trying to find space in the gym between the track teams and JV/varsity baseball and softball. It's hard to find in hour in the gym. I have to compliment the girls for being so flexible because we have been moving practice times and places."

The wins did come though, specifically 12 straight wins to open the season. The Lady Trojans won the St. Teresa Invitational. Charleston did so in defeating Decatur Lutheran 8-0, Mount Zion in penalty kicks, and St. Teresa 2-0. It was the third straight year Charleston defeated Mount Zion at this tournament in overtime. Charleston won their home opener, an 8-0 game over Urbana. Then, the team traveled to Centralia for a 6-0 win.

That was followed with an 8-0 victory over Olney. Fisher scored two of Charleston's six first half goals, making it up to her coach. In observance of Good Friday, Fisher showed up 30 minutes late. "I didn't get a whole lot of time to warm up, so I didn't get to play a whole lot," said Fisher. "I had to go to church." Stranz wasn't too upset about it. "We were without Catherine Smith too, but it's no problem they missed since it's a church service," said Stranz. "They came in ready to go when they showed up. I'm just happy to get a game in honestly."

In their rematch, St. Teresa slapped Charleston with their first goal allowed of the season. Winning 1-0 at halftime, Charleston dominated in the second half to win 4-1. After that, Charleston followed with wins over Mattoon, Champaign Centennial, Decatur MacArthur,

Urbana University, and Salem. Moving onto their Lady Trojan Invitational that brought in strong foes in Champaign Central, Dunlap, and Mattoon, Charleston still stood undefeated at 12-0-0.

Charleston's win streak wasn't necessarily broken, but a tie to Champaign Central stopped the run of "W's." Kristen Gisondi only had one save recorded, but it was the one that mattered. Champaign Central's Emica Quigley snuck past a Charleston defender and had a one-on-one break-a-way with Gisondi. The senior's decision to come out of the box proved true as she laid out to stop the line drive shot and keep Charleston tied 0-0. "She is there for the clutch moments," said Stranz. "A lot of the times, she gets bored back there, but when it's time to shine, she is there to make the play."

Needing two goals in the final 4:11 to rally to tie Dunlap added another tie for Charleston. Carlson scored the first goal with 4:11 remaining. Then, with 1:06 left, Burgess netted her first goal of the tournament to keep this undefeated season alive. Charleston bounced back with a 5-0 win over Mattoon. It was their 12th shutout in 15 games. Burgess, Fisher, and both Gisondis (Kristen and Sarah) made the all-tournament team.

The Lady Trojans clinched the first ever Apollo Conference championship. It was the first year the Apollo Conference had enough teams with Charleston, Mattoon, Mount Zion, and Salem fielding teams. Charleston clinched the championship with a win over Mount Zion in overtime. Wins over Monticello, Urbana University, and Danville ended the regular season. Charleston nearly defeated Mahomet-Seymour but had to settle for a 2-2 tie after Mahomet tied it with under four minutes to play.

Off to Regionals as the number one seed, Charleston opted to go with a new formation late in the season. "We're going to try to change a few things up and this will give us a chance to test it out," Stranz said. "We have been doing well but after playing Mahomet-Seymour (in a 2-2 tie last week) I think I need to have another formation and we'll try it (tonight)."

Charleston mowed past Decatur MacArthur 7-0. Hjort and Chioma Obia scored two goals. Carlson, Burgess, and Shelby Linder added a goal as well. The win set up a Coles County clash for the Regional Championship. The Lady Trojans had defeated Mattoon twice already this season, but the third time wasn't going to be easy. Charleston sneaked past Mattoon with a 1-0 win. Christine Ryan's goal with 14:33 left in the second half was enough for Charleston to win the Regional title.

The new formations growing pains were shown for a team that came into the game averaging five goals a game. "We are working on a new formation that should work," said Stranz. "We were doing things in slow motion so they can get the movements. We stuck with it in the first half. I wish we could have started in the middle of the season and flip flopped."

The game nearly went into overtime. With 45 seconds remaining, Mattoon's record setting goal scorer, Lexi Rainwater, found herself in a one-on-one situation with Kristen Gisondi in goal. A bad bounce took the ball away from Rainwater, and Gisondi made it in time to bat the ball away, sealing the victory. "I'm walking away frustrated," said Stranz. "I'm glad we got the win, but we didn't look like a regional champion."

The win sent Charleston to the Normal West Sectional. The drive was nearly two hours with their first opponent being Morris, a sub-.500 team that won their Regional. Charleston was up against the wind in the first half but was able to command a 2-0 halftime lead. Four corner kicks began the game for Morris but was able to connect. Then, about two minutes later, Carlson drove down the field to set up Fisher for the first goal. Then, Hjort was able to launch a

30-yard kick for a goal that sailed through the wind. "I was trying to shoot but I didn't expect it to go in," she said. "I expected Ali or Christine to get it. When it went in I was surprised."

By no means was the game complete with the 2-0 lead. Morris had come back from a 2-0 deficit to beat Yorkville 3-2 in their regional championship. "Two-zero is a dangerous score," the Charleston coach said. "I would have liked to have gotten a third goal a little sooner." That third goal game from Burgess with under five minutes to play to seal the game. "We've done well in the second half in games against (Champaign) Centennial and Mount Zion," Stranz said. "We maintained control and were able to have success. It worked out extremely well. We're doing a lot better passing."

Playing in their first ever sectional championship, Charleston was faced with the monstrous task in Normal West. The Big 12 Conference champions came into the game with a 21-4-2 record and were playing for the sectional title on their home field. "This will probably be the strongest team we've played," Stranz said. "We've played some teams with some good players but they have three or four girls who are really good

One of those girls was Tess Marcodes. The junior defender wowed fans with her cartwheel like throw-ins to set up two goals as well as throw a goal in herself in the first half. It didn't help that freshman, Katie Lorenz, added two goals in a 7-1 victory over Charleston. "They have a good, physical team," said Stranz. "We dropped our heads a little bit after the flips throws because we knew it shouldn't have happened. It cost us and took us out of the game."

The Normal West coach was a little blunter with his assessment of the game. "Not to discourage Charleston because they are a good team, but the thing with them is I don't think they were ready for this level of skill and ability," said West coach Val Walker. "We lost four games, but we play Chicago teams, and high competition. My recommendation is to toughen up their schedule."

Hjort scored an equalizer on an assist from Chioma Obia, but the 1-1 tie was a distant memory when Normal West held a 4-1 halftime lead. Marcodes set up Rachel Weber for a goal with a throw-in. Then, Marcodes literally threw in a goal herself. The ball took a deep bounce and bounced over Gisondi in goal. Three second half goals ended Charleston's best season in school history. "They were a good team," said Stranz. "We look to be back. We know what we need to work on."

The season concluded a 19-1-3 record for the Lady Trojans. Fisher led the team with 22 goals and 10 assists and was named to the all-state team. Carlson had 15 goals and nine assists. Burgess had a breakout junior season with 18 goals. Hjort finished her last season with 13 goals. Fisher, Burgess, and Kristin Gisondi were named to the Herald & Review first team all-area team. Sarah Gisondi, Hjort, Pritschet, and Carlson were named to the second team. Marucco and Cody Martin made the honorable mention team. The team set a new record in goals scored with 104 goals. They also broke the shutouts record with 16. The old record of 12 had stood since 2001.

School Record Tying Squad Falls in Regional Title in 2014

Charleston might have had one of their deepest teams on the offensive side in years with 64 goals returning between players Madi Fisher, Ali Carlson, Makenzie Burgess, and Sarah Gisondi, all seniors. The year started off on the wrong foot, losing out on a St. Teresa

Tournament title by falling to Mt. Zion 2-1. The Lady Trojans responded by rattling off 14 straight wins before falling to Dunlap 3-1 in the Charleston Spring Classic.

Charleston mowed down the Apollo Conference, winning the conference for a second year in a row with a 3-0 win over Mattoon, 7-0 win over Salem, and a 3-1 revenge win over Mt. Zion. Charleston headed into their own Regional with a 18-2-0 record, which netted the one seed. After an 8-0 win over Monticello, it set up a match against Champaign St. Thomas More.

Both teams faced adversity when Charleston's field was deemed unplayable due to rain. This setup a chance in placement with the game being played on Eastern Illinois University's substitute field. Charleston even held a 1-0 halftime lead when Ali Carlson drilled a goal from a pass from Chioma Obia and Madi Fisher. However, everything began to crumble in the second half.

All-Apollo defender Cody Martin had to leave the game with an ankle injury. With 25:13 remaining in the game, Louisette Lukusa hit the game-tying goal. About eight minutes later, Ronda Harsbarger put in the go-ahead goal. Then, 58 seconds later, Lukusa had a break-a-way and finished that, and with 8:44 remaining, the Charleston defense scored on their own goal at St. Thomas More upset the Trojans 4-1.

Stranz told JG-TC sports editor Brian Nielsen after the game, "I still think we are the better team. But we didn't show it today. She's (Lukusa) physical. The first part of the game we were able to score and keep her in check. We got the bruises and fouls from that. She's got the speed and did a fine job. We made a few mistakes and it cost us."

The best offensive team in history had to end their season with no hardware. The 2014 squad broke a school record for goals in a season with 105. Five girls had at least 13 goals or more. On the defensive side, the team allowed just 15 goals all season.

Five members of the team went on to play college soccer. Fisher and Carlson went on to play at Eastern Illinois University, Burgess went on to play at Kaskaskia College, Sarah Gisondi joined her sister Kristen at Monmouth College, and Martin went to Heartland College. Stranz was named the IHSSA Coach of the Year, while Fisher was an All-State selection. Fisher finished the year with 27 goals and 21 assists. Her assists total was just one assist away from tying the school record.

Trojans Girls Softball
(1981-2018)

Trojans Girls Softball
(1981-2018)

You can't talk about CHS softball without talking about Karen Karch. The former math teacher and softball coach was a pioneer for CHS softball. Karch helped start the program and led the team from 1981 to 2012, totaling 435 career wins, and 427 career losses in 32 years. Her 435 career wins are tied for 35th all-time in IHSA history.

Karch led Charleston to Apollo Conference titles in 1984 and 1985, while leading the team to Regional titles in 1985, 1986, and 1994. Keep in mind that CHS was playing softball powerhouses Mattoon and Mt. Zion multiple times a year. The two programs combined for 25 Regional titles, eight Sectional Championships, a 4th place and state-runner up finish, making them a formidable opponent for Charleston.

In 2012, Karch had the home field named after her, which was well deserving honor. When Karch began coaching in 1981, the team did not have a field. Karch lived near Carl Sandberg Elementary, and the school provided the team a field. Karch had a lot of maintenance with the field though. Many times, she had to bring her own gardening hose and siphon the field that pooled in left field. Karch also had to fend of neighbored dogs from walking across the field and picking up rocks and glass that laid around the field. The field also had no fence for the dugout, and just two benches for spectating.

The Lady Trojans tried playing at Lanman Field and Baker Field for a while. When trying to borrow Seaton Complex, Karch was told the team could not practice there because the fields were meant for the youth teams. It took until 2004 when CHS started complex additions and the softball team was presented their own home softball field. When asked about her thoughts about having the field be named "Karen Karch Field," the longtime coach showed some emotion that was similar to when she was first presented an athletic uniform for the first time. Karch grew up an era where girls were not provided opportunities to play sports.

"I don't even know what to say," Karch told Journal Gazette-Times Courier sports editor Brian Nielsen. "Just having a field of our own was wonderful. It is very humbling. For them to think of me enough to do this is very humbling."

Karch did not just battle field issues during her tenure as head coach, but also the discrimination of being a woman. In her earlier years, Karch told Nielsen she was glad that one of her many assistant coaches was a male. "He had more leeway when it came to talking to male umpires," Karch told Nielsen. "They did not even let me ask a question. I couldn't say as much as a male, so I would send Dave McGrady out to yell and he could say as much as he wanted."

Karch was inducted into the Illinois Coaches Association Softball Hall of Fame in the winter of 2013. She was inducted in the same class as longtime coaching counterpart Dave McDowell, who spent 28 seasons coaching at Mattoon High School. Karch joked about how great it was to be inducted with him. She told Nielsen, "When I was writing my bio for the Hall of Fame, I thought about saying how many times we won the Apollo or the Regional, but then I thought how many more times Dave McDowell and Greg Blakey (Mt. Zion coach) had."

Through all her years, it was not the regular season or postseason success that Karch was most proud of. It was the fact that her Charleston teams were cited by the IHSA for the

Sport a Winning Attitude award three times, an award that recognizes teams for good sportsmanship. "In my early years, I probably lacked sportsmanship skills," Karch told Nielsen. "I let my temper get the best of me. Over the years, I tried to live that reputation down, so when were recognized, I felt really good about that."

There have been some good players throughout Karch's 32 years. Lori Beals is still ranked in the IHSA record book for hitting three triples in a game against Mt. Zion on May 8, 1993. She is tied with several other players for second most in a game all-time. A couple of Parkland College recruits enjoyed success at Charleston. Erin James, class of 2001, stole a career record 114 bases. She currently ranks as the No. 1, No. 2, and No. 3 spots for stolen bases in a season. Ami Simpson, class of 2010, still holds the record for wins in a season with 18. Simpson used to hold the record for runs batted in for a season until that record was broken in 2018.

Braddi Reed is another name thrown around as one of the best pitchers in CHS history. Reed still holds the record for earned run average in a season (1.77), strikeouts (144), shutouts (5), and strikeouts in a game (16). Reed graduated in 2009 and played at Olney Central Community College. Vanessa James is on the best fielders in school history, holding the two spots in the all-time list for assists. James graduated in 2006 and played at Lake Land College for two years before playing two more years at the University of Louisville.

Simpson's teammate Kaylie Pruett held the single season runs record until 2018 by scoring 49 times during Charleston's then-single season record 24-8 win team. Pruett enjoyed a four-year career playing at Eastern Illinois University. The Pruett family has been big into softball for years, coaching many Charleston Chill teams.

After the Karch era ended, former track coach Blain Mayhall stepped in as the Charleston Middle School coach and then quickly accepted the high school position. Mayhall as rebuilt Charleston softball. After taking over the CMS team, Mayhall has gone 84-26 with a 3rd place state finish in 2015, and a 2nd place finish in 2014. For the high school, in Mayhall's fifth season, the team tied the school record for wins in 2017, while having the best ever-team in 2018 by going 31-5 (more on that team down below).

During the six-year run at the high school, Mayhall owns a 125-59 record. Charleston broke a 24-year Regional title drought and won their first Apollo Conference Championship since 1985. Players for Mayhall have broken 21 of 36 possible individual school records and 14 of 24 possible team records. The 2018 team recorded the first ever Sweet 16 finish in Charleston history.

Girls Softball (Taken from IHSA Website)

Season	Class	Titles	Place	Won	Lost	Tied	Coach
1980-81				2	10		Karen Karch
1981-82				9	8		Karen Karch
1982-83				5	9		Karen Karch
1983-84				16	4		Karen Karch
1984-85	AA	R		21	5		Karen Karch
1985-86	AA	R		15	15		Karen Karch

Year				W	L	Coach
1986-87				15	12	Karen Karch
1987-88				9	18	Karen Karch
1988-89				5	10	Karen Karch
1989-90				13	15	Karen Karch
1990-91				7	18	Karen Karch
1991-92				13	11	Karen Karch
1992-93				17	7	Karen Karch
1993-94	AA	R		16	14	Karen Karch
1994-95				12	17	Karen Karch
1995-96				7	16	Karen Karch
1996-97				15	14	Karen Karch
1997-98				6	18	Karen Karch
1998-99				13	16	Karen Karch
1999-00				18	12	Karen Karch
2000-01				17	15	Karen Karch
2001-02				11	14	Karen Karch
2002-03				13	17	Karen Karch
2003-04				18	14	Karen Karch
2004-05				17	18	Karen Karch
2005-06				16	19	Karen Karch
2006-07				11	21	Karen Karch
2007-08				20	13	Karen Karch
2008-09				21	12	Karen Karch
2009-10				24	8	Karen Karch
2010-11				17	14	Karen Karch
2011-12				16	13	Karen Karch
			Coach Total	435	427	32 yr .505
2012-13				17	14	Blain Mayhall
2013-14				19	11	Blain Mayhall
2014-15				16	14	Blain Mayhall
2015-16				18	10	Blain Mayhall
2016-17				24	5	Blain Mayhall
2017-18	3A	R		31	5	Blain Mayhall
			Coach Total	125	59	6 yr .679
			School Total	560	486	38 yr .535

CHARLESTON SOFTBALL RECORDS

Batting Average in a Season
.610, Ally O'Dell-2017
.609, Brandi Akins-1993
.564, Erin James-1999
.562, Macey McElravy-2017
.556, Macey McElravy-2018

.523, Reagan McGahey-2018
.515, Mara Crimmins-1989
.509, Vanessa James-2006

At Bats in a Season
130, Reagan McGahey-2018
126, Macey McElravy-2018
126, Natalie Gordon-2018
124, Ramsey Armstrong-2018
124, Vanessa James-2005
120, S. Vaughn-2005

Runs Scored in a Season
63, Reagan McGahey-2018
49, Natalie Gordon-2018
49, Macey McElravy-2018
48, Kaylie Pruett-2010
45, Haley Sparks-2010

Hits in a Season
70, Macey McElravy-2018
68, Reagan McGahey-2018
63, Macey McElravy-2017
57, Ramsey Armstrong-2018
57, Erin James-1999
56, Natalie Gordon-2018
56, Vanessa James-2005
56, Vanessa James-2006
50, Mara Crimmins-1989

Doubles in a Season
14, Reagan McGahey-2018
13, Macey McElravy-2018
13, Ramsey Armstrong-2018
13, Haley Sparks-2010
13, Macey McElravy-2017
13, Sam Maxey-2010

Triples in a Season
10, Mara Crimmins-1989
8, Natalie Gordon-2018
8, Reagan McGahey-2018
8, Erin Whitley-1985
7, Erin Whitley-1984
7, C. Clark-2004

Home Runs in a Season
15, Macey McElravy-2018
13, Reagan McGahey-2018
9, Macey McElravy-2017
7, Ramsey Armstrong-2018

6, Rachel Doty-2011

Stolen Bases in a Season
48, Erin James-2001
35, Erin James-2000
31, Erin James-1999
23, C. Babbs-1996
23, C. Babbs-1997

Sacrifices in a Season
18- Haley Cooley-2014
11, Ali Finn-2012
8, Courtney Campbell-2006

Most Base on Balls
27, Katherine Kennedy-2014
26, T. Helton-1987
26, S. Dell-1993

RBI's in a Season
63, Reagan McGahey-2018
56, Macey McElravy-2018
44, Ami Simpson-2010
42, S. Wall-1996
37, Ramsey Armstrong-2018
37, Ally O'Dell-2015
37, Macey McElravy-2017

On Base Percentage in a Season
.594, Macey McElravy-2018
.573, Macey McElravy-2017
.563, Reagan McGahey-2018
.557, Mara Crimmins-1989
.552, Erin James-1999

Slugging % in a Season
1.054, Reagan McGahey-2018
1.032, Macey McElravy-2018
.920, Macey McElravy-2017
.781, Ally O'Dell-2015
.750, Ramsey Armstrong-2018

OPS(ON BASE + SLUGGING % IN A SEASON
1.626, Macey McElravy-2018
1.617, Reagan McGahey-2018
1.492, Macey McElravy-2017
1.277, Ally O'Dell-2015
1.275, Ramsey Armstrong-2018

Wins in a Season

18, Ami Simpson-2010
15, Emily Price-2018
14, Trevy Emmerich-1985
13, Braddi Reed-2008
13, Carly Hunt-2005

Strike Outs in a Season
144, Braddi Reed-2008
127, Braddi Reed-2009
122, Carly Hunt-2005
105, Dee Campbell-2018
105, Cerven-1995

Fewest Hits Allowed in a Season
48, Dee Campbell-2018
59, Ami Simpson-2008
60, Kelly. Barr-2015
61, Madison Morecraft-2017
65, Braddi Reed-2006

Innings Pitched in a Season
157.0, Carly Hunt-2005
146.0, Ami Simpson-2010
137.67, Amanda Fuller-2014

Fewest Runs Allowed in a Season
21, Madison Morecraft-2017
23, Dee Campbell-2018
26, Braddi Reed-2006

Fewest Earned Runs Allowed in a Season
16, Dee Campbell-2018
17, Madison. Morecraft-2017
18, Carly Hunt-2004

Fewest Walks Allowed in a Season
4, Emily. Price-2017
5, D. Finley-2005
8, Paige Olmsted-2011

Fewest Wild Pitches Thrown
0, Macey. McElravy, M. Morecraft,-2017
1, Emily Price-2017
1, Dee Campbell-2018
1, Kelly Barr-2015

Putouts in a Season
292, Courtney Campbell-2006
285, Courtney Campbell-2005
272, Hannah Dowling-2009

Assists in a Season
101, Vanessa James-2005
92, Vanessa James-2006
91, Terrika Price-2013

Career Hits
173, Natalie Gordon (2015-2018)
171, Macey McElravy (2016-2018)
164, Vanessa.James (2003-2006)
148, Megan O'Dell (2009-2012)
146, Ally O'Dell (2014-2017)

Career Home Runs
28, Macey McElravy (2016-2018)
16, Ally O'Dell (2014-2017)
12, Abby Youngblood (2012-2015)
13, Reagan McGahey (2018)
9, M. O'Dell (2009-2012)
8, Ramsey Armstrong (2017-2018)

Career Runs Scored
135, Natalie Gordon (2015-2018)
112, Ally O'Dell (2014-2017)
111, Kailey Pruett (2007-2010)
99, Macey McElravy (2016-2018)
94, Terrika Price (2010-2013)
94, Megan O'Dell (2009-2012)

Career RBI
118, M. McElravy (2016-2018)
112, Megan O'Dell (2009-2012)
107, Ally O'Dell (2014-2017)
89, Ami Simpson (2007-2010)
78, Abby Youngblood (2012-2015)

Career Doubles
44, Macey McElravy (2016-2018)
36, Megan O'Dell (2009-2012)
34, Ally O'Dell (2014-2017)
28, Hannah Dowling (2006-2009)
26, Ami Simpson (2007-2010)

Career Triples
17, Natalie Gordon (2015-2018)
15, Erin Whitley (1982-1985)
15, Mara Crimmons (1986-1989)
14, Ally O'Dell (2014-2017)

11, Terrika Price (2010-2013)   Katherine Kennedy- .335 (2014-2016)

Career Batting Average (minimum 260 at bats)
Ally O'Dell- .443 (2014-2017)
Vanessa James- .439 (2004-2006)
Natalie Gordon- .420 (2015-2018)
Megan O'Dell- .393 (2009-2012)
Terrika Price- .392 (2010-2013)
Kelly Barr- . 388 (2013-2015)
Haley Sparks- .349 (2008-2010)
Sam Maxey- .347 (2008-2011)
Abby Youngblood- .344 (2013-2015)

Charleston Softball Records

Most Wins: 31, 2018
Apollo Conference Titles: 1984, 1985, 2018
Regional Titles: 1985, 1986, 1994, 2018
Most Coaching Wins: 435, Karen Karch (1981-2012)

2018 Squad Best of All-Time

The Charleston softball team looked to take the next step in 2018. The junior class had finished 2nd in the state as 8th graders, while the sophomore class finished 4th as 8th graders. After tying the school record for wins in 2017 by going 24-5, the team was ousted in Apollo contention and in the Regional title game. Coach Blain Mayhall told Journal Gazette-Times Courier reporter Justin Rust before the season, "They are looking to take one game at a time. We are going to focus on game at a time. The girls are focused on the next step. They had a good year last season, but there is still plenty of room for improvement. They are focused on getting better each day."

Charleston did lose one of their better bats from 2017 in Allyson O'Dell, who set a single season record for batting average with .610. However, the lineup was still stacked. Senior Natalie Gordon was back for a fourth year in the leadoff spot and committed to Lake Land College before the season started. Junior Macey McElravey was back after hitting nine home runs as a sophomore. Sophomore Ramsey Armstrong finished her freshman year strong, while freshman Reagan McGahey was already in the starting lineup.

In the pitching circle, McElravey and Madison Morecraft were Apollo Conference selections as pitchers, while sophomores Emily Price and Dee Campbell were seasoned pitchers. "Macey and Emily look good again," Mayhall told Rust. "Madi is dealing with some issues and we hope to get her back really soon and ready to look like the ace she was last season. We are really excited about Dee Campbell. She is focused and ready to take the next step."

Campbell wasted no time in her first start of the season by no-hitting Danville in four innings in a 10-0 mercy rule victory. "It feels good," Campbell told Rust after the game. "I have not thrown one of those in a while, so it feels good to be back. I just got back from an injury. I didn't expect to throw my movement pitches that good, but they were working today and were really effective." Campbell was not done as she threw another no-hitter against Lincoln later in the season.

Charleston began the Apollo Conference title chase by beating Mattoon 11-1 and 3-2. It was the first time in the 38-year program history that Charleston swept Mattoon in a season. "It's exciting for the girls," Mayhall told Rust. "They deserve it. The girls' energy and camaraderie are a lot different than teams I have had in the past. This is a fun group to be around."

Charleston followed that week by blowing out Lincoln as Campbell threw her second no-hitter of the season in the second game of an 18-0, 10-0 Saturday. After the romps, it setup a week with two state ranked opponents in Cumberland and Windsor-Stewardson-Strasburg.

Cumberland entered the contest as the No. 13 ranked team in the Class 1A, while Charleston was ranked No. 20 in Class 3A. McGahey hit a two-run home run to get the Charleston offense going and the team never looked back, winning 7-1. Gordon was 4-4, while Price pitched the complete game allowing the one run. Two days later, Charleston was matched up against WSS, who came in as the No. 10 ranked team in Class 1A, and it was a game that the JG-TC area will surely remember.

WSS held a 5-0 lead going into the fourth inning. McElravey's three run home run started a four run fifth inning to tie the game. WSS went on to score two more runs in the sixth to take a 7-5 advantage, but Charleston scored two more runs thanks to an RBI single from Gordon, and a suicide squeeze bunt from Payton Melton to score Hannah Harpster. The game went to extra innings. CHS loaded the bases with no outs in the ninth. WSS pitcher, Megan Schlechte, struck out the next two batters, but CHS took advantage of a bobbled grounder as Olivia Lane scored the game winning run to win the 8-7 contest.

"I hear people say that is a 1A school, but in central Illinois, it's a great area for softball and they are living proof of that," Mayhall told Rust. "I expect to see them in the state tournament." Mayhall was right as WSS won the Class 1A state championship.

Charleston dropped their lone Apollo game of the year by splitting with Taylorville but came back ready to play against another state ranked team. Casey-Westfield came into the game ranked as the No. 8 team in Class 2A, and Charleston would play comeback kids once again in a matter of a week. Charleston trailed 9-4 after five innings, and 9-7 after six innings. Charleston was down to two outs in the seventh, but Melton and Gordon hit back-to-back RBI doubles to tie the game. McGahey and McElravey added RBI singles in the inning as Charleston won 11-9.

"I said the bad news is that we are down 4-0, but the good news is that we have been down before, and it was just last week," Mayhall said to Journal Gazette-Times Courier reporter Mike Monahan. "If they don't get along like they do this year, we don't win those games. I have been a part of teams that do not get along. This is such a fun group to be around."

The fun continued for Charleston as the team rattled off 16 straight wins, which included sweeping the rest of the Apollo season over Effingham, Mt. Zion, and Mahomet-Seymour. It also included a 10 RBI game by McGahey in a 20-0 win over Urbana on April 23rd, 2018. The effort is ranked tied for 13th most RBI in a game in IHSA history. Mt. Zion tested Charleston as the Lady Trojans had to comeback in both games. In game one, Charleston trailed 4-2 in the seventh inning and 6-4 in the ninth inning before winning 7-6. Charleston trailed 6-0 in game two before taking that game 8-6. Charleston clinched their Apollo since 1985 by defeating Mahomet-Seymour 8-2 and 9-2 the following week.

Coach Mayhall credited the two seniors on the team in Gordon and Kaitlyn Coffey, two players Mayhall coached since seventh grade when he took over as the CMS softball coach. After that, Charleston lost three of their next four games going into Regional play, including a loss to St. Joseph-Ogdon and a pair to Pontiac.

However, Charleston cruised past Decatur MacArthur 21-0 in the Regional opener. This setup another round versus Effingham. Charleston leaned on their ace in Price, as she pitched a complete game shutout, allowing five hits, while walking one as Charleston beat Effingham 5-0 to win their first Regional title since 1994. It was the team's 30th win. McElravy powered Charleston with a two-home run, three RBI afternoon. Charleston followed that win with a 14-3 pounding on Mahomet-Seymour in the Sectional semi-final to advance to their first ever Sweet 16.

The Sectional Championship featured a classic as Mt. Zion and Charleston met for the third time this season. Charleston came back from 1-0, 5-1, and 7-5 deficits in the game to send the game to extra innings. The game featured a three-run home from McGahey to lead CHS to tie the game at 5-all, while Armstrong hit a two-run home run in the seventh inning to tie the game at 7-7.

The magic ran out for Charleston as Mt. Zion scored four times in the eighth inning and CHS had no answer with a final score of 11-7. "I can walk of the field proud of what we did because we did not do anything to lose the game," Mayhall told Rust after the game. "They did some things to win it. That is what you want any time you compete in a sport. You want to give yourself the best chance to win. I am extremely proud of these ladies and have been all year."

The 31-5 season set a single season record for wins in a season. Records were broken left and right. The freshman McGahey had perhaps the best ever season by a CHS freshman. McGahey set single season records in at bats (130), runs scored (63), doubles (14), RBI (63), and slugging percentage (1.054). McElravy joined the hit parade by setting single season records in hits (70), home runs (15), and on base percentage (.594). Campbell had a stellar sophomore season in the pitching circle by setting single season records in fewest runs allowed (23), fewest earned runs allowed (16), no-hitters (2), and strikeouts per inning (11.57).

The team set single season records in wins (31), runs scored (326), hits (448), doubles (88), triples (25), home runs (40), and strikeouts (230). The team's 448 hits and 88 doubles were ranked 21st most in a season in IHSA history. The team featured six on the All-Apollo list. Campbell and Price were both first team selections as pitchers. Joining them on the first team was Gordon, McElravey, and McGahey. Armstrong made the second team.

Trojans Girls Tennis
(1978-2018)

Trojans Girls Tennis
(1978-2018)

The first tennis team was in 1978 under the leadership of Vicki Preston. Preston served as the coach for 10 years before leaving in 1987. During her time, it is believed that she finished with the best win-loss mark in school history in dual meets. Preston compiled a 107-27 record while coaching at Charleston. After the first season, the tennis team began to see some success. In year two, Kathy Taitt, and Robin Koch qualified for state the first doubles team. Taitt eventually signed with the Eastern Illinois University tennis team. Then, in 1980, sister Jennifer Taitt qualified as the first singles player.

In 1981, CHS enjoyed an undefeated 14-0 season. Then, in 1982, the team went 13-1 despite having nine freshmen playing. Taitt led the team with a 13-1 singles record. The following season Taitt qualified for state for the fourth consecutive year. She is just one of three players in CHS history to every qualify for state all four years. In 1984, Carol Snyder was named Singles Player of the Year by Sparks Sports Magazine. She finished ranked 10th in the Middle Illinois Tennis Association. After her final season in 1985, Snyder finished with a career 60-10 record in singles competition. With the likes of Taitt and Snyder, CHS won the Apollo Conference four straight years from 1981 to 1984.

After Preston left, longtime biology teacher Ron Easter took over for four years. In 1990, Kristie Haberer might have fought the toughest conditions to make the state tournament. Battling 20-30 mile per hour winds and a wind chill of zero, Haberer found a way to make state in singles play. The next season, Kristy Sims qualified for the state tournament. Sims is on record as the last state representative for nine years. She enjoyed a long tennis career at Eastern Illinois University.

IHSA did not start keeping track of sectional results until 1996. The best finish by a team was in 2001 when the trio of Kristen Horney, Carlie Titus, and Jessica Matthews led the team to a 76th finish at the IHSA state tournament. CHS only had two state qualifiers for the next eight seasons. Once coach Amy Harrington took over in 2007, the team began to see more success. This was in part to Class of 2013 grad Kelsie Abolt. Abolt finisher her career qualifying for state all four years, twice in doubles and twice in singles. Her most memorable season would be in 2012 as her and Madi Fisher led the team to their first Apollo Conference since 1984. Abolt and Fisher didn't play college tennis as Abolt pole vaulted for a year at Eastern Illinois University, while Fisher signed on at EIU for soccer. Harrington coached until 2014.

From 2013-2016, Meagan Flight secured her legacy in CHS history by qualifying for state all four years. Flight is the only member on record to win a singles match at state. Flight signed with Illinois Springfield.

CHS Tennis Records

Apollo Conference Titles: 1981, 1982, 1983, 1984, 2012
Sectional Titles: None

State Qualifiers

1970s: Robin Koch & Kathy Taitt (doubles)-1979;

1980s: Jennifer Taitt (singles)-1980; Jennifer Taitt (singles)-1981; Jennifer Taitt (singles)-1982; Jennifer Taitt (singles)-1983; Carol Snyder (singles)-1984; Hillary Hagedorm & Kristen Weidner (doubles)1984; Claire Sanders (singles)-1986; Gina Suthikant & Kristen Brown (doubles)-1987; Terra Preston (singles)-1987 Claire Sanders & Terra Preston (doubles)-1988;

1990s: Kristie Haberer (singles)-1990; Kristy Simms (singles)-1991;

2000s: Kristen Horney (singles)-2000; Kristen Horney (singles)-2001; Carlie Titus & Jessica Matthews (doubles)-2001; Nikki Chambers (singles)-2003; Shannon Kelly & Beth Laube (doubles)-2005; Alysha Spencer & Kelsie Abolt (doubles)-2009;

2010s: Kelsie Abolt (singles)-2010; Kelsie Abolt (singles)-2011; Kelsie Abolt & Madi Fisher (doubles)-2012; Maegan Flight (singles)-2012; Maegan Flight (singles)-2013; Maegan Flight (singles)-2014; Haley Cooley (singles)-2014; Kayla Albin & Eva Bacon (doubles)-2014; Maegan Flight (singles)-2015; Kayla Albin & Eva Bacon (doubles)-2015

Trojans Girls Track & Field
(1973-2018)

Trojans Girls Track & Field
(1973-2018)

As recently in 2018, the track was named after coach Sharon Brinkmeyer. The recognition was well deserved after Brinkmeyer served as the track coach from 1979 to 1993. Despite Charleston's Apollo Conference championship win streak not starting with her, Brinkmeyer is credited to molding Charleston into the powerhouse that they became in the Apollo Conference. Starting with coach Ellen Whale, Charleston track teams won the Apollo Conference for 31 straight years from 1977 to 2007.

When Brinkmeyer took over, Charleston saw one of the greatest six year runs in the 80s. From 1980 to 1986, CHS lost just one dual or tri meet, which came in 1984. A lot of that had to do with the runners. In 1980, Carman Allen set the school record for the 800 with a 2:26. Allen was a part of the school record 4X200 that featured Pam Harshbarger, Kelly Nelms and Patty Patterson, while the school record 4X400 featured Harshbarger, Allen, Patterson, and LeAnna Hummell. Allen's record did not last long in the 800 as Carol Chapman set the new mark in 1984 by placing ninth at the state meet. Her 2:16 record and her 5:08 mile record, both set in 1984, are still records today. This was the lone year that CHS has won a sectional plaque.

The current 300-meter low hurdle record holder, Sheila Lenihan, was named Most Outstanding Class AA Athlete at Decatur Area's Best in 1985, a year that featured eight girls going to state for CHS. Lenihan followed that performance by breaking her own school record with a 45.4 in 1986. However, Molly Jackson, the current 3200-meter record holder, might have outshined. Jackson broke the school record of Janet Steel and finished third. Steele was a member of the Eastern Illinois University cross country and track team after high school. Jackson's sister, Amy, also qualified for the 3200-meter run. She battled a back injury for three weeks, and then came back with a strong performance in the sectional.

From 1988 to 1991, CHS featured one of the best dynamic duos in field events in Kim Double and Holly Pearcy. Pearcy broke her school record in shot put and discus, and earned a seventh place, all-state finish in shot put in 1990. On the other hand, Double was considered the best high jumper in school history until about two years ago. Double jumped 5-6, which stood as the school record until 2017. She finished all-state twice.

The 90s featured the best relay teams in school history. The 1994 squad still holds the record in the 4X200 and 4X400 meter relay, while the 1995 squad holds the record in the 4X800 meter relay. It came to no surprise that Collen Vandever, Shalimar Lewis, and Kendra Perkins are a part of those relays. All three were dominating the Apollo since their freshman years, including Perkins who was a three-time state qualifier in the 1600-meter run.

Tawnjai Ames finished an outstanding career in 1997. She broke Pearcy's record in the shot put and discus in 1996. She finished fourth in the shot put at state that year, while finishing sixth in discuss in 1997. She is still the record holder today. Lisa Woodruff joined Ames at state and just missed the state finals in the discus. Top 12 moved to Saturday, and Woodruff was 14th overall despite winning her heat. Leslie Spitz was another standout that year by breaking the school record in the 100-meter hurdles.

CHS won the Apollo for ten more years, but most of the records stood pat until Gena Nance broke the school record in the 400-meter dash in 2007. Nance, the daughter of successful cross-country coach Gene Nance, qualified for the state tournament three times, twice as a member of the 4X800 and once for the 400-meter dash.

From 2008 to 2013, only four girls qualified for the state tournament. Ashley Snoddy was a three-time state qualifier in the high jump from 2009 to 2011. Miranda Hankins qualified for the long jump in 2010 and 2011. Hankins might have qualified three times, but she gave a teammate the ultimate opportunity. As a freshman in 2009, Hankins had one final jump and was in third place with a jump of 16-4 1/2. Teammate Maybella Reinbolt was in second place as a senior with a jump o 16-6 1/2. On her final jump, Hankins jogged through the takeoff board, so that Reinbolt was secured a sport at the state tournament. Kelsi Abolt, who qualified for state in 2010, 2012, and 2013, broke the school record in the pole vault and finished sixth at state her senior season.

Charleston captured their first Apollo title in nearly ten years by winning in 2016. The team was led by Morgan Sherwood who won three events and would have won four events if she didn't finish second to a future all-state high jumper in teammate Sarah Flight. Sherwood was a multi-all state finisher and broke the school record in the triple jump. Other records that fell in 2016 included the 400-meter dash record by Hope Griffin, and the 4X100 meter relay record. The 4X800 meter relay of Megan Woodruff, Elizabeth Buescher, Hope Griffin, and Julia Griffin finished 11th at state finals, and missed all-state by five seconds.

Flight, who is to be a senior in 2019, is the current high jump record holder. She tied Becky Kaiser for the highest finish ever by finishing second in the high jump in 2017. Paige Minor joined Flight that year on the podium as she finished eighth. It was the first time that CHS had two individuals on the podium in the same event.

Becky Kaiser: The Best CHS Runner Ever

The sprinter from the class of 1978 is historically the best runner to ever wear a Lady Trojan uniform. Kaiser goes by Becky Clayton today, but her maiden name is still hanging in the gym in the CHS records. Clayton was a five-time all-state selection when she ran at Charleston. This included a third-place finish in the 50-yard dash in 1975, third place finish in the long jump and second place finishing in 1976, and a fourth-place finish in the 100-meter dash and third place finishing in the long jump in 1978.

Clayton would have likely added to that resume, but she sustained a muscle strain in her hip during her junior season in 1977. "I remember being frustrated, but that is what injuries do," Kaiser (Clayton) told Erik Hall who was doing a special feature on the 31-teams that won the Apollo Conference for the Journal Gazette-Times Courier. "I remember getting an ultrasound. It was the first time I ever got an ultrasound. I remember trying off and on training at practice and having some trouble, backing off, and getting frustrated. Coach Whale was fine. She was very understanding of it all."

Clayton showed how athletic she was at the time. Running the first time since her injury at the Apollo Meet, Clayton helped a 440 (now known as the 4X100) shed an entire second off their time from five days ago. Clayton eventually became a three-time NCAA All-American at the University of Illinois.

"She was an awesome athlete," Vicky (Bumpus) Hinds, a member of the 1977 class, told Hall. "I don't think really any of us knew at the time how good she was. She was just one of the girls, and never treated us any different. In our 440 relay, I had to hand off to her. It always scared me to death. When you said, 'go,' she was like wow. You are struggling your hardest to just get her the baton. Then, to watch her win the race was always awesome."

Like all-state mother, like all-state daughter

Kim Sherwood, current CMS teacher and Charleston Booster Club president, who was formally known as Kim Double, was the best high jumper in CHS History until Sarah Flight broke her school record in 2017. However, Sherwood was a two time all state high jumper, placing fifth in 1989 and fourth in 1991. Fast forward to 25 years later, her daughter, Morgan, became a two time all state track athlete as well. In 2016, Morgan finished ninth in the triple jump and sixth in the discus. She also finished 11th in the long jump and qualified for the meet in the high jump but did not make finals.

Sibling Rivalry

How about this family Thanksgiving? Taylor Garrett, who finished all-state in the 800-meter run his senior season, placed eighth. His younger sister, Megan, capped her freshman season by placing sixth in the 800-meter run to also capture all-state. However, her brother might be able to poke fun at his sister, who did not even think she was going to be able to run on Saturday. Garrett forgot her bib number at home, but her brothers and dad were able to find it in time. Garrett responded with her best race and was in 11th place with 200 meters to go before kicking her way to sixth on the final turn.

Charleston Girls Track & Field Record Holders

Event	Name	Time/Finish	Year
100 Meter	Becky Kaiser	11.6	1978
200 Meter	Becky Kaiser	25.0	1976
400 Meter	Hope Griffin	1:00.16	2016
800 Meter	Carol Chapman	2:16.0	1984
1600 Meter	Carol Chapman	5:08.4	1984
3200 Meter	Molly Jackson	10:59.3	1985
100 High Hurdles	Leslie Spitz	16.0	1997
300 Low Hurdles	Sheila Lenihan	45.4	1986
4X100 Relay	Michaela McBride Makenna Wilson Sharifa Hurtault Paige Minor	50.05	2016
4X200 Relay	Alisha Brown Jonica Craft Rebekah Clark Autumn Carrell	1:46.47	1994

4X400 Relay	Tara Horsman Rebekah Clark Colleen Vandever Kendra Perkins	4:05.01	1994
4X800 Relay	Shalimar Lewis Emily Vandever Tara Horsman Colleen Vandever	9:41.96	1995
Shot Put	Tawnjai Ames	42-08.5	1996
Discus	Tawnjai Ames	133-10	1996
Long Jump	Becky Kaiser	18-08.25	1978
Triple Jump	Morgan Sherwood	36-11	2016
Pole Vault	Kelsie Abolt	10-3	2013
High Jump	Sarah Flight	5-06.5	2017

Charleston Girl's Track All-State Winners

Name	Year	Class	Place	Event
Kelsie Abolt	2012-13	2A	6	pole vault
Tawnjai Ames	1995-96	AA	4	discus throw
	1996-97	AA	6	shot put
Carol Chapman	1983-84	AA	7	800-meter run
Jonica Craft	1994-95	AA	8	long jump
Kim Double	1988-89	AA	5t	high jump
	1990-91	AA	4	high jump
Sarah Flight	2016-17	2A	2	high jump
Megan Garrett	2017-18	2A	6	800-meter run
Molly Jackson	1985-86	AA	3	3200-meter run
Becky Kaiser	1974-75		3	50-yard dash
	1975-76		3	long jump
			2	100-yard dash
	1977-78	AA	4	100-yard dash
			3	long jump
Sheila Lenihan	1984-85	AA	3	100-meter low hurdles
	1985-86	AA	6	300-meter low hurdles
Paige Minor	2016-17	2A	8	high jump
Grace Oetting	2014-15	2A	9	3200-meter run
Holly Percy	1989-90	AA	7	shot put
Morgan Sherwood	2015-16	2A	9	triple jump
			6	discus throw
Janet Steele	1976-77		4	2-mile run
	1978-79	AA	7	2-mile run
Makenna Wilson	2016-17	2A	8	shot put
			3	discus throw

Trojans Girls Volleyball
(1976-2018)

Trojans Girls Volleyball
(1976-2018)

The first ever volleyball season came in 1976 with Ellen Whale as the coach. The Lady Trojans were 7-3 and won the District Championship before falling to Taylorville in the sectional. Doyte Hogue took over a year later and led Charleston to their first ever Apollo Conference Tournament Championship. Charleston swept Newton and Robinson to meet Mt. Zion in the championship. Mt. Zion won the first set 20-10, but Charleston knocked off the Lady Braves 20-18 and 20-12 to mount the comeback.

Hogue left after that one season and longtime coach Karen Karch took over. This would be Karch's first stint as head coach, which would end up being a 12-year run. Karch led Charleston to the school's second straight Apollo Tournament Championship in 1978 by sweeping Mt. Zion, Newton, and Decatur Lakeview. In 1981, Charleston set the then-school record for wins with a 20-5 season and the school's third Apollo Tournament Championship. The 1981 campaign featured a stretch in which Charleston won 14 of their 15 games played but fell to Mattoon in the District Tournament.

The 1982 season featured another Apollo Tournament Championship and a 16-8 record. This was Effingham's first year in the conference, but Charleston still knocked them off 15-11, 15-11 in the title match. Jana Oetting and Toni McNutt were gamers for the Lady Trojans. Oetting finished with a 48.30% hitting percentage, while McNutt led the team in aces for two straight seasons.

Jamie Edwards led the 1983 squad that won their first ever Regional title. Charleston defeated Mattoon in three sets by winning the last two 15-3 and 15-12. CHS also won a game in Sectional play by defeating Highland 15-5, 3-15, 15-8. The 1983 squad is the last CHS team to win a game in Sectional play. Charleston eventually lost to Carbondale 9-15, 15-10, 15-2.

It was not until 1990 that CHS would emerge a competitive team. The 13-11 team won the Apollo by beating Robinson, Taylorville, Mt. Zion, and Newton. Karch stepped down as head coach after this season but returned after two years in 1993.

After four non-winning seasons, Karch finished her volleyball coaching career with another Regional title. The 18-11-3 team knocked off Mattoon 16-14, 15-5 and Mt. Carmel 15-11, 15-13 in Regional play before falling to Salem 15-10, 15-8 in the Sectional. Gena Harrison led all servers with a 98.5% serving percentage. Anna Wheeler was the team's main hitter with 393 good attacks.

In 2004, and Sarah Weidner's lone season as coach, the CHS squad won another Apollo title. The Lady Trojans repeated in 2005 as coach Steve Pamperin came back after coaching the 2003 team. The Lady Trojans set a school record for wins in a season with a 23-3 record, including a stretch of winning 16 of 17 games. However, the Regional drought continued after CHS lost to Springfield High 25-23, 25-23.

In 2006, the team reloaded with another 20-win season, the last recorded 20-win season up to date. CHS was denied the Apollo and a Regional. Effingham beat Charleston both times that season, while Mattoon beat Charleston 25-23 in the third set to clinch a Regional.

Kenzie Keefer was a household name during those 20-win seasons. Keefer is the lone CHS player to ever be named the Decatur Herald & Review Player of the Year when she won in

2006. Keefer was the all-time record holder for kills, and the single season record holder until each were broken down the line. Avery Drake led the team in hitting percentage, while Maddie Young was the career record holder for assists at one point.

Since 2006, Charleston has recorded just four winning seasons, but some talented players have played in Baker Gym. In 2009, Brandi Coffey set the then-record for assists in a single season. In 2010, Kenzie Eveland recorded over 300 digs as a sophomore, and eventually finished as the then-career record holder. In 2011, Caitlin Wend set the school record for assists in game with 42. In 2012, Aryel Phinney left as the career points record holder and played at Lake Land College for two years. Thirteen school records fell during the 2014 season. The most exciting record that fell was when Lauren Nadler recorded 21 kills in a game as Charleston defeated Mattoon 25-23, 23-25, 25-23, which was the first win over Mattoon since 2006. Nadler is the all-time career kills leader with 577. Allie Endlsey set the single season record for assists and aces, while Ally Harrell set the record for hitting percentage.

Natalie Gordon became the first ever CHS volleyball player to record over 1,000 career assists in 2017, finishing with 1,032 career assists. Makenna Wilson became the first ever CHS volleyball player to record over 300 kills in a single season in 2016, finishing with 317. Mia Ruffolo set the new single season record for digs in 2017. Charleston holds a 503-532 record all time in 41 years of competitive play.

Girls Volleyball (Taken from IHSA Website)

Season	Class	Titles	Place	Won	Lost	Tied	Coach
1976-77		D					
1978-79				14	5		Karen Karch
1979-80				11	7		Karen Karch
1980-81				14	8		Karen Karch
1981-82				20	5		Karen Karch
1982-83				16	8		Karen Karch
1983-84	AA	R		15	10		Karen Karch
1985-86				8	16		Karen Karch
1986-87				10	15		Karen Karch
1987-88				10	14		Karen Karch
1988-89				3	21		Karen Karch
1989-90				9	14		Karen Karch
1990-91				13	11		Karen Karch
			Coach Total	143	134		12 yr .516
1991-92				8	13		Barb Heitka
1992-93				3	21		Barb Heitka
			Coach Total	11	34		2 yr .244
1993-94				12	15		Karen Karch
1994-95				10	16		Karen Karch
1995-96				10	18		Karen Karch
1996-97				14	14		Karen Karch

Year				Wins	Losses		Coach
1997-98	AA	R		18	11		Karen Karch
			Coach Total	64	74		5 yr .464
1998-99				15	14		Kim Sherwood
1999-00				10	17		Kim Sherwood
2000-01				15	15		Kim Sherwood
2001-02				12	17		Kim Sherwood
2002-03				9	14		Kim Sherwood
			Coach Total	61	77		5 yr .442
2003-04				9	16		Steve Pamperin
			Coach Total	9	16		1 yr .360
2004-05				19	7		Sarah Weidner
			Coach Total	19	7		1 yr .731
2005-06				23	3		Steve Pamperin
2006-07				20	5		Steve Pamperin
			Coach Total	43	8		2 yr .843
2007-08				11	13		Beth Anne Lancaster
2008-09				12	16		Beth Anne Lancaster
2009-10				17	12		Beth Anne Lancaster
2010-11				15	13		Beth Anne Lancaster
2011-12				10	17		Beth Anne Lancaster
			Coach Total	65	71		5 yr .478
2012-13				12	13		Kelsey Orr
			Coach Total	12	13		1 yr .480
2013-14				15	13		Susan Babers
			Coach Total	15	13		1 yr .536
2014-15				17	14		Justin Tomaska
2015-16				8	20		Justin Tomaska
2016-17				9	23		Justin Tomaska
2017-18				10	21		Justin Tomaska
			Coach Total	44	78		4 yr .361
			School Total	486	525		39 yr .481

Charleston Volleyball Records

Individual Single Game
Points: Natalie Gordon, 20, 2016
Aces: Allie Endsley, 7, 2014
Assists: Caitlin Wend, 42, 2011
Kills: Lauren Nadler, 21, 2014
Hitting Percentage: Ally Harrell, .800, 2014
Blocks: Makenna Wilson, Alicia Valdez, 5, 2016

Digs: Mia Ruffolo, 31, 2017
Receive Percentage: Makenna Wilson, Paige Wilson, Catherine Smith, 2.67, 2016

Individual Single Season
Points: Aryel Phinney, 179, 2011
Aces, Allie Endsley, 45, 2014
Assists: Allie Endsley, 577, 2014
Kills: Makenna Wilson, 317, 2016
Hitting Percentage: Ally Harrell, .262, 2014
Blocks: Stephanie Harper, 75, 2007
Digs: Mia Ruffolo, 457, 2017
Receive Percentage: Catherine Smith, 2.01, 2015

Individual Career
Points: Allie Endsley, 340, 2011-2014
Aces, Makenna Wilson, 80, 2013-2016
Assists: Natalie Gordon, 1,032, 2014-2017
Kills: Lauren Nadler, 577, 2011-2014
Hitting Percentage: Dakota Crowder, .249, 2012-2015
Blocks: Stephanie Harper, 154, 2006-2008
Digs: Mia Ruffolo, 778, 2015-2017
Receive Percentage: Catherine Smith, 2.01, 2012-2015

Charleston Volleyball Records
Most Wins: 23, 2005
Apollo Conference Titles: 1977, 1978, 1981, 1982, 1990, 2004, 2005
District Titles: 1976
Regional Titles: 1983, 1997
Most Coaching Wins: Karen Karch 143 (1978-1991, 1993-1997)

Speech and Drama

Tina Winings could go down as one of the, if not the greatest, speech coach in Illinois. Winings has been coaching drama, group interpretation, and speech individual events since 1984. Her resume includes taking 14 teams to state in drama, four state finishes in drama, 14 Sectional titles in group interpretation, 30 state qualifying teams in group interpretation, and 21 Regional titles in speech. Despite not being dubbed as "athletes," these individuals over the course of years have brought home more plaques than any other team on the athletic field. Viewers can see Mrs. Wining's old classroom where many of these are displayed.

This also includes six individuals who have been state champion in their respective events. These individuals include Catalina Hernandez in 2005 in oratorical declaration, Corey Schultz in 2006 in verse, Ben Leddy in 2006 in prose and 2007 in verse, Kevin Giffin in 2008 in prose and in 2009 in poetry reading, Jordan Cornwell in 2014 in prose, and Emma Walker in 2015 in oratorical declaration.

Drama Records

Sectional Championships: 1960, 1961, 1985, 1987, 1991, 1994, 2003, 2004, 2005
State Qualifiers: 1960, 1961, 1985, 1987, 1991, 1993, 1994, 1995, 1997, 2003, 2004, 2005, 2007, 2014
State Finishes: 1991 (2nd Place), 1994 (3rd Place), 2003 (3rd Place), 2005 (3rd Place)

Group Interpretation Records

Sectional Championships: 1989, 1990, 1991, 1992, 2000, 2001, 2002, 2003, 2005, 2006, 2008, 2012, 2013, 2015
State Qualifiers: 1984, 1986, 1987, 1988, 1989, 1990, 1991, 1992, 1994, 1996, 1997, 1998, 1999, 2000, 2001, 2002, 2003, 2004, 2005, 2006, 2007, 2008, 2009, 2010, 2012, 2013, 2014, 2015, 2017, 2018
State Finishes: 2002 (2nd Place)

Speech Individual Events

District Championship: 1966, 1968, 1971
Regional Championship: 1985, 1986, 1987, 1988, 1989, 1990, 1991, 1992, 1993, 1995, 1996, 1997, 1998, 1999, 2004, 2005, 2006, 2009, 2010, 2011, 2015
Sectional Championships: 1985, 1989, 1999
State Finishes: 2009 (3rd Place)

All-Apollo Award

The All-Apollo Award is an award that is given to the school that wins the most out of all competing sports. Points are taken from the Apollo Conference schools from all fall, winter, and spring sports. Charleston has been very successful in winning this award. Charleston won the award every year from the 1972-1973 season to the 1990-1991 season. Then, the school won the award each year from the 1993-1994 season to the 1997-1998 season. The team won the award again during the 2001-2002 season, 2002-2003 season, and the 2011-2012 season.

This Is Worth Mentioning!

- Charleston has featured a scholastic bowl team since at least 1987. John Schmitz led the first team to state with a 24-8 record. Scholastic bowl is when two teams answer questions over numerous topics with the hopes of answering the most questions correct. It is a battle of brains. Charleston's team qualified for state in 1987 under Schmitz, and then again in 1988 under the coaching of Cindy Bezruki. The two teams are the only to win Sectional Championships. CHS scholastic bowl teams have won Regional Championships in 2007, 2009, 2012, and 2015.

- Charleston has offered competitive cheer. Three CHS teams have qualified for the competitive cheer state competition. The 2006 and 2007 state qualifiers were led by Jan Spitz as coach, while the 2009 team was led by Lindsey Titus. Charleston has also offered a chess team since at least 1997.

- Charleston has offered dance since at least 1988 as the Lady Trojans have been coached dance by Mary Buchar. Buchar has coached the team since 1988, totaling 30 years of coaching dance teams. In 1998, the Charleston dance team was the IDTA Class AA Pom/Dance state champion. CHS ended the year ranked 42nd at nationals in Orlando, Florida. Charleston has fared success in the Class AA High Kick category, bringing home third in 2007, third in 2010, third in 2011, second in 2015, and third in 2018. In 2015, the team placed second in the hip hop category.

- Trey Katz, a member of the CHS class of 2011, was a standout gymnast during his high school days. Katz participated in the double mini trampoline and qualified for world competitions his sophomore, junior, and senior year. In 2009, Katz placed seventh when he went to St. Petersburg, Russia. In 2010, he finished ninth when he competed in Metz, France. In 2011, Katz won the bronze medal in Birmingham, England. Today, Katz is a coach at Kris Powers Gym in Shelbyville, Illinois, where many of his athletes have competed at the national and world competition. He married his high school sweetheart, Makayla Galbreath (Katz), a former CHS cheerleader as they live in Charleston with their daughter, Karsyn.

- Brett Pfeiffer, a member of the CHS class of 2017, accomplished a feat that not many athletes in the state of Illinois can say. Pfeiffer signed a weightlifting scholarship with

Northern Michigan University. Only a handful of kids in the history of Illinois have signed a weightlifting scholarship. Pfeiffer had many accolades, including representing USA in the Youth Pan American Weightlifting Championships in Guatemala in 2016.

- Despite CHS never offering a badminton team, there is plenty of history in the sport that comes from Charleston. Former CHS quarterback, Kevin Hussey, excelled in badminton. His father, Bob Hussey, was the Eastern Illinois University women's coach until the NCAA stopped making it a sport. Hussey went on to be a standout, which included participating in the World Championships at Calgary, Canada in 1985 and Beijing, China in 1987. His sons carried out the tradition. In 2006, CHS senior, Ben Hussey, was chosen as one of nine individuals to represent the United States 19-U team at the World Juniors championships in Incheong, Korea. In 2010, Quinn Hussey qualified for the Pan American Junior Championships for the United States national team.

- CHS offers swim teams for the boys and girls. Only one individual has ever participated in the state swim meet on both sides. That was Laura Pentzien in 2013. As a senior, Pentzien qualified for the 200-yard free style. Her father, Dwight Pentzien, has served as the girl's coach for many seasons, while longtime Charleston lawyer and current State's Attorney, Brian Bower has served as the boy's coach for many years. The team swims at Eastern Illinois University's pool.

- In 2003, an article written by Brooke Johnson for the JG-TC wrote about a special bond among CHS athletes, and one junior. Michael Bielefeldt, a member of the CHS class of 2004, moved down from the Chicago area in 2002. Bielefeldt has autism and did not develop speech until he was eight. While lacking in social skills at the time, he was not lacking in his love for sports, which caught the attention of a group of boys. John Dively, Ryan Shick, Jon Hutti, Curt Hinds, Dallas Bartz, Nick Meissen, Erik Werden, Andrew Shick, and others were among those who reached out to Bielefeldt and started a close-knit friendship. Today, more commonly known as "Mr. B" is a diehard CHS fan, who is also one of my good friends, and someone I consider family. Our Sundays in the fall consist of our famous pregame show at circuit judge Mitch Shick's house, where we are assigned football announcers and we make our NFL picks for the weeks. Thanks to a special friendship in high school, Mr. B is one of the best Charleston superfans.

- Long time ago, CHS offered a debate team. The team does not exist anymore but did win a Sectional title as a team in 1947.

- Charleston has been blessed with talented band directors over the years. John Daum served as the CHS band director during the 1970s and up to his retirement in 1988. He was the founder of the Charleston Community Band, who plays concerts at Kiwanis Park during the summer. The Daum Amphitheater was dedicated in his honor when he passed away in 2013. Daum served as mentor to Joe McArthur, who served as a band director at CHS or CMS for 22 years after Daum retired. In collaboration with former Illinois governor, Jim Edgar, and the Charleston community, the Charleston Marching

Trojans marched in the 1996 National Independence Day parade in Washington D.C. as Illinois' sole representative band. McArthur passed away in 2016.

Ginger Stanfield is another Charleston household name in the music department. Stanfield served as a band director in Charleston, primarily at Jefferson Elementary, for 34 years until she retired in 2013. She is not the director of the Charleston Community Band. Current band director, Lane Cruit (formerly known as Laney Grimes) has taught at CHS for 11 years and has organized trips for the band to perform at University of Illinois' Memorial Field and at Disney World in Orlando, Florida.

- Charleston has also been lucky on the vocal side as well. Charleston's former choir teacher at CMS, Debby Rappe, served the music industry for nearly 30 years. Rappe was a big influence in helping with Charleston musicals, which are typically performed in the spring. Julianne Sharp, the current choir instructor, has served CHS for the last 11 years. Sharp has turned music into something popular at CHS. Since her arrival in 2007, her students have visited the Rock n Roll Hall of Fame, Broadway in New York, and the Acapella Festival in Ohio. Charleston has a well-known acapella group, while many choir participants have sung the National Anthem at the IHSA state track meets.

- Jim Pogue has operated walkup songs for Charleston baseball games for many years. His son, John, was a longtime JV baseball coach after graduating CHS in 2009. While John was coaching football, him and his father calculated tackle totals.

- In 1974, Brian Whalin of Charleston was awarded the George Huff Award for proficiency and scholarship in fencing at the University of Illinois. Whalin had finished fourth in the epee (sword) to lead Illinois to a third straight Big Ten Conference championship.

- In 1935, the Charleston football field and track were finished. The first game was held that same year where Bill Henry scored the first ever touchdown in a 39-0 win over Paris. For three years, the field was named the "Charleston Athletic Field." A contest to name the new athletic grounds was held at Charleston High School in 1938. Mary Negley won a $5.00 prize for the naming of Trojan Hill. The latter name came in honor of the donor of the land. Later in 1938, night football was introduced to Trojan Hill.

- Current Jefferson Elementary principal Rob Ulm is an ultra-marathon runner. Ulm was also a two-time Boston Marathon qualifier. Ulm has completed at least 10 races of 100 or more miles. In 2014, Ulm completed one of the toughest races in the world. The Badwater 135 is a race that stretches from California to Nevada, and features runs up mountains. What Ulm called his "lowest point of the race" was around mile 59. While climbing 9,000 feet, Ulm took a break, and the race director biked by and told Ulm he - better keep moving because of a chance of seeing scorpions. With three stops, Ulm created the 135-mile race in 44 hours, 57 minutes, and 10 seconds.

- Ken Baker, the class of 1968 and son of coaching great Merv Baker, enjoyed a long career as an NFL official. Baker worked his way up from coaching high school football games to the Big 10 Conference. From 1991 to 2001, Baker served as an official. After hanging up the whistle in 2001 due to health concerns with his mother, Baker returned in 2003 as a replay official, where he served up to his retirement in 2011. Baker worked 14 playoff games in his career. The big one was the 2008 Super Bowl where the New York Giants upset the New England Patriots, a game where David Tyree made a catch against his helmet in the final minutes, which ended up as the game winning touchdown. In 2010, Baker was an official for an NFL playoff game between the New Orleans Saints and Minnesota Vikings, where head coaches Sean Payton and Brad Childress were both Eastern Illinois University alums. He also was an official during the Pro Bowl game in which CHS alum Jeff Gossett was a punter.

We are the voice for Charleston Athletics

The game winning home run...the interception

that sealed the deal...the bucket at the buzzer...

This is where memories like these are made.

Live on the radio, streamed at MyRadioLink.com,

the MyRadioLink app, and Amazon Alexa.

Nell Wiseman began teaching in 1959 at Charleston High School and taught for 58 years until her death in 2017. Mrs. Wiseman was a caring, generous, and energetic individual who always went the extra mile for her students. Nell was married to her husband, Robert, for 65 years. She will be forever missed.

-Page dedicated by Robert Wiseman

In tribute to coach Merv Baker for placing Charleston High's athletic teams on a level highly respected both on and off the athletic field. Coach Baker was a role model that athletes and students respected. Baker gave everything to the city of Charleston and always went above and beyond until his death in 2009. He loved his athletes as many still remember him today. Present coaches strive to be like Coach Baker. Thanks for coming to Charleston coach!

-Page dedicated by former CHS students and athletes

Charleston High School Class of 2011

- J. Alexander
- Z. Anderson
- M. Barharlou-Quivey
- L. Baji
- A. Bales
- B. Banning
- M. Batson
- J. Bays
- L. Beabout
- C. Beals
- M. Black
- C. Blagg
- J. Bloomquist
- C. Bough
- S. Bower
- V. Brown
- S. Buell
- L. Burgett
- Z. Burton
- C. Butler
- D. Caputo
- G. Centers
- J. Chapman
- A. Chui
- P. Chouinard
- E. Clark
- M. Cline
- M. Coffey
- C. Colman
- B. Cook
- C. Cooper
- M. Corrie
- B. Craft
- R. Dau
- K. Daubs
- J. Daugherty
- Q. Davis
- R. Davis
- K. Diaz
- R. Doty
- W. Dundee
- K. Dunlap
- A. Durbin
- L. Ebbert
- K. Ebel
- E. Elam
- B. Elliott
- E. Emmett
- M. Endsley
- R. Endsley
- S. Esarey
- A. Esker
- P. Eveland
- C. Faires
- H. Fairley
- L. Fairley
- S. Farkas
- K. Felgenhauer
- M. Fellers
- M. Ferguson
- A. Finley
- D. Finney
- B. Fitzpatrick
- C. Flores
- B. Ford
- A. Foster
- J. Fricke
- N. Fritz
- S. Fritz
- B. Furry
- J. Garcia
- A. Garrard
- J.M. Gordon
- J. D. Gordon
- V. Gossett
- K. Grant
- C. Haddix
- D. Haller
- A. Hart
- C. Hartman
- H. Hasbargen
- F. Haugh
- H. Haun
- J. Hawkins
- A. Hayes
- L. Hayes
- A. Heise
- T. Hiser
- T. Homann
- M. Huddleston
- B. Irwin
- S. Izadi
- I. Jackson
- H. Jacobs
- N. Jensen
- A. Johnson
- D. Johnson
- L. Johnson
- T. Katz
- D. Keck
- E. Kinsel
- A. Krutsinger
- M. Kuhn
- C. Kwak
- J. Lahr
- G. Lanham
- L. Lawrence
- K. Lawson
- Z. Lawson
- J. Lebrecht
- E. Leighty
- T. Lester
- N. Lowe
- D. Lowry
- A. Lunt
- S. Malman
- D. Mason
- S. Maxey
- C. McGinness
- J. McPherson
- S. Meeker
- K. Mendez
- V. Metzler
- I. Mier
- J. Miller
- L. Miller
- P. Miller
- S. Miller
- C. Morris
- C. Mossman-Canfield
- J. Murphy
- R. Nelson
- C. Norman
- J. Ogborn
- N. Olsen
- S. Overstreet
- C. Paap
- S. Pluard
- B. Popham
- C. Preston
- M. Rakow
- M. Randall
- M. Reid
- Z. Rhodes
- K. Ridgeway
- T. Robinson
- B. Roy-Rankin
- P. Schwartz
- Z. Schwerman
- G. Shafer
- A. Shelton
- R. Shepherd
- A. Shick
- L. Slaughter
- A. Smiley
- T. Smiley
- A.J. Smith
- A.R. Smith
- T. Smith
- A. Snoddy
- M. Spence
- H. Stear
- T. Steiskal
- A. Stephens
- L. Stepp
- A. Sweeney
- C. Swies
- M. Swinford
- K. Taylor
- D. Thoele
- A. Thomason
- L. Thomason
- C. Thompson
- H. Thompson
- H. Titus
- S. Trigg
- S. Tucker
- D. Tylman
- C. Unkraut
- E. Van Der Graaf
- M. Van Popering
- A. Vassay
- N. Vilardo
- A. Wagner
- B. Waldvogel
- B. Warner
- S. Watson
- K. Wesley
- J. Wheeler
- V. Williams
- K. Williams-McGinness
- J. Wright
- M. Young

Page dedicated by the Class of 2011

You deserve a comfortable dental experience and Dr. Havlik can help you achieve that!

The Booster Club is a not for profit organization served solely by volunteers who have supported Charleston Athletics since 1974. Our purpose is to promote and encourage interscholastic athletics and associated activities of Charleston Unit School District No. 1. We raise and distribute funds for boys' and girls' athletics at both CHS and CMS. These funds go directly to our student athletes in the form of uniforms, warm-ups, and miscellaneous equipment. Go Trojans!

Cross County Mall

Enjoy shopping in Mattoon's Cross County Mall, enclosed and climate-controlled for year-round shopping comfort. The mall is located in Mattoon on Illinois Route 16 and Interstate 57 and contains more than 300,000 square feet of convenient shopping and restaurants. Open Monday - Saturday 10:00 AM to 9:00 PM and Sunday Noon to 5:00 PM.

thomaschemicals.com
sales@thomaschemicals.com

MADE IN MATTOON, IL BY OUR SKILLED TEAM, OUR CUSTOM CLEANERS ARE BIODEGRADABLE AND SAFE TO USE. WE PRIDE OURSELVES ON MAKING ENVIRONMENTALLY RESPONSIBLE PRODUCTS WITHOUT SACRIFICING QUALITY. FOR AUTOMOTIVE, INDUSTRIAL, OR EVERYDAY USE- SEE WHAT THOMAS CHEMICALS CAN DO FOR YOU!

MYERSCOUGH AUTOMOTIVE
217-345-5373

With over 20 years of experience working on Ford, General Motors, and Chrysler, we will make sure that your vehicle is safe and reliable to drive. Since 2010 the first year Myerscough Automotive was open, we have become experienced with Toyota, Honda, Nissan, Volkswagen, BMW, Hyundai, and Classic vehicles. We are equipped to handle any vehicle that has a repair need.

Building a home is one of the largest investments you will ever make. This decision should be entrusted to a builder who values this commitment with fairness and honesty. Call us at 217-345-5511, or visit us at 1611A Redbud Road, Charleston, Illinois 61920.

Petersen Properties & EIU4Rent, Offering clean, affordable housing in both Charleston and Mattoon. We lease to working professionals and retirees in our community, as well as to students and staff from EIU and Lakeland College. Check out the variety of nice properties on our website www.eiu4rent.com!!
Go Trojans!!

Insulation Service supports Charleston athletics. Go Trojans!

LAMBO'S

We specialize in delivery of gas, diesel, alcohol, and bio products to retail locations and bulk storage locations in Illinois, Indiana, Missouri, Iowa, and Kentucky. We have been in business since 1992. During our 23 years in business we have maintained a great reputation of an efficient trucking company with a very high safety rating. We offer competitive pricing and focus on developing strong relationships with our customers and our professional drivers.

Mark D. Esarey, OD
Darcy L. Duzan, OD
Derek B. Hennig, OD

217-345-6600

1700 18th Street
Charleston, IL 61920

GOOD LUCK

Kevin & Rosie Ebel

Merritt & Chelsie Bennett

Wood Rentals, Jim Wood, Realtor, Managing Broker

Jordan Rakes

Bill & Sue Yocum

The Littleford Family

Sign Appeal

Trey & Makayla Katz

Alex Finley

Clark & Suzanna Fairley

Lorenz Wholesale

First Mid Bank & Trust

Adams Memorial

Hutti Chiropractic

Animal Medical Center